Born in Heaven, Made on Earth

Born in Heaven, Made on Earth

The Making of the Cult Image in the Ancient Near East

Edited by

MICHAEL B. DICK

EISENBRAUNS
Winona Lake, Indiana
1999

Printed in the United States of America.

Cataloging in Publication Data

Born in heaven, made on earth : the making of the cult image in the ancient Near East / edited by Michael B. Dick.
p. cm.
Includes bibliographical references.
ISBN 1-57506-024-8 (cloth)
1. Rites and ceremonies—Middle East. 2. Idols and images—Middle East.
I. Dick, Michael Brennan, 1943– .
BL1060.B67 1999
291.2′18—dc21 99-12840
CIP

The paper used in this publication meets the minimum requirements of the American National Standard for Information Sciences—Permanence of Paper for Printed Library Materials, ANSI Z39.48-1984.♾™

Contents

Introduction

Michael B. Dick

In 1977, after receiving my doctorate from The Johns Hopkins University, I asked one of my teachers for suggestions about a new research project. I had completed my Ph.D. dissertation on the Book of Job but lacked Job's proverbial patience to persevere with the book bearing his name as I began my new academic career. Professor Delbert R. Hillers told me that he had found it curious that the strictures against the cult image in the Hebrew Bible focused on the *making* of the cult statue. The moment of the image's construction particularly earned legal prohibition and prophetic scorn. Professor Hillers suggested that I study not only the biblical texts against the making of the statue but that I also study as many *realia* as I could both about the making of the cult statue in the Near East and about its subsequent induction as the presence of the deity. Such an investigation should include information about the statue's form and construction and about the status of the artisans who worked on it. As a postdoctoral student at Johns Hopkins, I devoted the entire year (1977–1978) to this topic, and it has remained a focus of my attention for the last fifteen years. Although heavy teaching loads have always claimed the greater part of my attention, whenever free on grant from the National Endowment for the Humanities or on sabbatical from Siena College, I have devoted my time to Hillers's suggestion.

My research in this area soon convinced me of the importance of the Mesopotamian *mīs pî* ritual used to "give birth" to the god represented by the cult image. Dr. Jerrold Cooper of Johns Hopkins introduced me to Christopher Walker of the British Museum, who had written his Oxford University dissertation on this rite. Christopher kindly made his dissertation available to me, and I have spent several weeks in the Tablet Room of the British Museum working on the countless exemplars of the ritual and incantation tablets of that ritual.

More than ten years ago, Christopher and I talked about working on two related publications: first of all, a popular (*haute vulgarisation*) work on the making and dedication of the cult image in the ancient Near East (Mesopotamia and Egypt); and second, the critical edition of the ritual *mīs pî* in its various versions.

Our first task was the popular work, envisioned as a collection of integrated essays. I worked on the biblical dimension and cooperated with Christopher on the Babylonian materials. I contacted a friend of mine from Johns Hopkins, Dr. David Lorton, to work on the Egyptian counterpart of the ritual. We also intended to treat the broader significance of the theology of the cult image, a topic admirably dealt with by David Lorton. A colleague of mine from Siena College, Dr. James Dalton, reviewed some of my material and was struck by how resonant it was with his research on India. A classmate of his from the University of Chicago had written a book on the cult image in southern India called *Gods of Flesh, Gods of Stone.* I contacted Dr. Waghorne and sent her my research on the dedication of the cult image in Assyria and Babylon. Subsequently, I asked her to contribute a modern component to our book.[1] Her extensive work on the making and dedication of the cult image in contemporary south India demonstrates the persistence of both the making of the image and of a ritual needed to give it birth as the god/goddess.

This was more than ten years ago! All four of us had intensive job responsibilities that delayed our individual contributions. Finally, all has come together and here the reader has the fruits of this long collaborative labor. This book is the "popular work" that Christopher and I envisioned a decade ago.

The Cult Image

> Through the study of icons and their construction we are able to perceive some of the most vital impulses underlying religious experience. Sacred images are products of the human imagination—they are constructed according to systematic rules, and then they are infused with sacrality and kept "alive" by highly controlled behaviors intended to retain the "spirit in matter." An analysis of this process of constructing sacred images, and the corollary process of their destruction, reveals to us something paradoxical and intriguing about human religion (Preston 1985: 9).

The study of the icon plays a crucial role in the comparative study of religion.[2] Attitudes (positive or negative) toward the concretization of the deity represented by the

1. Her contribution in this volume also documents the persistent ability of the biblical prophetic parodies to define the issues. As Waghorne demonstrates, the eighteenth- and nineteenth-century encounters between Hindu India and Christian England were greatly influenced by this biblical topos.

2. There is an excellent treatment of the comparative method by Longman (1991: 23–36). Longman's chapter surveys past excesses from pan-Babylonianism to the rejection of any cultural comparisons. W. W. Hallo's use of a "contextual" approach, followed in his volumes of *Scripture in Context,* offers helpful examples of a more mature comparative method that not only values similarities but differences.

cult image reveal significant positions about the divine presence, about immanence and transcendence, about the very nature of the deity. Struggles between iconodule and iconoclast have marked Judaism, Christianity, and Islam. Within Christianity itself[3] there have been countless strident conflicts: two main periods of Byzantine iconoclasm, the Carolingian period, and the Protestant Reformation.[4] The battle can even be detected in the old Pilgrim cemetery in Boston, where the earliest gravestones carefully eschewed any representative art.

All of these religions have been particularly affected by the seminal iconoclastic struggle in the Hebrew Bible. During the Babylonian Exile (6th century B.C.E.), Israel had come into intimate contact with the Babylonian iconodule. Many of the Bible's most strident parodies of making an image of the god stem from this period. Even many of the Deuteronomistic legal prohibitions of making a cult image probably stem from the post-Exilic period. These texts from the Hebrew Scriptures suggest at least a rudimentary awareness of Babylonian rituals for inducting a cult image. Furthermore, Israel's continuous contacts with Egypt to the south demand that we also investigate the making and dedication of the cult statue in Egypt. Although most of the arguments adduced by Second Isaiah are also found in roughly contemporary Hellenistic literature,[5] the biblical position became pivotal for Western culture, for it influenced Judaism, Christianity, and Islam. The Byzantine Emperors Leo III and Constantine V both rooted their virulently iconoclastic movements in the Old Testament. Even Islamic-Christian polemics centered on interpretation of the Hebrew Bible on idolatry (Sourdel 1966). Internal Christian struggles during the Reformation often dealt with idolatry; these conflicts had clear ramifications for the broader issue of sacramentality.

The biblical attacks on the cult image had further implications for the West's encounter with Eastern religions in the nineteenth and twentieth centuries. Because of its long iconoclastic history, England had trouble relating to India during the last century. In the 1840s, when the East India Trading Company assumed the role of protector of India's shrines, many in Parliament denounced as "idolatrous" England's expenses in protecting cult images! Even scholars had problems explaining how such an urbane, literate society as India could still practice so-called "primitive idolatry." Many books on Hinduism seem forced to consider the cult image (*mūrti*) as an insignificant element of that religion, a position more indebted to the scholar's western background than Indian truth (see Waghorne 1985: 1–7). And so biblical polemics against the cult image have been crucial for both western religions themselves and for their interaction with eastern religions.

3. For a study of Christian iconoclasm during the Byzantine, Carolingian, and Reformation periods, see Martin 1936; Pelikan 1974; Gero 1975; Eire 1986.

4. Compare the interior of the Roman Catholic church Chiesa del Gesù and the Protestant Schloss Chapel in Torgau, Germany.

5. See my chapter, "Prophetic Parodies of Making the Cult Image," in this volume.

Cult Image as Product of Human Hands

The apocryphal Letter of Jeremiah, written around the second or third century B.C.E., attacks the making and worship of the cult image as a mere 'work of human hands' (ἔργα χειρῶν ἀνθρώπων), which is contrasted with the 'work of God' (καὶ οὐδὲν θεοῦ ἔργον). This topos ("How can the product of human hands be a god?") is at the heart of the biblical assault on the divine statue. After investigating the biblical parodies, this book returns to the ancient worship of the cult image and to query the very iconodules parodied by works such as Second Isaiah and the Letter of Jeremiah. How do the great ancient religions of Babylon and Egypt and the Hinduism of modern India explain that a statue crafted by human artisans can embody the God/Goddess? Could either of these Israelite authors have put the theological issue more bluntly than the Assyrian King Esarhaddon (680–669 B.C.E.) himself:

> Whose right is it, O great gods, to create gods and goddesses in a place where humans dare not trespass? . . . Is it the right of deaf and blind human beings who are ignorant of themselves and remain in ignorance throughout their lives? The making of (images of) the gods and goddesses is your right, it is in your hands.

Three of the chapters included in this volume discuss the making and dedication of the cult image in Mesopotamia, Egypt, and contemporary South India, respectively. The Babylonian ritual procedures used for preparing the statue of a deity for functional use were known by the general title of 'mouth-washing' (Babylonian *mīs pî*, Sumerian KA.LUḪ.Ù.DA), or sometimes 'mouth-opening' (Babylonian *pit pî*, Sumerian KA.DUḪ.Ù.DA). Surviving texts document both the ritual used (ritual tablet) and the many Sumerian and Babylonian incantations that accompanied and gave effect to the ritual. In Egypt, the full name of the ritual was "Performing the Opening of the Mouth in the workshop for the statue (*tut*) of the God." Although early Christian literature often refers to similar Greek and Latin rites (ἵδρυσις, *dedicatio*),[6] it is not clear that such rites existed.[7] In any case, unlike their Mesopotamian and Egyptian predecessors, they have not survived. And so the Mesopotamian ritual and incantations of *mīs pî* and the Egyptian "Opening of the Mouth" remain among the best documented ancient religious texts exploring the role of the cult image for the iconodule. Furthermore the theology reflected by these texts probably formed the antipode against which the influential biblical parodies railed.[8] Thus they form one side of an early religious debate whose consequences have proved momentous.

6. See Minucius Felix, *Octavius* XXII, 5 and Arnobius, *Adversus Nationes* VI, 17.

7. See Barasch 1992: 48 nn. 76, 77; Burkert 1985: 91: "There are no magical rites to give life to the cult image as in Babylon."

8. In my article, "Prophetic Parodies of Making the Cult Image" (below), I argue that many of the passages in Second Isaiah suggest at least an awareness of Babylonian religious practice. Other Old Testament scholars have made similar observations. If the anonymous Second Isaiah had been an Israelite priest exiled to Babylon, this could provide the occasion for such familiarity.

Waghorne's treatment of the Hindu ritual *mahakumpabhiṣēka* shows the perdurance of the need to enliven the statue made by humans to make it the object and recipient of *latria.* The inclusion of this modern study does not imply "influence" or "borrowing." Although there are documented influences between India and Mesopotamia from prehistoric times, the inclusion of Waghorne's chapter makes no such assumptions. Instead, this sort of modern ritual demonstrates the continuing theological necessity to "consecrate" the image made by human hands to give it a rebirth as a God/ Goddess. Despite the fact that Hindus also suffered the judgment of Israel's prophets, the making and dedication of the cult statue continues in modern, technological India with increasing frequency.[9]

Of course, the order of chapters in this volume necessarily reflects an editorial plan. I have reluctantly chosen a sequence that begins with my "Prophetic Parodies of Making the Cult Image." I am aware that I risk the accusation that I am thereby forcing the *status quaestionis* into a biblical formulation. However, Second Isaiah and other biblical prophets have undeniably posed the issue in its most trenchant form: How can anything made by human hands be a God? The other three essays, in the order of Mesopotamia ("The Induction of the Cult Image in Mesopotamia"), Egypt ("The Theology of Cult Statues in Ancient Egypt"), and modern India ("The Divine Image in Contemporary South India: The Renaissance of a Once Maligned Tradition"), form the believers' response to the Bible.

The title of this book, *Born in Heaven, Made on Earth,* paraphrases the Akkadian bilingual incantation found in STT 200:11–19 and reflects the critical theological synergy between heaven and earth reflected in making the cult image.

I would like to thank the National Endowment for the Humanities, Siena College, and the Jewish Christian Institute at Siena College, whose generous funds assisted the editing of this work.

The excellent studies on the cult image by Angelika Berlejung appeared too late to be integrated into this book. However, I have included her works in the following bibliography. Her 1998 book, based on her Heidelberg dissertation, contains a helpful bibliography as well. Ironically, her works refer to articles in this volume, because I sent her earlier drafts of my article on prophetic parodies and the article jointly authored by Christopher Walker and me on the induction of the cult image. In some cases, our opinions—here in final form—differ (have matured, I trust) from those sent her in draft more than three years ago.

9. I have witnessed this ritual even in Albany, N.Y.

Bibliography

Arnobius

1949 *The Case Against the Pagans [Adversus Nationes].* Trans. George E. McCracken. Ancient Christian Writers 7–8. Westminister, Md.: Newman.

Barasch, Moshe
1992 *Icon: Studies in the History of an Idea.* New York: New York University Press.

Berlejung, Angelika
1996a "Der Handwerker als Theologe: Zur Mentalitäts- und Traditionsgeschichte eines altorientalischen und alttestamentlichen Berufstands." *Vetus Testamentum* 46: 145–68.
1996b "Die Macht der Insignien: Überlegungen zu einem Ritual der Investitur des Königs und dessen königsideologischen Implikationen." *Ugarit-Forschungen* 28: 1–36.
1997 "Washing the Mouth: The Consecration of Divine Images in Mesopotamia." Pp. 45–72 in *The Image and the Book,* ed. K. van der Toorn. Leuven: Peeters.
1998 *Die Theologie der Bilder: Herstellung und Einweihung von Kultbildern in Mesopotamien und die alttestamentliche Bilderpolemik.* Orbis Biblicus et Orientalis 162. Fribourg: Universitätsverlag.

Burkert, Walter
1985 *Greek Religion.* Trans. John Raffian. Cambridge: Harvard University Press.

Gero, Stephen
1973 "The 'Libri Carolini' and the Image Controversy." *Greek Orthodox Theological Review* 18: 7–34.

Eire, Carlos M. N.
1986 *War Against the Idols: The Reformation of Worship from Erasmus to Calvin.* Cambridge: Cambridge University Press.

Hallo, William W. et al., eds.
1980 *Scripture in Context: Essays on the Comparative Method.* Pittsburgh: Pickwick.
1983 *Scripture in Context II: More Essays on the Comparative Method.* Winona Lake, Ind: Eisenbrauns.
1990 *The Bible in the Light of Cuneiform Literature: Scripture in Context III.* Ancient Near Eastern Texts and Studies 8. Lewiston, N.Y.: Edwin Mellen.

Longman III, Tremper
1991 *Fictional Akkadian Autobiography: A Generic and Comparative Study.* Winona Lake, Ind.: Eisenbrauns.

Martin, Edward James
1930 *A History of the Iconoclastic Controversy.* London: SPCK.

Minuscius Felix
1931 *Octavius.* Trans. Gerard H. Rendall. Loeb Classical Library. London: William Heinemann.

Pelikan, Jaroslav
1974 *The Spirit of Eastern Christiandom (600–700).* Chicago: University of Chicago Press.

Preston, James J.
1985 "Creation of the Sacred Image: Apotheosis and Destruction in Hinduism," Pp. 9–30 in *Gods of Flesh, Gods of Stone,* ed. Joanne Punzo Waghorne and Norman Cutler. Chambersburg, Penn.: Anima.

Sourdel, Dominique
1966 "Un pamphlet musulman anonyme d'époque Abbaside contre les chrétiens." *Revue des Études Islamiques* 34: 29.

Waghorne, Joanne Punzo, and Cutler, Norman, eds.
1985 *Gods of Flesh, Gods of Stone.* Chambersburg, Penn.: Anima.

Prophetic Parodies of Making the Cult Image

MICHAEL B. DICK

This chapter examines the idol parodies in the Hebrew Bible, which are mainly but not exclusively restricted to the so-called Exilic and post-Exilic prophets (7th–6th centuries B.C.E.). There are enough thematic similarities among these texts for us to treat them synchronically, with only a cursory examination of the history behind this tradition.[1] This study will also isolate and treat the three main characteristics of the iconoclastic arguments found in these prophetic parodies; as we shall see, these three objections were also in fact discussed by later Hellenistic authors, whether pagan, Jewish, or Christian. The biblical iconoclastic texts, however, acquire extraordinary significance because they set the stage for many of the later arguments within Judaism, Christianity, and Islam. Indeed, as we see in J. Waghorne's article in this volume, many of the arguments used in the 19th-century British Empire against the iconodule of India were anticipated 2500 years earlier by the Hebrew Prophet.

According to Christoph Dohmen's recent examination of the Israelite legal prohibition against cult images (his so-called *Bilderverbot*), there are five different types of texts in the Hebrew Bible that deal with cult images (Dohmen 1987: 38):[2]

1. Wolfgang M. W. Roth (1975: 21–47) considers these texts to be a separate literary genre (pp. 21–22). However, this approach too often ignores the close rhetorical/literary ties between these passages and their immediate literary context and it exaggerates their formal similarities. Preuss (1971) and R. Clifford (1980) argue that these passages constitute a "literary motif." However, some of these parodies appear to have circulated independently before being inserted into their present prophetic context.

2. Christoph Dohmen wisely differentiates the *Bild* ('image'), *Götterbild* ('divine image'), and *Kultbild* ('cult image') (pp. 36–37). However, since most of the prophetic texts talk about the "function" of the divine image, we are justified in speaking of a cult image. My treatment of the legal texts in the Bible (the *Bilderverbot*) is considerably indebted to the work of Dohmen.

1. Narratives that happen to mention images, which, however, do not play a major role in the stories;
2. Texts in the Deuteronomistic History or the Chronicler that deal with cult reform;
3. Prophetic texts that focus their polemics against the worship and making of cult images, such as those found in Deutero-Isaiah, Jeremiah 10, and late wisdom texts;
4. Prophetic texts that mention cult images but are primarily interested in conflicts with non-Israelite religions and their gods;
5. The legal commandments prohibiting cult images (*Bilderverbot*): Exod 20:4, 23; 34:17; Lev 19:4; 26:1; Deut 4:15ff.; 27:15. These especially include the Decalogue in its various versions.

Because Dohmen has done an excellent job in dealing with the fifth category, the legal texts,[3] this chapter will concentrate on the third category of texts, the specific prophetic parodies against the making of cult images. However, we shall set the stage for our main treatment of the prophetic passages by reviewing both the archaeological data and the broader legal texts (*Bilderverbot*) that reflect on Israel's attitudes toward the cult statue. These two reviews relate essentially to the prophetic idol parodies, since both recent excavations and current textual studies of the Decalogue suggest that the strict aniconic monotheism that lay behind Deutero-Isaiah's and Jeremiah's polemic only triumphed as a late response to the theological crises of the Babylonian Exile (586 B.C.E.).[4]

Dohmen's careful study of the evolution of the prohibitions against the cult image suggests that they were largely the product of 6th-century redaction. The theological stresses of 586 B.C.E. assured both the triumph of Yahwistic monotheism and of aniconic worship: Yahweh's cult had probably always been aniconic, but now there were no gods but Yahweh, so there was utterly no room for any cult image! The prophetic parodies respond to the same contemporary crises. Although they stem from different traditions, the legal and the prophetic understandings of a monotheistic and aniconic Yahwism cope with the same catastrophe. The archaeological evidence also seems to support a gradual evolution of an aniconic religion in Israel.

After the following examination of both the archaeological data and the Decalogue and other legal texts prohibiting the cult image (the so-called *Bilderverbot*), we shall treat the relevant parodies in Hosea, Isaiah, Jeremiah, and Deutero-Isaiah. In turn, these prophetic texts will be examined against the background of passages drawn

3. For reviews of his book, which is a publication of his 1984–85 Bonn dissertation, see Brueggemann 1987: 314–15; Gnuse 1987: 111–12.

4. See the recent study of Manfried Dietrich and Oswald Loretz (1992: 183–84): "Als Ergebnis konnte festgehalten werden, daß die beiden ersten Gebote des Dakalogs als Schlußpunkte einer lange Entwicklung anzusehen sind, die nicht am Anfang der Geschichte Israels, sondern am Beginn des exilisch-nachexilischen Judentums stehen. . . ."

broadly both from Greece and the ancient Near East. The comparative texts are of two distinct types. Some texts at times support the biblical parodies, raising similar objections, while others counter the parodies with the iconodule's *apologia imaginis.* Among the latter texts are the particularly relevant comparative materials from Mesopotamia, which are treated in the article on the Opening of the Mouth Ritual (see below, pp. 55–121). Because the biblical satires focus their attention precisely on the making of images, the Babylonian and Assyrian historical and religious texts that focus on the making and dedication of the cult/divine image[5] are particularly relevant, because they demonstrate how a contemporary worshiper would respond to the theological objections raised by the Israelite prophet.

T. Mettinger's (1995) discussion of aniconism in Israel[6] has made a clear and helpful contribution to scholarly debate. It will be useful to adopt the terminology presented in his study.

> I shall use the term "aniconism" as referring to cults where there is no iconic representation of the deity (anthropomorphic or theriomorphic) serving as the dominant or central cultic symbol, that is, where we are concerned with either (a) an aniconic symbol or (b) sacred emptiness. I shall call the first of these two types "material aniconism" and the second "empty-space aniconism" (Mettinger 1995: 19).

Mettinger also distinguishes between de facto aniconism and programmatic aniconism. In the former, there is an indifference to or mere absence of images; in the latter there is a conscious repudiation of images and iconoclasm (1995: 18). Clearly, the prophetic idol parodies exhibit characteristics of programmatic aniconism.

The following cursory treatment of the archaeological data and of the Decalogue and the legal texts shows how difficult it is to date the emergence of aniconism, de facto or programmatic, in Israel. Neither the artifacts recently found nor contemporary research on biblical texts allow us to form confident hypotheses about the "image of Yahweh" in Israelite religion.

---

5. The date, provenience, and lexicon of the parodies in Deutero-Isaiah in fact suggest an acquaintance—even if only superficial—with the Babylonian practice of making and dedicating the cult image. The prophetic polemics against making the cult image reached a peak during post-Exilic times and may have been influenced by Israel's new contact with Babylon (see Dietrich and Loretz 1992: 3). These parodies are not completely off the mark, and even so eminent an Assyriologist as Thorkild Jacobsen commented (1987: 15):

> A scathing sarcastic indictment indeed, but keenly observed and . . . literally true. . . . Must we, then, accept the prophets' verdict as it stands and conclude that the ancient Mesopotamians, a highly intelligent and civilized people, failed so utterly to consider in their heart that they would fall down to a block of wood?

6. See the excellent review of Mettinger's book in T. Lewis's *JAOS* article (Lewis 1998). I am grateful to Professor Lewis for making his article available to me. His careful overview of the archaeological data has had a clear influence on the final version of this chapter.

Archaeological Evidence for the Cult Image in Israel

The archaeological data[7] for cult images in ancient Israel are often at odds with the textual evidence but do provide a hermeneutic to help us read the biblical text with greater acumen (Dever 1991).[8] The complexity of recent finds reminds us that the biblical prohibitions and the roughly contemporary prophetic parodies are the end result of a long development within Israelite religion and date from the last prophetic and Deuteronomistic phases of the Exilic and post-Exilic periods (7th–5th centuries B.C.E.).[9] Recent biblical studies by B. Lang (1981), H. Vorländer (1981), M. Smith (1981), M. S. Smith (1990), and R. Albertz (1994a, 1994b) suggest that Israel's monotheism, which so dominates the present text of the Hebrew Bible, represents the eventual triumph of a small "Yahweh-alone" group over the exigencies of the Exile following the destruction of Jerusalem in 586 B.C.E.[10] This victorious group played such a dominant role in editing the Hebrew Bible that their final triumph has been anachronistically regarded as both normative and universal during the entire preceding biblical period from 1200 to 600 B.C.E.

In actuality, earlier Israelite religion probably had several different regional manifestations (see the "Yahweh of Samaria" and the "Yahweh of Teman" in the Kuntillet Ajrud Inscriptions from the late 9th to the mid-8th century[11]) and probably tended toward henotheism or monolatry rather than monotheism.[12] These differing expressions of Yahwism confessed that the state God Yahweh might be the chief deity in the state cult but probably also acknowledged other divine beings in the pantheon (Halpern 1987: 94), perhaps a female Asherah (Dever 1995: 113).[13] The main deity Yahweh

7. Lewis's article (1998) presents an excellent survey of the archaeological evidence (or lack of it) for Yahweh images. To his survey should be added Uehlinger's (1994) study of fragments of a cult image of a deity found at Dan. In any case, this is not an image of Yahweh. There is also a brief survey of Iron Age divine figures by Keel (1995: 152–58). The 1983 report of W. Dever (1983: 574) still stands, namely, that no male images have been found from the Iron Age that could be identified with Yahweh.

8. However, note Keel's valuable caveat (1995: 272 n. 237) that we should avoid the "typical Jewish-Christian tradition" of assigning priority to the word and of seeing the picture as mere "illustration" of the text.

9. Some scholars, however, do place these prohibitions earlier; for example, B. Halpern (1987: 87) thinks that Exod 20:19–23 is premonarchic. M. Weinfeld (1991: 262–63) argues for the Mosaic origins of the Decalogue.

10. Note the title of Vorländer's essay, "Der Monotheismus Israels als Antwort auf die Krise des Exils" ["The Monotheism of Israel as a Response to the Crisis of the Exile"].

11. For the date of Kuntillet Ajrud, see Keel 1995: 280–81.

12. For a discussion of "monotheism," see Loretz 1994: 508 n. 110.

13. The coexistence of the Canaanite goddess Asherah in Israel as Yahweh's *paredros* during Iron Age I and II is not as clear as many studies would have us believe (Hadley 1994; M. S. Smith 1990: 88–94).

was probably de facto aniconic[14] from the beginning (Obbink 1929: 264–74; Pfeiffer 1926: 211–22; Dus 1961: 37–50),[15] although the reasons for such an unusual practice are no longer clear (Hendel 1988: 367–72).[16] However, there were other images within the cult; in fact, the later *Bilderverbot* themselves reveal that there must have been images that eventually had to be prohibited. As the "Yahweh-alone" movement grew and came to dominate Israel's religion, Israel's iconography diminished. We shall see in the next section that the *Bilderverbot* gradually expanded to exclude most of the iconography that had been permitted centuries earlier at the time of Solomon and his temple cult.[17]

Recent excavations tend to support this hypothetic diachrony of Israelite religion, for no image that can with certainty be identified with Yahweh has been found in an Israelite stratum, and other iconography gradually diminishes through the course of the Iron Age I and II (1200–600 B.C.E.). Although there are frequent finds of anthropomorphic deities, male and female, during the Late Bronze Age (up to 1200 B.C.E.),[18] the situation clearly changes by the beginning of the Israelite period (Iron Age I and II). "It may be significant that no representations of a male deity in terra cotta, metal, or stone have ever been found in clear Iron Age contexts . . ." (Dever 1983: 574). Only one figurine has been found that could possibly be a cult image from the Israelite period. At 11th-century Hazor an enthroned bronze figurine was found in a clay jar that probably served as a foundation deposit for an early Israelite cult site.[19]

Another discovery from the early period (12th century), a bronze bull, was found by A. Mazar at an open-air hilltop shrine about five miles east of Dothan. At this site, which he calls a *bamah* (Dever 1987: 233), Mazar found a bronze bull that might represent Yahweh, who is often called אביר יעקב 'the bull of Jacob' (Ps 132:2) and who was probably worshiped in the Northern Kingdom of Israel (ca. 900–622 B.C.E.) at the shrine of Bethel as a calf (עגל). However, certainty here is almost impossible, since

14. However, Israelite religion probably did not become programmatically aniconic until the reforms of the Deuteronomist and the prophetic parodies.

15. Some scholars argue from biblical passages that depict Yahweh in a temple-like scene (Ps 17:15; Isaiah 6) that at some stage there might have been a Yahweh image. However, see M. S. Smith 1988: 171–83. Dietrich and Loretz (1992: 108) are not sure that this aniconic status of Yahweh should a priori be accepted as true from the beginning.

16. Mettinger (1995) sees aniconism as a phenomenon shared with other parts of the Northwest Semitic world. See the careful review of this seminal book by Lewis (1998).

17. For an exhaustive study of the evidence of this type of Israelite imagery and art, see Schoer 1987.

18. See references in Hendel 1988: 367 n. 8.

19. For bibliography on this find and on the discussion of whether it represents Yahweh, see Hallo 1983: 1–2. In a series of articles G. W. Ahlström has claimed that the statue represents an Israelite god, which O. Keel has disputed. However, W. Dever is undoubtedly correct when he points out that the El-like bronze statuette, although found in "Israelite" Hazor XI dating to the 12th century, was part of a hoard in a votive jar and therefore probably was a holdover from the earlier, pre-Israelite, Late Bronze Age (1983: 583).

the Canaanite deity El was also represented as a bull; although many of El's attributes (as well as those of his consort, Asherah!) were later transferred to Yahweh, for any particular artifact, especially from this early period, it is not possible to determine whether Yahweh or El was represented by the bull.[20]

Yahweh's bull iconography has also been said to lie behind the controversial pictures on Pithos A found at the northern Sinai way-station Kuntillet Ajrud, a site that dates around 800–775 B.C.E. Because the inscriptions on the large Pithos A refer to "Yahweh of Samaria" and because the names end in the Israelite dialectal *-yw* (and not in the Judahite *-yhw*), the caravansary en route between Gaza and Elath probably dates from the reign of Israel's Jehoash (ca. 801–786), when the Northern Kingdom with its capital at Samaria had briefly overrun southern Judah. The inscriptions[21] use an epistolary style (Keel 1995: 257) to invoke a blessing "By Yahweh and His Asherah."[22] The painting on Pithos A portrays three figures (Keel 1995: 241 M, N, O), two standing, and a third seated, playing a lyre. Some have identified the larger figure (Keel's M) as a theriomorphic portrayal of Yahweh with ears of a bull and a tail; the figure next to him, according to some, would be his consort Asherah, with a bull's tail (not a penis) between her legs (Coogan 1987: 119). This interpretation is thoroughly flawed. First of all, it is methodologically unsound to require that the pictures correspond to the inscriptions; second, the figures are clearly two portrayals of the Egyptian god Bes. It is possible that the second figure is Beset, the female version of Bes, but the pair of Bes and Beset is not known prior to Ptolemaic Egypt (Keel 1995: 247). Thus, we do not have a portrayal of Yahweh at Kuntillet Ajrud. It is not clear who the lyre-player is: human or divine, male or female. In any case, the seated lyre-player is not likely to be Asherah either. In short, the intriguing pictures and inscriptions on these pithoi do not alter our lack of Yahweh imagery from Iron Age Israel.

Despite these controversial exceptions, Israel's religion appears to preserve its aniconic character despite the archaeologist's spade. In fact, much of the latest evidence supports the idea that the Hebrew Bible's prohibition against the icon gradually expanded, an expansion that will be traced below. Although the premonarchical and

20. See Dohmen 1987: 147–53 for an excursus on the bull cult in Israel, especially at Bethel; and Schroer 1987: 81–104.

21. It has been all too common to interpret the pictures on both pithoi by means of the inscriptions, that is, to assume that the pictures must be identified by the inscriptions. However, it is not clear that the inscriptions and pictures on Pithos A are related (Hadley 1995: 246–47), because the second Bes-figure (Keel 1995: 241 fig. "M") overlaps the inscription. It is also quite possible that not all of the figures on Pithos A were drawn by the same hand.

22. The translation עשרתה as 'his Asherah' is complicated, for it is not clear to what or to whom 'Asherah' refers; see McCarter 1987: 143–49 and Keel 1995: 259–63 for a discussion of the possibilities; also, see the book by Dietrich and Loretz (1992). Hadley's argument (1995: 248) appears to be compelling: that 'Asherah' here refers to the tree-symbol often accompanying Yahweh, not the Canaanite goddess Asherah (also see Lemaire 1995: 148). In fact, the 'asherah' is probably portrayed on the pithos as the tree encompassed by two caprids (Keel's E, F, and G in 1995: 239). This 'asherah' might be the one referred to in 1 Kgs 16:33. The sacred tree might at one time have been related to the goddess, but it is unclear whether this nexus continued on into the Israelite Iron Age (Keel 1995: 263).

early monarchical periods (1200–950) made frequent use of artistic motifs such as the bull, lion, and cherub, these become progressively less frequent in excavations from the later periods of the divided monarchy (920–722).[23]

The Evolution of the Bilderverbot in the Old Testament

The classical formulations of the *Bilderverbot* are found in the Decalogue, Exod 20:3–4 and Deut 5:7–8.

Exod 20:3–4

לֹא תַעֲשֶׂה־לְךָ פֶסֶל וְכָל־תְּמוּנָה אֲשֶׁר
בַּשָּׁמַיִם מִמַּעַל וַאֲשֶׁר בָּאָרֶץ מִתָּחַת וַאֲשֶׁר
בַּמַּיִם מִתַּחַת לָאָרֶץ׃

You shall not make for yourself an idol, and the form of anything that is in heaven above, or that is on the earth beneath, or that is in the water under the earth.

Deut 5:8

לֹא־תַעֲשֶׂה־לְךָ פֶסֶל כָּל־תְּמוּנָה אֲשֶׁר
בַּשָּׁמַיִם מִמַּעַל וַאֲשֶׁר בָּאָרֶץ מִתָּחַת וַאֲשֶׁר
בַּמַּיִם מִתַּחַת לָאָרֶץ׃

You shall not make for yourself an idol, the form of anything that is in the heaven above, or that is on the earth beneath, or that is in the water under the earth.

The syntactical irregularities in these texts strongly suggest that this pivotal commandment has undergone an evolution. Perhaps an original לא תעשה לך פסל 'you shall not make for yourself an idol' has undergone a later broadening by the addition of a כל־תמונה 'any form', perhaps derived from the Deuteronomistic parenesis in Deuteronomy 4. In any case, the *Bilderverbot* as recorded in Exodus and Deuteronomy seems to be the end of a long development and not its beginning. I have followed the diachrony suggested by C. Dohmen.

1. Dohmen's Reconstruction

Dohmen begins with his reconstruction of Exod 20:23b+24a:

> Gods of silver and gods of gold you shall not make for yourself; an altar of earth you shall make for me.

Dohmen thinks that this hypothetical original[24] is not really a command against cult images but only conservative cult law that sought to prohibit forms of worship alien to a "nomadic" (sic!) tradition. It should be noted that this commandment does not interdict the worship of images or their establishment but rather only the "making"

23. See Holladay 1987: 295–99 for an excellent review of the contrast between textual and archaeological evidence.

24. Many scholars challenge Dohmen's assertion of the originality of Exod 20: 23–24. R. Albertz (1994: 64 n. 129) sees this claim as mistakenly based on the assumption that the Book of the Covenant is early; Albertz would instead date it to the 8th century, after Hosea. Mettinger (195:138) takes it as a Deuteronomistic redaction. Halpern (1987: 87), however, takes this verse as "premonarchic."

of gold and silver statues. The combination of the two, the prohibitive and the injunctive, clarify the intent of the commandment: "Rather than cult images let there be sacrifices and blood rites" (Dohmen 1987: 238). This suggests that there was a cultural-sociological difference between the cult practice of the urbanites and that of the seminomadic and more conservative rural population.[25] Dietrich and Loretz have summarized several traditional reasons for Israel's aniconic tradition:

> . . . an expression of primitive aversion to images, a particular preference of the Israelites for "hearing" (over "seeing"), a peculiarly Israelite spirituality in its concept of the deity, the Israelite sense of awe before the divinity, Yahweh's jealousy of the Canaanite gods, the prohibition against other gods, cultural poverty resulting from the desert experience, animosity towards luxury items among prophetic-Levitical circles, the dependence of the Yahwistic religion on the aniconic worship of an early Semitic main god (1992: 106–7).

In a recent article, R. S. Hendel (1988: 365–82)[26] has suggested a related but distinct argument for Israel's aniconic religion. Hendel documents the close connection between the royal iconography and the portrayal of such main Canaanite deities as El. In the ancient Near East the earthly king, who was at times described as the "image/statue" of the god, was the embodiment of the main god. Ancient Israel had such a deep hostility toward the institution of the monarchy that it could consequently have adopted an aniconic representation of its god to reflect that he had no royal counterpart. W. W. Hallo (1988: 54–66) has argued that the appearance of the life-sized divine cult statue in Mesopotamia may have been in response to the worship of a deified king such as Naram-Sin (ca. 2230 B.C.E.).

James M. Kennedy (1987: 138–44) also roots Israel's aniconic tradition in the social fabric of ancient Israel. The cult of the divine image could command a large amount of the economic resources of a country and provide an ideological basis for a

25. O. Keel (1977: 40) has also commented that there are many examples of aniconic cults in the border areas of the major ancient Near Eastern "Hochkulturen." The main thesis of Mettinger's book (1995) is that there are other examples in the West Semitic world of both material and programmatic aniconism. Although Dohmen seems aware of recent objections to the word *nomadic*, which is really unsuitable for describing the early Israelites (see Brueggemann 1987: 315), he persists in using it.

26. This article contains a good bibliography on the image and Israelite religion. Hendel follows W. Zimmerli (1974: 234–42), who begins his examination of Israelite religion with the alleged earliest form of the Decalogue (Exod 20:4): אל תעשׂה־לך פסל 'You shall not make for yourself an image'. M. Weinfeld (1991: 262–63) defends the Mosaic origins of this command; M. S. Smith (1990: 148) dates it to the first half of the monarchy; however, most contemporary scholars concur with R. Albertz's assessment (1994: 61): "hardly much earlier than the Deuteronomistic reform (622 B.C.E.)." Dohmen, however, claims that the verse of the Book of the Covenant (Exod 20:23) that mentions images of precious metals (gold and silver) is the earliest formulation. If Dohmen is correct, this would support his argument that there is a tension between two cultures exemplified in the Yahwistic objection to the wealthy religious panoply of the Canaanites.

priestly-royalist hierarchy. Israel's rejection of the cult image would undercut this kind of development.[27]

If we look for a time when Israel was in transition from an early nonurban to an urban culture, then we must consider the early days of the monarchy. Conservative reactions quite often focused on the cultic realm. After a generation, the conservative movement became a totally new system identical with neither the older nonurban nor the newer urban culture.[28] Speaking of Exod 20:23–24, Dohmen concluded (1987: 244): "Such a commandment would have had no rationale within the nomadic lifestyle itself; it emerged rather from a conflict between cultures." The next step was the development of a prohibition of a certain type of worship (i.e., one with gold and silver images) to one prohibiting images themselves. Although this step is significant, it is verbally quite close to Exod 20:23.

2. The Early Monarchy

Texts from this period are rare, and we must extrapolate from both earlier and later data. In particular, we are interested in early judgments about such early cult representations as the Ark, Cherubim in the Solomonic Temple, and the bull cult of Bethel.

Traditions about the Ark are so complicated that it is quite difficult to arrive at the exact meaning of the tradition. There is little consensus either about the origin or about the meaning of the Ark: was it War Palladium or Divine Throne? The different understandings of the Ark can be appreciated when all of the different names of the Ark are considered: **ארון הברית** 'Ark of the Covenant', **ארון הברית יהוה** 'Ark of the Covenant of Yahweh', **ארון אלהים** 'Ark of God', and **ארון העדות** 'Ark of the Testimony'. The common denominator at all times, however, seems to have been that the Ark symbolized the presence of God, whether in war (1 Samuel 4ff.) or in the Temple. The Ark itself was aniconic and stemmed from a time when the image played no role in the cult.[29] When David moved the Ark to Jerusalem (see Psalm 132), it immediately conferred on that non-Israelite city an unchallenged cultic centrality. When the construction of the Temple was discussed in 1 Kings 6, the Ark was placed where the main cult statue would normally be located. In later texts the position of the Ark was subordinated to that of the Cherubim, which were often described in conjunction with the Ark (1 Kgs 8:7; 2 Chr 3:8ff.). According to O. Keel (1977: 23–29), the Cherubim functioned not as watchers and protective spirits but rather as bearers of the

27. "By rejecting idolatry Israel got rid of the sacral mechanisms that directed via sacrifice large amounts of material productivity into the control of religious and political hierarchies" (Kennedy 1987: 142).

28. "Das Bewußtsein aber der ursprünglichen Andersartigkeit gegenüber der städtisch-bäuerlichen Kultur der kanaanäischen Landesbewohner als wesentliches Element dimorphischer Struktur bleibt auch nach der Änderung der Lebensweise in der Seßhaftwerdung erhalten" (Otto 1984: 73).

29. Mettinger (1995: 196) sees the story about the Philistine capture of the Ark (1 Sam 5:1–5) as an indication that programmatic aniconism is quite old. According to Mettinger, this text has not been given enough attention in these discussions.

divinity—hence the idea of the Cherubim as the throne of Yahweh. Keel perceives this concept, like the Solomonic Temple itself, as Canaanite-Phoenician (Keel 1977: 29–30). Thus both the Ark and the Cherubim conveyed the theology of the presence of the invisible God, although they stemmed from different sources. And so Solomon effected a compromise in his combination of (a) the Cherub-throne and temple-type from the Canaanite-Phoenicians and (b) the empty throne from the theology of the Ark, although the Ark did not fit in well with the Temple (see Janowski 1991: 231–64). This demonstrates the perduring impact of the early rural aniconic cult.

There is then no evidence of hostility toward all represention al art. There were other symbols in the cult, such as the bronze serpent (נחשתן) attributed to Moses and Jeroboam's bull (עגל). When Jeroboam wished to establish a rival for the Jerusalem Temple, he set up the bull postament in Bethel, and it probably served like the Jerusalem Cherubim as part of the throne for the invisible Yahweh. However, there is no indisputable evidence, textual or archaeological, in the early monarchy for a cult image of Yahweh himself.

3. Orthodox Yahwistic Faith and the First Image Polemics

During the 9th century there are reports of cult reforms under Kings Asa (910–869 B.C.E.) (1 Kgs 15:9–14) and Jehosaphat (870–848 B.C.E.) (1 Kgs 22:41–51); however, closer analysis suggests that these reports are retrojections of the Deuteronomistic reforms that actually occurred more than two centuries later. Nevertheless, at this time we have evidence of the next important phase in the development of the *Bilderverbot.*

The prophet Elijah played an important role in the emergence of an intolerant monolatry from the earlier integrating monolatry. The 9th-century struggles between orthodox Yahwism and the religion of the Canaanite Baal centered around the Northern prophet Elijah and his successor Elisha. This conflict peaked in the account of the incident at Mount Carmel (1 Kings 18), which originally dealt with the exclusive worship of Yahweh (18:21, הלך אחרי 'to walk after').

Elijah's position seems to have been consistent with the tradition of the introduction to the Book of the Covenant (Exod 20:23b+24a), for the demand in Exodus 20 for a particular cultic expression without cult image but with sacrifice and blood rituals found its realization on Mount Carmel, where Israel's return to exclusive worship of Yahweh was followed by sacrifice. Exod 20:23 had already presupposed a "separation" from other cult practice, for the negative formulation of the prohibition presupposed the existence of the forbidden. And so the conservative interests of the Book of the Covenant (Exod 20:22–23:33) formulate the presupposition for the later demands of monolatry (see Exod 22:19: זבח לאלהים יחרם בלתי ליהוה לבדו 'he who sacrifices to gods other than Yahweh alone shall be destroyed').[30]

30. Exod 22:19 is complicated. First of all, the text itself is unclear; many would follow the Samaritan and other MSS to read לאלהים אחרים 'other gods' (Loretz 1994: 498). Albertz (1994: 263

Elijah then is both initiator and restorer. In response to the syncretism of the 9th century, he emerged as the champion of intolerant monolatry. Out of the older cultic requirements, he created the basis for the later prohibition against foreign gods. Elijah insisted on the fundamental decision: Yahweh *or* Baal, not Yahweh *and* Baal. Although there was not yet a conflict about different cult objects, nevertheless, the later polemics against images was to have its roots in this 9th-century development.[31]

The next crucial stage can be seen in the prophet Hosea, who lived in the middle of the 8th century. At the center of his message against syncretism stood the demand for exclusive worship of Yahweh and the rejection of all other gods. This is particularly clear in 13:4 (see 12:10):

> And I am Yahweh your God from the land of Egypt; and you shall not know any gods besides me, and there is no savior but me.

For Hosea the effects of religious syncretism extended from cultic practice (2:7–15, 4:4–9, 5:1–17) to the use of amulettes and divine statues, which he called עצבים 'idols' (4:17, 8:4, 13:2, 14:9) because of the paronomasia involving the two different verbal roots עצב I 'to build, shape' and עצב II 'to be sickly'. Although we still do not find the developed polemics against the cult image of later times, Hosea's criticism of the עצבים represents an important step in that direction.[32] From the time of Hosea on, the עצבים would be the foreign gods of the non-Israelites. Hosea acknowledges the ambivalence of the image: because the iconography cannot distinguish the specific elements of the Yahweh cult from the Baal cult, the polyvalent image must remain contrary to his radical demand for exclusive worship of Yahweh. This ambiguity also led to the first condemnation of the Bethel bull cult, because that image remained ambiguous and could easily be incorporated into Baal worship.

For Hosea the critique of the עצבים 'idols' and of the עגל 'bull' was merely an extension of the intolerant monolatry of Elijah; every image posed a threat, because it could quickly become self-important and thereby offer the danger of assimilation to other peoples and religions. A temptation of this kind would be particularly acute in the absence of any native Yahwistic iconography, for any image would have to be ambivalent.

4. *From the First Criticism of Images to the Second Commandment*

Beginning in the middle of the 8th century and through the fall of Samaria in 722 B.C.E., the seductiveness of Assyrian religion created a further crisis in the South. However, the 7th and 8th centuries were decisive for the emergence of the *Bilderverbot.* The original relationship between the cult and criticism of images persisted,

n. 108) dates the verse to the 8th century and Exod 34:14 to the 7th. Von Rad (1962: 498 n. 47) suggests that Exod 22:19 gives an impression of being older than Exod 20:3.

31. The JE version of Exodus 32 reveals the connection between the exclusive following of Yahweh and the first criticism of images.

32. It is not clear whether passages such as Hos 8:6, 11:2, 13:2, 14:4 are original or secondary; see Nissinen 1991: 159, 161–63, 165–66; Dietrich and Loretz 1992: 90.

for it was precisely the cultic reforms of Hezekiah and the centralization of the cult under Josiah that led to the prohibition of images. The reform of Hezekiah (2 Kings 18–20) rid the Temple of the old נחשתן 'bronze serpent' (2 Kgs 18:4). Although the text attributes this symbol to Moses himself—a claim that could not have originated with the Deuteronomistic Historian—it was probably its ambiguity that made the נחשתן 'bronze serpent' suspect, for the snake played a role in Assyrian religion.[33] There still does not seem to have been general hostility to artistic representations in the 7th century. Although some scholars argue on the basis of seals from the 7th century, which generally prefer inscriptions to images,[34] that there was already a commandment against images, this evidence is complex and needs further research in both prosopology and in the use of seals. Manasseh, Hezekiah's son, reversed his father's reforms and reintroduced many foreign cults. The Deuteronomic movement possibly originated as a response to Manasseh's syncretism. The Deuteronomistic insistence on the exclusivity of Yahweh and on the theology of election led to strong tendencies toward separation. The claim of the Northern prophet Hosea that images were too ambiguous developed within the Deuteronomistic theology to the demand that every image or cult object that could point toward another god was to be rejected.

> You shall not plant any tree as an Asherah next to the altar of Yahweh your God which you shall construct; nor shall you erect a Massebah, which Yahweh your God hates (Deut 16:21–22).

In this double commandment, the Deuteronomist prohibited both the syncretic addition of a foreign cult object or goddess (עשׁרה) and the use of a hitherto acceptable pillar (מצבה) because of its potential for misuse. Behind this lay the concern to establish the distinctiveness of Yahwistic belief and the exclusivity of worship of Yahweh rather than to prohibit images in general (see also the command to destroy such objects in Exod 34:13; Deut 7:5, 12:3). The reform of King Josiah (2 Kings 22–23) was based on the agenda of the Deuteronomist. The destruction of the Asherahs and Massebahs in the accounts of Josiah's reform (2 Kgs 23:4–20, 24) was not done in accord with some law against images (*Bilderverbot*) but rather out of the demand of Yahwistic religion for exclusivity.

One of the earliest versions of a specific *Bilderverbot* is found in an early form of Deut 5:8: לא תעשׂה־לך פסל 'You shall not make for yourself an image'. This verse, which has undergone an extensive redactional history, is probably a reaction to the crises during the last days of the Judahite monarchy. Deut 5:8 was clearly rooted (a) in the tradition of an imageless Yahwistic religion expressed in the earlier Exod 20:23; (b) in the antisyncretic Northern prophetic movements of the 9th century; and (c) in Hosea's suspicion of images. Because there are no allusions to such a command in the

33. The "bronze serpent" has also been connected with the worship of Asherah (see Olyan 1988: 70; Spieckermann 1982: 172–75). However, as we have seen, worship of the Canaanite goddess Asherah during the Israelite monarchy is problematic.

34. Sauer 1966: 1789.

reports of Josiah's reform, Deut 5:8 probably stems from the later Deuteronomistic movement at the beginning of the Exile (Dohmen 1987: 270–71).

The wording of Deut 5:8 with its עשׂה 'to make' and its *dativus commodi* 'for yourself' could be indebted to the older Exod 20:23 from the Book of the Covenant; however, the object of the verb עשׂה 'to make' has been changed from 'gods of silver and gold' to פסל 'cult image'. This substitution could have been influenced by the recent experience with Manasseh, who set up a פסל 'cult image' in the temple (2 Kgs 21:7).[35]

The use of פסל in Deut 5:8 then expanded the application from the 'silver and gold gods' of the older Exod 20:23 to any representation prepared for the cult, and it also recalled the historical crisis of Manasseh. Deut 5:8 has probably also been influenced by the JE version of Exodus 32,[36] which united the twin concerns of prohibition of images and worship of other gods. This earliest form of the *Bilderverbot* was not yet a broad prohibition against all representational art but only against the cult image.

The older version of the Decalogue embraced both a prohibition of foreign gods and of cult images, inasmuch as both have now been redacted as one of ten commandments. This is quite clear when we compare Deut 5:8 with the parallel (but later) text in Exod 20:4. The first difference is that in Deut 5:8 כל תמונה 'every representation' is added asyndetically to פסל 'cult image', whereas in Exod 20:4 the copulative ו is added. The reading in Deut 5:8 is a *lectio difficilior* and therefore is apt to be original.[37] The significance of these two readings becomes clearer when we look at the following verse (Deut 5:9a // Exod 20:5a): לא־תשתחוה להם ולא תעבדם 'you shall not bow down to them and shall not serve them'. Zimmerli (1963: 236–38) first pointed out that the plural object suffixes skip over the second commandment and refer to the אלהים אחרים 'other gods' in Deut 5:7 and Exod 20:3, so that the prohibition against cult images "stands totally in the shadow of the prohibition against other gods [first commandment] and together with this was treated as one commandment" (p. 241). However, Hossfeld (1982: 23–24) has shown that this is true only of the verse in Deuteronomy, since here the כל תמונה 'every representation' stands as an explicative in apposition to פסל 'cult image'; however, in the Exodus version the copulative creates

35. The parallel text in 2 Chr 33:15 reads פסל סמל 'image of the idol'; if Nah 1:14 ומסכה פסל refers to the cult object set up by Manasseh, then this incident could have influenced the choice of vocabulary in Deut 5:8.

36. The "JE version" of Exodus 32 refers to the widely accepted proposal of the Documentary Hypothesis that the first several books of the Hebrew Bible (Old Testament) were comprised of several different written sources that were combined at different times until the finished stage of these books was reached around 450 B.C.E. The J (Yahwist) version of Israel's sacred history possibly originated in the Davidic-Solomonic court of Jerusalem around 950, whereas the Elohistic (E) source is usually attributed to Northern tradents writing around 850 B.C.E. These two versions were combined (JE) after the destruction of the Northern Kingdom by the Assyrians in 722, whereupon the E source was probably brought south to Jerusalem, where it was integrated into the J document.

37. However, see Weinfeld 1991: 291: "As it turns out, neither Hossfeld's thesis about the priority of the Deuteronomic version of the Decalogue nor his reasoning about the development of the formulation of the two discussed commandments can be sustained."

two direct objects פסל תמונה 'image and every representation', and so the plural suffixes in v. 5a refer back to these, not to the foreign gods. It is clear that the editor of Exodus was aware of the significance of his ו 'and', for he then must join the two "covet commandments" as one in order to keep the number of commandments at ten.

5. *The Evolution of the Second Commandment of the Decalogue*

The evolution of the commandment against cult images is to be found in further Deuteronomistic redactions. According to Dohmen, the Deuteronomist expanded the original version of Exod 20:23b:

> Gods of silver and gods of gold you shall not make for yourself; an altar of earth you shall make for me.

The Deuteronomist added v. 23a to the original v. 23b; לא תעשׂון אתי 'you shall not make besides me' was prefaced as a conscious ellipsis: 'You shall make nothing besides me: silver and golden gods you shall not make' (Dohmen 1987: 157). This combination, then, constructed a "double commandment" condemning both the worship of foreign gods and making images. Verse 23a now stands akin to Lev 26:1 and other passages that afford priority to the *Bilderverbot* over the *Fremdgötterverbot.*[38] When the Deuteronomistic editor combined the Book of the Covenant with the Sinai theophany, he changed the important commandment in v. 23b to the plural to extend the prohibitions to the entire people and then added v. 23a to combine the two commandments.

The Deuteronomistic editor also redacted the JE version of the "Golden Calf" story in Exodus 32, both to place it in parallelism with Deuteronomy 9 and to retell it as a violation of the *Bilderverbot,* for Exod 32:31 now clearly recalls the new, expanded introduction to the Book of the Covenant (20:23ab):

> And Moses returned to Yahweh and said, "Alas, this people has committed a great sin: they have made for themselves gods of gold" (32:31).

The Second Commandment emerged during the Exile as the chief defense of the newly emerged monotheism. The *Bilderverbot* had originally arisen as a special instance of the commandment against other gods, but now it was to dominate. This development is clear in Lev 26:1.

> You shall not make for yourselves idols, and cult images and massebah you shall not set up for yourselves, and a worked stone you shall not place in your land to bow down to it because I am Yahweh your God.

This verse stands at a very important position in the Holiness Code (Leviticus 19–26). Lev 26:3 concludes the Code with its blessings and curses. Verses 1–2 introduce

38. Dohmen also claims that the use of the *nun paragogicum* (תעשׂון) is stylistically characteristic of the Deuteronomist but rarely used by the Priestly editor.

the Blessings and Curses of Leviticus 26 rather than finish out the commandments in Leviticus 25. The text of Leviticus 19 was framed by vv. 2 and 37, since v. 2 began with the formula: "You shall be holy because I Yahweh your God am holy," and v. 37 ended with the general parenesis: "You shall observe all my statutes and all my ordinances and do them: I am Yahweh." Lev 19:2 and 26:1 probably established a larger framework for the entire Holiness Code, for in Leviticus 19 the most important commandments are repeated in 19:4 and 19:30, and both of these are resumed in Lev 26:1–2.

If the vetitive in Lev 19:4 dismissed foreign gods as אלילים 'idols', then Lev 26:1 went a step further and identified them with their images, for this verse said they were not to be made (עשׂה). Thus the commandment against other gods is enveloped by and subordinated to the prohibition against cult images, which is stressed by the multiplication of direct objects: משׂכית 'cut stone', אבן 'stone', פסל 'cult image', מצבה 'massebah'.

During the late Exilic period there also was a tendency to expand this prohibition to all artistic representations, the final stage in the evolution of the *Bilderverbot* in the Hebrew Bible. This stage is particularly evident in Deut 4:16–25, which reveals a complex redaction (Knapp).

> Lest you worship and make for yourselves a cult image, a representation of any statue, a representation of a male or female, a representation of any beast on the earth, a representation of any winged bird in the heavens, a representation of anything that crawls on the land, a representation of any fish which is in the waters under the earth, . . . Lest you forget the covenant of Yahweh your God which he made with you and make for yourselves a cult image, the form of anything . . . and bow down, and you make a cult image, the form of anything.

D. Knapp sees two main blocks of material in Deuteronomy 4: (a) vv. 1–4, 9–14 and (b) a continuation in vv. 15–16a+ (without סמל) and vv. 19–28. Knapp sees the same hand at work in the counterpart passage in Deuteronomy 29. Thus he sees Deuteronomy 4 as a late Deuteronomistic text that was preceded by Deuteronomy 1–3, 5, and 12ff. If we follow Knapp's analysis, then the original (Deut 4:1–4, 9–14) did not contain a commandment against making images. In this text, the simple demand is hearing and obedience to the word: "Then Yahweh your God spoke to you from the midst of the fire; you heard the sound of words, but you did not see any form—only a sound (Deut 4:12). The editor who expanded on this did so to eliminate the other possibility of תמונה 'form' (vv. 15, 16a+19–28): פסל תמונת כל, which is translated by Dohmen (p. 205) "that you make yourselves no cult image, the form of anything." This text also is a witness to the stage in which the commandment against images has overshadowed the commandment against worship of other gods (cf. Deut 4:28 and Deut 19:15ff.).

There also has been a further development in Deut 4:16a+ 17–18, which displays vocabulary from the 6th century B.C.E. Priestly editor. In this regard especially note סמל 'figure/image', the addition of which has caused some syntactical problems.

There were, therefore, two stages of development: (1) originally, the phrase read פסל תמונת כל 'cult image, the form of anything'; (2) later, probably a Priestly editor added סמל 'figure', creating the new expression תמונה כל סמל as a development of the term פסל: 'and no cult image for yourselves, the representation of any type of statue'. In the final form two different things are prohibited, while the original apposition תמונה כל 'form of anything' only explained the word פסל 'cult image'. Therefore, the text was expanded to list various types of תבנית 'likeness' (vv. 16b–18). The original prohibition against cult images was then extended to embrace all types of cult objects, whether anthropomorphic or zoomorphic, and symbols, posts, and so on.

There were then three stages to the growth of Deuteronomy 4:

1. In the original text (vv. 1–4, 9–14) there was no reference to a prohibition against cult images.
2. The first expansion of Deuteronomy 4 (vv. 15–16a+19–28) expanded on the original paranesis against vision (v. 12) and developed from it a paranesis on the Decalogue prohibition against cult images, thereby establishing a causal relationship. This expansion with its תמונת כל 'image of anything' also crept into the versions of the Decalogue.
3 The second expansion from a Priestly redactor (P) expanded this paranesis still more (vv. 16a+ [only סמל] b, 17–18) and thereby expanded the prohibition of the cult image to a prohibition of any artistic representation.

I have briefly traced the development of the biblical legal prohibition of the cultic use of the image, which has set the stage for the main study of the late prophetic attacks against making images (= Dohmen's type 3 text). However, none of these trenchant prophetic parodies specifically cites legal texts in either the Decalogue or the other laws that we have just examined.[39] The prophets prefer to appeal to weaknesses perceived as inherent to iconolatria. Indeed, their insights appear to have been widespread, since these same criticisms were voiced in independent Hellenistic thought; and the weaknesses in iconolatria highlighted by the prophetic parodies were almost defensively given special attention in the rituals accompanying the making and induction of the cult image in ancient Mesopotamia.

The Prophetic Parodies

The main passages in the Hebrew prophets dealing with the human crafting of the cult image are found in Jeremiah (10:1–6) and Deutero-Isaiah (40:19–20; 41:5–14; 44:6–22); however, there are less-sustained arguments in such minor prophets as

39. Unless we note that both legal texts and parodies focus on the 'making' (עשׂה) of the cult image. Furthermore, some prophetic texts combine their idol parodies with השתחוה 'bow down', which might reveal an indebtedness to late versions of the *Bilderverbot*; see Micah 5:12; Isa 2:8, 20; Jer 1:16.

Hosea (8:4–6; 13:2–3), Micah (5:12–13), and Habakkuk (2:18–19). Echoes of these prophetic texts can also be found in the books of Judges (17–18), Psalms (115:3–9; 135:15–18), and such apocrypha as the Letter of Jeremiah and the Wisdom of Solomon (13–15).

Let us examine the texts of some of these main passages, all of which date to the same period as the latest stages of redaction of the *Bilderverbot* discussed above.

Jeremiah 10:3–15

Jer 10:3–15[40] is a poetic passage that appears in significantly different versions in the Masoretic Text (Hebrew) and in the Septuagint (Greek). The Greek verse that corresponds to the MT 10:9 is found between vv. 4 and 5 in the Septuagint, which also omits the MT's vv. 6–8 and 10. It is impossible to arrive at the "original" form of the text, because the Greek and Hebrew probably witness alternate forms of the Jeremianic tradition.[41] The authenticity of the passage, that is, whether Jeremiah himself wrote this idol parody, remains problematic. Although scholarship is divided on this issue, the thesis put forward by Robert Carroll in his recent commentary (1986) is persuasive: the book of Jeremiah represents a long and complicated literary evolution that precludes our ability to trace any section back to the "historical Jeremiah." We cannot be more precise about the dating of this passage; it could be either late pre-Exilic or Exilic. As we shall see, the arguments in Jeremiah against cult images are similar to the ones found in Deutero-Isaiah, a fact that suggests a post-Exilic date for the Jeremianic material.[42] However, in almost every case, these idol parodies seem originally to have had their own existence and to have been inserted into their present prophetic context. Later insertion may also help explain the apparent lack of precision in the parodies in their present context. Typical of this type of parody (e.g., Isa 44:9–20) is the frequent change between singular and plural: vv. 3–4 singular, vv. 5–9 plural, and v. 14 singular and plural.

This passage documents the various stages in the preparation of a full plastic cult image: (1) first the wooden core of the statue is prepared (v. 3); (2) next, the cores are plated with gold and silver (vv. 4a, 9a, 14); (3) then the image is fastened to its base

40. See Ackroyd 1963: 385–90; Andrew 1982: 128–30; Davidson n.d.: 41–58; Holladay 1986: 321–37; Margaliot 1980: 295–308; Overholt 1965: 1–12; Schroer 1987: 197–210; Wambacq 1974: 57–62.

41. Hebrew manuscripts of Jeremiah found at Qumran often agree with the text form of the Septuagint rather than with the present Masoretic Hebrew Text (e.g., 4QJer^{b}). However, 4QJer^{a} agrees with the MT in that in this manuscript v. 9 is followed by v. 10. This suggests that the book of Jeremiah circulated in different Hebrew versions until quite late. The Greek then is probably a translation of a Hebrew *Vorlage* different from the one represented by the MT. We would never be able to determine which version of 10:3–16, the Greek or the MT, is more original (see Schroer 1987: 200).

42. Wambacq (1974: 57–62) has suggested that all except an orginal v. 2 stem from the years 300–298; however, these dates seem too late.

(v. 4b); (4) finally, the statue is clothed (v. 9b). This passage mentions three different craftsmen. The supervisory craftsman is the חרש, who is described in v. 3 more specifically as a carpenter.[43] In vv. 9 and 14 the craftman is the goldsmith (צורף), who works with hammered silver (כסף מרקע) and as a jeweler[44] (נסכו, v. 14).

The overall purpose of the passage 10:1–16 is to contrast Yahweh with the idols: the gods are identified with their cult images. Thus, the idols are '*works* of the craftsman' (מעשׂה חרש) and '*works* of the wisemen' (מעשׂה חכמים) in v. 9; however, 'Yahweh *has made* the earth with his power' (עשׂה ארץ בכחו), he 'has established the world with *his wisdom*' (בחכמתו).

Jer 10:3–15

3 כִּי־חֻקּוֹת הָעַמִּים הֶבֶל הוּא כִּי־עֵץ
מִיַּעַר כְּרָתוֹ מַעֲשֵׂה יְדֵי־חָרָשׁ בַּמַּעֲצָד׃
4 בְּכֶסֶף וּבְזָהָב יְיַפֵּהוּ בְּמַסְמְרוֹת
וּבְמַקָּבוֹת יְחַזְּקוּם וְלוֹא יָפִיק׃
5 כְּתֹמֶר מִקְשָׁה הֵמָּה וְלֹא יְדַבֵּרוּ
נָשׂוֹא יִנָּשׂוֹא

3 For the customs[a] of the people are false. He
cuts a tree from the forest, the work of the hands
of a craftsman, with a chisel.[b] 4 He decorates[c] it
with silver and gold; with nails and hammers
they[d] set them firmly in place so they don't
topple over.[e] 5 Their idols are beaten gold,[f] and
they cannot speak; they have to be carried,

a. For a similar use of חקות to mean 'religious customs', see Lev 18:3.

b. Verse 3 מעצד is probably a chisel. See Isa 44:12, where מעצד seems to be used as a tool for the iron worker. In Ugaritic economic texts (e.g., 2048 passim) this word is always paired with a hammer. The only tool that could be used both by an iron worker (see note on Isa 44:12 for contemporary iron technology) and a wood worker and is also linked with a hammer is the chisel. (However, A. Fitzgerald [1989: 445] understands מקבת as 'hole', thus 'mortise'. Although the technology used in wooden statues did make use of mortises and tenons, it seems that the pair 'hammer and nails' is too well attested elsewhere.) See Schroer 1987: 203; he sees the מעצד as an 'adze'. The verbal root for this tool is found in the Gezer calendar's *yrḥ ʿṣd pšt* 'month of harvesting flax' and in Akkadian *eṣēdu* 'to harvest'.

c. The MT (and LXX) reads 'decorate it' from פרה in the *Piel*, but the Syriac and Targum read יְצַפֵּהוּ 'to plate it' from Hebrew *Piel* צפה 'to cover with plate' (see 1 Kgs 6:20).

d. The shift from singular to plural, both of the idols and of their makers, is disturbing: vv. 3–4 singular, vv. 5–9 plural, v. 14 singular and plural. This inconcinnity seems to be part of the genre, for it is also found in Isa 44:15 (see Holter 1995: 174). See Holladay 1986: 325; Schroer 1987: 209 n. 216. Perhaps this reinforces the identity of image and maker: as the one changes in number, so does the other.

e. Fitzgerald 1989: 445. Fitzgerald takes במסמרות as the "pegs by which in fact cast metal statues were normally attached to wooden bases" (1989: 444). Hebrew מקבת II means 'hole', in this case the mortise chiseled into the wood base to support the statue (see Fitzgerald 1989: 445 n. 53). Although there are clear examples of mortise and tenon joints in ancient woodworking, this same word

43. The carpenter is often called חרש עץ (2 Sam 5:11; 2 Kgs 12:12; Isa 44:13; 1 Chr 14:1).

44. This is the real meaning of נסכו rather than 'to pour' (see Dohmen 1983: 39–42).

כִּי לֹא יִצְעָדוּ אַל־תִּירְאוּ מֵהֶם
כִּי־לֹא יָרֵעוּ וְגַם־הֵיטֵיב אֵין אוֹתָם׃
8 וּבְאַחַת יִבְעֲרוּ וְיִכְסָלוּ מוּסַר הֲבָלִים
עֵץ הוּא׃ 9 כֶּסֶף מְרֻקָּע מִתַּרְשִׁישׁ יוּבָא
וְזָהָב מֵאוּפָז מַעֲשֵׂה חָרָשׁ וִידֵי צוֹרֵף
תְּכֵלֶת וְאַרְגָּמָן לְבוּשָׁם מַעֲשֵׂה חֲכָמִים
כֻּלָּם׃ 14 נִבְעַר כָּל־אָדָם מִדַּעַת הֹבִישׁ
כָּל־צוֹרֵף מִפָּסֶל כִּי שֶׁקֶר נִסְכּוֹ
וְלֹא־רוּחַ בָּם׃ 15 הֶבֶל הֵמָּה מַעֲשֵׂה
תַּעְתֻּעִים בְּעֵת פְּקֻדָּתָם יֹאבֵדוּ׃

for they cannot walk.[g] Be not afraid of them, for
they cannot do evil, neither is it in them to do
good. . . . 8 In summary, they are dull[h] and foolish—the instruction of a nothing! (After all) it is
only wood. 9 Hammered silver is imported from
Tarshish, and gold from Ophir.[i] They are the
work of the craftsman and of the hands of the
goldsmith; their clothing is violet and purple:[j]
they are all the work of skilled men. . . . 14 Every
man is stupid and without knowledge; every goldsmith is put to shame by his idols; for his images[k]
are false, and there is no breath in them.[l] 15 They
are worthless, a work of delusion; at the time of
their punishment they shall perish.

---

is clearly a 'hammer' in Isa 44:12. Schroer (1987: 203 n. 185) thinks that 'hammer and nails' here refers to joining pieces of wood or to attaching the statue to its pedestal. Wis 13:15 seems to be a midrash on this passage from Jeremiah; it understands the text as referring to the attachment of the statue to its pedestal. Since this passage is clearly satirical and exaggerates the proverbial instability of the statue (Isa 40:20, 41:7; Wis 13:15–16; Ep Jer 27), it may indeed be that the author wants the reader to imagine the comical, though technologically inaccurate, step of affixing the statue to its base with a spike! The process described probably does not refer to the affixing of precious metal plating to the wood, although nails were used for this purpose in 2 Chr 3:9.

f. Verse 5: Rather than MT כְּתֹמֶר מִקְשָׁה 'like a scarecrow in a cucumber patch', perhaps we should read כתם מכשה, the Hebrew word for gold and 'hammered work' used of זהב 'gold' or כסף 'silver' in Exod 25:31, 36; 37:17, 22. This could be the origin of the LXX ἀργύριον τορευτόν 'chased silver'. However, see Ep Jer 69: 'like a scarecrow (προβασκάνιον) in a cucumber field'. This image of course would also work in the parody in this passage: the scarecrow was the only allowable image in aniconic Israel (Holladay 1986: 331).

g. The incantations of the *mīs pî* ritual stress the statue's ability to "walk"!

h. Perhaps there is a pun here on the two meanings of Hebrew בער I: 'to burn' (as does wood!) and II: 'to be dull'. This possibility is reinforced by Theodotion's revision of the LXX: 'For at once the hearts of the foolish shall be burned up and be weak; it is wood' (see Holladay 1986: 332).

i. Verse 9: It is not clear whether we should read the MT מאופז as the *Hophal* participle of פזז 'purify' (see 1 Kgs 10:18, 2 Chr 2:17) or should emend to the legendary location of אופיר 'Ophir', either in Arabia or in East Africa. There is an 8th-century B.C.E. ostracon from Tell Qasile, an Israelite port a little north of Tel Aviv, that refers to זהב אפר 'gold of Ophir'. Ophir and gold are paired together eight times in the Hebrew Bible; see Schroer 1987: 205.

j. See Ezek 16:18 for a mention of the clothing of statues, a common practice in Mesopotamia (Matsushima 1993) and Egypt.

k. The MT reads נִסְכּוֹ 'his image'; the Greek reads 'he has poured out' (ἐχώνευσαν); perhaps we should read נְסָכָו 'he worked on it as a jeweler' or נָסְכוּ 'they worked on "falsehood" as jewelers' (I understand the root נסך as 'to work as a jeweler').

l. This "breath" seems to be the equivalent of the Egyptian *ka* described in Lorton's article.

3 ὅτι τὰ νόμιμα τῶν ἐθνῶν μάταια· ξύλον ἐστὶν ἐκ τοῦ δρυμοῦ ἐκκεκομμένον, ἔργον τέκτονος καὶ χώνευμα· 4 ἀργυρίῳ καὶ χρυσίῳ κεκαλλωπισμένα ἐστίν· ἐν σφύραις καὶ ἥλοις ἐστερέωσαν αὐτά, καὶ οὐ κινητήσονται· 9 ἀργύριον τορευτόν ἐστιν, οὐ πορεύσονται· ἀργύριον προσβλητὸν ἀπὸ Θαρσις ἥξει, χρυσίον Μωφαζ καὶ χεὶρ χρυσοχόων, ἔργα τεχνιτῶν πάντα· ὑάκινθον καὶ πορφύραν ἐνδύσουσιν αὐτά· 5 αἰρόμενα ἀρθήσονται, ὅτι οὐκ ἐπιβήσονται. μὴ φοβηθῆτε αὐτά, ὅτι οὐ μὴ κακοποιήσωσιν, καὶ ἀγαθὸν οὐκ ἔστιν ἐν αὐτοῖς. 14 ἐμωράνθη πᾶς ἄνθρωπος ἀπὸ γνώσεως, κατῃσχύνθη πᾶς χρυσοχόος ἐπὶ τοῖς γλυπτοῖς αὐτοῦ, ὅτι ψευδῆ ἐχώνευσαν, οὐκ ἔστιν πνεῦμα ἐν αὐτοῖς· 15 μάταιά ἐστιν, ἔργα ἐμπεπαιγμένα, ἐν καιρῷ ἐπισκοπῆς αὐτῶν ἀπολοῦνται.

3 . . . For the customs of the peoples are empty. For it is wood cut from the forest, a work of the craftsman and a product of the foundry. 4 With silver and gold are they embellished; with hammer and nails they fasten them so that they do not move. 9 Chased silver they are; they will not move. Hammered silver comes from Tarshish, gold of "Mophaz," a work of the goldsmith—they are all works of craftsmen! Blue and royal purple clothes they put on them; 5 they have to be carried, since they cannot walk. Do not fear them, because they cannot do evil, and good is not in them. . . . 14 As a fool stands every man without knowledge: every goldsmith will be ashamed of his statues, for they have poured out lies; there is no spirit in them. 15 They are foolish, works to be mocked; at the time of their judgment, they will perish.

Isaiah 40:18–20 and 41:6–7

Should these two passages[45] be treated together? Fitzgerald (1989: 431) has made a good case for regarding these two sections as belonging to a single technical description of the construction of a metal figurine, decorated with both precious metal plating and inlays and set on a wooden base. Thus, three craftsmen are involved in making a single statue; the two parts both deal with the successive stages, and each ends with an attempt to make the statue stable:

> The caster (*ḥrš*) encourages the worker in precious metals (*ṣrp*); the worker in precious metals (*mḥlyq ptyš*) encourages the wood worker (*hwlm pʿm*) as the statue is passed from one worker to the next (Fitzgerald 1989: 443).

Fitzgerald's methodology is refreshing, for he interprets the passage based on knowledge of technical processes gained from the study of ancient Near Eastern (mainly

45. See Elliger 1978: 59–81, 107–8, 128–31; Fitzgerald 1989: 426–46; Hutter 1987: 31–36; Williamson 1986: 1–20; Holter 1995: 33–126.

Egyptian) metal figurines. However, he cannot account for the "displacement" of these two sections other than by "a copyist's carelessness."

Although these two sections may originally have belonged together and in fact shall be so treated here, there can be no real doubt that both sections have been thoroughly integrated into their present context (see Clifford 1980: 450–64; Holter 1995: 71–78, 105–21). In the former passage (Isa 40:18–20), the idol-maker plates (יְרַקְּעֶנּוּ) the image with gold, whereas in 42:5 and 44:24, Yahweh 'crafts' (רֹקַע) the earth (Holter 1995: 54–55)! The craftsman chooses (יִבְחָר) wood that will not rot (40:19), but Yahweh 'chooses' Israel (בְּחַרְתִּיךָ) in 41:8. The latter passage (41:6–7) is now part of a trial scene (41:1–10), which in turn is part of the larger literary unit, 41:1–42:4 (Melugin 1976: 95–96). As in Jeremiah 10, several of the words used of idol-makers in 41:6–7 (יעזרו, חזק, אמר) are also used of Yahweh in the larger context: the craftsmen must assist each other (יעזרו), but Yahweh has assisted Israel (אף־עזרתיך: 41:10, 13, 14); the craftsmen 'speak' (אמר) to each other, but Yahweh speaks (41:9) to Israel; the workers 'fortify' (חזק) each other, while Yahweh 'fortifies' Israel (החזקתיך: 41:9).

> The powerless deities and the idols who image them on earth are vividly contrasted with the powerful Yahweh and his servant on earth, Israel. The lifeless idols on earth mirror perfectly the powerless deities in heaven. Servant Israel, coming to life by the words and presence of Yahweh, effectively images the power of its deity Yahweh. . . . Thus in this passage the trial has been used in order to show that alone among the nations only favored Israel is the chosen locus of divine justice. Somehow the nations will recognize Yahweh's unique power reflected in servant Israel (Clifford 1980: 454).

There are several similarities between the following passage in Deutero-Isaiah and Jeremiah 10 (Schroer 1987: 211).

1. In Isa 40:19 פסל 'statue' is joined with נסך 'to cast' as in Jer 10:14; however, in the case of Jeremiah the subject of the verb is the צורף 'goldsmith' not the חרשׁ.
2. As in Jer 10:9, Isa 40:19 speaks of hammered (רקע) metal (silver in Jeremiah, gold in Isaiah) used by the smith (צרף).
3. As in Jer 10:4, one of the main problems confronting the makers of cult images is the stabilization of the figure (לא ימוט, ולא יפיק).
4. In both passages, the 'skill' of the craftsmen (חרשׁ חכם, מעשׂה חכמים) is mentioned.

These rhetorical and verbal similarities and the fact that the editor/author of Second Isaiah has seemingly split a single descriptive parody and inserted the parts into two passages, which have been crafted verbally to tie in with the inserts, suggest that these parodies were once independent.[46]

46. Elliger (1978: 66) calls this passage, whose theme is the preparation of the cult image, a subspecies (*Untergattung*) of the *Spottlied* (poetic parody, lampoon).

Isa 40:18–20; 41:6–7

18 וְאֶל־מִי תְּדַמְּיוּן אֵל וּמַה־דְּמוּת
תַּעַרְכוּ לוֹ 19 הַפֶּסֶל נָסַךְ חָרָשׁ וְצֹרֵף
בַּזָּהָב יְרַקְּעֶנּוּ וּרְתֻקוֹת כֶּסֶף צוֹרֵף׃
20 הַמְסֻכָּן תְּרוּמָה עֵץ לֹא־יִרְקַב
יִבְחָר חָרָשׁ חָכָם

18 But to whom will you liken God, or what likeness[a] will you set alongside him? 19 An idol[b] perhaps? One on which a craftsman has worked[c] and a goldsmith then overlays with gold,[d] and inlays[e] with silver wire?[f] 20 As for sissoo-wood,[g] he[h]

---

a. The use of דמות here could recall Gen 1:26 (see Gilbert 1973: 87; Holter 1995: 79–89). In Genesis (Gen 1:18), God, like the craftsman in Isa 41:7, pronounces his work "good."

b. The ־ה on פסל can be taken as the interrogative rather than the article; see Fitzgerald 1989: 436. However, Holter's argument from parallel structure (1995: 38) that we should retain the Masoretic pointing and take this as an article seems persuasive.

c. For the tenses in this passage, see Fitzgerald 1989: 436. 1QIsa[a] reads ואעשׂה מסך for MT נסך. Elliger takes מסך as a verb, an alloform of נסך. Thus, ויעשׂה is a variant used also in the versions (LXX, Syriac, Targum); since the versions take חרש as a carpenter (LXX τέκτων, ST נגרא), MT נסך is thought to be inappropriate. However, LXX τέκτων is often used of workers in metal (1 Kgs 13:19.). I take the verb נסך as meaning 'to work on as a jeweler' (Dohmen 1983: 39–42).

d. 19b T: וקינאה בדהב מחפיליה 'and the smith plates it with gold'; S וקיניה בדהבה קרמה 'and the smith plates it with gold'; see Jer 10:9: כֶּתֶם מְרֻקָּע 'beaten gold'. The versions think of a wooden statue plated with gold.

e. Fitzgerald (1989: 434) understands the root צרף here as 'to arrange, join together'; מַרְצֶפֶת, רִצְפָּה seem to mean 'pavement' made of fitted stones. Two techniques were used to apply precious metal to a cast statue: gold (foil) could be applied to the surface (רקע); wire could be forced (צרף, 'inlaid') into prepared channels. Either צרף or יצרוף could be read here; however, a simple metathesis in the presence of the sibilant could also explain the MT צורף from a putative רוֹצֵף. Interestingly, Qa has two metatheses here: יבשק, ירבק.

f. 19c is missing in the LXX; S וסאמא צריפא קבע בה 'and he fastens purified silver on it'. T ליה ושישלן דכסף קינאה מאהיד 'and the smith fastens silver chains on it'; V 'laminis argenteis argentarius. . . .' Fitzgerald (1989: 439–40) understands רתקות as the drawn wire used for inlay (for eyebrows, lips, etc.): 'things squeezed (by drawing through a wiredrawer)'. Or the silver could be used for the jewelry, such as a wire necklace or bracelet seen on some metal statues (Schroer 1987: Abb. 80, 81).

g. As in the case of the beginning of v. 19, the initial ־ה is the article, which emphasizes the direct object. For the different approaches to this phrase, see Williamson 1986 and Holter 1995: 41–45. I take מסכן as a type of tree (neo-Babylonian *mesukannu*), a view already anticipated as early as Jerome ("In Hebraeo dicitur amsuchan; quod genus ligni est imputribile, quo vel maxime idola fiunt") and the Targum (אוֹרָן בָּרֵי 'he shapes, cuts a pine, fir tree'). Saʾadya identified it as an 'oak'. Zimmern (1894) drew attention to Akkadian *musukkanu* wood, which he thought meant 'palm'. (Campbell Thompson thought it meant 'mulberry'.) The NEB transposes *terumah* (read as *terimah*) to the end of v. 19 and reads "Is it an image which a craftsman sets up, and a goldsmith covers with plate and fits with studs of silver as a costly gift? Or is it mulberry-wood that will not rot which a man chooses?" Gershevitch has definitely identified the wood as Sissoo-wood. (For bibliography on *musukkanu*, see Cohen 1978: 133 n. 67.) This suggestion was adopted by Millard and Snook, but they translated *terumah* as plinth or podium (← RWM).

h. Fitzgerald (1989: 437) understands the subject of יבחר and יבקש as 'the worker in fine metals'. The text seems to presume a factory setting where artisans of various types are gathered. "The worker in fine metals after gilding the figurine selects wood for a base and after choosing a wood passes the wood and gilded statue on to him down the ('assembly line') to prepare the base and mount

יְבַקֶּשׁ־לוֹ לְהָכִין פֶּסֶל לֹא יִמּוֹט׃
41:6 אִישׁ אֶת־רֵעֵהוּ יַעְזֹרוּ
וּלְאָחִיו יֹאמַר חֲזָק׃ 7 וַיְחַזֵּק חָרָשׁ
אֶת־צֹרֵף מַחֲלִיק

chooses (that for) a platform[i] [wood that will not rot];[j] he seeks out a skilful[k] [wood] craftsman to set up[l] an image that will not fall.[m] 41:6 Each one helps his co-worker and says to his companion, "Take courage!" 7 The craftsman encourages

---

the figurine." Schroer (1987: 212) thinks that there is an abrupt change in subject between v. 19 and v. 20. She theorizes that v. 20 stemmed from an originally different parody that described a wooden sculpture. She does not accept the idea that there is a reference here to a wooden pedestal: "Andererseits steht im Text von einem solchen Podest leider nichts, und daß ausgerechnet für ein Podest besonderes Holz gewählt werden soll, ist merkwürdig." However, we have an almost exact description of such a wooden statue pedestal in an inscription of Esarhaddon, where a wooden pedestal (*šubtu*) of musukannu wood (!) is provided for a cult image (Borger 1956: §53: AsBbA, 84:39). This passage also adds the comment about musukannu-wood that it does not rot (*iṣṣe darê*). Furthermore, in lexical lists, the *kigallu* (another Akkadian word for pedestal) is often of wood: giš.ki.gal.

i. With Fitzgerald (and others), I take Hebrew תרומה to be derived from רום 'to be high', i.e., the wooden platform into which metal figurines were fixed by having their tenons pushed into mortises carved in the wood (see Elliger 1978: 79–80). This is the equivalent of the Babylonian *šubtu* or *kigallu.*

j. The phrase עץ לא ירקב 'wood that will not rot' is frequently dismissed as a gloss; however, in this case, we should be cautious, for *musukannu* wood is frequently described in Akkadian as *iṣṣi dārûti* 'a wood that is everlasting'; cf. CAD D 118.

k. The craftsmen in Deutero-Isaiah are חכם in two senses: (1) they are skilled in their craft, but (2) they are knowledgeable in the sacred mysteries (*TDOT* 4.378 and Isa 3:3). Esarhaddon prayed that he might have similar craftsmen to work on the restoration of the cult images of Babylon (Borger 1956: §53, AsBbA Rs. 2–38): "(18) Endow the skilled (*enqūti*) craftsmen (DUMU.MEŠ) *ummâni*) whom you ordered to complete this task with as high an understanding as Ea, their creator. (19) Teach them skills by your exalted word; (20) make all their handiwork succeed through the craft of Ninshiku."

l. Hebrew להכין perfectly describes wedging the tenon on the cast figurine into its wooden base so that it can now stand up. Many examples of this joining are shown in ANEP no. 480 and Schroer 1987: Abb. 82–83; metal figurines attached to an original wooden base have survived in Egypt (see Roeder 1956: 2.528).

m. Pausanius (2d century C.E.) records in his *Graeciae Descriptio* (3:15.10–11) that several cult statues were fastened down with chains so that they couldn't move. He also comments that the Athenians were content with a Wingless Victory who could not fly away (3.15.7). They were, however, also vulnerable to toppling over. Pausanias says that the delapidation of the shrine of Larisian Zeus on Mount Larisa was epitomized by the fact that "the *agalma*, which is made of wood, no longer stands on its pedestal" (2:24.3: τὸ δὲ ἄγαλμα ξύλου πεποιημένον οὐκέτι ἑστηκὸς ἦν ἐπὶ τῷ βάθρῳ). In Limnaeum the statue of Artemis Orthia is also called Lygodesma because it was found in a thicket of willows (λύγος) that entwined around the image and kept it upright (ὀρθόν; 3.16.7–11).

There are references in Mesopotamian literature to statues' toppling from their pedestals: *šumma ṣalam šarri . . . lu ṣalam abīšu . . . imqutma ittešbir* 'If a statue of a king or of his father should fall and break' (*RAcc* 38 rev. 14). Many statues in both Egypt (cf. Khaf-Re valley temple at Giza) and Assyria (cf. statue of Ashurnasirpal now on display in the Metropolitan Museum) were set in a deep depression in their pedestals to counteract toppling. (A controversial text *AR*, II, §§795, 796 even suggests that Sennacherib was assasinated by a falling statue; but cf. Hallo 1991: 163.)

פַּטִּישׁ אֶת־הוֹלֶם פָּעַם אֹמֵר לַדֶּבֶק טוֹב הוּא וַיְחַזְּקֵהוּ בְמַסְמְרִים לֹא יִמּוֹט׃	the goldsmith, and he who smooths with[n] the planisher[o] [encourages] him who hammers the footing;[p] he[q] says of the fit, "It is good"; then after he has jammed[r] it tightly in place with pegs,[s] it cannot be moved.

n. See Joüon §126h for the omission of the preposition ־ב.

o. For this understanding of Hebrew מחליק פטיש, see Fitzgerald 1989: 443–44. He understands this to refer to the 'planishing' process (Hebrew חלק 'smooth') whereby goldleaf was applied to the metal surface of the figurine (see also Schroer 1987: 213). This craftsman then is the equivalent of the צרף 'goldsmith' in 40:19.

p. That is, the carpenter.

q. The subject of the verbs אמר and ויחזקהו is the carpenter.

r. The verb חזק can mean in the *Piel* 'to be firmly grasped'; Fitzgerald (1989: 444) refers to Isa 54:2: ויתדתיך חזקי 'make firm [in the ground] your tent stakes!' Here then it refers to making the tenon of the figurine firm in the mortise of its wooden base.

s. במסמרים is usually understood to mean 'nails'; however, Fitzgerald (1989: 444) argues that nails pounded into a wooden base were not used to stabilize metal figurines such as the text describes up to this point. According to Fitzgerald, this word probably describes the metal tongue (tenon) that was left on the figurine from casting and was now inserted into the mortise in the wooden base to stabilize it (see Schroer 1987: Abb. 82–83.) However, this term could refer to wooden pegs tapped or wedged in to stabilize the mortise and tenon. If these verses originally referred to a wooden statue, then nails would be used to affix metal plates to it (see Schroer 1987: 214 n. 232), as was done to a wooden statue of the Egyptian pharaoh Pepi I.

Isaiah 44:9–22

Isa 44:9–20[47] is the most extensive parody on the manufacturing of a cult image in the Hebrew Bible. It is part of a legal judgment speech (*Gerichtsrede*), which is apparent from the statement in 44:7: "Who is like me?[48] Let him stand up[49] and speak; let him tell it and bring his case to me."[50] The legal speech continues into vv. 21–22. Into this courtroom setting have been inserted vv. 9–20 as proof of Yahweh's incomparability. According to Elliger and Westermann, these verses are a taunt song (*Spottlied*).

Some scholars insist that this section (vv. 9–20) is not a unity because of internal inconsistencies (see Roth 1975: 23 n.12).[51] For example, Elliger (1978: 422) sees the

47. See Thomas 1971: 319–30.

48. This rhetorical מי is also found at the beginning of 40:41.

49. This is found in LXX στήτω καί.

50. On ערך as a legal term, see Scholnick 1922: 353 n. 3.

51. However, as we have already seen in Jeremiah 10, the alternation between singular and plural seems to be part of this genre.

Spottlied (vv. 9–20) as coming from three different non–Deutero-Isaian post-Exilic sources:

1. The plural frame: vv. 9–11 and 18 (perhaps also vv. 12–13 as a quotation).
2. The addition: vv. 14–17.
3. The final addition: vv. 19–20.

Westermann divides this taunt song into two parts (1977: 147–48). Verses 9–12, the matrix of the song, are a general verdict against the making and worshiping of idols. Such people should be put to shame! Verses 13–19 expand on the manufacture of the images; and v. 20 returns to the motif of *shame.*

In any case, as pointed out by Richard Clifford (1980: 460–63) and Knut Holter (1995: 190–202), vv. 9–20 are thoroughly integrated into their context. Several *mots cachets* achieve this interweaving. The 'idol crafters' (יֹצְרֵי־פֶסֶל) of v. 9 are contrasted with Yahweh in v. 2 'who crafts you from the womb and helps you' (מבטן יעזרך ויצרך) and v. 24. In v. 8 Israel is told to 'fear not' (אל־תפחדו); however, in v. 11 the idol-makers are afraid (יפחדו). Throughout the taunt song, the verb עשׂה describes the fruitless (v. 10b) activity of the idol-maker (vv. 13, 15, 17, 19). But Yahweh proclaims in v. 24: אנכי יהוה עשׂה כל 'I am Yahweh who is making all'. Yahweh can say to Israel in v. 21: 'You are my servant' (עבדי־אתה); the iconodule in v. 17d says to his block of wood, 'You are my god' (אלי אתה). In v. 8 Israel is Yahweh's witness (ואתם עדי), which contrasts with the witnesses of the idols (עדיהם) in v. 9. Furthermore, in v. 15 the image-maker "makes"[52] a god (אַף־יִפְעַל־אֵל); contrast this with Yahweh's actions in 43:12–13, a passage that uses many of the words of Isa 44:9–22:

וְאַתֶּם עֵדַי נְאֻם־יְהוָה וַאֲנִי־אֵל׃ גַּם־מִיּוֹם אֲנִי הוּא וְאֵין מִיָּדִי מַצִּיל אֶפְעַל וּמִי יְשִׁיבֶנָּה׃ ס	12 You are my witnesses, says Yahweh, and I am God! 13 and also from today on I am he, there is no one who can deliver you from my hand; I work and who can restrain it?

> Comparison between the nations and Israel as they line up before Yahweh is central to the chapter. The idol passage, with its vivid narratives, accentuates the infinite series of purposeless acts imposed upon the nations. Israel can easily fulfill its role as witness by recalling that Yahweh is the first and the last and is bound to it by creation and redemption (Clifford 1980: 463).

There is confusion in the text about the sequence of activities, especially beginning in v. 14, where the infinitive construct seems overly abrupt. More importantly, this seems to be an instance of *hysteron proteron* in that it is after the carpenter has carved

52. The Hebrew verb פעל is mostly poetic and late (Schroer 1987: 217 n. 238); this may suggest that our passage is more "poetic" than technically accurate.

the image (v. 13) that he goes to the forest to cut and nurture the wood (v. 14)![53] Although this awkwardness could be explained as an inelegant splicing of two separate descriptions, other possibilities suggest themselves. First of all, it is methodologically precarious to fault a parody for its logic! However, more importantly, Deutero-Isaiah may refer here to the actual ritual sequence of the Babylonian *mīs pî* ritual. In the *mīs pî* ceremony, after the statue had been crafted in the temple atelier (*bīt mummi*), it was brought to the river bank, where it was ritually retrogressed to the time it began as a tree and watered so that it could be reborn (see Jacobsen 1987: 25–26). This section of Deutero-Isaiah does refer to the Akkadian wood *erēnu* (cedar) and to an encyclopedic list of rare woods and therefore might be aware of the ritual in its broadest outline and be mocking its apparently unnatural sequence.

Isa 44:9–22

9 יֹצְרֵי־פֶסֶל כֻּלָּם תֹּהוּ וַחֲמוּדֵיהֶם
בַּל־יוֹעִילוּ וְעֵדֵיהֶם הֵמָּה בַּל־יִרְאוּ
וּבַל־יֵדְעוּ לְמַעַן יֵבֹשׁוּ׃ 10 מִי־יָצַר
אֵל וּפֶסֶל נָסָךְ לְבִלְתִּי הוֹעִיל׃

9 All[a] who craft[b] idols are nothing,[c] and the things
they delight in do not profit; their[d] witnesses
they[e] neither see[f] nor know, that they may be put
to shame. 10 Who[g] crafts a god or who would
cast an image that is profitable for nothing?

a. Deutero-Isaiah seems to use כלם almost in the sense of 'the whole sorry lot': 40:26, 41:29, 42:22, 44:11, 45:16, 49:18, 50:9.

b. The fashioners of idols (יצרי־פסל) are contrasted with Yahweh, who fashions (ויצרך) Israel in 44:2.

c. This reference to idol crafters as 'nothings' (תהו) recalls the situation in Gen 1:2 before creation. Similar language is used in 1 Sam 12:21 and Isa 41:29. The language in Samuel is not typically Deuteronomistic and may be a later addition to the text (McCarter 1980: 217; Stoebe 1973: 234, 239).

d. The suffix 'their' refers back to those who craft idols. The idols bear witness about their makers (Holter 1995: 136).

e. The MT המה has *puncta extraordinaria* (GK §5n, BL §6 r, s); Qa has the word written above the line; the word probably is a dittography and should be omitted.

f. This motif echoes the Deuteronomistic polemic against the cult image, namely, that they have eyes but do not see (Deut 4:28), an argument also developed in Ps 115:5. The iconodule was also aware of this danger, for in the *mīs pî* ceremony, he states: "this statue without its mouth opened cannot smell incense, cannot eat food, cannot drink water. . . ." (STT 200:43).

g. Some take the מי at the beginning of v. 10 as an indefinite pronoun 'whoever'; see Preuss (1971: 209 n. 90): "Wer einen Gott bilden will, hat nur ein Götzenbild gegossen." See also Thomas 1971: 320. However, rhetorical questions are frequent at the beginning of idol parodies (Holter 1995: 138 n. 25). The identity of the god and statue are also found in vv. 15c and 17.

53. Schroer 1987: 216: "Vv. 14–17 sind zudem nicht sehr logisch nach der Notiz von der Fertigstellung des Bildes angefügt." A similar "illogical" order can be found in an Egyptian tomb representation of the making of two anthropoid sarcophagai cited by Lorton (see p. 158) in his chapter in this volume. Here the performance of the "opening of the mouth" ceremony and the felling of the tree are combined in the same tableau.

11 הֵן כָּל־חֲבֵרָיו יֵבֹשׁוּ וְחָרָשִׁים הֵמָּה
מֵאָדָם יִתְקַבְּצוּ כֻלָּם יַעַמְדוּ יִפְחֲדוּ
יֵבֹשׁוּ יָחַד׃ 12 חָרַשׁ בַּרְזֶל מַעֲצָד

11 Now, since [h] all his fellows [i] shall be put to shame, and the craftsmen are but human;[j] let them all assemble, let them stand forth, they shall be terrified,[k] they shall be put to shame together.
12 The ironsmith works [l] with[m] a chisel[n] over the

h. Verse 11: The הן opens the juridical procedings (see 41:11, 24, 29). See Waltke and O'Connor 1990: 40.2.1c.

i. MT חבריו, Qa חובריו, S אומניהון, T פלחיהון 'their worshipers'; probably guild members. Elliger (1978: 424) understands the term not as 'guild members' (Penna, Thomas) but as the statue's companions, i.e., worshipers (Fohrer, McKenzie). However, 'his fellows' (חבריו) probably refers to the fellow members of his craft guild. These are the equivalent of the *mārē ummâni* in the *mīs pî* ritual (cf. the cognate of the Akkadian in the S!). In Deutero-Isaiah, like חרש, חבר is also used of Babylonian enchantments in Isa 47:9, 12; these double uses may be intentional (Holter 1995: 144 n. 38).

j. However, in the Mesopotamian *mīs pî* ceremony, the workmen must swear an oath that they did not craft the image but that the appropriate craft deity (e.g., Kusibanda) had.

k. The craftsmen should be terrified (יפחדו); Israel, however, is assured by Yahweh in v. 8 not to be terrified (אל־תפחדו).

l. The Hebrew text 'the iron-worker a chisel' is obviously deficient; it seems to lack a verb. People have suggested such verbs as עשׂה 'makes', חרשׁ 'engraves' (therefore a haplography), and חָצֵשׁ 'cleaves'. The phrase 'iron-worker' seems secure, since it forms a parallel with the חרש עצים 'woodworker' in v. 13. Perhaps the least radical suggestion would be to read יפעל for MT ופעל and to take that verb as the verb governing all of v. 12a: 'The ironworker with a chisel works in the coals'. This would then refer to the iron-worker chiseling the slag from a lump of wrought iron that must be kept in the coals in order to work on it; at that time, technology could not achieve adequate temperature to cast iron; craftsmen could only fashion lumps of heated iron (wrought iron). Or the מעצד could be the direct object of the verb יפעל, which is usually transitive. In this case the tool would, as in Jeremiah 10, be a carpenter's tool that the iron-smith tempers in the coals in preparation for the carpenter's use. This latter possibility has the advantages that it integrates the work of the two craftsmen and appreciates the fact that we know of no iron work on ancient Near Eastern cult images. Perhaps the example of iron was chosen for an ironic function: the material worked on is stronger than the worker! Holter (1995: 15) finds it "unnatural" to go back to the making of a tool rather than to the making of an image, as the context would seem to require.

m. On the omission of the preposition ־ב presupposed by this translation, see Joüon §133i. However, as stated above, MT מעצד could be the direct object of the verb: 'he works the chisel in the coals'.

n. As we have already seen, מעצד is a problem. In Jer 10:3 the word refers to an implement apparently used for wood-working. Elliger speculates: (עִצֵּד) גֹּלֶם עָצַד 'schneidet die Urform aus'. This word is deleted by Duhm, Steinmann, Penna, North, Fohrer, and McKenzie or else is used as the base for emendations: מֶה עָצֵב 'What trouble!' Clifford (1980: 461) takes מעצד as the verb עצד 'incises' (see the Gezer Calendar) preceded by an enclitic mem on ברזל. However, both מעצד and מעקב are found listed together in Ugaritic text 2048.3, 8, 10, 12, 14. The מעצד could refer to a small chisel used to break off chunks of wrought iron from its slag; the chunks are then hammered over the coals into the final shape. It is doubtful that the technology of the time allowed for anything other than wrought iron. This would explain the appearance of these two tools in the Ugaritic text, since hammer and chisel are a natural semantic pair.

LXX ὤξυνε τέκτων σίδηρον (Delitzsch, Gesenius, Thomas, Bonnard = חָרָשׁ ברזל יחֵד/הֵחֵד). S לטשׁ פרזלא נגרא, like the LXX, thinks of a carpenter sharpening his iron. (LXX continues carpenter notion with additions.) T thinks of a smith (נפחא) who makes an axe out of iron. V 'faber ferrarius' = MT.

וּפֹעֵל בַּפֶּחָם וּבַמַּקָּבוֹת יִצְּרֵהוּ
וַיִּפְעָלֵהוּ בִּזְרוֹעַ כֹּחוֹ גַּם־רָעֵב
וְאֵין כֹּחַ לֹא־שָׁתָה מַיִם וַיִּיעָף׃
13 חָרַשׁ עֵצִים נָטָה קָו יְתָאֳרֵהוּ
בַשֶּׂרֶד יַעֲשֵׂהוּ בַּמַּקְצֻעוֹת וּבַמְּחוּגָה
יְתָאֳרֵהוּ וַיַּעֲשֵׂהוּ כְּתַבְנִית אִישׁ
כְּתִפְאֶרֶת אָדָם לָשֶׁבֶת בָּיִת׃
14 לִכְרָת־לוֹ אֲרָזִים וַיִּקַּח תִּרְזָה
וְאַלּוֹן וַיְאַמֶּץ־לוֹ בַּעֲצֵי־יָעַר נָטַע
אֹרֶן וְגֶשֶׁם יְגַדֵּל׃

coals; he shapes it with hammers, and forges it with his strong arm; he becomes hungry and his strength fails, he drinks no water and is faint.[o]
13 The carpenter[p] stretches a line,[q] he marks it out with a stylus;[r] he makes[s] it with planes,[t] and marks it with a compass; he shapes it into the figure of a man, with the beauty of a man, to dwell in a house.[u]
14 He goes out to cut[v] down cedars; he chooses an ilex tree[w] or an oak and secures it for himself[x] among the trees of the forest;

---

o. Verse 12: Preuss (1971: 210): "Der Spott hat dabei zwei Zeilrichtungen. Einmal geht es um die menschliche Tätigkeit selber: Wo so gearbeitet wird, kann doch kein 'Gott' herauskommen! Und zweitens wird das Material und vor allem dessen sonstige Verwendung in anderen Bereichen und zu anderen Zwecken aufs Korn genommen: Wie kann daraus und auf diese Weise ein angemessenes Gottesbild, ein Gott werden?"

p. Verse 13: LXX: Ἐκλεξάμενος τέκτων ξύλον ἔστησεν αὐτὸ ἐν μέτρῳ καὶ ἐν κόλλῃ ἐρρύθμισεν αὐτό, καὶ ἐποίησεν αὐτό ὡς μορφὴν ἀνδρὸς καὶ ὡς ὡραιότητα ἀνθρώπου στῆσαι αὐτὸ ἐν οἴκῳ 'The carpenter, having chosen a piece of wood, marks it out with a rule and fits it with glue, and makes it as the form of a man and as the beauty of a man, to set it up in the house'.

S: גבא נגרא קיסא 'the carpenter selects wood'; 'he measures/anoints it' (ומשׁחה); ובתתא דבקה 'and with glue he joins it' (= LXX).

T: 'The carpenter marks (נפיץ) the wood with the string'; ליה במשקולתא 'and he separates it with the plumbline'; מגזיליה באוזמילא 'he cuts it out with a knife'; ובנצורין מאחיד ליה 'he fastens it with clamps'.

V: 'artifex lignarius extendit normam' 'formavit illud in runcina (plane)'. 'fecit illud in angularibus (T-square), et in circino tornavit'.

q. The plumb line (קו) is generally used in the Hebrew Bible in connection with large projects (e.g., 2 Kgs 21:13); perhaps its use here is ironic (Horace, *Ars Poetica* 139: parturient montes, nascetur ridiculus mus).

r. שֶׂרֶד 'a stylus' (Aquila παραγραφίς).

s. The MT of v. 13 repeats יַעֲשֵׂהוּ 'he makes it'; perhaps it would be better to read יְשַׁעֵהוּ 'he smooths it', here from the verb שׁעע 'to make smooth'. On the other hand, the verb עשׂה 'to make' is a frequent motif in this passage as well as in all idol parodies (Dick 1984: 237–38; Holter 1995: 161–63).

t. מַקְצֻעָה Baumgartner: 'wood scraper' ← קצע.

u. Hebrew לשבת בית can refer to either a private house or the temple; the choice depends on what type of divine image is meant.

v. Verse 14: Elliger (1978: 419) "[the ungrammatical insertion of לכרת] dürfte ein Hinweis darauf sein, daß der Zitator (14–17) nicht identisch ist mit dem Verfasser der jetzt voraufgehenden Sätze." D. Winton Thomas: הלך לכרת לו 'He goeth to cut him down. . . '. This suggestion has been accepted by Clifford (1980: 461 n. 28).

w. תרזה 'ilex?' (cf. Arabic *taraza* 'be hard').

x. אמץ Cohen 1978: 45 n. 185: 'secures for himself'; see Ps 80:16 and parallel in v. 16 אמצת לך.

15 וְהָיָה לְאָדָם לְבָעֵר וַיִּקַּח מֵהֶם וַיָּחָם
אַף־יַשִּׂיק וְאָפָה לָחֶם אַף־יִפְעַל־אֵל
וַיִּשְׁתָּחוּ עָשָׂהוּ פֶסֶל וַיִּסְגָּד־לָמוֹ׃
16 חֶצְיוֹ שָׂרַף בְּמוֹ־אֵשׁ עַל־חֶצְיוֹ
בָּשָׂר יֹאכֵל יִצְלֶה צָלִי וְיִשְׂבָּע
אַף־יָחֹם וְיֹאמַר הֶאָח חַמּוֹתִי רָאִיתִי
אוּר׃ 17 וּשְׁאֵרִיתוֹ לְאֵל עָשָׂה לְפִסְלוֹ
יִסְגָּוד־לוֹ וְיִשְׁתַּחוּ וְיִתְפַּלֵּל אֵלָיו
וְיֹאמַר הַצִּילֵנִי כִּי אֵלִי אָתָּה׃ 18 לֹא
יָדְעוּ וְלֹא יָבִינוּ כִּי טַח מֵרְאוֹת עֵינֵיהֶם
מֵהַשְׂכִּיל לִבֹּתָם׃ 19 וְלֹא־יָשִׁיב
אֶל־לִבּוֹ וְלֹא דַעַת וְלֹא־תְבוּנָה לֵאמֹר
חֶצְיוֹ שָׂרַפְתִּי בְמוֹ־אֵשׁ וְאַף אָפִיתִי
עַל־גֶּחָלָיו לֶחֶם אֶצְלֶה בָשָׂר וְאֹכֵל
וְיִתְרוֹ לְתוֹעֵבָה אֶעֱשֶׂה לְבוּל עֵץ
אֶסְגּוֹד׃ 20 רֹעֶה אֵפֶר לֵב הוּתַל הִטָּהוּ
וְלֹא־יַצִּיל אֶת־נַפְשׁוֹ וְלֹא יֹאמַר
הֲלוֹא שֶׁקֶר בִּימִינִי׃ ס 21 זְכָר־אֵלֶּה
יַעֲקֹב וְיִשְׂרָאֵל כִּי עַבְדִּי־אָתָּה
יְצַרְתִּיךָ עֶבֶד־לִי אַתָּה יִשְׂרָאֵל לֹא
תִנָּשֵׁנִי׃ 22 מָחִיתִי כָעָב פְּשָׁעֶיךָ וְכֶעָנָן
חַטֹּאותֶיךָ שׁוּבָה אֵלַי כִּי גְאַלְתִּיךָ׃

he plants a cedar[y] and the rain nourishes it.
15 Then it becomes fuel for a man; he takes a
part of it and warms himself, he kindles a fire and
bakes bread; also he makes a god and people worship it; he makes an image and falls down before
it. 16 Half of it he burns in the fire; over the half
he eats meat, he roasts[z] meat and is satisfied; also
he warms himself and says, "Aha, I am warm, I
have experienced the fire!" 17 And the rest of it
he makes into a god, his idol; and falls down to it
and worships it; he prays to it and says, "Deliver
me, for thou art my god!"[aa] 18 They know not,
nor do they discern; for their eyes are covered, so
that they cannot see, and their minds, so that
they cannot understand. 19 No one considers,
nor is there knowledge or discernment to say,
"Half of it I burned in the fire, I also baked bread
on its coals, I roasted flesh and have eaten; and
shall I make the residue of it an abomination?
Shall I fall down before a block of wood?"[ab] 20
He feeds on ashes; a deluded mind has led him
astray, and he cannot deliver himself or say, "Is
there not a lie in my right hand?" 21 Remember
these things, O Jacob, and Israel, for you are my
servant; I crafted you,[ac] you are my servant;

---

y. MT ארן: Probably = Akk *erēnu* 'cedar' (see Cohen 1978: 44–45). According to texts cited by Cohen, *erēnu* was used both for figurines (Maqlu IX 39–40: *ṣalam erēni*) and for burning in the cult (SBH 144:20). Although Cohen could not find this word in *mīs pî* texts, it can be found both as a wood and as balsam in such rituals. However, the small ן־ in writing ארן may suggest scribal uncertainty about the word, which some read as the more common Hebrew word ארז. Christopher North (1964: 138) finds that "the Hebrew is clumsy and catalogical"; however, such lists of woods are typical among the ritual materials in the *mīs pî* ritual.

z. The MT יאכל יצלה 'he eats (then) he roasts' presents an odd sequence that many commentators and versions (LXX, Syriac) suggest should be reversed to establish a more logical order. However, much about this entire spoof is nonsequential: he goes to cut, then chooses the wood, then plants it (exact reverse of a more logical sequence!); and the 'halves' here do not really "add up."

aa. Verse 17: Note the pun with the roots צלה 'roast' (vv. 16, 19) and נצל 'save' in v. 17!

ab. Verse 19: לבול עץ אסגוד. See Akk. *bulu*: *bulu* is glossed *iṣ-ṣu la-bi-ru* 'old wood'; Qa לבלוי עץ; S פתכרא דקיסא 'idol of wood'; T לבלי אץ 'to something destroyed out of wood'; V 'ante truncum ligni'.

ac. Yahweh is the subject of the verb יצר 'fashion', not the object of the idol-maker's fashioning, as at the beginning of this passage (v. 9).

> O Israel, you will not be forgotten by me. 22 I have swept away your transgressions like a cloud, and your sins like mist; return to me, for I have redeemed you.

The Prophetic Argument and the Ancient World

The principal arguments of the Israelite prophets against fashioning the cult image were also taken up by roughly contemporary Hellenistic rationalists. Their arguments center on three distinct but closely interrelated points:[54]

1. First, the prophets identify the cult image with the deity him/herself. The gods are as corruptible and vulnerable as the materials from which the image has been constructed.
2. Second, the prophets challenge how a product of human hands could be considered divine.
3. Third, the prophets parody the profane raw materials out of which the divine image has been made.[55]

Identity of Image and Deity

In Hos 14:4[56] the people pledge that they will never again identify their god with the product of their own hands: ולא־נאמר עוד אלהינו למעשׂה ידינו 'Never again will we say, "Our god!" to the work of our hands'. In the *rîb*, that is, legal accusation, in Jeremiah 2, the prophet challenged the people to turn to the gods that they had made for themselves: ואיה אלהיך אשר עשׂית לך 'Where are your gods that you made for yourselves?'

---

54. Isa 44:13 further argues that these images are anthropmorphic, כתבנית איש כתפארת אדם 'like the form of a man, like the beauty of a human', and thus hardly divine—an argument later developed by the Book of Wisdom, which also mocks their zoomorphic form (Wis 13:14). For a further treatment of this theme in Wisdom, see Gilbert 1973: 84–88. This objection was of course also found in Greek literature as early as Xenophanes, who maintained that the deity was not like humans in form or in thought: οὔ τι δέμας θνητοῖσιν ὁμοίος οὐδὲ νόημα '(a god) in no way similar to humans either in flesh or in thought' (Fr. 23, Clement, *Strom* V, 109, I; see Clerc 1915: 91).

55. Preuss 1971: 210: "Der Spott hat dabei zwei Zeilrichtungen. Einmal geht es um die menschliche Tätigkeit selber: Wo so gearbeitet wird, kann doch kein 'Gott' herauskommen! Und zweitens wird das Material und vor allem dessen sonstige Verwendung in anderen Bereichen und zu anderen Zwecken aufs Korn genommen: Wie kann daraus und auf diese Weise ein angemessenes Gottesbild, ein Gott werden?"

56. See my article (Dick 1998). Mettinger (1995: 21–22) advances this discussion with his recourse to C. Peirce's semiotics.

Almost two centuries later, Deutero-Isaiah paralleled the יצרי־פסל 'fashioners of a cult image' (44:9) with the יצר אל 'one who fashioned a god' (v. 10). In 44:15c the anonymous prophet scoffs: אף־יפאל־אל וישתחו עשׂהו פסל ויסגד־למו 'And he made a *god* and worshiped it; he constructed a *cult statue* and venerated it'. We encounter the same confusion of statue and deity two verses later: ושאריתו לאל עשׂה לפסלו 'And the rest of it [the log] he made into a god for a cult image'.

Similar satirical identifications can be found in such nonprophetic passages as Judg 18:24, where Micah laments the loss of his cult image/god: ויאמר את־אלהי אשר־עשׂיתי לקחתם 'and he said, "You took my god which I made".' In 1 Sam 5:1–5 Dagon himself (and not his statue) is said to fall before the Ark of Yahweh.

In Greek literature we find identical objections to the confusion of the god and the image.[57] The pious iconodule laments the identification; the satirist ridicules it. Diogenes (*Vitae Philosophorum* 2.116) reports that Stilpo of Megara, who taught at Athens around 320 B.C.E., once pointed to the famous chryselephantine statue of Athena and asked a man if that were the goddess Athena, the one of Zeus. When the man replied, "Yes," Stilpo countered that it was Athena of Phidias, not of Zeus, and therefore it was not a god (οὐκ ἄρα, εἶπε, θεός).

Few biblical texts can equal the satirical wit of Lucian (second century C.E.) in his *Juppiter Tragoidus* 7: Zeus, presiding over the assembly of the gods, seats them according to their material and workmanship: those of gold in the front row, followed by those of silver, then ivory, bronze, and lastly those of stone. Zeus does afford special honors to those made by Phidias, Alcamenes, or Myron. However, the ἄτεχνοι 'uncrafted' are ordered to huddle together apart from the rest.[58]

---

57. Plutarch in *De Iside et Osiride* (379C–D) laments the popular confusion among the poorly educated between the divine image and the deity itself:

> ὅθεν ἄριστα λέγεται παρὰ τοῖς φιλοσόφοις τὸ τοὺς μὴ μανθάνοντας ὀρθῶς ἀκούειν ὀνομάτων κακῶς χρῆσθαι καὶ τοῖς πράγμασιν· ὥσπερ Ἑλλήνων οἱ τὰ χαλκᾶ καὶ τὰ γραπτὰ καὶ λίθινα μὴ μαθόντες μηδ᾽ ἐθισθέντες ἀγαλματα καὶ τιμὰς θεῶν ἀλλὰ θεοὺς καλεῖν, εἶπα τολμῶντες λέγειν, ὅτι τὴν ᾿Αθηνᾶν Λαχάρης ἐξέδυσε, τὸν δ᾽ ᾿Απόλλωνα χρυσοῦς βοστρύχους ἔχοντα Διονύσιος ἀπέκειρεν, ὁ δὲ Ζεὺς ὁ Καπετώλιος περὶ τὸν ἐμφύλιον πόλεμον ἐνεπρήσθη καὶ διεφθάρη. . . .
>
> There is an excellent saying among the philosophers that those who do not learn to understand words correctly also fail to use the objects properly. And so there are Greeks who have not learned or accustomed themselves to calling works of bronze, painting, and stone "images" made to honor the gods; rather they call these objects themselves "gods." And so they dare to say that Lachares undressed Athena, and that Dionysius gave a haircut to Apollo of the golden locks, and that Zeus on the Capitoline Hill was burnt and destroyed during the civil war.

For further bibliography, see Clerc 1915: 112 n. 2.

58. *Juppiter Tragodus* 7:1:

> Εὖ γε, ὦ Ἑρμῆ, ἄριστα κεκήρυκταί σοι, καὶ συνίασι γὰρ ἤδη· ὥστε παραλαμβάνων κάθιζε αὐτοὺς κατὰ τὴν ἀξίαν ἕκαστον, ὡς ἂν ὕλης ἢ τέξνης ἔχῃ, ἐν προεδρίᾳ μὲν τοὺς χρυσοῦς, ἔτα επὶ τούτοις οἱ τοὺς αργυροῦς, εἶτα ἑξῆς ὁπόσοι ἐλεφάντινοι, εἶτα τοὺς

The Greek iconodule, however, could be thoroughly aware of the difference between the deity and its image. The second-century rhetorician Dio Chrysostom in his Olympic Discourse used contemporary psychology to explain the presence of the god in his/her image. Just as the human body is the vessel for the φρόνησις and λόγος 'reason and intelligence', so the image made by the craftsman is merely the vessel for the divine spirit.[59]

ἀνθρώπινον σῶμα ὡς ἀγγεῖον φρονήσεως καὶ λόγου θεῷ προσάπτοντες, ἐνδεία καὶ ἀπορίᾳ παραδείγματος τῷ φανερῷ τε καὶ εἰκαστῷ τὸ ἀνείκαστον καὶ ἀφανὲς ἐνδείκνυσθαι ζητοῦντες, συμβόλου δυνάμει χρώμενοι. . . .

(men) attributing to a god a human body as a vessel for understanding and rationality for lack of a better illustration seeking to illustrate by that which is visible and a representation of that which is both invisible and unrepresentable using a symbol (Dis XII 59).

There is no question that cuneiform texts from Mesopotamia, both historical and religious, can refer to the statue as if it simply were the god him/herself. The multiple peregrinations of Babylon's statue of Marduk due to raids were often phrased as if the God Marduk went on a journey. And so the Kassite king of Babylon Agumkakrime (1602–1585 B.C.E.) talks of Marduk's return—not the statue's—from captivity in Hana:[60]

When the Great Gods told by their pure word Marduk the Lord of Esangila and of Babylon to return to Babylon, Marduk determined to return to Babylon. . . . I planned and paid close attention and made him ready to take back to Babylon; I supported Marduk who loves my reign. I consulted King Shamash through a lamb of the *bārû*-priest, and I sent to a far country to the land of Ḫana so that they might take Marduk and Ṣarpanitu who love my reign by the hand; and so I brought them back to Esangila and to Babylon. In the temple which Shamash carefully fixed (by oracle) I returned them (V R pl. 33 col i 44–ii 21; see K.4348+ K.4149+ K.4203+ Sm 27).[61]

Earlier journeys of Marduk are recounted in the theologically important "Prophecy of Marduk" reconstructed by R. Borger from fragments of a large tablet from Nineveh

---

χαλκοῦς ἢ λιθίνους, καὶ ἐν αὐτοῖς τούτοις οἱ Φειδίου μὲν ἢ 'Αλκαμένους ἢ Μύρωνος ἢ τῶν ὁμοίωβ τεχνιτῶν προτετιμήσθων, οἱ συρφετώδεις δὲ οὗτοι καὶ ἄτεχνοι πόρρω που συνωσθέντες σιωπῇ ἀναπληρούντων μόνον τὴν ἐκκλησίαν·

59. This explanation of the relationship between the cult image and the deity (as body to the soul) was particularly prevalent among the neoplatonists. See the 5th Oration of the Emperor Julian; cf. Bernhardt 1956: 29–30, and von Geffcken 1916–19: 294–98.

60. Perhaps we should read Ḫatti (*ḫa-ti-i*) instead of *ḫa-ni-i*. Landsberger 1954: 65 n. 160: "Die Emendation *mat Ḫatti* 'Land der Hittiter' für Ḫani erscheint zwingend." Babylon had just been plundered by the Hittite Mursilis. Since this inscription exists only in a later copy, many have questioned its authenticty. Cf. Landsberger 1928–29: 312; 1954: 67–68, 116; Borger 1971a: 17; Weidner 1959–60: 138. For abbreviations of the cuneiform literature, see Borger 1967.

61. See Jensen as cited in Schrader, *Keilschriftliche Bibliothek* 3/1, 134–52, with literature.

and a duplicate from Ashur. This document catalogues the trips of Marduk, that is, his *statue*, with the Hittites, the Elamites, and the Assyrians (Borger 1971a: 3–24; see esp. 7:21′–7:24′).

The identification of deity and cult statue can probably be traced to the earliest days of Mesopotamian religion. Even as early as pre-Sargonic Lagash (before 2000 B.C.E.), month names could be identified in terms of "moving the (statue of the) gods": itu-^{d}ba-ba$_{6}$ é-gibila$_{x}$-na-ì-gingin-a 'month in which the goddess Baba goes to her new temple' (MDP 243). Uruk IV and Jemdet Nasr (ca. 3200–2800 B.C.E.) glyptic art showed the deity, hidden in a shrine, being conveyed by boat on such a journey (UVB XVII, 29, pl. 26a, b, e).[62] By the early Ur I period (ca. 2500 B.C.E.), the deity itself in human form, undoubtedly the cult image, was portrayed on the boat.[63] Even though early pre-Sargonic inscriptions (before 2300 B.C.E.) cite offerings to the statue of a king (alan/dúl lugal), the earliest mention of a statue of a deity (alan ^{d}X) is found in the Isin Dynasty (ca. 2020–1790 B.C.E.). A. Spycket (1968) argues that the absence of the phrase alan ^{d}X 'statue of the god X' before the second millennium suggests that cult images did not emerge before this time.[64]

Later Babylonian texts, for example, the Babylonian Chronicles, frequently mention the taking of a god to Babylon, which of course identifies the deity with its cult statue. In 626 B.C.E., just before Naboplossar became king of Babylon, "the gods of Kish went to Babylon."[65] Another passage in the Babylonian Chronicle mentions *Ilāni šūt Uruk u nišēšu ītekmū* 'they took away the gods of Uruk and its inhabitants' (CT 34 48 iii 3 [NB chron]).[66]

Nevertheless, the Mesopotamians clearly maintained a distinction between the god and his/her statue.[67] The destruction of a cult statue did not entail the destruction of the deity. When the statue of Shamash at Sippar was destroyed (CT 34 48 i 7–8 *usaḫḫū uḫalliqū*) by Sutean raiders under Simbar-Shipak (ca. 1026–1009 B.C.E.),[68] worship of Shamash could still continue, using a symbolic equivalent, a

62. Presumably all of these journeys and processions refer to travels undertaken by the cult image identified with the god/goddess. For the skimpy archaeological evidence for cult statues in Mesopotamia, see Seidl 1980–83: 307–19; Curtis 1990: 30–56.

63. For further information, see Opificius 1957–71: 463–66; Sauren 1969a: 214–36; Sjöberg 1957–71: 480–83; Boehmer 1957–71: 479–80. A similar transportation of the gods took place in Syria; see du Buisson 1970: 50; Fleischer 1973: 364; Lucian, *De Dea Syria*, #47.

64. See the reviews of Sauren (1969b: 117) and Pettinato (1969: 213), and the comments of Lambert (1990: 123–25).

65. Chronicle 2:6 (Grayson 1975: 88). See Hallo 1983: 14–15. For this practice in ancient Assyria, see Cogan 1974, esp. chap. 2.

66. For a portrayal of the robbery of captured gods (i.e., images), see Barnett and Falkner 1962: pl. 92.

67. A similar distinction occurs in Egypt, as Lorton has shown (see p. 183). The *ka* could enter a funerary statue during the life of an individual without thereby diminishing him. "The *ka* was divisible without diminishment." The same holds true for the presence of the deity with his/her cult image.

68. See the boundary-stone inscription in King 1912: no. 36, BM 91000.

sun-disk (*nipḫu*), until the reign of Nabu-apla-iddina (ca. 887–855 B.C.E.). When Nabu-apla-iddina dedicated his new statue of Shamash, he washed its mouth "before Shamash":

> By means of the skill of Ea and of the workmanship of Ninildu (carpenter deity), Kusibanda (goldsmith deity), Ninkurra, Ninzadim (craft deities), with red gold and clear lapis-lazuli he fashioned the statue of Shamash the great Lord (*ṣa-lam* ᵈUTU EN GAL) with great care. With the rite of purification of Ea and Asalluḫi before Shamash (*ma-ḫar* ᵈUTU) in E-kar-zagina which is on the bank of the Euphrates he washed its mouth (*pi-šu im-si-ma*) (King 1912: no. 36, iv 14–27).[69]

This passage clearly differentiates the statue being dedicated from the deity before whom it was dedicated, and this despite the fact that this inscription earlier stated that the Suteans had effaced the great Lord Shamash himself (i 1–8).

Further, there was no problem with the same god having cult images in two different temples; thus Shamash had a statue in both Sippar and Larsa. Certain deities like the sun-god Shamash and the goddess Ishtar of the morning and evening star were also worshiped in their celestial bodies. Thus, some deities could be worshiped in their cult images—often in several different shrines—and in the sun or a star, and yet neither of these was considered identical with the god/goddess. Several cylinder seals from the Akkadian period (ca. 2300–2100 B.C.E.) provide visual evidence of the distinction between a cult image and the deity portrayed. One seal impression preserved in the École Biblique in Jerusalem (Amiet 1955: 411–13, pl. v.4) combines the clear depiction of gods (one enthroned, one seated) with a smaller cult statue in a *naos*. The gods and the statue are represented differently, the cult statue being half size. Another seal, several impressions of which are in the Louvre collection, shows the typical introduction scene, in which a god presents a worshiper to a seated deity, behind whom is the cult statue. The statue is a half-sized standing figure portrayed in profile as standing on one foot on a pedestal typical of Akkadian statuary in the round (Delaporte 1920: t. 103, p. 11, and pl. 9; see also Spycket 1968: 24 and Seidl 1980–83: 317).

Works of Human Hands

As we saw above, one of the the earliest reconstructed versions of the *Bilderverbot* probably read: "gods of silver and gods of gold you shall not make for yourself" (Exod 20:23; see Dohmen 1987: 176–77).[70] Like this hypothetical version from the Book of the Covenant, other apodictic formulations specifically mention the 'making' (עשה) of the image (Exod 20:3; Exod 34:17; Lev 19:4; Lev 26:1; Deut 4:16).

69. This inscription clearly refers to the statue as a *ṣalmu* 'statue': see the inscription on the picture to the left of the sun-disk: (1) *ṣa-lam* ᵈUTU EN GAL (2) *a-šib É-babbar-ra šá qe-reb Sippar*[ki] 'the statue of Shamash who dwells in the Ebabbar which is within Sippar'.

70. Also see Pettinato (1981: 169) for the making of gold and silver statues at Ebla.

The use of עשׂה 'to make' in these legal texts did not yet suggest the later prophetic parodies of the making of the cult image: How can a product of human craft represent the divine? This polemic use of עשׂה was, however, adumbrated in the story of Judges 17–18, which is difficult to date, because it is included in a section that displays considerable Deuteronomistic editing (Boling 1979: 36). The use of עשׂה 'make' in 17:4, 18:24, and 18:27, and the reference to צרף 'smith' in 17:14, represented an attempt to depreciate the image by calling attention to its origins in human craft (Preuss 1971: 65).[71]

The phrase מעשׂה ידך 'work of your hand' (or variations such as מעשׂה אדם 'human workmanship' or מעשׂה חרשׁ 'work of the craftsman') for the cult image are common in the prophets.[72] The earliest instance of its use is in Hos 13:2,[73] 14:4; cf. 8:6. Recalling the final form of the Decalogue, Mic 5:12, Isa 2:8, and Jer 1:16 combine the phrase with the verb השׁתחוה 'to bow down to'.

However, Jer 10:1–6 marks an early expansion of the argument against a human's making a god. Although it is not clear that the passage is authentic to Jeremiah,[74] the argument is not foreign to him, for in 16:20 he clearly juxtaposes אלהים and אדם.

היעשׂה־לו אדם אלהים והמה לא אלהים׃

Does a human make for himself a god? They are not gods!

Gods made by humans are therefore no gods! In Jer 10:1–16 the prophet polemicizes against the images by emphasizing their human origin,[75] which is stressed by an almost encyclopedic list of the materials of their fabrication and array (vv. 3, 4, 9), of the various artisans involved (חכם 'skilled workman', צרף 'metal smith', חרשׁ 'artisan'), and of the tools they used (vv. 3, 4). Their pitiful efforts are contrasted in v. 12 with the "workmanship" of Yahweh who, like the skilled artisans (v. 9), also employs skill (v. 12b); Yahweh's work, however, constructs (עשׂה) the universe!

---

71. Tertullian in his *De Idolatria* picks up on the topos of 'making' (4:1): "Idolum tam fieri quam coli deus prohibet. Quanto praecedit, ut fiat quod coli possit, tanto prius est, ne fiat, si coli non licet" (God forbids the making as much as the worship of the idol. If worship is forbidden, then, to the extent that making it precedes worship, does the prohibition to make it have priority over the prohibition to worship it.).

72. Its use in Deut 4:28 to refer to an idol is atypical, since the expression in Deuteronomy is generally used in a good sense: 'all that you do' (Preuss 1971: 132 n. 82).

73. I agree with Preuss (1971: 129 n. 6) and with Wildberger (1965: 103) that this phrase in Hosea is predeuteronomic; however, see Lang 1983: 32–33 for the opinion that the Hoseanic polemic against idols is *not* from Hosea.

74. Preuss (1971: 169), Overholt (1965: 1–12), and Holladay (1986: 326) argue for its authenticity. However, the very phrase "authentic to Jeremiah" is problematic in the extreme, for it presupposes more knowledge about the contribution to the book of Jeremiah by a historical personage called Jeremiah than we can probably ever achieve; see Carroll 1986: 33–50.

75. Preuss 1971: 169; see esp. 166–67: "[E]r das 'Wesen' der Bilder aufzeigt, indem er ihre Herstellung schildert."

The anonymous prophet Second Isaiah (chaps. 40–55 in the book of Isaiah), who probably wrote in exile in Babylon after the destruction of Jerusalem in 586 B.C.E., composed the most sustained parody of the making of the cult image. Human craftsmanship is stressed by the plethora of terms for different artisans: חרש 'artisan' (חרש ברזל 'iron worker', חרש עצים 'wood worker'), צרף 'smith', חכם 'skilled worker', מחליק פטיש 'one who smooths with a hammer', הולם פעם 'one who strikes the anvil', יצרי־פסל 'image fashioners', חבריו 'his fellow guild members'. These passages probably contain the most complete list of Israelite craftsmen in the Hebrew Bible. The verbs that describe their technical activities also stress their efforts as being human. Besides the more general verbs פעל and עשׂה 'make, construct', we find רקע 'pound out/plate', נסך 'function as a jeweler',[76] בחר 'choose', בקשׁ 'select', נטה קו 'to measure', תאר 'to shape'. Furthermore, we encounter a bewildering list of the tools of the craftsmen's trades: rivets, chisels, hammers, chalk, wood planes, and anvils.[77]

All of their exertions lead to exhaustion, famine, and thirst (Isa 44:12); they need to help and encourage each other (Isa 41:6). Yet despite their useless efforts (בל־יועילו), the craftsmen after all are simply humans: וחרשים המה מאדם (Isa 44:11).[78] Three of the most common Hebrew words for cult/divine image also suggest their origin in human craft: עצבים (see Dohmen 1987: 259–60),[79] פסל, and מסכה, the latter two words even constituting a frequent word pair.[80] The word פסל, often mistranslated 'graven image', probably does not suggest the precise method of manufacturing.[81] Dohmen's study of the word in the Hebrew Bible recommends the translation 'Kultbild' without reference to its construction (Dohmen 1987: 48–49); similarly, the Greek noun χόανον means simply 'statue', although derived from the root χόω 'to carve (wood)'. Although the noun מסכה is usually understood as a 'poured metal image' from the root נסך, Dohmen's research plausibly suggests that the term merely denotes a product of the metal-smith.[82] His workmanship was broader than either plating a wooden core or casting a metal statue; the images he worked on frequently wore gold or silver

76. For this meaning of נסך rather than the more traditional 'to pour (metal)', see Dohmen, *TWAT,* s.v.

77. For similar cynical observations about the mechanical complexity ("bars, bolts, nails, planks, wedges, etc.") of Greek cult images, see Lucian *Gallus* 24:26–40.

78. The prophetic parodies of idol manufacturers had not yet developed the accusation against the moral character of the craftsmen that we shall find later in Christian, Jewish, and pagan Greek literature, where they are frequently denounced as φαυλότατοι 'most evil' and μοχθηροὶ τὸ ἦθος 'wretched people' (Clerc 1915: 101 n. 4).

79. This word, a favorite in the book of Hosea, probably plays on the two different roots עצב I 'to shape' and עצב II 'to be sick, painful'.

80. Although it has been common to translate these last two terms as 'graven (i.e., carved) image' and 'cast statue', it is unlikely that we can be so specific about their construction. Similarly, the pair פסל ומסכה is erroneously thought to specify a wooden core covered with metal plating.

81. Many seek an explanation in the northwest Semitic root *psl* 'to carve, cut' witnessed in the Ugaritic worker *pslm*; see Dohmen 1987: 42–44 for bibliography.

82. See, however, the less plausible suggestion discussed by J. Fauer (1978: 11–12), who derives מסכה from סכה 'anoint with' and associates it with the anointing of statues during their consecration ceremony; supposedly it is also related to Hebrew נסך 'cultic libation'.

jewelry that could warrant the title מסכה. The pair פסל ומסכה is then a hendiadys for a 'cult image made by a jeweler', a meaning that probably extended even to single components of the phrase. It is interesting that with the possible exception of Daniel 3, the Hebrew Bible does not use the more neutral term צלם 'statue' either in the *Bilderverbot* or in the prophetic idol parodies.

The Greek philosopher Zeno, the fifth-century B.C.E. founder of the Stoa, echoed the objections of Deutero-Isaiah in the following citation from Clement of Alexandria's *Stromata*:

> λέγει δὲ καὶ Ζήνων ὁ τῆς Ζτωϊκῆς κτίστης αἱρεσεως ἐν τῷ τῆς πολιτεία βιβλίῳ μήτε ναοὺς δεῖν ποιεῖν μήτε ἀγάλματα· μηδὲν γὰρ εἶναι τῶν θεῶν ἄξιον κατασκεύασμα, καὶ γράφειν οὐ δέδιεν αὐταῖς λέξεσι τάδε· "ἱερά τε οἰκοδομεῖν οὐδὲν δεήσει· ἱερὸν γὰρ μὴ πολλοῦ ἄγιον οὐδὲν χρὴ νομίζειν· οὐδὲν δὲ πολλοῦ ἄξιον καὶ ἅγιον οἰκοδόμων ἔργον καὶ βαναύσων." 5.11.76

> Zeno, the founder of Stoicism, says in his Republic that there should be neither temples nor statues, for no product of human labor is worthy of the gods. He did not fear to write in his own words, "It is not fitting to construct temples, for a temple is not of much value and should not be called holy. For no product of human builders and handymen is of much value or holiness."

In 689 B.C.E., the Assyrian king Sennacherib became exasperated with Babylon's constant revolts against the Assyrian crown and devastated the city, destroying its temples.[83] It remains a point of dispute whether Sennacherib actually destroyed the Babylonian cult statue of Marduk or whether he merely led it into exile in Ashur.[84] In any case, during the reign of his son, Assyria's attitude toward recalcitrant Babylon ameliorated; Esarhaddon consulted the oracles and was commanded to return the divine statues—newly refurbished[85]—to their rebuilt shrines in Babylon.

In spite of the large number of inscriptions describing Esarhaddon's renewal and return of these statues to Babylon, it seems that he died prior to completing the task. Thus it was really his son Ashurbanipal who fulfilled the claims of his father Esarhaddon and returned Marduk to Babylon during the first year of his reign (668 B.C.E.; Streck 1916: 263:26; Borger 1972: 35).

---

83. For a description of Sennacherib's conflict with Babylon, see Brinkman 1973: 89–95. The texts describing the destruction that also contain his theological justification are listed in Miller and Roberts 1977: 14–15.

84. See Miller and Roberts 1977: 94 n. 124; especially note the extensive treatment of this topic in Landsberger 1965: 20–27; cf. Borger's review (1972: 33–37).

85. Whether the statues had to be completely remade or whether the old statues in Assyrian "exile" needed only to be refurbished depends on whether Sennacherib had utterly destroyed the cult images in 689 or had brought them as booty to Ashur. Landsberger 1965: 20 n. 26: "Die *tedishtu* von Götter(bilder) ist nicht eine gewönliche Reparatur, sondern ein hochheiliges Ritual, das zur Geheimlehre gehört und durch Mundwaschung und -öffnung besiegelt wird [Ebeling 1931: 100–114; Meier 1937–39: 42 Anm. 20]." See Cassin 1968: 111. Thus the long-documented history of the treatment of the Marduk statue in the Esangila in Babylon until the destruction of the image by the Persian king Xerxes probably concerns only a single statue.

A text dating from the latter days of the reign of Esarhaddon (Borger 1956: 81ff. [§53]) describes the process of renewing (or remaking) these cult images, from the first stage of consulting the oracles to their final installation in Babylon. This process could only be carried out when and precisely as the gods determined it. In the earlier case of Nabu-apla-iddina (887–855 B.C.E.), the statue of Shamash destroyed centuries earlier could not be replaced until Shamash miraculously revealed the appearance of the image. Earlier attempts by King Simmashshihu to consult Shamash about his appearance were unsuccessful. The moment of revelation lay with the god! Even the form of the statue had to be revealed; Nabu-appla-idina needed a *ṣirpu*, a clay plaque. We also have a series of dream texts in which the deity reveals his/her form to the worshiper (see Oppenheim 1956: 193, 354).[86] In the case of Esarhaddon, the oracles had to be consulted: "When in heaven and on earth signs favorable for the renewal of the (statue of) the gods occurred. . . ."[87]

It could readily be believed that a statue was divine when its appearance was miraculous. Pausanias tell us of instances of statues (in one case, Athene) falling from the heavens (1.26.6). However, to believe in the divinity of the statue was more difficult when the statue had not fallen from heaven but had merely emerged from the craftsmen's atelier (Clerc 1915: 31).

In the following text, also cited in the following chapter, Esarhaddon fully realized the theological problem stressed by the Israelite prophets, namely, of human artisans presuming to craft a divine image:

> (14) Whose right is it, O great Gods, to create gods and goddesses[88] in a place where humans dare not trespass? This task of refurbishing (the statues), which you have constantly been allotting me by oracle, is difficult! (15) Is it the right of deaf and blind human beings who are ignorant of themselves and remain in ignorance throughout their lives? (16) The making of the gods and goddesses is your right, it is in your hands; so I beseech you, create (the gods), and in your exalted holy of holies (17) may what you yourselves have in your heart be brought about in accordance

86. Pausanias (8.42.7) refers to a replacement for a wooden statue of Demeter destroyed in a fire. Oantas made a replacement only after its form had been revealed to him in a dream (καὶ κατὰ ὀνειράτων ὄψιν).

87. The astronomical sign was the heliacal rising of Jupiter. See Borger 1956: 17–18 for a detailed discussion of the omen (bibliography). Compare also the omen declaration delivered to Ashurbanipal in CT 35 pp. 13–15 (in CT obv., in Bauer 1933: 79–82, rev. line 23): "I commissioned you with the renewal of these (images of the) gods and of their temples." The astronomical omen had to be collaborated by a liver omen.

88. Dio Chrysostom in his Olympic Discourse delivered in 97 C.E., asked a similar question of the suitability of crafting the divine statue:

> εἰ δ᾽ αὖ τὸ πρέπον εἶδος καὶ τὴν ἀξίαν μορφήν τῆς θεοῦ φύσεως ἔδημιούργησας, ὕλῃ τε ἐπιτρεπεῖ χρησάμενος, ἀνδρός καὶ τἆλλα ποιήσας ὡς ἐποίησας, σκοπῶμεν τὰ νῦν·
>
> But we should now contemplate, whether the shape you crafted was suitable for a god and was its form worthy of the divine nature? For you not only used pleasing material but also presented a human form of marvelous beauty and size; and apart from its being a man's shape, you also made all the other attributes just as you have made them.

with your unalterable word. (18) Endow the skilled craftsmen whom you ordered to complete this task with as high an understanding as Ea, their creator. (19) Teach them skills by your exalted word; (20) make all their handiwork succeed through the craft of Ninšiku.

The creation of the god was a supreme act of synergy between heaven and earth (STT 200.11: *ina šamê ibbani ina erṣeti ibbanû*), for the statue had been produced by earthly and godly artisans (STT 200.19: [*ṣa*] *lam* [*bun*] *nanê ša īli u amēli*).[89] Mesopotamian religion subordinated the earthly craftsmen to the craftsmen of the gods in several ways. First of all, the *mārē ummânī mudê šipri* had to be designated by the great gods. Thus Esarhaddon in *Asarh* §53, 22–25, arranged diviners in groups: "to determine the experts who should do the work and their initiation . . . they ordered me to enter the *bīt mummi* in Ashur . . . they indicated to me the names of the artisans (fit) for completing the work."

We know from a late writing exercise tablet (VS XV Nr 1 = VAT 8571), which probably dates from the Seleucid period, although the Late Bronze and Persian periods cannot be excluded (Renger 1967: 112 n. 5), that many of these artisans (carpenters, jewelers, stonecutters, etc.) were classified as *ērib bīti* 'priests'. They were probably appointed by the *šatammu* 'bishop' and the *reš šarri bēl piqitti* 'royal commissioner and executive officer'[90] and would probably be consecrated by an ordination ritual, *gullubu*, which involved the ritual shaving of hair. These freemen, members of independent craft guilds at least by Neo-Babylonian times, would be appointed for specific restoration and construction tasks in the temple precincts.[91]

The work on the image would be done in the temple atelier (*bīt mummi*), also called in BBR 31 i line 23 'place where the god is made' (KI DINGIR DÙ-*ú*), which is probably the equivalent of Esarhaddon's 'where the gods are born' (*ašar nabnit* DINGIR.MEŠ) (Borger 1956: §53, 88, line 13). However, the theologically diminished role of these earthly craftsmen is best clarified in the "Mouth Washing" ritual itself and in its incantations, which are translated in the chapter on *mīs pî*. The statue had to be enlivened by the special ceremony called the KA.LUḪ.Ù.DA.DINGIR/*mīs pî* (pp. 55–121), equivalent to the Greek *hidrusis* or the Roman *dedicatio*.[92] Without this ritual, the statue was

89. Also, in ancient Egypt, the presence of the deity in the cult image was not a result of human effort but of the divine will and divine grace. See Lorton's discussion, pp. 184–85.

90. On the translation of the title of this latter official, see Weisberg 1967: 43; for a description of both offices, see Saggs 1959: esp. 36–37.

91. The "craftsmen charter" YBC 3499 (535/534 B.C.E.), which has been treated in detail by David B. Weisberg (1967), is an actual contract between the *šatammu* (Nidniti-Bel) and the *reš šarri bēl piqitti* (Nabu-aḫiddin) of the Eanna temple in Uruk and representatives of various craft guilds, called in line 22 [lu]*um-man-nu ša* É.AN.NA (carpenters, jewelers, and goldsmiths). The artisans agree to make repairs requiring silver, gold, bronze, and wood (lines 18–19).

92. For references to a rite for dedication of a cult image in Greece and Rome, see Bevan 1940: 31–35. Most of the references to the rite in the classical world are found in Christian sources (Minucius Felix, *Octavius* XXII, 5 and Arnobius, *Adversus Nationes* VI, 17); some classical scholars still question the existence of such rites in Greece and Rome (Burkert 1985: 91). For a full treatment of the Mesopotamian *mīs pî* ritual and a translation of various ritual tablets and some incantations, see pp. 55–121 in this volume.

only a dead product of human artisans: "This statue cannot smell incense, drink water, or eat food without the Opening of the Mouth!"[93]—a phrase reminiscent of Psalm 135 and Jer 10:5.

There is no need to discuss the Mesopotamian *mīs/pit pî* ritual here, since Christopher Walker and I treat it in detail in another chapter in this book. However, two elements in this rite directly concern the way Mesopotamian religion responds to the theological difficulties of humans' crafting a god, as highlighted in the prophetic parodies: (1) the workmen swear that they did not make the god; (2) the ritual traces the statue back to its origin in the orchard and then witnesses its "rebirth" as a divine product. First of all, the two-day rite takes great pains to demonstrate that the statue was really a product of Ea and to disassociate it from the human craftsmen in whose atelier it had been prepared. In "reality" it was the product of the craft deities. Although Deutero-Isaiah and Jeremiah portray the human artisan searching the forest for the right tree, in the Mouth Washing incantations, this role is performed by Igisigsig, the carpenter of Anum:

> Tamarisk, pure tree, growing up from a clean place, coming from a pure place, drinking water in abundance from the irrigation-channel; from its trunk gods are made, with its branches gods are cleansed. Igisigsig, the chief gardner of Anu, cut off its branches and took them (K.3511, 1–9).

After the reed hut and the cultic materials had been prepared on the river bank, the statue was processed from the *bīt mummi* to the river with the accompanying incantation, "From this day forth you shall walk before Ea, your father." On the bank the tools used by the artisans (an adze, chisel, saw) together with a gold and silver tortoise and turtle were bound up in the body of a sacrificed sheep and thrown into the river. The artisans were mere surrogates of Ea: upon the completion of their task, the tools were again consigned to the watery abode of Ea, who was the 'Image Fashioner' (nu-dím-mud).[94]

The next morning the artisans (*mārū ummânū mala ila šuāta iṭḫu*) are brought before the craft-gods Ninkurra, Kusibanda, Ninildu, and Ninzadim. Their hands are bound with a fillet and then are (symbolically) cut off with a tamarisk knife while each swears, "I swear that I [the smith] did not make you; Ninagal, Ea of the smith, made you" or "I [the carpenter] did not make you; Ninildu, Ea of the carpenter, made you," and so on.[95] "The meaning of what is here done is of course clear: the fact that the statue is the work of human hands is ritually denied and thus magically made nonexistent, nullified" (Jacobsen 1987: 23–24).[96]

93. STT 200:43.

94. See Luckenbill 1924: 81, lines 27–29: "To dedicate that canal . . . precious stones and a tortoise I presented to Ea Lord of springs and wells."

95. K.6324+ iv 4–12; compare IV R 25 ii 32–38, where the text refers to fillets of red and of blue wool. This is the Nineveh equivalent of the incantation in BM 45749 line 52. See also STT 200, 66–72. Bevan (1940: 79) quotes the Christian writer Isidorus of Pelusium (Epistles, iv, 207) that one of the Egyptian Ptolemies had a statue of Artemis made and then invited all the artisans to a

According to Jacobsen's (1987) persuasive analysis of the "Washing of the Mouth" rite, there are two ritual moments in the KA.LUḪ.Ù.DA: (1) as we have just seen, the statue is disassociated from the earthly workman; (2) it must then be "reborn" as the natural offspring of Ea/Nudimmud.

Profane Construction Materials

In Hos 8:4 the craftsmen use "their" gold and silver to make their images,[97] when in reality the precious metals were gifts from Yahweh (2:10).[98] The frequent pairing of כסף וזהב 'silver and gold' (Preuss 1971: 64–65) and of the Deuteronomistic האבן והעץ 'stone and tree' (Jer 2:27, 3:9; Hab 2:19) in the idol parodies highlights that these images are mere inert, dumb materials, with no רוח 'spirit/wind'[99] in them (Hab 2:18–19):[100]

---

dinner in a pit, whereupon he buried them alive to preserve the concept that this image had not been made by humans. Although this story is undoubtedly part of the Christian polemic against paganism, it does illustrate the problem of the existence of the artisans who made the statue "unmade by human hands."

96. Lorton in his chapter (below) on the cult image in Egypt contrasts this mode of "distancing" the human workers from the cult image with that used in the Egyptian cult (pp. 156–57).

97. Barasch 1992: 59–60: "Nowhere could the total incongruity between the god and its artistic image be made as manifest as when one considered the image as a material object. It is not surprising, then, that all the arguments against the belief in images—from Heraclitus to Arnobius—focus on the idol's material. Wherever the 'vanity' of the gods' images had to be shown, the corruptible nature of the materials of which the idols are made is vividly presented. The failure of the image to reveal the god becomes almost tangible when we consider the material aspect of the idol."

98. The same theology is found in the Old Greek of Isa 44:14, where the Greek translator has possibly mistaken ארן 'cedar' for אדן 'lord' and read ὃ ἐφύτευσεν κύριος καὶ ὑετος ἐμήκυνεν ('Which the Lord planted and the rain made sprout').

99. The objection of lack of 'spirit' recurs in Moslem iconoclastic literature: "anyone who has made an image of a living thing will be obliged on resurrection day to blow the spirit (*ar-rūḥ*) into his image." See Griffith 1985: 67–71.

100. Similarly, the Greeks, e.g., Plato, talk about the images as ἄψυχον 'dead, soulless'. See Plato's *Laws* 931A1. On the role of the 'wind/spirit' in giving life in both the OT and in Greek literature, see Bernhardt 1956: 18 n. 8. For the OT Apocrypha, see Wis 13:10:

> Ταλαίπωροι δὲ καὶ ἐν νεκροῖς αἱ ἐλπίδες αὐτῶν, οἵτινες ἐκάλεσαν θεοὺς ἔργα χειρῶν ἀνθρώπων
>
> Wretched men, whose hopes are *in dead things*, those who call work of human hands gods.

Wis 15:16-17:

> ἄνθρωπος γὰρ ἐποίησεν αὐτούς, καὶ τὸ πνεῦμα δεδανεισμένος ἔπλασεν αὐτούς· οὐδεὶς γὰρ αὐτῷ ὅμοιον ἄνθρωπος ἰσχύει πλάσαι θεόν· θνητὸς δὲ ὢν νεκρὸν ἐργάζεται χερσίν ἀνόμοις· κρείττων γάρ ἐστιν τῶν σεβασμάτων αὐτοῦ, ὧν αὐτὸς μὲν ἔζησεν, ἐκεῖνα δὲ οπὐδέποτε·
>
> For a human made them, and one whose own life breath is itself borrowed shaped them. No human can shape a god like himself. A mortal makes a dead thing with his lawless hands; but he surpasses the objects of his worship since he is alive, and they never were.

> What is the use of an image, or for its maker to carve it at all? It is a thing of metal, a lying oracle. What is the use of its maker trusting this and fashioning dumb idols? Woe to him who says to the piece of wood, "Wake up!"[101] to the dumb stone, "On your feet!" Plated it may be with gold and silver, but not a breath of life inside it.

This mosaic of arguments against the crafting of the divine statue probably refers to the ceremony by which the statue was enlivened, the Babylonian *mīs pî* ritual.

The second-century Christian apologist Athenagoras made similar objections against the cult image in his *Legatio* addressed to the Emperor. He refers to statues of Alexander, Neryllinus, and Proteus that were supposed to have performed miracles:

> πότερον οὖν ὁ Νερυλλῖνος καὶ ὁ Πρωτεὺς καὶ ὁ ᾿Αλέξανδρός εἰσιν οἱ ταῦτα ἐνεργοῦντες περὶ τὰ ἀγάλματα ἢ τῆς ὕλης ἡ σύστασις; ἀλλ᾿ ἡ μὲν ὕλη χαλκός ἐστιν, τί δὲ χαλκὸς δύναται καθ᾿ αὑτόν, ὃν μεταποιῆσαι πάλιν εἰς ἕτερον σχῆμα ἔξεστιν, ὡς τὸν ποδονιπτῆρα ὁ παρὰ τῷ Ἡροδότῳ ῎Αμασις;

> Is it then Neryllinus, and Proteus, and Alexander who accomplished these [miracles] in the statues? Or is it the nature of the matter itself? But the matter is bronze! What can bronze do of itself, which may be made again into a different form, as [Pharaoh] Amasis treated the footpan according to Herodotus? (*Legatio* 26).[102]

In the classical world, the metal statue that once occasioned awe could easily be remade into frying pans, bed pans, and so on. In the *Satires* of the Roman poet Juvenal (X, 56ff.) the bronze statue of the feared Sejanus, the agent of Tiberius, is hacked to pieces and remade into common household articles:

> and from that face which was but lately second in the entire world, are being fashioned pots, basins, frying pans and slop pails.

In Second Isaiah the almost encyclopedic list of exotic woods from which they are constructed (ארזים 'cedar', תרזה 'ilex?', ארן [Akk. *erēnu*] 'balsam', אלון 'oak', מסכן [Akkadian *mesukannu* or sissoo wood]) stresses that these statues are ultimately no more than a בול 'old hunk of wood' (Isa 44:19),[103] which must be carefully chosen so

---

101. The idea that the image was asleep and had to be awakened (on a daily basis!) was quite prevalent in Egypt, as Lorton's chapter illustrates (p. 139).

102. In the Byzantine iconoclastic movement, John Damascene (8th century) tries to refute the argument that man-made objects cannot convey divine power in order to justify the Byzantine icon (Barasch 1992: 208–9).

103. The Epistle of Jeremiah 19 refers to idols as no more than a beam from the temple: ὥσπερ δοκὸς τῶν ἐκ οἰκίας. A similar spoof on an idol as a block of wood is found in fragment 131 of the Syracusan comic Epicharmus (5th century B.C.E.): ἐκ παντὸς ξύλου κλοιός τε καὶ γένοιτο κὴκ τωὐτοῦ θεός 'From the same wood could be made either a dog collar or a god'. Also see Clement of Alexandria *Proptrepicus* 2.24:

> ὅ δ᾿ Ἡρακλέα ἐκ ξύλου λαβὼν κατεσκευασμένον (ἔτυχε δὲ ἕψων τι οἴκοι, οἷα εἰκός)· "Εἶα δή, ὦ Ἡράκλεις" εἶπεν· "νῦν σοι ἤδη καιρός, ὥσπερ Εὐρυσθεῖ, ἀτὰρ δὴ καὶ ἡμῖν ὑπουργῆσαι τὸν τρισκαιδέκατον τοῦτον ἆθλον καὶ Διαγόρᾳ τοὔψον παρασκευάσαι," κᾇτ᾿ αὐτὸν εἰς τὸ πῦρ ενέθηκεν ὡς ξύλον

that it will not rot (Isa 40:19–20). The prophet further satirizes the work of the idol-maker by stating that there is really no difference between the wood that becomes a "god" and the wood that heats the carpenter's meal (Isa 44:16).[104]

In his concern for types of woods, Second Isaiah perhaps here betrays his acquaintance with the Babylonian rite for the "Opening of the Mouth." It is undoubtedly not a coincidence that in these lists of different species of woods we have a clear indebtedness both to a Babylonian lexicon and to the preeminent role played by wood and the orchard in the Mesopotamian *mīs pî*.

In the *bīt mummi* the statue was a wooden plank (*gišṭuppu*),[105] a word reminiscent of Deutero-Isaiah's *bul* and the Epistle of Jeremiah's δοκὸς. However, as soon as it progressed to the river bank, the rite "magically set the clock back." The accompanying incantation, "From this day you walk with Ea your father," brought the statue back to the fertilizing waters of Ea, from which it was first nourished as a trunk of wood. The statue was first placed on the *burû*-reed mat facing the setting sun, the direction of death. The statue was then moved to an adjoining orchard (KIRI_6), where it was placed in a *šutukku*-hut; this time, it faced the east and awaited the sunrise of its "birthday." The priest filled a tamarisk trough with holy water, filled also with precious stones, plants, and oils.

> The waters from the river are the lifegiving waters of the "father," the river-god Ea, and represent his fructifying semen. The trough of tamarisk into which they are poured represents the womb of the "mother," the wood which is to conceive and to give birth to the cult statue. It is furnished, in addition to its own substance, wood,

---

> Somebody took a wooden image of Herakles (he happened to be cooking something at home) and said, "Herakles, now is the time for you to undergo for us your thirteenth labor as you did the twelve for Eurustheus and make this [dinner] ready for Diagoras." He then cast it into the fire as a piece of wood.
>
> See Athenagoras *Legatio* 4; and for an example from Latin literature, Horace *Sat* 1:8ff.
>
> *Olim truncus eram ficulnus, inutile lignum,*
> *cum faber, incertus scamnum faceretne Priapum,*
> *maluit esse deum.*
>
> Once I was a fig tree—useless wood, when a carpenter, who could not decide whether to make a stool or a god, decided on a god.

104. Herodotus (2.172) tells the story about Pharaoh Amasis who broke up his golden ποδανιπτήρ, which had been used for washing feet and as a chamber pot, to make an image that his people worshiped. This story was cited by Philo *de vita contemp* 7.

105. This is found in IV R ii 32–38 (= K.63a // K.3367). Jacobsen, "The Graven Image," 24: "The workmen who worked on the statue—which is referred to merely as a piece of wood, 'the plank' (*gišṭuppu*)—are present. . . ." The actual phrase, which I can only find in IV R ii is *a-na-ku la i-pu-šu* [lú]NAGAR GIŠ.DUB.NUN.NA DÙ-*šu*. Jacobsen understands the appellation NUN.NA as referring to Ea, i.e., the plank of Ea. However, this rite consecrates first a ceremonial boat for Nisku and then an *askaru*, and I am not sure how typical it is of other KA.LUḪ.Ù.DA rites. And so GIŠ.DUB, a word usually used of jewelry pieces, is really not used of a regular statue.

with other ingredients for a statue: precious stones, among them gold and silver ore (Jacobsen 1987: 25).

The trough is then placed on the brick of the birth goddess, who elsewhere is called ᵈtibira-dingir-re-ne-ka 'Copper caster of the gods' (Jacobsen 1976: 107 n. 135).[106] Around her stand the craftsman, who are now reduced to mere midwives. Symbolizing the birth, three *mašqû*-troughs are filled with blood. The statue faces the three gods Ea, Shamash, and Asalluḫi, and the following incantation greets the new day:

> [W]hen the god was made, the pure statue completed, the god was visible in all the lands; he is clothed in splendor, suited to lordliness, lordly, he is full of pride; he is surrounded with radiance; he is endowed with an awesome radiance, he shines out splendidly, the statue appears brilliantly. In heaven he was made, on earth he was made. This statue was made in the totality of heaven and earth. This statue grew up in the forest of *ḫašurru*-cedars; this statue came from the mountains, the pure place. This statue is the creation of both god and human. The statue has eyes which Ninkurru made; the statue has . . . which Ninagal made; the statue is of a form which Ninzadim made; the statue is of gold and silver which Kusibanda made; [the statue . . . which] Ninildu made; [the statue] (has) . . . which Ninzadim made. This statue is of [. . .], . . . *ḫulālu* stone, serpentine, calcite, [. . .], *elmešu*-stone, *antasurrû*-stone, [. . .]. By the work of the craftsman in metal and wood [. . .]. This statue Ninkurra, Ninagal, [Kusibanda], Ninildu (and) Ninzadim made. (Yet), this statue, not having undergone the rite of mouthwashing, cannot smell incense, eat food, drink water.[107]

These statues were as dead and immobile as the materials from which they were crafted. They may have had mouths, but they could not speak (Jer 10:5); noses, but they could not smell; feet, but they could not walk (Jer 10:5; Ps 115:3–9). Their only motion was their tendency to wobble (Jer 10:4) or to fall over (Isa 40:20; 41:7), so that they had to be fastened to the wall. However, it is clear from the *mīs pî* rite that a cultic attempt was made to have the statue "reborn"[108] with heavenly materials, and so raw products were placed in the tamarisk birth-trough. Furthermore, the rite is replete with countless incantations for the blessing of all the elements used in the ritual (*Kultmittelbeschwörungen*), asking that the materials be provided by the gods themselves: "In the great sanctuary of the heavens, the great gods have increased the bounty for the Opening of the Mouth of the gods" (79-7-8, 68 + K.3511, §iii, col. ii, lines 5–6).

---

106. For literature on this goddess, see Biggs 1967: 45ff.; Krecher 1966: 199ff.

107. STT 200:1–42; parallels in STT 201, K.2969, K.10132, Rm 421, IV R 25, K.3367. For this translation, see pp. 98–99 in this volume.

108. As Lorton points out in his article, despite the use of the Egyptian word "*mesi* (to be born)" of statues, it is not clear that the Egyptians saw the "enlivening" of the cult image as a birth (pp. 165–66 with n. 65). Lorton prefers to use the word "transvaluation" (p. 173).

Conclusion

As clever as these prophetic parodies were, they were both unoriginal and methodologically flawed. Each of the three biblical objections against making the cult image has parallels in other ancient literatures. Some of these passages, such as the Hellenistic satirist Lucian, spoof the cult image in language almost indistinguishable from Deutero-Isaiah, while other more reverent texts of the iconodule are thoroughly aware of these objections but attempt to resolve them either philosophically (Dio Chrysostom) or cultically (Opening of the Mouth Ritual).

However, Deutero-Isaiah's method is also flawed, for he has contrasted a phenomenological description of the Mesopotamian practice with a theological portrayal of Yahwism. His argument does not reflect the culpable ignorance of the Israelite religion about other religions (pace Kaufmann 1960: 2, 7) but a conscious distortion forged in polemic. The Mesopotamian could just as easily have parodied an obscure desert god who liked to live in an acacia box (the ark of the covenant), was constantly and whimsically changing his mind, and who was inordinantly fond of the smell of burning beef fat (Saggs 1978: 15).

Bibliography

Ackroyd, P. R.
1963 "Jeremiah X.1–16." *JTS* N.S. 14: 385–90.
Albertz, R.
1994a *A History of Israelite Religion in the Old Testament Period.* 2 vols. Louisville: Westminster/John Knox.
1994b "Monotheismus in der israelitischen Religionsgeschichte." Pp. 77–96 in W. Dietrich and M. Klopfenstein (eds), *Ein Gott allein? JHVH-Verehrung und biblischer Monotheismus im Kontext der israelitischen und altorientalischen Religionsgeschichte.* OBO 139. Göttingen: Vandenhoeck & Ruprecht.
Amiet, P.
1955 "Cylindres-sceaux conservés à Jérusalem." *RB* 62: 407–13.
Andrew, M. E.
1982 "The Authorship of Jeremiah 10:1–16." *ZAW* 94: 128–30.
Barasch, Moshe
1992 *Icon.* New York: New York University.
Barnett, R. D., and M. Falkner
1962 *The Sculptures of Assur-nasir-apli (883–859 B.C.) Tiglath-pileser III (745–727 B.C.) Esarhaddon (681–669 B.C.) from the Central and South-West Palaces at Nimrud.* London: British Museum.
Bauer, T.
1933 *Das Inschriftenwerk Assurbanipals.* Leipzig.
Bernhardt, Karl-Heinz
1956 *Gott und Bild.* Berlin: Evangelische Verlagsanstalt.

Bevan, Edwyn
1940 *Holy Images: An Inquiry into Idolatry and Image-Worship in Ancient Paganism and in Christianity.* London: George Allen.
Biggs, R.
1967 *Šà.zi.ga: Ancient Mesopotamian Potency Incantations.* Texts from Cuneiform Sources 2. Locust Valley, N.Y.: Augustin.
Boehmer, R. M.
1957–71 "Götterprozession in der Bildkunst." *RlA* 3.479–80.
Boling, R.
1979 *Judges.* AB 6A. Garden City, N.Y.: Doubleday.
Borger, R.
1956 *Die Inschriften Asarhaddons Königs von Assyrien.* AfO Beiheft 9. Graz.
1957–58 "Die Inschriften Asarhaddons (AfO Beiheft 9), Nachtrage und Verbesserungen." *AfO* 18: 113ff.
1971 "Gott Marduk und Gott-König Shulgi als Propheten: Zwei prophetische Texte." *BiOr* 28: 3–24.
1971b "Das Tempelbau-Ritual." *ZA* 61:72–80.
1972 Review of *Brief eines Bischofs von Esagila an König Asarhaddon,* by B. Landsberger. *BiOr* 29: 33–37.
Brinkman, J. A.
1973 "Sennacherib's Babylonian Problem: An Interpretation." *JCS* 25: 89–95.
Brueggemann, W.
1987 Review of *Das Bilderverbot: Seine Entstehung und Seine Entwicklung im Alten Testament,* by Christoph Dohmen. *JBL* 106: 314–15.
Burkert, Walter
1985 *Greek Religion.* Trans. by John Raffian. Cambridge: Harvard University Press.
Cagni, L.
1969 *L'Epopea di Erra.* Studi Semitici 34. Rome.
Carroll, R.
1986 *The Book of Jeremiah.* Old Testament Library. Philadelphia: Westminster.
Cassin, E.
1968 *La spendeur divine: Introduction à l'étude de la mentalité mésopotamienne.* Paris.
Clerc, C.
1915 *Les théories relatives au culte des images.* Paris.
Clifford, R.
1980 "The Function of Idol Passages in Second Isaiah." *CBQ* 42: 450–64.
Cogan, M.
1974 *Imperialism and Religion: Assyria, Judah, and Israel in the Eighth and Seventh Centuries B.C.E.* SBLMS 19. Missoula: Scholars Press.
Cohen, H. R.
1978 *Biblical Hapax Legomena in the Light of Akkadian and Ugaritic.* SBLDS 37. Missoula: Scholars Press.
Coogan, Michael
1987 "Canaanite Origins and Lineage: Reflections on the Religion of Ancient Israel." Pp. 115–24 in Patrick Miller, Jr., et al. (eds.), *Ancient Israelite Religion.* Philadelphia: Fortress.

Curtis, E. M.
1990 "Images in Mesopotamia and the Bible." Pp. 31–56 in William Hallo et al. (eds.), *The Bible in the Light of Cuneiform Literature: Scripture in Context III.* Lewiston: Mellen.
Davidson, R.
1976 "Jeremiah X 1–16." *Transactions of the Glasgow University Oriental Society* 25: 41–58.
Delaporte, L.
1920 *Catalogue des cylindres . . . du Louvre,* vol. 1. Paris.
Dever, W.
1983 "Material Remains and the Cult in Ancient Israel: An Essay in Archaeological Systematics." Pp. 571–87 in C. Meyers and M. O'Connor (eds.), *The Word of the Lord Shall Go Forth: Essays in Honor of David Noel Freedman in Celebration of His Sixtieth Birthday.* Winona Lake, Ind.: Eisenbrauns.
1987 "The Contribution of Archaeology to the Study of Canaanite and Early Israelite Religion." Pp. 209–48 in Patrick Miller, Jr., et al. (eds.), *Ancient Israelite Religion.* Philadelphia: Fortress.
1991 "Unresolved Issues in the Early History of Israel: Toward a Synthesis of Archaeological and Textual Reconstructions." Pp. 195–208 in D. Jobling, P. Day, and G. Sheppard (eds.), *The Bible and the Politics of Exegesis.* Cleveland: Pilgrim.
1995 "Ancient Israelite Religion: How to Reconcile the Differing Textual and Artifactual Portraits." Pp. 105–25 in W. Dietrich and M. Klopfenstein (eds.), *Ein Gott allein? JHVH-Verehrung und biblischer Monotheismus im Kontext der israelitischen und altorientalischen Religionsgeschichte.* OBO 139. Göttingen: Vandenhoeck & Ruprecht.
Dick, M.
1984 "Prophetic Poiesis and the Verbal Icon." *CBQ* 46: 226–46.
1998 "The Relationship between the Cult Image and the Deity in Mesopotamia." Pp. 111–16 in Jiří Prosecký (ed.), Intellectual Life of the Ancient Near East. Prague: Academy of Sciences of the Czech Republic Oriental Institute.
Dietrich, Manfried, and Oswald Loretz
1992 *"Yahwe und seine Aschera": Anthropomorphisches Kultbild in Mesopotamien, Ugarit, und Israel.* Ugaritisch-Biblische Literatur 9. Münster: Ugarit-Verlag.
Dohmen, Christoph
1983 "Ein kanaanäischer Schmiedeterminus (NSK)." *UF* 15: 39–42.
1987 *Das Bilderverbot: Seine Entstehung und Seine Entwicklung im Alten Testament.* 2d ed. BBB 62. Bonn: Athenäum.
Du Mesnil du Buisson, R.
1970 "Études sur les dieux phéniciens." *Études préliminaires aux religions orientales dans l'Empire romain* 14: 50.
Dus, J.
1961 "Das zweite Gebot." *Communio Viatorum* 4: 37–50.
Ebeling, Erich
1931 Tod und Leben nach den Vorstellungen der Babylonier. Berlin and Lepizig.
Elliger, K.
1978 *Deuterojesaja.* BKAT 11/1. Neukirchen-Vluyn: Neukirchener Verlag.

Fauer, J.
1978 "The Biblical Idea of Idolatry." *JQR* 69: 1–15.
Fitzgerald, A.
1989 "The Technology of Isaiah 40:19–20 + 41:6–7." *CBQ* 51: 426–46.
Fleischer, R.
1973 *Artemis von Ephesos und Verwandte Kultstatuen aus Anatolien und Syrien.* Leiden: Brill.
Geffcken, J. von
1916–19 "Der Bilderstreit des heidnischen Altertums." *Archiv für Religionswissenschaft* 19: 294–98.
Gilbert, M.
1973 *La Critique des dieux dans le livre de la Sagesse (Sg 13–15).* AB 53. Rome: Pontifical Biblical Institute.
Gnuse, R.
1987 Review of *Das Bilderverbot: Seine Entstehung und Seine Entwicklung im Alten Testament,* by Christoph Dohmen. *CBQ* 49: 111–12.
Grayson, A. K.
1975 *Assyrian and Babylonian Chronicles.* Texts from Cuneiform Sources 5. Locust Valley, NY: J. J. Augustin.
Griffith, Signey
1985 "Theodore Abū Qurrah's Arabic Tract on the Christian Practice of Venerating Images." *JAOS* 105: 67–71.
Hadley, J.
1994 "Yahweh and 'His Asherah': Archaeological and Textual Evidence from the Cult of the Goddess." Pp. 235–68 in W. Dietrich and M. Klopfenstein (eds.), *Ein Gott allein? JHVH-Verehrung und biblischer Monotheismus im Kontext der israelitischen und altorientalischen Religionsgeschichte.* OBO 139. Göttingen: Vandenhoeck & Ruprecht.
Hallo, W. W.
1983 "Cult Statue and Divine Image: A Preliminary Study." Pp. 1–17 in William Hallo, James Moyer, and Leo Purdue (eds.), *Scripture in Context II: More Essays on the Comparative Method.* Winona Lake, Ind.: Eisenbrauns.
1988 "Texts, Statues and the Cult of the Divine King." Pp. 54–66 in *Congress Volume: Jerusalem, 1986.* VTSup 40. Leiden: Brill.
1991 "The Death of Kings: Traditional Historiography in Contextual Perspective." Pp. 148–65 in Mordechai Cogan and Israel Ephʿal (eds.), *Ah, Assyria . . . : Studies in Assyrian History and Ancient Near Eastern Historiography Presented to Hayim Tadmor.* Jerusalem: Magnes.
Halpern, B.
1987 "'Brisker Pipes than Poetry': The Development of Israelite Monotheism." Pp. 77–115 in J. Neusner, B. Levine, and E. Frerichs (eds.), *Judaic Perspectives in Ancient Israel.* Philadelphia: Fortress.
Hendel, Ronald S.
1988 "The Social Origins of the Aniconic Tradition in Early Israel." *CBQ* 50: 365–82.
Holladay, John S. Jr.
1987 "Religion in Israel and Judah under the Monarchy: An Explicitly Archaeological Approach." Pp. 249–99 in Patrick Miller, Jr., et al. (eds.), *Ancient Israelite Religion.* Philadelphia: Fortress.

Holladay, W.
1986 *Jeremiah 1.* Hermeneia. Philadelphia: Fortress.
Holter, K.
1995 *Second Isaiah's Idol-Fabrication Passages.* BET 28. Frankfurt am Main: Peter Lang.
Hossfeld, F. L.
1982 *Der Dekalog: Seine späten Fassungen, die originale Komposition und seine Vorstufen.* OBO 45. Freiburg and Göttingen.
Hutter, M.
1987 "Jes 40:20: Kulturgeschichtliche Notizen zu einer Crux." *BN* 36: 31–36.
Jacobsen, T.
1976 *The Treasures of Darkness: A History of Mesopotamian Religion.* New Haven: Yale University Press.
1987 "The Graven Image." Pp. 15–32 in P. Miller, Jr., et al. (eds.), *Ancient Israelite Religion.* Philadelphia: Fortress.
Janowski, B.
1991 "Keruben und Zion: Thesen zur Enstehung der Zionstradition." Pp. 231–64 in D. R. Damiels (ed.), *Ernten, was man sät: Festschrift für Klaus Koch zu seinem 65. Geburtstag.* Neukirchen-Vluyn: Neukirchner Verlag.
Kaufmann, Y.
1960 *The Religion of Israel.* Chicago: University of Chicago Press.
Keel, O.
1977 *Jahwe-Visionen und Siegelkunst: Eine neue Deutung der Majestätsschilderungen in Jes 6, Ez 1 und 10 und Sach 4.* SBS 84/85. Stuttgart: Katholisches Bibelwerk.
Keel, O., and Uehlinger, C.
1995 *Göttinnen, Götter und Gottessymbole: Neue Erkenntnisse zur Religionsgeschichte Kanaans und Israels aufgrund bislang unerschlossener ikonographischer Quellen.* Quaestiones Disputatae 134. Freiburg: Herder.
Kennedy, J. M.
1987 "The Social Background of Early Israel's Rejection of Cultic Images." *Biblical Theology Bulletin* 17: 138–44.
King, L. W.
1912 *Babylonian Boundary Stones and Memorial Tablets in the British Museum.* London.
Knapp, D.
No Date *Untersuchungen zu Deut 4.* Arbeitstitel. Ph.D. Disseration, Göttingen. Cited in C. Dohmen, *Das Bilderverbot.*
Krecher, J.
1966 *Sumerische Kultlyrik.* Wiesbaden: Harrassowitz.
Lambert, W. G.
1969 *Atra-ḫasis: The Babylonian Story of the Flood.* London: Oxford University Press.
1990 "Ancient Mesopotamian Gods: Superstition, Philosophy, Theology." *Revue de l'Histoire des Religions* 207: 115–30.
Landsberger, B.
1928–29 "Das 'Gute Wort'." *MAOG* 4: 312
1954 "Assyrische Königsliste und 'Dunkles Zeitalter.'" *JCS* 8: 31ff., 47ff., 106ff.
1955 "Remarks on the Archive of the Soldier Ubarum." *JCS* 9: 121–31.
1965 *Brief eines Bischofs von Esagila an König Asarhaddon.* MKNAW N.S. 28/6. Amsterdam.

Lang, B.
1981 "Die Jahwe-allein Bewegung." Pp. 47–83 in B. Lang (ed.), *Der Einzige Gott: Die Geburt des biblischen Monotheismus.* Munich: Kosel.
1983 *Monotheism and the Prophetic Minority: An Essay in Biblical History and Sociology.* Sheffield: Almond.

Lemaire, A.
1994 "Déesses et Dieux de Syrie-palestine d'après les Inscriptions." Pp. 127–58 in W. Dietrich and M. Klopfenstein (eds.), *Ein Gott allein? JHVH-Verehrung und biblischer Monotheismus im Kontext der israelitischen und altorientalischen Religionsgeschichte.* OBO 139. Göttingen: Vandenhoeck & Ruprecht.

Lewis, T. J.
1998 "Divine Images and Iconism in Ancient Israel." *JAOS* 118: 36–53.

Loretz, O.
1994 "Das 'Ahnen- und Götterstatuen-Verbot' im Dekalog und die Einzigkeit Jahwes: Zum Begriff des Göttlichen in altorientalischen und alttestamentlichen Quellen." Pp. 491–527 in W. Dietrich and M. Klopfenstein (eds.), *Ein Gott allein? JHVH-Verehrung und biblischer Monotheismus im Kontext der israelitischen und altorientalischen Religionsgeschichte.* OBO 139. Göttingen: Vandenhoeck & Ruprecht.

Luckenbill, D. D.
1924 *The Annals of Sennacherib.* OIP 2. Chicago: University of Chicago Press.

McCarter, P. Kyle, Jr.
1980 *I Samuel.* AB 8. Garden City, N.Y.: Doubleday.
1987 "Aspects of the Religion of the Israelite Monarchy: Biblical and Epigraphic Data." Pp. 137–55 in P. D. Miller, Jr., et al. (eds.), *Ancient Israelite Religion.* Philadelphia: Fortress.

Machinist, P.
1991 "The Question of Distinctiveness in Ancient Israel: An Essay." Pp. 196–212 in M. Cogan and I. Eph'al (eds.), *Ah Assyria . . . Studies in Assyrian History and Ancient Near Eastern Historiography Presented to Hayim Tadmor.* Scripta Hierosolymitana 33. Jerusalem: Magnes.

Margaliot, M.
1980 "Jeremiah X 1–16: A Re-examination." *VT* 30: 295–308.

Matsushima, E.
1993 "Divine Statues in Ancient Mesopotamia: Their Fashioning and Clothing and Their Interaction with the Society." Pp. 209–19 in E. Matsushima (ed.), *Official Cult and Popular Religion in the Ancient Near East.* Heidelberg: C. Winter.

Meier, Gerhard
1937–39 "Die Ritualtafel der Serie 'Mundwaschung'." *AfO* 12: 40ff.

Melugin, R.
1976 *The Formation of Isaiah 40–50.* Berlin: de Gruyter.

Mettinger, T.
1995 *No Graven Image? Israelite Aniconism in Its Ancient Near Eastern Context.* ConBibOT 42. Stockholm: Alqvist & Wiksell.

Miller Jr., P. D., and Roberts, J. J. M.
1977 *The Hand of the Lord: A Reassessment of the "Ark Narrative" of 1 Samuel.* Johns Hopkins Near Eastern Studies. Baltimore: Johns Hopkins University Press.

Nissinen, M.
1991 *Prophetie, Redaktion und Fortschreibung im Hoseabuch: Studien zum Werdegang eines Prophetenbuches im Lichte von Hos 4 und 11.* AOAT 231. Kevelaer: Butzon & Bercker / Neukirchen-Vluyn: Neukirchener Verlag.

Obbink, H. T.
1929 "Jahwebilder." *ZAW* 47: 264–74.

Olyan, Saul M.
1988 *Asherah and the Cult of Yaheweh in Israel.* SBLMS 34. Atlanta: Scholars Press.

Opificius, R.
1957–71 "Götterboot." *RlA* 3.463–66.

Oppenheim, A. L.
1956 *The Interpretation of Dreams in the Ancient Near East.* Philadelphia: American Philosophical Society.

Otto, E.
1984 "Historisches Geschehen-Überlieferung-Erklärungsmodell: Sozial-historische Grundsatz- und Einzelprobleme in der Geschichtsschreibung des frühen Israel—Eine Antwort auf N. P. Lemches Beitrag zur Diskussion um eine Sozialgeschichte Israels." *BN* 23: 63–80.

Overholt, T. W.
1965 "The Falsehood of Idolatry: An Interpretation of Jer. X 1–16." *JTS* N.S. 16: 1–12.

Pettinato, G.
1969 Review of *Les statues de culte dans les textes Mésopotamiens des origines à la 1re dynastie de Babylon* by A. Spycket. *BiOr* 26: 212–16.
1981 *The Archives of Ebla.* New York: Doubleday.

Pfeiffer, R. H.
1926 "Images of Yahweh." *JBL* 45: 211–22.

Preuss
1971 *Verspottung fremder Religionen im Alten Testament.* BWANT 92. Stuttgart: Kohlhammer.

Renger, J.
1967 "Untersuchungen zum Priestertum der altbabylonischen Zeit, 1. Teil." *ZA* 58: 110.

Roeder, G.
1956 *Ägyptische Bronzefiguren.* Staatliche Museen zu Berlin: Mitteilungen aus der Ägyptischen Sammlung 5–6. Berlin: Staatliche Museen.

Roth, Wolfgang M. W.
1975 "For Life He Appeals to Death (Wis 13:18): A Study of Old Testament Idol Parodies." *CBQ* 37: 21–47.

Saggs, H. W. F.
1959 "Two . . . Officials." *Sumer* 15: 36–37.
1978 *The Encounter with the Divine in Mesopotamia and Israel.* London: Athlone.

Sauer, G.
1966 "Siegel." Pp. 1786–90 in B. Reicke and L. Rost (eds.), *Biblisch-Historisches Handwörterbuch.* Göttingen: Vandenhoeck & Ruprecht.

Sauren, H.
1969a "Besuchfahrten der Götter in Sumer." *Or* 38: 214–36.

1969b Review of *Les statues de culte dans les textes Mésopotamiens des origines à la 1re dynastie de Babylon* by A. Spycket. *JSS* 14: 116–19.

Scholnick, S. H.

1992 "The Meaning of Mišpāṭ (Justice) in the Book of Job." Pp. 349–58 in Roy B. Zuck (ed.), *Sitting with Job*. Grand Rapids: Baker.

Schroer, S.

1987 *In Israel gab es Bilder: Nachtrichten von darstellender Kunst im Alten Testament.* OBO 74. Göttingen: Vandenhoeck & Ruprecht.

Seidl, U.

1980–83 "Kultbild." *RlA* 5.307–19.

Sjöberg, A. W.

1957–71 "Götterreisen." *RlA* 3.480–83.

Smith, M. S.

1981 "Religiöse Parteien bei den Israeliten vor 587." Pp. 9–46 in B. Lang (ed.), *Der einzige Gott: Die Geburt des biblischen Monotheismus.* Munich: Kosel.

1988 "'Seeing God' in the Psalms: The Background to the Beatific Vision in the Hebrew Bible." *CBQ* 50: 171–83.

1990 *The Early History of God: Yahweh and the Other Deities in Ancient Israel.* San Francisco: Harper.

Spieckermann, H.

1982 *Juda unter Assur in der Sargonidenzeit.* Göttingen:Vandenhoeck & Ruprecht.

Spycket, A.

1968 *Les statues de culte dans les textes Mésopotamiens des origines à la 1re dynastie de Babylon.* Cahiers de la Revue Biblique 9. Paris: Gabalda.

Stoebe, Hans Joachim

1973 *Das erste Buch Samuelis.* KAT 8/1. Gütersloh: Gütersloher Verlagshaus.

Streck, M.

1916 *Assurbanipal und die letzen assyrischen Könige.* VAB 7. Leipzig: Hinrichs.

Thomas, D. W.

1971 "Isaiah XLIV.9–20: A Translation and Commentary." Pp. 319–30 in A. Caquot and M. Philonenko (eds.), *Hommages à André Dupont-Sommer.* Paris: Adrien-Maisonneuve.

Uehlinger, C.

1994 "Eine anthropomorphe Kultstatue des Gottes von Dan." *BN* 72: 85–100.

Vorländer, H.

1981 "Der Monotheismus Israels als Antwort auf die Krise des Exils." Pp. 84–113 in B. Lang (ed.), *Der Einzige Gott: Die Geburt des biblischen Monotheismus.* Munich: Kosel.

Waltke, B. K., and M. O'Connor

1990 *An Introduction to Biblical Hebrew Syntax.* Winona Lake, Ind.: Eisenbrauns.

Wambacq, B. N.

1974 "Jérémie X,1–16." *RB* 81: 57–62.

Weidner, Ernst.

1959–60 "Die älteren Kassiten-Könige." *AfO* 19: 138.

Weinfeld, M.

1991 *Deuteronomy 1–11.* AB 5. New York: Doubleday.

Weisberg, David B.
1967 *Guild Structure and Political Allegiance in Early Achaemenid Mesopotamia.* Yale Near Eastern Researches 1. New Haven: Yale University Press.

Westermann, C.
1977 *Isaiah 40–66.* OTL. Philadelphia: Westminster.

Wildberger, H.
1965–72 *Jesaja: I Teilband, Jesaja 1–12.* BKAT 10. Neukirchen-Vluyn: Neukirchener.

Williamson, H. G. M.
1986 "Isaiah 40,20: A Case of Not Seeing the Wood for the Trees." *Biblica* 67: 1–20.

Zimmerli, W.
1950 "Das zweite Gebot." Pp. 550–63 in W. Baumgarten (ed.), *Festschrift A. Bertholet.* Tübingen: Mohr (= pp. 234–49 in *Gottes Offenbarung.* Munich, 1963)
1974 "Das Bilderverbot in der Geschichte des alten Israel." *Studien zur alttestamentlichen Theologie und Prophetie.* TBü 19. Munich: Chr. Kaiser.

The Induction of the Cult Image in Ancient Mesopotamia: The Mesopotamian <u>mīs pî</u> Ritual

CHRISTOPHER WALKER AND MICHAEL B. DICK

49 πῶς οὖν οὐκ ἔστιν αἰσθέσθαι ὅτι οὐκ
εἰσιν θεοί, οἳ οὔτε σῴζουσιν ἑαυτοὺς ἐκ
πολέμου οὔτε ἐκ κακῶν; 50 ὑπάρχοντα
γὰρ ξύλινα καὶ περίχρυσα καὶ περιάργυρα
γνωσθήσεται μετὰ ταῦτα ὅτι ἐστὶν ψευδῆ·
51 τοῖς ἔθνεσι πᾶσα τοῖς τε βασιλεῦσι
φανερὸν ἔσται ὅτι οὐκ εἰσι θεοὶ ἀλλὰ ἔργα
χειρῶν ἀνθρώπων, καὶ οὐδὲν θεοῦ ἔργον
ἐν αὐτοῖς ἐστιν.

49 How then can one fail to see that these
are not gods, for they cannot save themselves
from war or calamity? 50 Since they are
made of wood and overlaid with gold and
silver, it will afterward be known that they
are false. 51 It will be manifest to all the
nations and kings that they are not gods but
the work of men's hands, and that there is no
work of God in them. [Epistle of Jeremiah]

The apocryphal Letter of Jeremiah, written around the second or third century B.C.E., attacks the making and worship of the cult image as a mere 'work of human hands', which is contrasted with the 'work of God'. Forms of this argument have played an important role in the history of religions and have formed the basis for iconoclastic movements within Judaism, Christianity, and Islam. This paper returns to the ancient worship of the cult image and queries the very iconodule parodied by works such as the Letter of Jeremiah about his/her own theology concerning the cult statue. More specifically, we shall investigate Mesopotamian texts dealing with the making and dedication of the divine statue in Assyria and Babylonia. These Mesopotamian texts address precisely the point considered by Deutero-Isaiah and the Letter of Jeremiah to be the most vulnerable in the worship of the divine image, namely, the human making of the divine image. Could either of these Israelite authors have put

For complete abbreviations and references, see Borger 1967, CAD, and AHw.

the theological issue more bluntly than the Assyrian king Esarhaddon: "Whose right is it, O great gods, to create gods and goddesses in a place where humans dare not trespass?"

The Babylonian ritual[1] procedures for preparing the statue of a deity for use were known by the general title of 'mouth-washing' (Babylonian *mīs pî*), or sometimes 'mouth-opening' (Babylonian *pit pî*). Surviving texts document both the ritual used (ritual tablet) and the many Sumerian and Babylonian incantations that accompanied and gave effect to the ritual. By such rituals, which Winter (1992: 17) calls rites of constitution, "the material form [of the statue] was animated, the representation not standing for but actually manifesting the presence of the subject represented. The image was then indeed empowered to speak, or to see, or to act, through various culturally-subscribed channels (Winter 1992: 13)."[2]

Previous Studies

The first partial publication of the ritual on the basis of Neo-Assyrian copies was given by Heinrich Zimmern (1896–1901). In a later publication (1906) Zimmern commented on the general concept of mouth-washing and discussed two of the relevant incantation texts. Aylward M. Blackman (1924) published Stephen Langdon's English translation of the Assyrian text, together with a discussion of other evidence from religious and historical texts. A year later an almost complete copy of the Babylonian

1. For a brief discussion of *ritual*, see Winter 1992: 16–17.

2. M. Dick: The theology of the presence of the deity in the cult image in Mesopotamia seems to me, a Roman Catholic, to be similar to the Catholic theology of the "real presence" of Jesus within the Eucharist. The divine Lord Jesus is confessed to be really present within the Eucharistic bread and is thought to be equally present on altars around the world, just as, for example, Shamash could be really present in Sippar or Babylon. The destruction of the statue of Shamash in Sippar did not destroy the god Shamash any more than the destruction of the Eucharistic Host destroys Jesus. By a ritual combining words and acts, the bread "made by human hands" becomes for Catholics the Divine Jesus.

[Figure 1—opposite] FRAGMENT OF A TERRACOTTA STATUE OF A GOD. U. 16993; BM 122934: "Fragment of a terracotta statue in the round. . . . Ht. of fragment, 0.18 m. The head and shoulders only, and the left arm down to the elbow, are preserved. The figure is that of a god, wearing the high horned mitre and a sheepskin cloak; he was seated in a chair of which part of the back remains. The modeling of the figure is exceptionally fine and the preservation is unusually good; the whole had been painted with a thick gesso-like paint which had decayed and swelled, but parts of it could be saved; the flesh of the face and arms were red, the beard and the hair black, the skin robe apparently white with black lines between the locks of the fleece, the crown yellow and the necklace of red and yellow beads alternately; the chair back was black." Woolley and Mallowan, *Ur Excavations VII* (1976), pl. 63; p. 247. Courtesy of the Trustees of the British Museum.

text of the ritual was published by Sidney Smith (1925).[3] Erich Ebeling (1931) gave a fresh edition (in German) of the Babylonian ritual text and the first publication of an Assyrian ritual, found in the German excavations at Ashur, which tells of the restoration and rededication of a damaged statue.[4] C. B. F. Walker's unpublished Oxford B.Phil. thesis, *Material for a Reconstruction of the mīs pî Ritual* (Oxford, 1966), surveyed the current state of knowledge and gave the first edition of many of the incantations that accompanied the ritual.[5] Thorkild Jacobsen (1987) attempted to penetrate the religious ideas and logic behind the Babylonian ritual. Our study gives a fresh presentation of the basic sources of the ritual and a few of the more important incantations.[6]

Historical References

Historical references to the ritual are regrettably few. Sumerian administrative texts of the time of the Ur III dynasty (2113–2006 B.C.E.) refer to the provision of flour, other ritual commodities, and a reed hut for the ritual of opening the mouth of a statue of Gudea (2150 B.C.E.), the dead and deified ruler of Lagash (Civil 1967: 211; Steinkeller 1984: 40).

Thereafter the next reference[7] is from the time of Nabu-apal-iddina, king of Babylon in the mid-ninth century B.C.E.[8] This stone tablet, which dates to the thirty-first year of the reign of Nabu-apla-iddina (ca. 887–855), a contemporary of the Assyrian king Ashurnasirpal II, was found by H. Rassam at Abu Habba (Sippar) in 1881. Two hundred years before this Babylonian king, in the time of Simbar-Shipak (ca. 1026–1009 B.C.E.), the Sutians had destroyed the cult image of Shamash. In the

3. Smith's translation was reprinted in Hooke 1953: 116–20.

4. This is cited as Text 4 herein. Ebeling subsequently (1937) published corrections to the first edition. Of the other texts edited by Ebeling under the title "Riten für die 'Mundoffnung'," one (no. 28) is irrelevant and the other (no. 29) is not a ritual text but a school text quoting a series of extracts from the series *mīs pî*.

5. We (Walker and Dick) are currently working on the publication of the critical edition of the ritual.

6. For other recent discussions of the cult image in Mesopotamia with some references to the *mīs pî* ritual, see Hallo 1983; Curtis 1990; Winter 1992.

7. There is a controversial Neo-Assyrian text (K.4348+4149+4203+Sm.27), supposedly a copy of an original attributed to the Kassite king Agum-kakrime (ca. 1590 B.C.E.), which elaborately describes the renewal of a statue of Marduk by craftsmen. Landsberger considered it apocryphal (1928–29: 312; 1954: 68), but E. Weidner judged it genuine (1959–60: 138).

8. King 1912: 120–27 no. 26 (BM 91000) iv 22-8; Rashid 1967: 297–309; Gelb 1949: 348 n. 12; Brinkman 1968: 348 (24.2.3), 189f. (Brinkman defends the historicity of the stone tablet [cf. n. 1159]; Labat 1970: 77 n. 2, 115ff., 251; Ellis 1968: 105; Barrelet 1968: 38f.

[Figure 2—opposite] NABU-APLA-IDDINA AND THE SIPPAR STATUE OF SHAMASH. L. W. King 1912: 120–27 no. 26 (BM 91000).

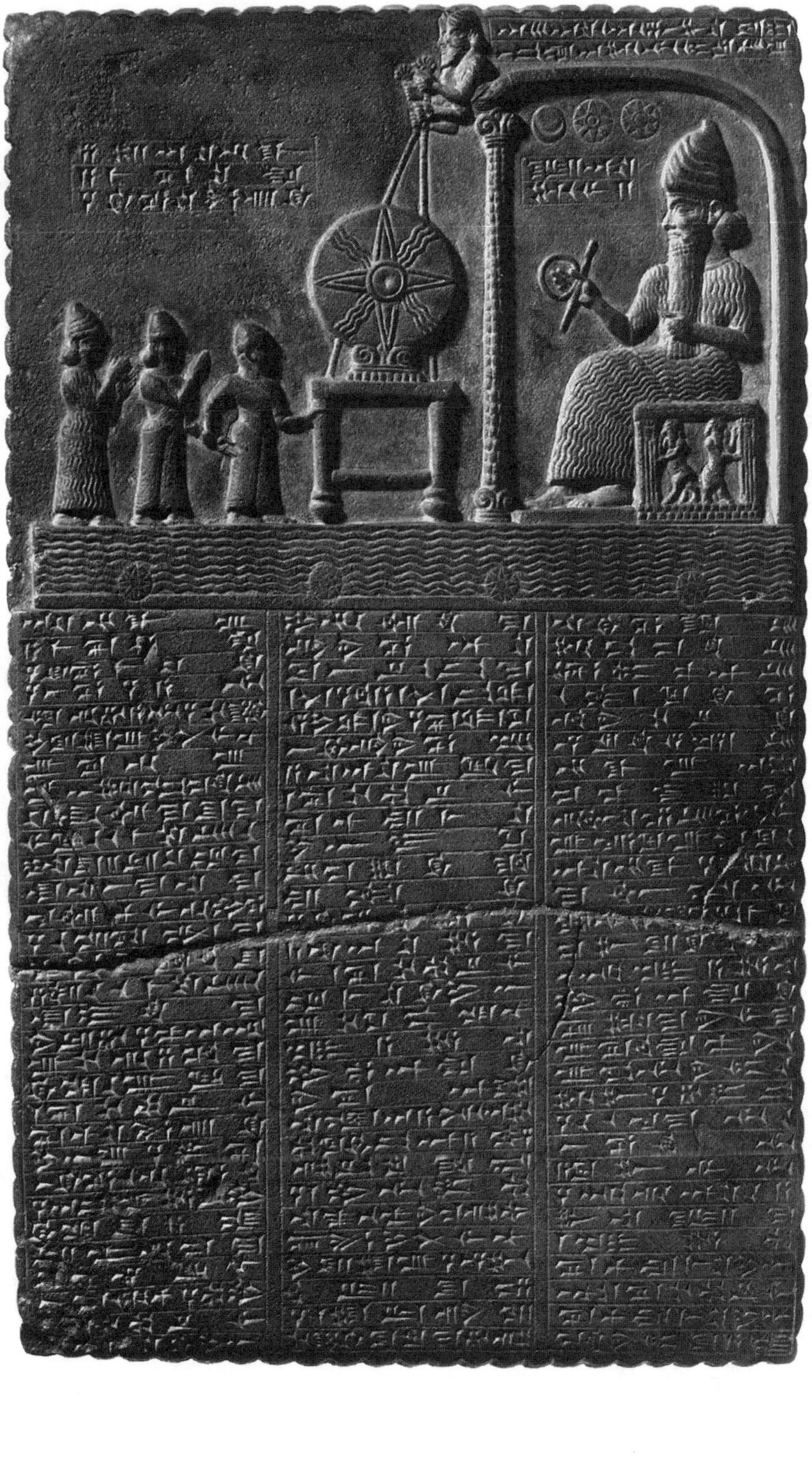

[Figure 3] STATUE OF A SMITING GOD ON AN ALTAR. BM 102562; hematite; 2.2 × 0.9 cm., Old Babylonian. "Three deities (one badly chipped) face an altar on which stands the statue of the smiting storm god overcoming an enemy and flanked by statues of attendant deities and worshippers." Dominique Collon, *First Impressions: Cylinder Seals in the Ancient Near East* (London: British Museum Publications, 1987) 175, no. 809. "Seal 809 depicts the focus of worship, the cult-statue of the main deity on its dais, surrounded by other statues."

[Figure 4] STATUE OF THE GODDESS ISHTAR. BM 130694; hematite; 2.7 × 1.5 cm.; Collon, no. 167. Old Babylonian. The consistent use on seals of the same frontal view of Ishtar suggests that they are representing a specific well-known cult statue; cf. Collon, no. 165 (BM 86267). For a description of the seal, see D. Collon, *Near Eastern Seals* (London: British Museum Publications, 1990), 47.

interim the loss of the statue had been compensated for by use of a sun-disk (*nipḫu*) as a symbolic equivalent. Now at last a replica of the original image has been (divinely) revealed and Nabu-apla-iddina orders a new cult statue to be fashioned and ritually dedicated.

[Figure 5] STATUE OF THE GOD SHAMASH UNDER A BALDACHINO. Collon, no. 765; Nippur (scribal quarter), Iraq. IM; pink limestone; 3.7 × 2.5 cm.; McCowan et al. 1967: pl. 109:11. Akkadian Period (2334–2193 B.C.E.). "He [Šamaš/Utu] is also shown under a baldachino supported by twisted columns, with bull-men holding the gateposts. This probably depicts a famous shrine." Compare the portrayal on the later Sippar Shamash statue of Nabu-apla-iddina (fig. 2).

Column III

19. A relief of his (Shamash) image,[9]
20. an impression of baked clay,[10]
21. his figure and his insignia,[11]
22. on the opposite side of
23. the Euphrates
24. on the west bank
25. was discovered.[12]
26. And Nabu-nadin-shum,
27. the priest of Sippar, the diviner,
28. descendent of Ekur-shum-ushabshi,
29. the priest of Sippar, the diviner,
30. that relief of the image

9. Akkadian: *ú-ṣur-ti ṣal-mi-šú*; this is perhaps equivalent to GIŠ.ḪUR in the Nineveh Ritual Tablet line 197 and in line 57 of the Babylonian Ritual (see below, pp. 80 and 96).

10. M.-Th. Barrelet (1968: 39) is probably correct in translating the Akkadian *ṣir-pu* as "un presage (estampage)"; contrast the CAD's translation 'kiln-fired' (CAD Ṣ 209). This *ṣirpu* would then be the technical name for the clay impression that accompanied the stone tablet.

11. Text: GAR-*šu* 'his figure': a similar use of the noun *šiknu* (GAR) is found in Borger 1956: 23: "the gods and godddesses whose appearance (*šiknu*) has deteriorated."

12. The finding of the model was a "pious fraud" (W. G. Lambert 1957–58: 398). "The god and the statue were so closely related that when the latter was lost nothing could be done to replace it. Šamaš had gone. The providential finding of the model alone made possible the manufacture of a totally new statue, for had one been made without a model, it would not have been Šamaš" (p. 399).

Column IV

1. to Nabu-apla-iddina,
2. the king, his lord, showed;
3. and Nabu-apla-iddina,
4. the king of Babylon,
5. who the fashioning of such an image,
6. had given him (Nabu-nadin-shum) as a command,
7. and had entrusted to him,
8. beheld that image and
9. his countenance was glad,
10. and joyful was
11. his spirit.
12. To fashion that image
13. he (the king) directed his attention.
14. Then through the craft[13] of Ea,
15. by the skill of Ninildu,[14]
16. Kusibanda,[15]
17. Ninkurra[16] and Ninzadim,[17]
18. with red gold
19. and bright lapis lazuli,

---

13. For this meaning of *nemēqu* 'craft' rather than 'wisdom', see Landsberger 1965: 22 n. 29.

14. Nin-íldu (on the name, see Emesal vocabulary, MSL 4, 7 n. 42; Cagni, *Erra*, 195, for bibliography) was the patron deity of carpenters (Tallqvist 1938: 408; IV R 25 ii 27). Among the deity's epithets are "the Great Carpenter of Heaven/Anum" (K.9879, an incantation cited in Cagni, *Erra*, 192) and "Bearer of the Axe" (*Erra* I 156). In IV R 25 ii 25–28, a *mīs pî* ritual, the carpenter declares that Ninildu, Ea of the carpenters [cf. CT 25 47 Rm 483:5], made it (a lunar disk), I (the carpenter) did not make it." Cf. *Racc* 54, n. 36. In IV R 18 37ff., Ea gives orders to Ninildu for the construction of divine implements.

15. Kusibanda was the patron of goldsmiths (*kutimmu*) and also, as were all of the artisan gods and goddesses, an *Erscheinungsform* of Ea: [d]é-a *ša* [lú]*ku-ti-me* (CT 24 43:118). The importance of Kusibanda for the making of images is illustrated by the epithet found in the Erra Epic (I 158): "Creator of the (images of) god and man (*ba-an* DINGIR *i* LÚ)." Theologically, it was not the human *kutimmu* who made the divine image, but Kusibanda: "[i]t was Kusibanda, Ea the divine patron of the goldsmith, who made it, I (the *kutimmu*) did not make the figurine" (IV R 25 ii 23–25). For the materials with which Kusibanda works, see II R 58 n. 6 lines 66–67.

16. Ninkurra is the patron deity of the stonecutters; in some texts she is considered an *Erscheinungsform* of the master-builder Ea. See Tallqvist 1938: 411, for examples. In II R 58 n. 6 (*mīs pî* tablet 1/2, lines 68–69, Ninkurra brings the precious stones (*dušu*, *ḫulalu*, *muššaru*) from the mountains (ḫur-sag-ta).

17. Ninzadim ([d]*Nin-zá-dím*) was the patron deity of the lapidaries and was also considered an *Erscheinungsform* of Ea (CT 25 48:14). IV R 25 iv 43–44 (a *mīs pî* ritual): "Ninzadim has treated you (a lunar disk) tenderly with his pure hands" (translation from CAD K 541b). In the Kalû Ritual (*Racc* 46 = BE 13987) Ea created in the Apsu the gods Ninildu, Ninsimug, and Arazu to complete the construction of the divine temples (line 29); Ea then created Kusibanda, Ninzadim, and Ninkurra in order to manufacture the metal work for the decoration of the temples (line 31; cf. CAD

20. the image of Shamash, the great lord,
21. he (the king) carefully prepared.
22. With the rites of purification
23. of Ea and Asalluḫi
24. before Shamash
25. in the temple E-kar-zaginna[18]
26. which is on the bank of the Euphrates,
27. he (the king) washed the (statue's) mouth
28. Then he (the statue/Shamash) took up his dwelling.

A Neo-Assyrian letter to the king of Assyria records the renewal and consecration of statues by mouth-washing: "I renewed the statues in the house of Bal(a)ṭāju (and) performed the 'mouth-washing' ceremony (KA.LUḪ.Ù.DA)." [19] The editor of this text suggests that the event referred to is to be connected with the renewal and consecration of Babylonian deities in the year 671/670, described by Esarhaddon in one of his inscriptions.

In 689 B.C.E. the Assyrian king Sennacherib had become exasperated with Babylon's constant revolts against the Assyrian crown, and he devastated the city, destroying its temples.[20] It remains a point of dispute whether Sennacherib actually destroyed the Babylonian cult statue of Marduk or whether he merely transported it into exile in Ashur.[21] In any case, during the reign of his son, Assyria's attitude toward the

E 242a). The role of these artisan deities is quite explicit in the incantation K.9879+ Rm.2,209+ 80-7-19, 119 cited by Cagni, *Erra*, 192:

> Ninildu, the great carpenter of Anum,
> with his flashing axe and with his pure hands
> will construct the perfect stable throne of his lordship.
> Ninagal, the great metalworker (simug gal) of Anum,
> will plate it with silver and gold (lines 7–14).

These divine workers are the *marê ummâni* 'craftsmen' par excellence. In Borger 1956: 89 §57, lines 21–24, they are possibly identified with the *apkallu* (*apkallu* here is singular; so Borger [1956: 89] prefers to identify it with Adapa).

18. On the translation of KAR ZA.GÌN.NA as 'Quay of Splendor', see Cassin 1968: 114–15. The temple of the Quay of Splendor (É KAR ZA.GÌN.NA) was located on the bank of the Euphrates (line 26). According to Moran (1959: 259 n. 7), this temple lay within the Esangila complex in Babylon near the east bank of the Euphrates. Ea, the dweller of the Apsu, was lord of this temple. In K.10924 this temple is called the "Gateway to the Apsu" (KÁ ZU + AB). See Borger 1956: 89; *RlA* 2 320 (Ebeling); Luckenbill 1907–8: 307; and George 1993: 108, for further references.

19. Parpola 1970: no. 188 (83-1-18, 50 = ABL 970); further discussion in AOAT 5/2, p. 184.

20. For a summary of these events and the cuneiform texts related to them, see Miller and Roberts 1977: 14–15; Porter 1987.

21. For a discussion of this point, see Landsberger 1965: 20–27. The Bavian Inscription (Luckenbill 1924: 83, line 48) and Sennacherib's *bīt akītu* inscription (Luckenbill 1924: 137:36f.) suggest that the statues of the gods were smashed and demolished; however, other inscriptions allude to the presence of Marduk (i.e., his statue) before Ashur (Streck 1916: 242 lines 24–26).

recalcitrant Babylon ameliorated; Esarhaddon consulted the oracles and was commanded to return the divine statues, newly refurbished, to their rebuilt shrines in Babylon.[22]

In spite of the large number of inscriptions describing Esarhaddon's renewal and return of these statues to Babylon, it seems that he actually died prior to completing the task.[23] According to the Babylonian Chronicles, it was really his son Ashurbanipal who fulfilled the claims of his father Esarhaddon and returned Marduk to Babylon during the first year of his reign (668 B.C.E.).[24]

The following text from the latter days of the reign of Esarhaddon describes the process of renewing (or remaking) the cult images from the very first stage of consulting the oracles to their final installation.[25]

Esarhaddon's Renewal of the Gods

(2.) When in heaven and on earth signs favorable for the renewal of the (statue of) the gods occurred,[26] (9) then I, Esarhaddon, king of the universe, king of the Land of Ashur, (10) the apple of Ashur's eye, the beloved of the great gods, with the great intelligence and vast understanding, (11) which the great Nudimmud,[27] the wise man of the gods, bestowed on me, (12) with the wisdom which Ashur and Marduk entrusted to me when they made me aware of the renewal of (the statue of) the great gods, (13) with lifting of hands, prayers, and supplication, (I) prayed to the divinities Ashur, king of the gods and to the great Lord Marduk:

> (14) "Whose right is it, O great gods, to create gods and goddesses[28] in a place where man dare not trespass? This task of refurbishing (the statues), which you have constantly been alloting to me (by oracle), is difficult! (15) Is it the right of deaf and blind human beings who are ignorant of themselves and remain in ig-

22. For the dates of the various Esarhaddon inscriptions dealing with the renewal of the gods, see Porter 1987: 281 n. 26.

23. Apparently Sennacherib actually began to return them and reached as far as Labbanat, about twenty miles north of Babylon, before being forced to withdraw because of plotters waiting in the town of Dūr-Kurigalzu. See Porter 1987: 257–58.

24. Chronicle 1, 34–36; and Chronicle 14, 31–37. See TCS 5.

25. Borger 1956: §53; AsBbA Rs. 2–38. For difficulties in using Borger's edition, see Porter 1987: 300–304.

26. The astronomical sign was the heliacal rising of Jupiter. See Borger 1956: 17–18 for a detailed discussion of the omen (plus bibliography). Compare the omen declaration delivered to Ashurbanipal in CT 35 pls. 13–15 (obverse, but in Bauer 1933: 79–82 "reverse") line 23: 'I commissioned you with the renewal of these (images of the) gods and of their temples' (*ud-du-uš* DINGIR.MEŠ *šá-a-tu-[nu a-d]i eš-ri-e-ti-šú-nu ap-qid-da qa-tuk-ka*).

27. Ea, the god of craftsmen, enjoys the epithet ^{d}nu-dím-mud 'image fashioner'. See Jacobsen 1976: 111 n. 157. See Thomsen 1984: 56 §53 for a different understanding of this divine name.

28. Text: [*i*]*t-ti man-ni* DINGIR.MEŠ GAL.MEŠ *ba-nu-u* DINGIR.MEŠ *u* ^{d}*ištar*; cf. the translation of Landsberger 1965: 21: "Wem steht es zu, o ihr grössen Götter und Göttinen zu schaffen. . . ?"

norance thoughout their lives?[29] (16) The making of (images of) the gods and goddesses is your right, it is in your hands; so I beseech you, create (the gods), and in your exalted holy of holies (17) may what you yourselves have in your heart be brought about in accordance with your unalterable word. (18) Endow the skilled (*enqūti*) craftsmen (DUMU.MEŠ *ummâni*) whom you ordered to complete this task with as high an understanding as Ea, their creator. (19) Teach them skills by your exalted word; (20) make all their handiwork succeed through the craft of Ninshiku."[30]

(21) I arranged diviners in groups in order to obtain a reliable oracular pronouncement about entering the *bīt mummi*. I performed divination (in order to determine whether the renewal should be done) in Ashur, Babylon, (or) Nineveh. (22) To determine the experts who should do the work and their initiation, I decided that each group should decide for itself separately; (23) and still all the extispicies were in perfect agreement; they gave me a reliable, positive answer. (24) They ordered me to enter the *bīt mummi* in Ashur, the capital city, the dwelling of Ashur, Father of the gods; (25) they indicated to me the names of the artisans (fit) for completing the work. By authority of a reassuring and favorable oracle, the diviners ordered me to do this work as follows: (26) "Do it quickly, pay attention, and be careful; do not let up, do not direct your attention elsewhere." (27) I trusted their positive and unchangeable oracle; I placed full reliance (on it).

In a favorable month, on a propitious day (28) in the month of Shabatti, the favorite month of Enlil, I entered the *bīt mummi*, the place where refurbishing was done, which the gods had chosen. (29) I brought carpenters, goldsmiths, metalworkers, stonecutters—skilled artisans knowledgeable in the mysteries—into the temple which Šamaš and Adad had indicated through divination. (30) I installed the craftsmen there. Red gold, mined in the mountains, which no one had as yet worked for artistic purposes, countless precious stones, (31) not yet cut . . . , native to the mountains and upon which Ea had generously bestowed his splendor[31] so that they might be fit for the lordly deities, (32) I prepared in abundance for the shrines of the great gods, my lords, and for the bejewelling of their divinity. I gave (all these costly materials) into the pure hands[32] (of the craftsmen). (32–33) I had a crown made of red gold and precious stones—the symbol of the lordship of my lord Ashur, king of the

29. The Akkadian *warkatam parāsum* is a classic crux interpretum:

Borger 1956: 82:	"und ihre Lebenstage nicht ergründen."
Borger 1957–58: 117:	"Hier ist doch nur die Übersetzung 'den Willen (der Götter) befragen, erforschen' möglich."
Landsberger 1955: 126 n. 25:	*warkat* + person or object *parāsum* always means 'to take care of'.
Von Soden, AHw 831:	"etwas genau prüfen und klären."

30. The god ᵈnin-ši-kù (Akkadian Niššiku) is Ea (AHw 796b). On the writing of this late form (not found in Kassite times), see Lambert 1969: 148–49.

31. On the splendor (ME.LÁM/*melammu*) of the gods, see Cassin 1968.

32. See Erra Epic II 20 (Cagni 1969). Here the god Ea says that Marduk 'has given (the artisans) understanding and has purified their hands' (*uz-ni iš-ruk-šu-nu-ti-ma qa-ti-šú-nu ú-lal-li*).

gods; then I returned it to its (proper) place. This crown, clad in awe, (34) full of dignity, bearing brilliance, covered with light, greatly pleased Ashur, the great lord, so that his heart was content and his face gleamed. (35) Bēl, Bēltiyya, Bēlet-Bābili, Ea, Madānu—the great gods—were ceremoniously born[33] within the Ešarra, the temple of their father (Ashur);[34] (36) and their appearance was beautiful. With red *šāriru*-gold, the product of Arallu, ore from the mountains, I decorated their images. (37) With splendid ornaments and precious jewelry I adorned their necks and filled their breasts,[35] exactly as the great lord Marduk wanted and as pleased queen Šarpanitu. (38) They (the artisans) made the statues of their great divinity even more artistic than before. They made them extremely beautiful, and they provided them with an awe-inspiring force, and they made them shine like the sun.

Transport of the Gods to Babylon[36]

(18) (The gods) traveled the road to Babylon, a festive way. From Ashur to the quay (19) at Babylon, every third of a double-mile piles of brushwood were lit, at every double-mile fat bulls were slaughtered. (20) And I, Esarhaddon, led the great god in procession; I processed with joy before him. (21) I brought them joyfully into the heart of Babylon, the city of their honor. Into the orchards, among the canals and (22) parterres of the temple E-kar-zaginna, the pure place, they entered by means of the office of the *apkallu*, (23) 'mouth-washing' (KA.LUḪ.Ù.DA)', 'mouth-opening' (KA.DUḪ.Ù.DA), washing and purification, before the stars of heaven, before Ea, Šamaš, Asalluḫi, (24) Bēlit-ilī, Kusu, Ningirim, Ninkurra, Ninagal, Kusibanda, Ninildu, and Ninzadim. . . .

A final reference to the ritual occurs in an inscription of Ashurbanipal that, inter alia, describes the restoration to Babylon of a divine statue by Ashurbanipal's brother Šamaš-šum-ukin, the king of Babylon.[37] The description of proceedings is somewhat damaged but is clearly influenced by the inscription of Esarhaddon just described

33. '. . . were born' (*im-ma-al-du*). The use of forms of (*w*)*alādu* 'to give birth' for the making of cult statues occasioned a dispute between R. Borger and B. Landsberger on the precise connotation of (*w*)*alādu.* The issue of the 'birth of the god' will be discussed at the end of this chapter.

34. As Porter correctly emphasizes (1987: 241–42), this statement has profound political implication. Marduk is now 'reborn' as the son of Ashur, the father of the gods (*ab ilāni*); Marduk is now his first born (*aplu rēštu*). By their rebirth they have been incorporated into the Assyrian pantheon, albeit in a role subordinate to Ashur.

35. The importance of jewelry for the necks and breasts of cult statues is exemplified by their frequency in the inventories of the gods Ninegal and Shamash at Qatna (fifteenth century B.C.E.); see Bottéro 1949. For a representation of a statue wearing such jewelry, see the plaque found in the temple of the goddesses Kititum at Ischali (Dynasty of Larsa, 20th–19th centuries B.C.E.) in Frankfort 1936: 85.

36. Borger 1956: §57, 20–24 and §60, AsBbE and AsBbH.

37. K.2694+ 3050 col. iii; Streck 1916: II, 264–69, lines 19–22; translation in Luckenbill *ARAB* 2.381–82 §989.

above. A 'mouth-washing' (KA.LUḪ.Ù.DA) takes place in the orchards and parterres of E-kar-zaginna, before the stars of heaven, before Ea and Šamaš.

Date and Source of The Texts

At present there is no extant source material for the reconstruction of the *mīs pî* ritual and its accompanying incantations from the third or second millennia B.C.E. All of the available sources for both the ritual tablet and for the accompanying incantations are of Neo-Assyrian or Neo/Late-Babylonian date (eighth–fifth centuries B.C.E., but second century for some fragments from Uruk). They come from Nineveh, Ashur, Sultantepe (Turkey), Hama (Syria), Babylon, Sippar, Nippur, and Uruk.

The large majority of texts come from Nineveh and date to the seventh century B.C.E., many of the incantation tablets having colophons that mark them as belonging to the royal library of Ashurbanipal. One fragment in Babylonian script from Nineveh (K.3472) could conceivably be earlier and is copied from an earlier original.[38] The colophons of tablets from Ashurbanipal's library do not often quote their sources. While some texts may have circulated in Assyria for centuries, it is known that copies of many compositions were deliberately collected for the king by his agents in Babylonia.[39]

The Neo-Assyrian tablets from Ashur, KAR 229 (tablet 1/2?) and VAT 10038 (tablet 4) and 10569 (tablet 1/2?) are of eighth–seventh century B.C.E. date.[40] The tablets from Sultantepe, STT 198 and 199 (tablet 1/2), 200 and 201 (tablet 3), 208 and 209 (tablet 1/2) date to the seventh century B.C.E. (see Gurney 1952: 25–26; Lloyd and Gökçe 1953: 31). The one tablet from Hama (Hama 6 A 343, tablet 3) is to be dated to the eighth or ninth century B.C.E.[41]

Of the texts from Babylon, BM 34828 (tablet 4) and BE 15526 (= VAT 17039, tablet 4) are undatable Neo-Babylonian fragments. BM 45749, the Babylonian ritual tablet, has a colophon that indicates that it was copied by Iddina-Nabû, the son of Luḫdu-Nabû, the *mašmaššu*-priest, from a red-burnt tablet of Nabû-etel-ilāni, the son of Dābibī, the incantation-priest(?). Neither of these scribes is known from other texts or is otherwise datable.

38. Cf. also K.3367 (no colophon), part of the incantation for washing the mouth of the *uskaru*, in Babylonian script.

39. (1) Parpola 1983: 1–29; (2) Moren 1980: 190–91, on CT 54 nos. 57 (K.3034+) and 106 (K.5440+ = ABL 1321 [part]), two letters to an Assyrian king concerning the copying of literary texts, including a mouth-washing ritual, suggests that they were written to Ashurbanipal from Ur (cf. Dietrich [1967–68: 67 and 95–96], who suggested a date in the reign of Sargon or Sennacherib).

40. According to personal letter (May 4, 1993) from Stefan M. Maul of the Freie Universität of Berlin, both VAT 10038 and 10569 come from Ashur. VAT 10038 comes from a "small library in the Old Palace"; although 10569 comes from Ashur, its exact site remains unclear.

41. Laessøe (1956: 60) gives as the *terminus ante quem* 720 B.C.E., the year in which Hama was conquered by the armies of Sargon II, but notes that at least some of the tablets found in Building III at Hama should be dated to the ninth century B.C.E.

The Neo-Babylonian archives from Sippar are datable to the seventh–fifth centuries B.C.E. The colophon of the Neo-Babylonian Sippar tablet BM 65594 (tablet 4 of *mīs pî*) indicates that it was copied by Nabû-kuzub-ilāni, the apprentice *mašmaššu*-priest. The only other tablet containing this name in the colophon is a late Assyrian (seventh century B.C.E.) tablet from Nineveh, Rm 349 (CT 18, 28; 5R 41 rev. 32). Thus this Sippar tablet is not at present more closely datable. The same applies to the recently excavated tablet IM 124645 (= Sippar 177/2340, tablet 3).

The Neo-Babylonian school texts from Nippur containing extracts from *mīs pî* (CBS 8802 = PBS 12/1 6; CBS 4506 = PBS 12/1 no 7; CBS 4507 = PBS 1/2 no. 116) are undatable. Of the fragments from Uruk, VAT 14494 (LKTU 19, tablet 5 of *mīs pî*) is to be dated roughly to the seventh–fifth centuries B.C.E.,[42] while W.20030/97 (tablet 1/2 of *mīs pî*?) belongs to a group of tablets datable to the Seleucid Period (third–second centuries B.C.E.; see van Dijk 1980: 13; cf. Mayer 1978: 458).

The Ritual Series mīs pî and Its Incantations: Structure

Mesopotamian rituals typically consist of prescribed ritual actions (ritual tablet) to be accompanied by the recitations of incantations in Sumerian and Akkadian. Many rituals, particularly those designed to be used in medical or apotropaic contexts, are relatively brief and the texts simply allude to the titles of the incantations to be used. Others, especially major cultic rituals, are of considerable complexity, with the ritual actions spread out over one or more days, the instructions written out on a numbered series of tablets, and the text of the incantations given in full. The mouth-washing ritual, *mīs pî*, falls into this latter category. In an arrangement that may seem peculiar to modern readers, the incantations were presented first, followed by the ritual within which they were to be used.[43] This arrangement is paralleled in other ritual series.[44]

Peg Boden (1993), a doctoral student from The Johns Hopkins University, has provided an insightful analysis of *mīs pî* as an example of a ritual of transition. The rite uses language of gestation and birth to recreate ritually the cult statue as the god. In fact, the Sumerian title of the ritual "For Washing the Mouth" may allude to the action of the midwife as she cleanses and opens the breathing passage of the newborn at birth. As Boden shows, the ritual follows the typical tripartite format of rites of transition: (1) separation of the individual from current status [preliminal rites]; (2) reshaping, intended to prepare the individual for its new status [liminal rites]; (3) reintroduction of the changed individual [postliminal rites].

42. See Falkenstein's remarks in LKTU, p. 1.

43. This is demonstrated by the fragment K.10531, which has the end of an incantation, followed by the catch-line *e-nu-ma* KA DINGIR LUḪ-*ú ina* UD ŠE.GA, and by the order of the extracts in the Philadelphia school tablets PBS 12/1 nos. 6 and 7.

44. For example, probably Šurpu, 'Burning'; cf. Lambert 1959–60: 122.

As with so many other texts, no complete copy of *mīs pî* survives, so it has to be reconstructed from many small fragments. Fortunately, many of these duplicate each other, and it is evident that, at least at Nineveh, the royal libraries contained several copies of the whole text. In attempting to reconstruct a complete ritual series, one hopes that the incantation texts will follow the order of the incantations listed in the ritual texts. In the case of *mīs pî*, the available ritual texts from Nineveh and Babylon offer different arrangements of the ritual and its incantations, and even the nature and order of incantations in the ritual text from Nineveh does not seem to be consistent with the fragments of incantation texts found at Nineveh. Some assistance in the reconstruction of the order of the incantations is given by two Late Babylonian school tablets in Philadelphia (PBS 12/1 nos. 6 and 7), which quote extracts from several tablets of the series.

Only two fragments of incantation tablets have colophons indicating the number of the tablet within the series. These numbers determine present efforts to label the different tablets. Thus tablet 4 is identified as such by the colophon of BM 65594 (IM 4-KÀM LUḪ *pi-i-ia*); it can be fairly fully reconstructed and contains a group of incantations cited by the ritual tablets (BM 45749 lines 53–54, 56–61). The preceding group of incantations (BM 45749 lines 46–48), which can also be substantially reconstructed, becomes tablet 3, although no surviving fragment bears this number. The materials available for the reconstruction of tablets 1–2 are more fragmentary and in part inconsistent with the ritual texts; STT 199 could correspond to the first tablet of incantations, according to BM 45749 (lines 3–14), but its incantations appear in a completely different order in the Nineveh ritual.

The catch-line of tablet 4 identifies the first incantation of tablet 5 (én aga-maḫ aga ní-gal-a ri- [a], cited on BM 65594 and K.2445+), and again a large part of tablet 5 can be reconstructed from fragments from Nineveh (incantations corresponding to BM 45749 lines 55–56 and 60). The catch-line of tablet 5 identifies the first incantation of the next tablet (én e-sír-ra gin-a-ni-ta, cited on Rm 2,154 and K.4866). This incantation can be almost completely reconstructed from fragments of several single-column tablets at Nineveh and is the only incantation on these tablets. Logically one would expect these fragments to be copies of tablet 6. However, one other fragment of a single-column tablet from Nineveh, K.6031 (CT 17, 40), contains the catch-line én e-sír-ra gin-a-ni-ta, followed by the colophon DUB 7-KÀM-MA LUḪ KA; thus, the tablets containing én e-sír-ra gin-a-ni-ta should be copies of tablet 8. Since all the surviving material for tablets 3–5 from Nineveh appears to belong to double column tablets, it may be that we have parts of two different editions of the text at Nineveh. Some of the possible Nineveh fragments of tablet 1–2 are also written on single-column tablets.

The evidence presently available seems to be consistent with the proposition that there was a series of six incantation tablets circulating in Babylonia and a series of eight incantation tablets at Nineveh, the two series differing somewhat in their content and neither apparently being fully consistent with the ritual texts.

Growth and Development of the Ritual

Given the historical reference to the mouth-opening of a statue of Gudea of Lagaš (ca. 2200 B.C.E.), it is reasonable to suppose that some part, at least, of the surviving ritual and incantations known from Neo-Assyrian and Neo/Late-Babylonian texts goes back to the third millennium B.C.E. According to Hallo (1970: 120), many if not all of the neo-Sumerian hymns to deities were composed to be recited at the induction of the deity's cult statue.[45] These same hymns would then be regularly recited during the major festivals and processions of the statue. Ur III texts from Tello record offerings, usually in the third month, for the 'opening of the mouth' (ka-duḫ-ḫa) of the Gudea statues; this suggests that the ritual could be performed regularly (Winter 1992: 37 n. 12).[46]

One aspect of the ritual, the cutting of the hands of the craftsmen with knives of tamarisk wood, has a somewhat "primitive" air, but because it is evidently symbolic, it may not tell us anything about earlier ritual practices. The only clear-cut evidence of any historical development of the ritual is found in the differences between the texts from Nineveh and the one from Babylon. The order of events is rearranged and so is the order and identity of the incantations used, but pending a complete reconstruction, it is not yet apparent to what extent these features reflect a different understanding of the ritual. The addition in the Babylonian text of sacrifices to a long list of astral deities is an interesting change, but in the absence of a date for the tablet and of detailed diachronic studies of astrological developments in Babylonia, it is hard either to evaluate the variation or to suggest that it has consequences for understanding the ritual.

Although one cannot yet untangle the various strands of the ritual to show how it developed, it is worth pointing out that the whole essence of the ritual is contained in a single incantation, én u_4 dingir dím-ma (tablet 3; see STT 200).[47] Here is spelled out the proposition that the statue that has not had its mouth opened does not smell incense, does not eat food, and does not drink water. Water is to be prepared, along with various other substances. The statue is to be brought to an orchard next to a canal. The statue is to be purified with (water from) the holy-water basin (*egubbû*), and its mouth is to be opened four times with honey, ghee, cedar and cypress. Similar abbreviated statements are made in the incantations én è-a-zu-dè and én me-te bára-maḫ ki-tuš nam-tar-ra (tablet 4). It is worth noting that although the ritual texts repeatedly refer to mouth-washing and mouth-opening (KA.LUḪ.Ù.DA and KA.DUḪ.Ù.DA), and the term KA.DUḪ.Ù.DA (mouth-opening) appears in the rubric of several

45. "If so, they anticipated the later techniques of endowing these man-made objects with their supernatural powers by means of elaborate rituals known as mouth-washing and mouth-opening" (Hallo 1970: 120).

46. Steible (1991: 291) also considers the reading *ki . . . ka*[!]*-duḫ-ḫa-ba* in the inscription Ibbi-sin A 9–10 line 25 'the place where the mouth is opened'. Ibbi-Sin (2038–2004 B.C.E. was the last king of the Ur III dynasty.

47. See below for a translation of this bilingual incantation.

incantations, it is only in these three incantations that any explicit reference is made to mouth-opening with honey, ghee, cedar, and cypress. The concept of mouth-opening, which appears to have been the major consideration in the ritual for the statue of Gudea (and which plays a major part in Egyptian ritual), was evidently subordinated in the first millennium to the concept of mouth-washing (KA.LUḪ.Ù.DA).

Incantations such as those just referred to were evidently composed for use in the *mīs pî* ritual. Others, such as the incantations used to sanctify the various materials put in the *egubbû*, will have had use in a wider context and may have originated in another context. The Hama text attests to one of the *mīs pî* incantations being used independently of the complete ritual. K.3472 (in Babylonian script, duplicating much of tablet 5) has the colophon: *ṭup-pi ḫi-šiḫ-ti* URU_4 É DINGIR.RA DÙ-*šu e-nu-ma* URU_4 É [. . .] *ki-i* KA GIŠ *le-u*$_5$*-um* x[. . .] 'What is necessary for making the foundations of a god's temple: (catch-line) "When the foundations of a [god's] temple [. . .]": according to the text of a writing-board [. . .]'.[48] Although there is fragmentary evidence for the use in other rituals of a few of the incantations listed in the *mīs pî* ritual texts, the other rituals are so broken that we cannot at present judge for which context the incantations were first composed.

The concept of mouth-washing has been discussed by Jacobsen (1987). Mouth-washing was not confined to the ritual for the dedication of divine statues. It was used also in rituals for divine symbols (e.g., the *uskāru* crescent of the moon god),[49] for cultic impedimenta,[50] for the king himself (Meier 1937–39: 40ff.), and in a variety of other fragmentary ritual contexts.

The incantation "Ea, Shamash, and Asalluḫi" used on the second day of the ritual (Babylonian Ritual BM 45749 line 47, Nineveh Ritual line 144) is attested at Nineveh, Sippar,[51] and Hama in Syria. The Hama text, Hama 6 A 343, now in the Danish National Museum, Copenhagen, was first edited by J. Laessøe (1956: 60–67). He was aware of the incantation's possible connection with *mīs pî* but, not having access to the duplicate material available, he interpreted the second half of the incantation as a ritual for a man affected by snake-bite. The Hama copy ends with the lines: "I, so-and-so, son of so-and-so, am afraid, frightened and terrified. Against the evil of snakes." This sets it within the context of *namburbi* incantations. Laessøe correctly compared a parallel and partially duplicate *namburbi* incantation from Nineveh now edited by Caplice (1971: 156–58). Now that we have an almost complete text for the incantation and can give due weight to the incantation's references to cultic buildings and rituals (omitted in Caplice's incantation) and to the statue's eating and hearing, it seems apparent that the incantation in its present form was originally composed for use in

48. Note that this catch-line is the first line of K.3570 (Babylonian).

49. K.63a, 4R 25, which partly duplicates *mīs pî* tablet 3.

50. For example, the *tukannu* leather bag; see the rituals for the *barû*, Zimmern 1896–1901: 1–20.

51. A tablet from the recent Iraqi excavations has now been published by F. N. H. Al-Rawi and A. R. George, "Tablets from the Sippar Library V: An Incantation from *Mīs Pî*," *Iraq* 57 (1995) 225–28.

mīs pî or a similar dedicatory ritual and subsequently found a curious secondary use at Hama. Whether this version of the incantation has priority over Caplice's version remains an open question.

It is perhaps of some signficance that "Ea, Shamash, and Asalluḫi" is one of only two Akkadian incantations used in *mīs pî.* The other is én A.GÚB.BA *šá* ᵈkù-sù *u* ᵈnin-gìrima (Nineveh ritual line 46; not included in BM 45749), the text of which is at present completely unknown. Apart from these two, there are a number of short Akkadian declarations, prayers, or "whisperings" included in the ritual, all of which are written out in full on the Nineveh ritual tablet.

We have not provided a complete "score" of the cuneiform texts; a "score" will accompany our publication of the critical edition of the ritual series.

Translations

Below we have included translations of some representative texts.[52] First, there are three ritual tablets that describe both the ritual acts (Greek *drômena* or Akkadian

52. When reading the translations of the rituals and incantations that follow, it should be borne in mind that the translations of terms for plants, stones, and cultic appurtenances are in many cases provisional.

---

1. Babylonian Ritual Tablet BM 45749 (81-7-6, 162 + 234)

1. PRE-LIMINAL STAGE. Here the statue is physically isolated from both the temple workshop (*bīt mummi*) and the human workers who crafted it. This separation will enable its rebirth as the god. The setting sun marks the close of its former status; the statue now awaits the dawning of a new day.

Obverse

1 *enūma pī ili temessû ina ūmi mitgāri ina bīt mummi 2 egubbê tukân*

54. See Labat 1965: 91, #31. This menology lists the propitious times for renewing (*ú-diš*) a statue: "If during the month of Nisan (from the first to the thirtieth) a man restores the deteriorated statue of his god or goddess, then this man will live a long life and his god will speak favorably of him. If during the month of second Nisan DITTO, then death(?) will be in the house of that man."

55. "It (the *bīt mummu*) was the place where the statues and ornaments of the gods and the equipment and ornamental work of their temples were made or restored; the place where the newly

epištu) and at least the *incipit* of their incantations[53] (Greek *legomena* or Akkadian *šiptu*). Second, we have translated two incantations of different types. Sultantepe (STT) 200 was probably originally composed for the ritual and is one of its most important incantations; this tablet is quite illustrative of the ritual's theology. The excerpt from tablet 6 or 8 (numbering depends on the version) is clearly derivative, since it does not fit in its present context. This text has clearly been adapted from another context and shows the fluidity of many of the incantations in the *mīs pî* ritual: some of the incantations—probably originally from *mīs pî*—are reused in other rituals, whereas others have themselves been taken into *mīs pî* from elsewhere (e.g., this excerpt from 6/8).

[1] The Babylonian Ritual Tablet (BM 45749)
[2] The Ninevite Ritual Tablet
[3] Incantation "When the God was Made," STT 200.
[4] Excerpts from tablet 6/8 of the Ninevite *mīs pî.*
[5] TuL 27, a ritual tablet for the restoration of a damaged statue.

53. Generally, the *incipit* of a Sumerian incantation or the full text of an Akkadian invocation or incantation quoted in the ritual tablet is given in bold type.

Obverse

1 When you wash the mouth of a god, on a favorable day[54] in the *bīt mummi*,[55] you set up 2 holy-water vessels.

made images of the gods were magically animated and where the damaged images were reanimated by restoring them and by performing the prescribed rituals. . . . We may therefore call the *bīt mummu* the workshop of the temples; the expression is synonymous with the *bīt mārē ummâni* 'the house of the craftsmen'. . . . It was most likely a workshop and a technical training school" (Heidel 1948: 103).

2 *ṣubāta sāma maḫar ili u ṣubāta pēṣa ina imitti ili ana Ea u Asalluḫi*[56] *riksê tarakkas mīs pî*

3 *ila šuāta teppušma ana ili šuāti riksa tarakkas qātka tanaššima* **én an-na ní-bi-ta tu-ud-da-a**

4 *šalāšīšu tamannu šipta* ***ultu ūmi annî ana maḫar Ea abika tallak*** *ana maḫar ili šuāti šalāšīšu tamannuma*

5 *qāt ili taṣabbatma immera tu-šá-áš-ar-šú*[57] **én è-zu-dè min giš gin tir-⌈ta⌉** *ištu bīt mārē ummâni*

6 *ina gizillî ina maḫar ili šuāti adi kišad nāri tamannuma ina muḫḫi burê uššabma*

7 *īnēšu ana ereb šamši tašakkan šutukka tanaddi ana Ea Asalluḫi u ili šuāti riksē tarakkas*

8 *šikar rēštî mazâ*[58] *tanaqqi šapri immeri tepettema pāša pulukka šaššāra*

9 *raqqa šeleppâ ša kaspi u ḫurāṣi ana libbi tašakkan tašappima ana nāri tanaddi*

10 *ana maḫar Ea* **lugal umun engur** *šalāšīšu taqabbima qātka tanaššima* **én ᵈen-ki lugal abzu-ke$_4$** *šalāšīšu tamannuma*

11 *šikara šizba karāna u dišpa tanaqqi mīs pî teppušma šipta* ***ša illaka pīšu mesi***

12 *šalāšīšu taqabbima riksē tapaṭṭar qāt ili taṣabbatma ina kirî ina urigallê ina muḫḫi burê*

13 *ina tapsê kitî tušeššabšu īnēšu ana ṣīt šamši tašakkan*

56. The trinity of Ea, Shamash, and Asalluḫi is very common in purification rituals. Ea (Sumerian Enki) is the primary deity of purification rituals in which water plays such an important role, because he is the main god of "holy water" (*RLA* II, 376). The waters used in the mouth-washing ceremony are called 'the waters of incantation' (a nam.šub/*mê sipti*) in IV R 25 iv 52–53. Ea is also the god of Apsu and of the city of Eridu (see Burrows 1932: 231–52; *RLA* II, 378). Ea is likewise the patron deity of the craftsmen, in which role he enjoys the epithet ᵈNu.dím.mud 'Image fashioner' (see Jacobsen 1976: 111 n. 157).

On the reading of ᵈAsal.lú.ḫi, see Sjöberg 1969: 80 with bibliography. Originally, Asalluḫi was the god of ḪA.A^{ki}, a city near Eridu; his relation to Ea/Enki is clarified by his epithets: dumu abzu 'son of the Abzu', dumu-sag-eridu^{ki}-ga 'first-born of Erudi', dumu-sag-ᵈen-ki-ke$_4$ 'first born of Enki'. Asalluḫi was later identified with Marduk. On the naming of Marduk as Asalluḫi in Enuma Elish, see Jacobsen 1976: 182. Asalluḫi was the patron of exorcism (EN *a-ši-pu-ti*) who purifies heaven and earth (*mullil šamê u erṣeti*).

2 (You place) a red cloth in front of the god and a white cloth to the right of the god. For Ea and Asalluḫi you set up offering-tables. Mouth-washing

3 you perform on that god and for that god you set up an offering table. You raise your hand and the incantation, "Born in heaven by your own power,"

4 you recite three times. The incantation, "From today you go before your father Ea," you recite three times before that god, and

5 you take the hand of the god and. . . . . . a ram. The incantation, "As you grew up,[59] as you grew up from the forest," (while going) from the house of the craftsmen

6 with a torch in front of the god to the river bank you recite. Seat (him) on a reed-mat, and

7 you set his eyes toward sunset. You set up a reed-hut. For Ea, Asalluḫi and that god you set up offering-tables.

8 You libate best beer; you open the thigh of a ram, and an axe, a nail, a saw,

9 a tortoise and turtle of silver and gold you place inside; you bind it up and throw it into the river.[60]

10 Before Ea you pronounce three times, "King, lord of the deep," and raise your hands and recite three times the incantation, "Enki, king of the Apsu," and

11 beer, milk, wine (and) honey you libate. You perform mouth-washing, and the incantation, "He who comes, his mouth is washed,"

12 three times you pronounce and dismantle the offering-tables. You take the hand of that god, and in the orchard in the midst of the reed-standards on a reed-mat

13 on a linen cloth you seat him. You set his eyes toward sunrise.

---

57. The verbal root for *tu-šá-áš-ar-šú* is not clear. This word also appears in the Nineveh Ritual Tablet, line 65.

58. *šikar rēštî mazâ* for KAŠ.SAG LÙ.LÙ. See CAD M/1 439 KAŠ LÙ.LÙ.A = *mazû* (a type of beer).

59. Sumerian è is translated by Akkadian *šâḫu* 'to grow up' in the bilingual versions of this incantation.

60. The religious significance of this strange rite is to demonstrate that the artisans are merely surrogates of Ea: upon completion of the divine image, the tools are again consigned to the watery abode of Ea who is the 'image-fashioner'. The tortoise and the turtle of gold and silver are offerings for Ea, for whom both of these animals are sacred (*RLA* II 379a s.v. Enki; *RLA* III 488a s.v. Göttersymbole). The tortoise is frequently found in *kudurrus* representing Ea. The function of the tortoise in this passage is paralleled in Luckenbill (1907–8: 81, lines 27–29): "To dedicate that canal . . . precious stones and a tortoise I presented to Ea Lord of springs and wells."

2. Liminal stage. As it awaits the dawn, the statue undergoes a "divine gestation." The womb-like tamarisk trough is filled with the river's fructifying "semen" and other items used to make the statue and now used for its divine birth. The tamarisk trough is placed on the bricks of the Birth Goddess (line 23). The invocation of sets of nine deities may well recall the nine months of gestation.

13 *ana nāri tallakma maṣḫata ana nāri tanaddi*

14 *miḫḫa tanaqqi qātēka tanaššima* **én èš-abzu nam-tar-tar-e-dè**[61] **én kar abzu kar ⸢kù⸣-[ga-àm]**

15 *šulušā ina maḫar nāri tamannuma mê sebet agubbê tasâbma ina bīt Kusu tukān*

16 *ana libbi egubbê ša mīs pî bīna maštakal libbi iṣṣi sebet suḫuššē qan šalāli [qan appāri]*[62]

17 *qanâ ṣāba* G[I? x] x x [x x x] x *kibrīt* x [x x] *ṭābta erēna šurmēna burāša*

18 [*uḫula qar*]*nana, sikilla* GIŠ.Ì.GIŠ *šadâna ṣābita zalāqa*

19 [. . . . .] *muššara sāmta uqnâ pappardilâ papparmina dušâ*

20 [. . . . .] *annaka parzilla šamna šaman rūšti igulâ šaman erēni dišpa ḫimēta tanaddi*

21 [. . . . .] x *ša riksē riqqēšunu tanaddima tukân buginni bīni mê eggubî*

22 [*tumallima ana libbi*][63] *buginni sāmta uqna kaspa ḫurāṣa burāša šamna ḫalṣa tanaddima*

23 [x x x] *egubbê ina muḫḫi libitti ša Dingirmaḫ tukān*

24 [x x x] *egubbê tarakkasma mīs pî teppuš riksē tapaṭṭarma*

25 [*9 riksē*] *ana Anim Enlil Ea Sin Šamaš Adad Marduk Gula Ištar kakkabāni*

---

61. **én ⸢èš⸣ abzu ⸢nam-tar⸣-tar-e-dè**: Jacobsen (1987) translates, "Father, 'Waters below'! To determine destinies. . . ," suggesting the reading **én ⸢ad⸣ abzu**, but although the sign ⸢**èš**⸣ is broken on BM 45749 it is wholly preserved in the Nineveh ritual text line 19 (K.10060, exemplar D, and K.6883, exemplar E).

62. G[I.AMBAR(SUG)]: these signs, copied by Smith, are now almost wholly lost as a result of deterioration of the tablet before conservation in 1960.

63. The restoration of *tumalli ana libbi* is adopted from Ebeling 1931: 104.

64. According to J. Krecher (1966: 133–34), there are two deities named Kusu (^{d}*kù-sù*); the first is a female grain goddess, while the second—the one referred to here—was a god of exorcism and

13 You go to the river and throw meal into the river.

14 You libate *miḫḫu*-beer. You lift up your hands and the incantation, "Apsu-temple, to determine fates," (and) the incantation, "Quay of the Apsu, pure quay,"

15 three times each in front of the river you recite and water (for) seven holy-water basins you draw and place it in the chapel of Kusu.[64]

16 Into the holy-water basin of mouth-washing tamarisk, *maštakal*, date-palm-"heart," seven palm-shoots, *šalalu*-reed, *apparu*-reed,

17 fine/sweet reed, ..., sulphur, ... , salt, cedar, cypress, juniper,

18 ["horned alkali"], *sikillu*-plant, tree resin?, lodestone, *zalāqu*-stone,

19 [. . . . .] *muššaru*-stone, carnelian, lapis-lazuli, *pappardilu*-stone, *papparminu*-stone, *dušu*-stone,

20 [. . . . .] tin, iron, oil, salve-oil, perfumed$^?$ oil, cedar oil, honey (and) ghee you throw.

21 [. . . . .] of the offering-tables you lay down and arrange their aromatics. A trough of tamarisk wood with the waters of the holy-water basin

22 you fill, and into the trough carnelian, lapis-lazuli, silver beads, gold beads,[65] juniper (and) *ḫalṣu*-oil you throw, and

23 [. . .] holy-water-basins you set on the brick of Dingirmaḫ

24 [. . . . . .] the holy-water basins you set up, and perform mouth-washing. You dismantle the offering-table, and

25 9 offering-tables for Anu, Enlil, Ea, Sin, Shamash, Adad, Marduk, Gula (and) Ishtar, the stars

---

prayers. He was known as 'the chief exorcist of Enlil' (*šangammaḫu ša* ^{d}*Enlil*) and as the 'expert in ritually pure waters' (*ša mê ellūti idû*). See Tallqvist 1938: 344. However, the three gods Kusu, Ningirim, and Nisaba are all gods of reeds and grasses and according to Jacobsen (1976: 10) are "restorers of divine images." These three are associated in several liturgies (see Mullo Weir 1958: 372).

65. "Beads" for NA$_4$, see CAD K 246.

66. Dingirmaḫ is the equivalent of the Akkadian Bēlet-ili, the Mother-goddess. It is appropriate that the "mother of gods" be invoked in "enlivening" a statue of a god. Perhaps it is in this respect that she bears the title ^{d}tibira-dingir-re-ne-ka 'copper-caster of the gods' (see Jacobsen 1976: 107 n. 135).

26 [x x *ana*] *iltāni tarakkas* **én giš-šinig giš-kù-ga** *tamannuma mīs pî teppuš*

27 *9 riksē ana Ninmaḫ Kusu Ningirima Ninkurra Ninagal*
28 *Guškinbanda Ninildu Ninzadim u ili šuāti ana šūti tarakkas* KIMIN

29 *2 riksē ana Sagmegar u Delebat tarakkas* KIMIN
30 *2 riksē ana Sin u Kajamāni tarakkas* KIMIN
31 *3 riksē ana Šāḫiṭi Šiltāḫi Ṣalbatāni tarakkas* KIMIN
32 *6 riksē ana Zibānīti kakkab Šamši Epinni* ŠU.PA

33 *Eriqqi Eru Enzi tarakkas* KIMIN
34 *4 riksē ana Ikî Šinūnūti Anunīti Absinni tarakkas* KIMIN

35 *4 riksē ana* MUL.KU$_6$ MUL.GU.LA MUL.ERIDU^{ki} *Zuqaqīpi tarakkas* KIMIN

Reverse of the Tablet

36 *3 riksē ana šūt Anim šūt* [*Enlil u šūt Ea tarakkas* KIMIN]

37 *ina šēri ina libbi šutukkê ana Ea Šamaš u* [*Asalluḫi 3 kussê tanaddi*][67]

38 *ṣubat ḫuššî tatarraṣ kitâ ina muḫḫi tašaddad šalāšat paššūrē tarakkas*[68] [*suluppa sasqâ tasarraq*]
39 *miris dišpi ḫimēti tašakkan adagurra tukân* ⸢*šeššet*⸣[69] DUG [. . . . . .] x x

40 *tasaddir šamma bēra*[70] *tanaddi inib kirî tumaṣṣi*[71] *tukabbat*[72] x [x x] *tatarraṣ*

41 *šeam naḫla tasarraq nignak burāši tasarraq erēna ina qātīka tanaššima*

42 **én an-na ní-bi-ta tu-ud-da-a** *šalāšīšu tamannu* **én ⸢^{d}utu en⸣ [g]al an-ki-⸢bi-da⸣-ke$_4$**[73]
43 **én a nam-ti-⸢la⸣ i$_7$ íl-la-me-en** x x [x x x] x MEŠ x [x SU]M$^?$-*in*[74]

67. The end is restored from the Nineveh version, lines 110–11.

68. KEŠDA-*as*: for this orthography, compare line 52. The end of the line is restored from the Nineveh version line 111.

69. ⸢6⸣; the number is now more damaged than Smith's copy suggests. Smith's transliteration gives 6 as his preferred reading (rather than 7); there may be a connection with the number 6 in line 115 of the Nineveh text, and a mathematical connection with the 3 seats and 3 tables.

26 [. . . . . .], towards the north you set up. The incantation, "Tamarisk, pure wood," you recite, and you perform mouth-washing.

27 9 offering-tables for Ninmaḫ, Kusu, Ningirim, Ninkurra, Ninagal,

28 Kusibanda, Ninildu, Ninzadim and that god toward the south you set up, ditto.

29 2 offering tables for Jupiter and Venus you set up, ditto.

30 2 offering tables for the Moon and Saturn you set up, ditto.

31 3 offering tables for Mercury, Sirius (and) Mars you set up, ditto.

32 6 offering tables for the Balance (Libra) (which is) the star of Shamash, the Plough, "ŠU.PA,"

33 the Wagon (Ursa Major), Erî (Aquila), the Goat (Lyra) you set up, ditto.

34 4 offering tables for the Field (Pegasus), the Swallow (Pisces), Anunitum (Pisces) (and) the Barley-stalk (Spica/Virgo) you set up, ditto.

35 4 offering tables for the Fish(?), the Giant (Aquarius), Eridu (and) the Scorpion you set up, ditto.

Reverse of the Tablet

36 3 offering-tables for the (stars) of Anu, the (stars) of Enlil and the (stars) of Ea you set up, ditto.

37 In the morning within the reed-hut for Ea, Shamash and Asalluḫi you set three thrones.

38 You spread over them red cloth; you draw a linen (curtain) before them. You set up three tables; you sprinkle dates (and) meal.

39 You set in place a confection of honey (and) butter. You set up an *adagurru*-vessel. 6. . . . . .-jars

40 you set in line, you lay choice grasses down. You spread out fruit of the orchard, you. . . , ... you stretch out(?).

41 Sifted barley you scatter, a censer of juniper you sprinkle, cedar in your hand you raise, and

42 the incantation, "Born in heaven by his own power," you recite three times; the incantation, "Shamash, great lord of heaven and earth,"

43 the incantation, "Water of life, the river rising in flood . . . ," [you recite, and]. . . . . you give(?).

70. For Ú.BAR.

71. See AHw 1498a *(w)uṣṣû(m)*.

72. *tumaṣṣi tukabbat*: cf. CAD K 17b *tušarraḫ tukabbat*, as in the Nineveh version line 118.

73. **én ⌜^{d}utu en⌝ [g]al an-ki-⌜bi-da⌝-ke$_4$**: this incantation incipit is restored from PBS 12/1 no. 7 line 8; that tablet has other extracts from *mīs pî*. Cf. also line 134 of the Nineveh text.

74. The end of this line probably duplicates line 136 of the Nineveh text.

44 **én illu garza-bi aš-àm maš-àm** *tamannuma* x x x ⸢*na*$^?$⸣ *tanaqqi nignakka tasarraq*

45 *maṣḫāta ana pūt immeri tanaddima niqâ tanaqqi riksē t*[*u-x*]-⸢*li/tu*⸣-⸢*ma*$^?$⸣

3. POST-LIMINAL STAGE. The statue has now been reborn as the god and is reintroduced into the temple (line 60).

46 *mašmaššu ina šumēli ili šuāti ana maḫar Ea Šamaš u Asalluḫi izzazma* **én** ⸢**^{d}utu**⸣ **[di]-⸢ku$_5$⸣ maḫ** *imannu*

47 *šipta* ***Ea Šamaš u Asalluḫi*** *šalāšīšu immanu* **[é]n u$_4$ ⸢dingir⸣ [dím-m]a** *imannuma mīs pî teppuš*

48 *arkišu* **én alam kù me-gal šu-⸢ti-a⸣**[75] *tamannu/imannu takpirti tukappar*

49 *libša tulabbaš terêqamma mārē ummâni mala ila šuāta iṭḫû*

50 *u unūtsunu* [x x x] *Ninkurra Ninagal Guškinbanda*

51 *Nin*[*ildu Ninzadim tušazzassunūti*]*ma qātsunu ina paršigi*[76]

52 *tarakkas ina paṭri bīni tanakkis* [. . .] ***anāku la ēpuššu Ninagal Ea ša nappaḫi***[77] ***īpuššu*** *tušaqbi*

53 *īn ili šuāti tepette mašmaššu ina maḫar ili šuāti . . .* **[én] ⸢è⸣-a-zu-⸢dè⸣ ⸢min** ***ina šá-ḫi-ka*⸣** *imannu*

54 **én alam ki-kù-ga-ta ù-[tu-ud-da én] alam an-na ù-tu-⸢ud⸣-da**

55 **én ^{d}nin-íldu nagar-gal-an-n[a-ke$_4$ é]n ⸢túg⸣-[maḫ túg]-⸢níg⸣-lam-ma gada-babbar-ra**

56 **én aga-maḫ én giš-gu-za kù-ga** *imannuma ana maḫar* [x x] x **én ⸢gin⸣-na na-an-gub-bé-en** *imannu*

57 *šanû imannuma uṣurāti ušerrab*[78] *šalšu imannum*[*a* KI-^{d}UT]U DU x x *ina maḫar riksa*

75. *šu-ti-a*: sic. The Nineveh ritual tablet line 162 has *šu-du$_7$-a*.

76. Restored from line 175 of the Nineveh text.

77. ^{d}*nin-*⸢*á*$^?$⸣*-*[*gal*$^?$] ^{d}BE *šá* ⸢LÚ⸣.[SIMUG]: the traces of ⸢*á*$^?$⸣ are extremely uncertain, but the restoration follow the pattern of the Nineveh text lines 179ff.

78. The text reads TU-*rab* which suggests the Assyrian form *ušerrab* 'he makes enter', such as found in CAD E 269b.

44 The incantation, "The flood, its divine task is unique, is holy," you recite and. . . . . .you libate, a censer you sprinkle,

45 *masḫatu*-flour you place on the forehead of a ram and sacrifice (it); an offering-table you. . . . . .

46 The *mašmaššu*-priest stands on the left side of that god, before Ea, Shamash and Asalluḫi, and recites the incantation, "Shamash, exalted judge."

47 The incantation, "Ea, Shamash and Asalluḫi," he recites three times. The Incantation, "On the day when the god was created," he recites and you perform mouth-washing.

48 Afterwards the incantation, "Pure statue, suited(!) to great divine attributes," he recites; you wipe a wiping;

49 you whisper a whispering. You retire, and all of the craftsmen who approached that god

50 and their equipment [. . . . . . before(?)] Ninkurra, Ninagal, Kusibanda,

51 Ninildu (and) [Ninzadim you make them stand], and their hands with a "headband"

52 you bind and cut (them) with a knife of tamarisk wood. "I did not make him (the statue), Ninagal (who is) Ea (god) of the smith made him," you make (them) say.

53 You open the eye of that god. The *mašmaššu*-priest before that god . . . he recites the incantation, "In your growing up, in your growing up. . . . ,"[79]

54 the incantation, "Statue born in a pure place," the incantation, "Statue born in heaven,"

55 the incantation, "Ninildu, great carpenter of Anu," the incantation, "Exalted garment, ...garment of white linen,"

56 the incantation, "Exalted crown," (and) the incantation, "Holy throne," he recites, and before. . . . . the incantation, "Go, do not tarry," he recites;

57 the second version[80] he recites and he makes (him) enter the form;[81] the third version he recites and the *kiutukam* prayer[82] . . . . First the offering-tablc

79. In this incantation Sumerian **[én] ⌜è⌝-a-zu-⌜dè⌝** is translated by Akkadian *ina šá-ḫi-ka* (Akkadian *šâḫu/šiaḫu* 'to grow tall') also in BM 83023 (83-1-21, 186) (*mīs pî* 4, identified by M. J. Geller). The inclusion in the ritual text of the Akkadian translation is remarkable.

80. There are three different versions of this incantation from tablet 4 of the series (see BM 65594 for numbering); see K.2445+ lines 66–72 (version one); lines 73-B6 (second version); lines B7-19 (third version).

58 *ša ili šuāti tapaṭṭar arkišu ša Kusu u Ningirima tapaṭṭar arkišu ša ili mārē ummâni tapaṭṭar*[83]

59 *arkišu ša ilāni rabûti tapaṭṭar qāt ili taṣabbatma* **én gìr ki bal ⌜min⌝** x [x x x] **⌜én⌝ e-sír-⌜ra⌝ gin-a-ni-ta**

60 *adi bīt ili tamannuma ina bāb bit ili šuāti muḫḫura tušamḫar qāt ili taṣabbatma tušerrebma* **én lugal-mu šà-du$_{10}$-ga-zu-šè**

61 *adi papāḫi tamannu ila ina šubtīšu tušaššabma* **én unù kin-sig an-na-ke$_{4}$ én me-te bára-maḫ** *ina šubtīšu tamannu*

62 *ina imitti papāḫi šutukka tanaddi ana Ea u Asalluḫi riksa tarakkas riksa tušallamma*

63 *mīs pî ila šuāta teppušma ana ili šuāti riksa tarakkas mê buginni ila šuata tullama*

64 **én ^{d}asal-lú-ḫi dumu eridu^{ki}-ga-ke$_{4}$** *7-šú tamannuma ša ilūti tuṭaḫḫi*

65 *ina mušīti tašakkan ana kār apsî tallakma tuššab takpirtu ebbetu adi kār apsî tušallak*

---

66 *mūdû mūdâ likallim la mūdû la immar ikkib Enlil rabi Marduk*[84]

67 *kî pī ṭuppi gabari ṣirpi sāmi ša Nabû-etel-ilāni*

68 *mār dābibī* LÚ.KA.INIM.MA *Iddina-Nabû mār Luḫdu-Nabû*

69 *mašmaššu ana balaṭ napšātīšu arāk ūmēšu išṭurma*

70 *ina Esagila ukîn*

---

81. Some authors have suggested that the god is here invited to enter the "form" of the statue whereby it can become the divine presence (Winter 1992: 23). The beginning of the Nabu-apla-iddina text given above (III:19) refers to the finding of a model/form of the statue (*uṣurat ṣalmi*) of Shamash, which is the same word translated here as 'form'. However, if we read the Sumerogram GIŠ.ḪUR.ME as the Akkadian *gišhuru*, then it could also be a 'magic circle' (see *Šurpu* III 127) used in rituals: "Enter the circles." However, there have been no explicit references earlier to such circles, although they are referred to (*gi giš-ḫur-ḫur-re dingir-re-e-ne-ke$_{4}$* 'reed of the magic circles of the gods') in the *mīs pî* incantation found in STT 198:50. This incantation was recited on the first day

58 of that god you dismantle; afterwards you dismantle (the offering-table) of Kusu and Ningirima; afterwards you dismantle (the offering-table) of the gods of the craftsmen;

59 afterwards you dismantle the offering-table of the great gods. You take the hand of the god and the incantation, "The feet sprinting over the ground, the feet sprinting over the ground, ... ," (and) the incantation, "As he walked through the street,"[85]

60 all the way to that god's temple you recite. At the door of that god's temple you make an offering. You take the god's hand and make him enter, and the incantation, "My king, to your heart's content,"

61 (going) to the sanctuary you recite. You seat the god in his cella, and the incantation, "The celestial evening meal," and the incantation, "Fit for the august throne-dais," you recite in his cella.

62 On the right of the sanctuary you set up a reed-hut; for Ea and Asalluḫi you set up an offering-table; you complete the offering-table, and

63 on that god you perform mouth-washing, and for that god you set up an offering-table. With water (from) the trough you purify that god and

64 the incantation, "Asalluḫi, son of Eridu," you recite seven times, and bring near the trappings of divinity;

65 at night you set them (upon him). You go to the Kar-Apsi, and sit down; you make clean wiping extend to the Kar-Apsi.

---

66 The initiate may show it to the initiate. The uninitiated may not see it. Taboo of the great Enlil, Marduk.

67 According to the wording of a tablet, the copy of a red-burnt tablet of Nabû-etel-ilāni,

68 the son of Dabibi, the incantation-priest(?), has Iddina-Nabû, the son of Luḫdu-Nabû,

69 the *mašmaššu*-priest, for the life of his soul and for the prolonging of his days written (it) and

70 set it in Esangila.

---

of the ritual in conjunction with setting up the reed standard (*urigallu*) in a circle (see Nineveh Ritual Tablet, line 6).

82. The threefold incantation **gin-na na-an-gub-bé-en** found in tablet 4 of the *mīs pî* series is called a *kiutukam* prayer (*ka-inim-ma ki* ^{d}*utu-kam*).

83. Restored from line 203 of the Nineveh text.

84. See §151 in Hunger 1968 for a treatment of this colophon.

85. This entire incantation from *mīs pî* tablet 6 or 8 is given at the end of this chapter.

2. *Ninevite Ritual Text*

1 *enūma pī ili temessû*

2 *ina ūmi magri/mitgāri ina šērim ana ṣēri ana kirî ša kišād nāri tallakma*

3 *nipiḫ šamši tammarma kudurra takaddir*

4 *ana ālim tatârma isḫa tammar ina mišil bēr ūmi ana ṣēri tatârma*

5 *bilat qanê teleqqi*

6 *urigallē teppuš sūrta tusārma*

7 *šutukkē ana Ea Šamaš u Asalluḫi tanaddi*

8 **én gi-kù gi-gíd-da gi-giš-gi kù-ga**

9 **én im-kù-zu ^{d}asar-re abzu-a igi im-ma-an-sum**

10 *šulušā ana šutukkē tamannu*

11 [*šutukkē an*]*a Kusu Ningirima Dingirmaḫ tanaddi* [. . .]

12 *itât bīt ili šuāti . . . . . tanaddi*

13 *bīna libbi gišimmari erēni tanaddi*

14 . . . . . *bītâtu* . . . .

15 **én gi abzu-ta mú-a** *ana qan* . . . [. . .]

16 **én gi-šà-ga sikil-la ša$_6$-ga** *ana qan* [. . .]

17 **én zì nam-num-na sur-ra** *ana zisurrî* x [. . .]

18 *ana nāri tallakma maṣḫata ana nāri tanaddi miḫḫa tanaqqi*

19 *qātka tanaššima* **én èš-abzu nam tar-tar-[e-dè** . . .]

20 **[én k]ar abzu kar kù-g[a-àm** . . .]

21 **[én k]ar za-gín-na kar ^{d}en**. . . . [. . .]

22 *šulušā ina maḫar nāri tamannuma mê sebet agubbê*

23 *tasâb tatârma ina bīt Kusu ina mušīti agubbi*

24 [*ša* KA.LUḪ.Ù.D]A *bīna maš*[*takal libbi iṣ*]*ṣi*

25 *7 suḫuššē qan šalāli* [*qan appāri qanâ ṭāba*]

26 [. . . . .] *ṭābta e*[*rēna šurmēna burāša*]

27 [*uḫula qarnan*]*a, sikilla* GIŠ.Ì.GIŠ . . .

1 When you wash the mouth of a god,

2 on a favorable day in the morning you go into the countryside, to an orchard on the bank of a river, and

3 you watch for sunrise, you mark out a boundary.

4 You return to the city and inspect the appurtenances. At the first half double-hour of the day you return to the countryside and

5 you take a load of reeds,

6 make reed posts, set them up in a circle and

7 establish "reed-huts" for Ea, Shamash, and Asalluḫi.

8 The incantations "Pure reed, long reed, pure node of a reed"

9 (and) "Marduk saw your pure clay in the Apsu"

10 you recite three times each to the "reed-huts."

11 You establish ["reed-huts"] for Kusu, Ningirima (and) Dingirmaḫ [. . .]

12 around/alongside the temple of that god. . . . . .

13 tamarisk, date-palm-heart (and) cedar you arrange.

14 . . . . .temples. . . . .

15 The incantation "Reed grown from the Apsu" to the reed . . . [. . . . . . you recite];

16 the incantation "Reed whose heart is pure and good" to the reed [. . . . . . you recite];

17 the incantation "Flour nobly poured out" to the "magical circle of flour" . . . [you recite].

18 You go to the river and throw *maṣḫatu*-flour into the river. You libate *miḫḫu*-beer.

19 You lift up your hand[86] and the incantations "Apsu-temple, to determine fates . . . ,"

20 "Quay of the Apsu, pure quay . . . ,"

21 (and) "Lapis-lazuli quay, quay of En[ki] . . . ,"

22 three times each in front of the river you recite and water (for) seven holy-water basins

23 you draw. You return and in the chapel of Kusu at night the holy-water basin

24 of mouth-washing with tamarisk, *maštakal*, date-palm "heart,"

25 seven palm-shoots, *šalālu*-reed, *appāru*-reed, fine/sweet reed,

26 . . . . . , salt, cedar, cypress, juniper,

27 ["horned alkali"], *sikillu*-plant, tree resin? [you fill? . .],

86. See Gruber 1980: 60–84 for a discussion of the idiom *qāta našû*.

Probably no gap here, but in K.6324+ lines 8–27 are written as lines 8–33; to judge by BM 45749, 18 "line 34" should follow directly after "line 27," so there is some overlap here.

34 *šadâna ṣābita*. . . . .

35 *muššara sāmta uqnâ pappardilâ papparmina*

36 *dušâ kaspa ḫurāṣa erâ parzilla tumallima*

37 *šamna šaman rūšti igulâ šaman erēni dišpa ḫim*[*ēta* . . . . . .]

38 *šipāta peṣâta šipāta sāmāta šipāta uqnâta kišassu* [*tarakka*]*s*$^{?}$

39 *pursīti ṣeḫri bāba tukattam ēma tukattamū*

40 **én lugal an-na ki-sikil-la mu-un-šám-šám** *tamannu*

41 *nignakka gizillâ egubbâ tušbâʾšu*

42 *eqla*(?) *tullal qaqqara tašabbiṭ mê ellūti tasallaḫ*

43 *nignak burāši tašakkan šikara rēštâ*[87] *tanaqqi*

44 *3 zidubdubbè ana muḫḫi egubbî tanaddi*

45 **én ḫur-sag giš-tir šim-giš-erin-na-ke$_4$** *šalāšīšu tamannu*

46 *šipta* ***egubbû ša*** ^{d}***Kusu u*** ^{d}***Ningirima***

47 *ana maḫar egubbî šalāšīšu tamannu*

48 [**én**. . . . .]-**ta**$^{?}$ ^{d}**nidaba** *šalāšīšu tamannu*

49 [. . . . . *ana*] *maḫar egubbî riksa tarakkas*

50 *nîqa tanaqqi nignak burāši tašakkan*

51 *šikara rēštâ tanaqqi qātka tanaššima*

52 **én a kù-ga a i$_7$-idigna gub-ba**

53 *šalāšīšu ana maḫar egubbi tamannuma tuškên*

54 *ana bīt isḫi tatârma paṭīra tašakkan nāra tammar*

55 *ina bīt mārē ummâni ašar ilu ibbanû*

56 *qaqqara tašabbiṭ mê ellūti tasallaḫ ana Ea u Asalluḫi u ili šuāti*

57 *3 nignakkē burāši tašakkan šikara rēštâ tanaqqi*

58 *ila šuāta mīs pî pīt pî teppuš*

59 *nignakka gizillâ tušbâʾšu egubbê tullalšu*

87. The Akkadian for the Sumerogram KAŠ SAG is difficult, since both Akkadian *šikru* and *šikru reštû* are found. However, many NA rituals write KAŠ *reš-tu-ú* (see Thureau-Dangin 1921: 119, 19).

34 lodestone, ...

35 *muššaru*-stone, carnelian, lapis-lazuli, *pappardilu*-stone, *papparminu*-stone,

36 *dušu*-stone, silver, gold, copper (and) iron you fill, and

37 oil, salve-oil, perfumed? oil, cedar oil, honey and ghee [you . . .].

38 White wool, red wool (and) blue wool you bind around (?) its neck.

39 You close the mouth of a small *pursītu*-vessel. As you close it

40 you recite the incantation, "The king in heaven drew (water) in a pure place."

41 You swing over/move past him (the god) the censer, torch and holy-water basin,

42 you purify the area(?), you sweep the ground, you sprinkle pure water.

43 A censer of juniper you set in place, you libate best beer.

44 Three heaps of flour you set up on the holy-water vessel.

45 The incantation, "Mountain, forest of cedar-incense," you recite three times.

46 The incantation, "Holy-water vessel of Kusu and Ningirima,"

47 you recite three times before the holy-water vessel.

48 [The incantation, ". . . . . Nidaba," you recite three times.

49 [. . . . .] Before the holy-water vessel you set up an offering table.

50 You sacrifice a ram, you set up a censer of juniper.

51 You libate best beer, you raise your hand, and

52 the incantation, "Pure water which runs in the Tigris,"

53 you recite three times before the holy-water vessel and prostrate yourself.

54 You return to the house of appurtenances and set up a *paṭiru*-altar; you inspect the river (water).[88]

55 In the house of the craftsmen, where the god was created,

56 you sweep the ground, you sprinkle pure water. For Ea, Asalluḫi and that god

57 you set up 3 censers of juniper, you libate best beer.

58 On that god you perform mouth-washing (and) mouth-opening.

59 You swing over/move past him (the god) the censer (and) torch, you purify him with the holy-water basin.

88. The *bīt isḫi* was first mentioned in line 4. Is this water that is inspected the river water previously drawn (lines 22–23)?

59a **[én an-na] nì-bi-ta è-a** *šalāšīšu tamannu*

60 *ana ili šuāti kīam taqabbi*

---

61 ***ultu ūmi annî ana maḫar Ea abika tallak***
62 ***libbaka liṭīb kabattaka liḫdu***
63 ***Ea abika ana maḫrika rīšta limla***
64 *šalāšīšu taqabbima tuškênma*
65 *qāt ili taṣabbatma immera tu-šá-áš-ar-šú*
66 **én è-a-zu-dè [è-a-z]u-dè gal-a** *ištu bīt mārē* [*ummâni*]

67 *adi nāri ina maḫar ili ina gizillî tamannu*

---

68 *mārē ummâni mala ana ili šuāti* [*iṭḫû*]
69 *u unūssunu itti ili šuāti ana ṣēr*[*i* x x]
70 *ina kirî ša kišad nāri tukân*
71 [*ila šuāta i*]*na muḫḫi burî tušeššabma šutukkē tannadi*
72 [*ana*] *Ea u Asalluḫi paṭīra tukân*
73 *suluppē sasqâ tasarraq*
74 *miris dišpi ḫimēti* [*tašakkan*]
75 *nignak burāši tašakkan niqâ tanaqqi*
76 [. . . .*maz*]*â tanaqqima tušk*[*ên*]
77 [. . . . . .] *nignak burāši tašakkan šikara rēštâ tanaqqi*
78 [. . . . . .] *pāša pulukka šaššāra*
79 [*raqqa šeleppâ*] *ša kaspi u ḫurāṣi ana šabri immeri*
80 *tašakkan tašappima ana nāri tanaddi*

Gap of some lines

87 [. . . . .] x ŠIN *tu-*⌜*ta*⌝*-ú-*⌜*šú*⌝
88 [. . . . . . *šipta* ***ša illak***]***a pīšu mesi***
89 [. . . . . ***itti***] ***aḫḫēšu limmannu***
90 [. . . . . . ***pāša***] ***pulukka šaššāra ša mārē ummâni***
91 [. . . . . .] x-***ḫú-šú***[90] ***ina zumrīšu tabal***
92 [. . . . . .] ***ilu šuātu Ea pīšu mesi***
93 [. . . . . . ***itti***] ***aḫḫēšu munušu***
94 *šalāšīšu taqabbina maḫar Ea riksa tapaṭṭarma*

---

89. The same unknown root is found in BM 45749, line 5.
90. The gap can probably be restored as [*mala iṭ*]*ḫûšu* 'as many as worked on him (i.e., that god)'.

59a The incantation, "In heaven by your own power you are born," you recite three times.
60 You speak as follows to that god:

---

61 "From today you go before your father Ea.
62 Let your heart be pleased, let your mind be happy.
63 May Ea, your father, be full of joy with you."
64 You speak it three times and prostrate yourself, and
65 you take the hand of the god and[89] . . . . . . a ram.
66 The incantation, "As you go out, as you go out, great . . . ," (going) from the house of the craftsmen
67 to the river in front of the god with a torch you recite.

---

68 As many of the craftsmen as approached that god
69 and their equipment together with that god to the country [. . . . . .]
70 in the orchard on the river bank you place ⟨them⟩.
71 You seat that god on a reed-mat and establish reed-huts.
72 For Ea and Asalluḫi you place an offering-table;
73 you scatter dates, and meal;
74 [you set in place] a confection of honey and butter;
75 you set in place a censer of juniper, you sacrifice a ram.
76 You libate *mazû*-be[er] and prostrate yourself.[91]
77 [. . . . . .] you set in place a censer of juniper; you libate best beer.
78 [. . . . . .] an axe, a nail, a saw,
79 [a tortoise and turtle] of silver and gold into the thigh of a ram
80 you place; you bind it up and throw it into the river.

87 [. . . . .]. . . . .
88 [. . . . . . the incantation, "He who comes, his mouth is washed;
89 [. . . . . . with] his brothers let him be counted;
90 [. . . . . . the axe,] the nail (and) the saw of the craftsmen,
91 [as many as work]ed on him, take away in his[92] body!
92 [. . . . . .] that god, oh Ea, his mouth is washed;
93 [. . . . . . with] his brothers count him."
94 You recite (this) three times, and before Ea you dismantle the offering-table.

---

91. See Gruber 1980: 238–54 for a treatment of *šukênu.*
92. "His" refers to the sheep thrown into the river in line 80.

95 *qāt ili taṣabbatma ina kirî ina libbi šutukkê urigallê*

96 *ila šuāta ina muḫḫi burî ina tapsê kitî tušeššabšu*
97 *īnēšu ana ṣīt šamši tašakkamma itât ṣalmi šuāti*
98 *ini libbi šutukkê urigallê unūt ili mala ibaššū*

99 *u unūt mārē ummâni tanaddima terêqamma*

---

100 *ana Anim Enlil Ea Sin Šamaš*
101 *Adad Marduk Gula Ninsianna*
102 *9 nignakkē ana kakkab šimetān tašakkan riksa tarakkas*
103 *niqā tanaqqi šikara rēštâ tanaqqi*
104 *mīs pî pīt pî teppuš riksa tapaṭṭarma*

---

105 *ana Dingirmaḫ Kusu Ningirima Ninkurra*
106 *Ninagal Guškinbanda Ninildu Ninzadim u ili šuāti*
107 *9 nignakkē ana ilāni mušīti tašakkan šumšunu tazakkar*
108 *niqâ tanaqqi mīs pî pīt pî teppuš*

---

109 *ina šēri ina libbi šutukkê ana Ea Šamaš u Asalluḫi*
110 *3 kussê tanaddi ṣubat ḫuššî tatarraṣ kitâ ina muḫḫi tašaddad*

111 *3 paššūrē tarakkas suluppē sasqâ tasarraq*
112 *miris dišpi ḫimēti tašakkan*
113 *adagurra billata damqa tumalli*
114 *qanâ ṭāba u ša ina libbi tanakkisma ēma paššūrē tukân*
115 *6 kukkubē šikari rēstî tumallima i-ra-ta-a-an tasaddir*
116 *nignak burāši tašakkan 3 mašqī ša dami tasaddir*
117 *šamma bēra tanaddi 3 niqê peṣûti*[93] *kabrūti tatarraṣ*
118 *inib kirî tušarraḫ tukabbat*[94] *še'a rabâ* (ŠE.GAL) *naḫla*
119 *arki šammi bēri tasarraq*
120 *šipāta peṣâta šipāta sāmāta pušikka tabarra*
121 *uqnâta šīpāti šarāti tašakkan* [. . . . . .] *terêqamma*
122 [. . . . .] *Ninagal*

---

93. One manuscript reads UD.UD or DADAG, which could mean *ebbūti* 'pure', which might also be the intention here: *niqâ* DADAG *kabra tanakkis* 'You slaughter a pure, fattened sacrificial lamb' (BMS 40:9).

95 You take the hand of the god, and in the orchard in the midst of the reed-huts and reed-standards

96 you seat that god on a reed-mat on a linen cloth.

97 You set his eyes toward sunrise; and alongside that statue

98 in the midst of the reed-huts and reed-standards the equipment for the god, all of it,

99 and the equipment of the craftsmen you lay down, and you withdraw.

---

100 For Anu, Enlil, Ea, Sin, Shamash,

101 Adad, Marduk, Gula (and) Ninsianna

102 you set up 9 censers to the evening-star and set up an offering table;

103 you sacrifice a ram, you libate best beer,

104 you perform Mouth-Washing (and) Mouth-Opening. You dismantle the offering-table, and

---

105 for Dingirmaḫ, Kusu, Ningirima, Ninkurra,

106 Ninagal, Kusibanda, Ninildu, Ninzadim and that god

107 you set up 9 censers to the gods of the night, you name their names,

108 you sacrifice a ram, you perform Mouth-Washing and Mouth-Opening.

---

109 In the morning in the midst of the reed-huts for Ea, Shamash and Asalluḫi

110 you set three thrones. You spread over them red cloth; you draw a linen (curtain) before them.

111 You set up three tables; you sprinkle dates and meal.

112 You set in place a confection of honey and butter.

113 You fill an *adagurru*-vessel with good beer.

114 "Good" reed and its pulp you cut, and when/where you set the tables,

115 you fill 6 *kukkubu*-jars with best beer, and you set them in a row. . . .

116 you set in place a censer of juniper. You set three troughs of blood in a row.

117 Choice grasses you lay down; you lay out 3 white fattened sacrificial sheep.

118 The fruit of the orchard you praise and honor; sifted barley

119 you scatter behind the choice grasses.

120 White wool, red wool, combed wool, red-dyed wool,

121 blue wool, various(?) wools, fleece you set in place, . . . and retire.

122 [. . . . .] Ninagal

---

94. Compare BM 45749, line 40, *tumaṣṣi tukabbat.* We strongly suspect that we correctly understand neither passage.

123 [. . . . .] *Ninzadim*
124 [. . . . .*mārē*] *ummâni*
125 [. . . . .] . . . *tanaddi*
126 [. . . . . SA]R$^{?}$-*as*
127 [. . . . .] *gizillâ*

---

128 [. . . . .] *tullal*
129 [. . . . .] *nipḫa*? (SAR-*ḫa*)
130 [. . . . .]-⌜*ta*⌝ *te-ṣe-en*
131 *burāša tasarraq*
132 [. . . . .] *erēna ina qātika tanaššima*
133 **[én an-na n]í-bi-ta tu-ud-da-a** *tamannu*
134 **[én ^{d}utu e]n gal an-ki-bi-da-ke$_4$**
135 **[én a nam-ti-la i$_7$] íl-la-me-en** *tamannuma*
136 [. . . . .] *tanaddin*?
137 **[én illu garza-bi aš-àm maš-àm** 3-T]A$^{?}$.ÀM *tamannu*[*ma*]

138 [. . . . .] *tanaq*[*qi*]
138a [. . . . .] x x [x]

Depending on the arrangement of lines in K.6324+ there may be a gap here, but the total number of lines should be all right.

139 [. . . . .] x x x [. . .]
140 [. . . . .] *šu luḫ*$^{?}$ *ḫi* ⌜*tu*/*li*⌝ [. . .]
141 [x] x x [x] x *bīna maštakal*
142 *libbi iṣṣi* x x [. . .] x *ma qassu inaš*[*šima*]
143 **[én] ^{d}utu ⌜di⌝-ku$_5$ maḫ an-ki-[bi-da-ke$_4$]**
144 ***šipta Ea Šamaš u Asalluḫi*** *imannu*
145 x *annam anna maḫar Šamaš imannu*

---

146 [*ana*] *Kusu Ningirima Ninkurra*
147 *Ninagal Kusibanda Ninildu*
148 *Ninzadim nignak burāši tašakkan*
149 *niqâ tanaqqi šikara rēštâ tanaqqima*
150 *mīs pî pīt pî teppuš*
151 *nignakka gizillâ tušbâ'šu*
152 *egubbâ tullalšu terêqamma*

---

153 [. . . . .] x x *šá* [x]

123 [. . . . .] Ninzadim

124 [. . . . .] the craftsmen

125 [. . . . .] you lay down

126 [. . . . .]. . . . .

127 [. . . . .] a torch

---

128 [. . . . .] you purify.

129 [. . . . .] blaze?

130 [. . . . .] . . . you heap

131 you scatter juniper

132 [. . . . .] you raise cedar in your hand and

133 you recite the incantation, "Born in heaven by his own power,"

134 the incantation, "Shamash, great lord of heaven and earth,"

135 the incantation, "Water of life, the river rising in flood," you recite, and

136 [. . . . .] you give(?)

137 the incantation, "The flood, its divine task is unique, is holy," you recite three times, and

138 [. . . . .] you sacrifice/libate.

138a [. . . . .]. . . . .

139 [. . . . .]. . . . .

140 [. . . . .]. . . . .

141 [. . . . .] tamarisk, *maštakal*

142 date-palm "heart" . . . . raises his hand, [and]

143 the incantation, "Shamash, exalted judge of heaven and earth,"

144 (and) the incantation, "Ea, Shamash and Asalluḫi," he recites.

145 Thus(?) he recites before Shamash.

---

146 For Kusu, Ningirima, Ninkurra,

147 Ninagal, Kusibanda, Ninildu,

148 (and) Ninzadim you set in place a censer of juniper.

149 you sacrifice a ram, you libate best beer,

150 you perform mouth-washing (and) mouth-opening,

151 you make a censer (and) a torch move past him.

152 You purify him with a holy-water vessel (and) you retire, and

---

154 [. . . . .] *ma*? *kab* x

154a [. . . . .] x [x]

If K.6324+ and K.8656 are continuous, there is no gap.

155 [. . . . . *ḫi*] *mēta* [x x]

156 [. . . . .] x *maqqīta* ⌜*tukân*⌝ [x]

157 [. . . . .] *tašakkan niqâ tanaqqi*

158 [*imitta*] *ḫimṣa šumâ tuṭaḫḫa*

159 [x x x] *dišpa tanaqqi mašmaššu idi ili šuāti izzaz*

160 **[én u$_4$ di]ngir dím-ma** *imannuma/tamannuma tuškênma*

161 *mīs pî pīt pî teppuš*

162 [*arkišu*] **én alam kù me-gal šu-du$_7$-a** *tamannu/imannu*

163 *takpirtu u liḫšu*

---

164 [*ana libbi uzni*] *ša ili šuāti kīam taqabbi*[95]

165 ***[itti ilāni] aḫḫēka manâta***

166 [*ana libbi uzni immittišu*] *tulaḫḫaš*

---

167 ***ultu ūmi annî šimātīka ana ilūti limmanūma***

168 ***[itti ilāni aḫḫēka] tattamnu***

169 ***[ana šarri mūdi pīka] qurub***

170 ***[ana bītika . . . . . .] qurub***

171 ***[ana māti/šadî tabnû] napšer***

172 [*ana libbi uzni šumēlišu*] *tulaḫḫaš*

---

173 [*terêqamma mārū ummâni*] *mala ana ili šuāti itḫû*

174 [. . . . . . *Ninkurra*] *Ninagal Guškinbanda*

175 [*Ninildu*] *Ninzadim tušazzassunūtima*

176 [. . . . .]

177 [. . . . .]

178 [. . . . . .] x [. . . . .]

---

179 ***anāku lā ēpu[šu. . . . .]***

180 ***Ninagal Ea*** [. . . . .]

---

95. Lines 164–75 are restored from two copies of *mīs pî* tablet 3, Sm 290 (Laessøe, *Bit Rimki*, pl. 3) and K.13461 (unpublished).

155 [. . . . . g]hee [. . ?]

156 [. . . . .] . . ? you set up a libation vessel [? . . .]

157 [. . . . .] you set in place; you sacrifice a ram (and)

158 you present the shoulder, the *ḫimṣu*,[96] and the "roast";

159 [. . . . . .] you libate honey. The *mašmaššu*-priest stands beside that god;

160 He/you recite(s) the incantation, "On the day when the god was created," and you prostrate yourself and

161 you perform mouth-washing and mouth-opening.

162 Afterward you/he recite(s) the incantation, "Pure statue, suited to great divine attributes."

163 Wiping and whispered prayer.

---

164 Into the ear(s) of that god you speak as follows:

165 "You are counted among your brother gods,"

166 you whisper into his right ear.

---

167 "From today may your destiny be counted as divinity;

168 with your brother gods you are counted;

169 approach the king who knows your voice;

170 approach your temple. . . . . . ;

171 to the land/mountain where you were created be released,"

172 you whisper into his left ear.

---

173 You retire, and all the craftsmen who approached that god

174 [. . . . . . with (?) Ninkurra], Ninagal, Kusibanda,

175 [Ninildu] (and) Ninzadim you make them stand, and

---

179 (I swear) I did not make (the statue) [. . . . .];[97]

180 Ninagal, who is Ea [. . . . .];

---

96. CAD Ḫ 192 defines the *ḫimṣu* as "the fatty tissue around the intestines."

97. For the use of the negative *lā* with the subjunctive in the "assertorische Eid," see GAG §185.

181 ***anāku ul ēpuš anāku lā*** [. . . . .]
182 ***Ninildu Ea ilu ša nagāri lu*** x [. . . . . .]
183 ***anāku ul ēpuš anāku lā ēpušuma qa***-x [. . .]

184 ***Kusibanda Ea ilu ša kutimmi*** [. . . . . .]
185 ***Ninkurra Ea ilu ša*** x [. . . . . .]
186 ***Ninzadim Ea ilu*** [. . . . . .]

---

187 *mašmaššu ana maḫar ili šuāti* [. . . . . .]
188 **én è-a-zu-dè min gal-la** [. . . . . .]
189 **én alam ki-kù-ga-ta ⸢ù⸣-[tu-ud-da** . . . . . .]
190 **én alam an-ne ù-[tu-ud-da** . . . . . .]
191 **én ^{d}nin-íldu nagar-gal-a[n-na-ke$_4$** . . . . . .]
192 **én túg-maḫ túg-níg-lám-ma g[ada-babbar-ra** . . . . . .]
193 **én aga-maḫ ní-gal-[a ri-a** . . . . . .]
194 **én giš-gu-za kù-ga ^{d}nin-íldu nagar-ga[l-an-na-ke$_4$** . . . . . .]

---

195 **én gin-na na-an-gub-bé-en** *imannuma t*[*a*$^?$- . . . . . .]
196 **én gin-na na-an-gub-bé-en** *šanâ* [. . . . . .]
197 *uṣurāti* TU$^?$-[*rab* . . . . . .]
198 **én gin-na na-an-gub-bé-en** *šalša imannuma*
199 KI-^{d}UTU DU [. . . . . .]
200 *ina maḫar riksa ša ili šuāti tapaṭar*
201 *arkišu ša ilāni mārē ummâni tapaṭar*
202 *arkišu ša Kusu u Ningirima tapaṭar*
203 *arkišu ša ilāni rabûti tapaṭar*

---

204 [. . . . .] x x
Continuation lost

---

3. STT 200 Incantation

The incantation "When the god was made," used on the second day of the ritual and best preserved on the Sultantepe tablet STT 200, effectively contains a summary of the essential meaning and form of the mouth-washing/mouth-opening ritual. The statue of the deity shares in the lofty status of the deity him/herself. It is understood as

181 I did not make (the statue); (I swear) I did not [make (it);]
182 Ninildu, who is Ea the god of the carpenter [made it . . . . . .];
183 I did not make (the statue), (I swear) I did not make (it), . . . [. . . . .];
184 Kusibanda, who is Ea the god of the goldsmith [made it . . . . . .];
185 Ninkurra, who is Ea the god of [. . . . .]
186 Ninzadim, who is Ea the god of [. . . . .]

---

187 The *mašmaššu* before that god [. . . . .]
188 the incantation, "As you go out, as you go out, great . . . ," [. . .]
189 the incantation, "Statue born in a pure place . . . ," [. . .]
190 the incantation, "Statue born in heaven . . . ," [. . .]
191 the incantation, "Ninildu, great carpenter of Anu . . . ," [. . .]
192 the incantation, "Exalted garment,. . . . garment of white linen . . . ," [. . .]
193 the incantation, "Exalted crown. . . . . ," [. . .]
194 the incantation, "Holy throne, which Ninildu, great carpenter of Anu . . . ," [. . .]

---

195 The incantation, "Go, do not tarry," he recites [. . . . . .];
196 the second incantation, "Go, do not tarry," [he recites];
197 you make (him/the god?) enter the form[98] [. . . . .];
198 the third incantation, "Go, do not tarry," he recites, and
199 . . . . [. . . . .]
200 First you dismantle the offering-table of that god;
201 afterward you dismantle the offering-table of the gods of the craftsmen;
202 afterward you dismantle the offering-table of Kusu and Ningirima;
203 afterward you dismantle the offering-table of the great gods.

---

98. See comments on line 57 of the Babylonian Ritual tablet.

---

the joint creation of god and human. Human hands formed it from wood and adorned it with precious stones and metals, but the relevant gods inspired every aspect of their work and the workmanship is ascribed to the gods themselves. The finished statue cannot fully function as the deity's manifestation until its mouth has been opened.

In a convention common to Sumerian incantations of the so-called "Marduk-Ea-Type" (Falkenstein 1931: 44–67) Marduk (under his Sumerian name Asalluḫi) is described as seeing the problem and going to report it to his father Ea (Sumerian Enki), who advises him of the ritual necessary to put matters right. A basin of water is to be prepared with various cultic materials. The statue is to be brought out of a 'house of washing' (*bīt rimki*) in an orchard by a canal. The craftsmen and their tools are to be assembled and the hands of the craftsmen are to be cut off with a wooden knife (no doubt symbolically). That the imperative verbal forms end at this point shows that this is the end of Enki's advice. Thus the essentials are the preparation of the holy-water basin (*egubbû*) and the demonstration that the statue was not of human workmanship. The continuation of the incantation addresses the statue itself. The divine creation of the statue is again reiterated. The god Kusu, chief exorcist of Enlil, is declared to have purified the statue with the holy-water basin, censer, and torch. Marduk (Asalluḫi) is declared to have made it brilliant. Thus far, the actions of the *mīs pî* ritual have been summarized, with Kusu's purification apparently corresponding to the ritual's mouth-washing.

Then the incantation declares, "the wise man (*apkallu*) and the *abriqqu*-priest of Eridu with honey, butter, cedar, and cypress have opened your mouth twice seven times." Thus it is acknowledged that the essential act of mouth-opening is performed by human rather than divine agents. It is noticeable that the *apkallu* and *abriqqu* are not mentioned in our ritual texts.

The concluding prayer is common to many of the incantations of the *mīs pî* series. The rubric to the incantation, "Incantation: *šuilla* for opening the mouth of a god," is of interest in that the incantation has nothing in common with the genre of prayers normally referred to as *šuilla* ('lifting the hand').

The rubric emphasizes that the incantation is primarily concerned with the concept of mouth-opening rather than mouth-washing. Given the rather subordinate status of mouth-opening in the existing rituals, the incantation may reflect historically earlier cultic practices. The reference to the *apkallu* and *abriqqu* points in the same direction.

2. Incantation:[99] On the day when the god was created (and) the pure statue was completed,
4. the god was visible in all the lands.
6. He is clothed in splendor, suited to lordliness, lordly, he is full of pride,
8. he is surrounded with radiance, he is endowed with an awesome radiance,
10. he shines out splendidly, the statue appears brilliantly.
11. In heaven he was made, on earth he was made.

99. The line numbering skips because the text is bilingual (Akkadian and Sumerian); normally there is one line per language, but at times both languages an occupy the same line.

13. This statue was made in the totality of heaven and earth;
15. this statue grew up in the forest of *ḫashurru*-trees;
17. this statue came from the mountains, the pure place.
19. The statue is the creation of (both) god and human![100]
21. [The statue] has eyes which Ninkurru made;
23. [the statue has . . .] which Ninagal made,
25. the statue is of a form (*bunnannû*) which Ninzadim made,
27. the statue is of gold and silver which Kusibanda made,
28. [the statue . . . . . .] which Ninildu made,
30. [the statue. . . . . which] Ninzadim made.
32. This statue which [is made of] *ḫulālu*-stone, *ḫulāl-īni*-stone, *muššaru*-stone,

Lines 34 to 36 are broken; however they refer to the different semi-precious stones (*pappardilû*-stone, *elmešu*-stone, *antasurrû*-stone) from which the statue was made.

38. By the craft of the *qurqurru*-craftsman
40. this statue Ninkurra, Ninagal, [Kusibanda], Ninildu (and) Ninzadim [made].[101]
43. This statue without its mouth opened cannot smell incense, cannot eat food,
44. nor drink water.
45. Asalluḫi saw this (and repeated it) to his father Enki (in the Apsu),
46. "My Father, this statue without its mouth opened (cannot smell incense, cannot eat food, cannot drink water; show me what to do)."
47. Enki (answered) his son Asalluḫi: "My son, what do you not know? (What can I tell you?)
48. Asalluḫi, what do you not know? (What can I tell you?) Whatever I know (you also know). Go, my son!
50. Waters of the Apsu fetched from the midst of Eridu,
52. waters of the Tigris and Euphrates . . . from a pure place,
54. tamarisk, *maštakal*, heart of date-palm, *šalalu*-reed, multi-colored marsh-reed,
56. seven palm-shoots, juniper, white cedar throw into it.
58. In the garden at the pure canal of the orchard construct a "House of Washing (*bīt rimki*)."
60. Bring him (the statue) out to the "House of Washing" at the pure canal of the orchard.

100. See IV R 25 iii 21: "creation of the gods, work of humans!" The Akkadian of the duplicate text STT 201 reads "has the features of . . .'

101. Akkadian: 'This is the statue that . . .'

62. Bring this statue out before Shamash.
64. The axe that touched him, the hatchet that touched him, the saw that touched him, and the craftsmen (*marê ummâni*) who touched him you [. . .] there.
67. Bind their hands with bandages.
69. With a tamarisk sword cut off the fists of the *qurqurru*-workers who touched him."
71. This statue that the gods Ninkurra, Ninagal, Kusibanda, Ninildu, and Ninzadim have made,
74. Kusu, the chief exorcist of Enlil, with the holy-water basin, the censer, the cultic torch and with clean hands has purified.
76. Asalluḫi, the son of Eridu, has made brilliant.
78–80. The wise man (and) the *abriqqu*-priest of Eridu with honey, butter, cedar, and cypress have opened your mouth twice seven times.
81. May this god become pure like heaven, clean like earth, as brilliant as the center of heaven. Let the evil tongue stand aside.

INCANTATION—ŠU-ILLA PRAYER FOR THE OPENING OF THE MOUTH OF A GOD

---

83. When you have recited this, you pour a libation for Ea, Shamash, and Asalluḫi.
84. You prostrate yourself and recite three times the incantation, "Pure statue suited to great divine attributes."[102] Purifying and whispering.

4. *Mīs pî 6/8 Incantation*

One of the final incantations of the series according to the Babylonian ritual, perhaps the final incantation at Nineveh, to judge by the incantation tablets, is 'As he walked along the street' (**én e-sír-ra gin-a-ni-ta**). By contrast with most of the other *mīs pî* incantations from Nineveh, this one is inscribed on single-column tablets and is always the only incantation inscribed on the tablet. The incantation is recited as the statue is led in procession from the ceremonies on the river to its permanent home in the temple. It describes how Asalluḫi, taking a stroll through the town, observed the accidental pollution of an incantation priest and sought advice from his father Enki. Enki advised Asalluḫi to prepare a holy-water basin, as for the mouth-washing ritual, and to strew water from it through the streets to purify the town. The instructions given for the preparation of the holy-water basin parallel the instructions given in the ritual tablets and in tablet 3 in the incantation "On the day when the god was created" (STT 200, above).

---

102. **én alam-kù IM-gal šu-du$_4$-ti-a**. See BM 45749 lines 48–49 and K.6324 (Nineveh Ritual Text) line 162.

The effect of the incantation in the present ritual presumably is to guard against the inadvertent pollution of the divine statue on its journey to the temple. But the fact that the incantation refers to the pollution of an incantation-priest, rather than a statue, suggests that it was not originally composed for use in this ritual. There is evidence for some corruption of the text, in that while lines 16–22 make it clear that it is the incantation-priest who has become polluted, without the restoration of a reference to the incantation-priest who has become polluted at the beginning of line 5, it would be Asalluḫi himself who has become polluted.

1. Incantation: As he walked down the street,
2. as Asalluḫi walked down the street,
3. as he walked across the square,
4. as he walked across the street (and) the road,
5. ⟨an incantation-priest⟩ stepped in poured out washing water,
6. he set his foot in impure water,
7. he saw water (touched by) unwashed hands,
8. he met a woman whose hands were unclean,
9. he saw a young women whose hands were unwashed,
10. his hand touched a bewitched woman,
11. he met a man whose hands were unclean,
12. he saw a man whose hands were unwashed,
13. his hand touched man whose body was impure.
14. Asalluḫi saw it,
15. he repeated it to his father Enki in the Apsu,
16. "My father, the incantation-priest stepped in poured out washing water, he stepped (in it).
17. he set his foot in impure water,
18. he saw water (touched by) unwashed hands,
19. he met a woman whose hands were unclean,
20. he saw a young woman whose hands were unwashed,
21. his hand touched a bewitched woman,
22. he met a man whose hands were unclean,
23. he saw a man whose hands were unwashed,
24. his hand touched man whose body was impure.
25. Show me what to do."
26. Ea answered his son Marduk,
27. "My son, what do you not know? What can I add to you?
28. Marduk, what do you not know? What can I add to you?
29. Whatever I know you also know.

30. Go, my son, Marduk.
31. Take seven *šaḫarratu*-vessels brought from a large kiln.
32. At the mouths of the two rivers draw water.
33. Tamarisk, soapwort(?), young date palm, *šalālu*-reed, "horned" alkali, salt which opens the mouths of the gods,
34. cedar, cypress, *supālu*-juniper, boxwood, aromatics, *burāšu*-juniper, terebinth(?), white cedar,
35. red [. . .], cedar-oil, pure oil, excellent oil, oil of a *nikiptu* plant, white honey brought from its mountain/country of origin,
36. pure cow-fat, cow fat produced in a pure stall,
37. gold, silver, *ṣāriru*-gold, rock-crystal, serpentine,
38. *ḫulālu*-stone, carnelian, (and) lapis lazuli throw into the holy-water basin.
39. Set in place the pure holy-water basin of Eridu,
40. perform the rites of the Apsu,
41. recite your propitious incantation,
42. make that water fully perfect by the craft (of the purification-priest),
43. purify (it) by your pure incantation,
44. take a bucket, a dipper with a ring handle,
45. pour that water into it.
46. The holy-water basin that purifies the temple of the gods,
47. the holy-water basin that cleanses the temple of the gods,
48. the holy-water basin that makes bright the temple of the gods,
49. the holy-water basin that washes the mouth of the gods,
50. the holy-water basin that purifies the city,
51. the holy-water basin that cleanses the city,
52. the holy-water basin that makes the city shine,
53. take it and make it pass through the city,
54. make it pass through the city-square,
55. make it pass through street and alley,
56. make it pass through the city . . .
57. Shout . . .
58. 'Let the city (?) become pure,
59. let [. . .] become bright
60. let [. . .] become pure,
61. let [. . .] become bright.' "
62. The [. . .] of the gods
63. [. . .] may it be pure,
64. [. . .] may it be clean,

65. [. . .] may it be bright.
66. [May the evil tongue stand aside.]

5. *TuL No. 27*

The text[103] fundamentally falls into two parts: (1) an account of the procedures to be followed when it is determined that the statue of a god has fallen into disrepair and is to be sent to the *bīt mummi*, and (2) the ritual to be enacted in order to ensure the successful rebirth of the god (obverse 31–reverse 37). The separate nature of the two sections is underlined by the intervening prescription (obverse line 30) that the text is not to be shown to the uninitiated; such prescriptions frequently occur in the colophons of religious or magical texts.

The text evidently has a complicated manuscript history. Sources A, B, and E are Assyrian, and sources C and D are Babylonian. As with so many religious texts from Mesopotamia, the colophons of the surviving tablets (including A.418, from Ashur) indicate that they are copied from earlier sources from Babylonia. It could reasonably be deduced from the insertion of obverse line 30 (found so far in only one source) that this tablet, A.418 (or the original from which it had been copied), was in fact a compilation from more than one earlier tablet. But the following part of the text (after line 30) has an even more complicated history. We give here the text of A.418, partly restored from the various duplicates, concluding with its colophon. But of these duplicates, two (BM 47436 and BM 47445), which begin only with the text of A.418 reverse line 22′, insert after reverse line 37′ the note, "According to the text of the *giṭṭu*-tablet,"[104] and then add another 18 lines of ritual prescriptions (not reproduced here), ending with a colophon indicating that this text is taken from a second *giṭṭu*-tablet. A similar manuscript tradition is indicated by the fragmentary Nineveh exemplar K.8111 + 13266, which follows reverse line 37′ with a colophon and 8 additional lines of ritual before breaking off. Thus our material was at an earlier stage written on a series of at least three tablets, maybe more.

A	A.418 (Istanbul) Obverse 1–55, Reverse 1′–37′, colophon
B	K.3129+A 16941 (Chicago) Obverse 1–27
C	BM 47436 reverse 22′–37′, and continuation
C	BM 47445 reverse 22′–37′, and continuation
E	K.8111 + 1326 reverse 33′–37′, and continuation

Compare W.20030/3, W.20030/5, W.30030/98 for similarities.[105]

103. We name this text TuL no. 27 for easy reference after the primary edition of source A (A.418) by E. Ebeling (1931).

104. A *giṭṭu*-tablet is explained in CAD G 112a as "a one-column tablet with literary content."

105. See Mayer 1978: 443–58, esp. p. 444 n. 37, where the author notes the following similarities between the Warka texts and TuL 27: the use of *šipir ili* for divine statue, *ekurru* for the temple, the activity of the *kalû*, especially the singing of the lament *taqribāti*, the use of *abru*, and the reference to the king and his attendants.

[Figure 6] A.418 (= TuL 27) OBVERSE. Notice the drawings on this ritual tablet that show the position of cult objects during the ceremony. Duplicates (e.g., BM 47436, BM 47445) of this tablet show similar drawings. The authors have photographs of this tablet from different times since its discovery that witness the gradual deterioration (esp. of the lower left corner) of the tablet. Courtesy of the Istanbul Archaeological Museum.

[Figure 7] A.418 (= TuL 27) REVERSE. See description at figure 6.

[1.] [*šumma šipir*] ⌜*ili*⌝ *īnaḫma niqitta irta*[*ši*]

[2.] [. . . . .] . . . *libbīšu ubla*[106]

[3.] *ina qibīt Šamaš Adad u* ⌜*Marduk*⌝

[4.] [. . . . .] . . . *ina ūmi magri ina mūši kīma*[107] *šēpu parsat*

[5.] *ana maḫar* [*Ea* . . . . . .]*a tukattamšu*

[6.] *tuṣamma abra tanappaḫ taqribta tašakkan*

[7.] [*ila šuāti*] *ultu šubtīšu tanassaḫma kalû qaqqassu ipaṭṭar*

[8.] [*ira*]*ssu isappid*[108] *u* ʾ*ua iqabbi*

[9.] *ina amat tānēḫi* . . . *qassu iṣabbat*

[10.] *adi ina bīt Mummi irrubūma uššabū* ŠAR

[11.] . . . . . .*ina kisal bīt Mummi ašar ilu šuātu ašbu*

[12.] *abra ana Ea u* ⌜*Marduk*⌝ *tunammir*

[13.] *niqâ ana Ea u Marduk tanaqqi*

[14.] *niqâ ana ili šuāti tanaqqi taqribta tašakkan*

[15.] *šar māti qadi kimtīšu ina qaqqari ippalassaḫū*

[16.] *šutānuḫu lā ikallû*

[17.] *ālu u nišūšu ina sipdāti ina eperi ina maḫar ekurri*

[18.] *ippalassaḫū ummânī mudûti*

[19.] *ša zumrīšunu ebbū tušeššibšu*⟨*nu*⟩ *adi šipir ili šuāti iqattû*

[20.] *muḫḫurū takribāti kalû epēši ul ikalla*

[21.] *ūm šipir ili šuāti iqattû ina kišad nāri*

[22.] *ina maḫar Ea Šamaš u Asalluḫi pīšu tamessi*

[23.] *šumma šipir ili šuāti ša niqitta iršû*

[24.] *ana tēdišti la ṭâba ana ašrīšu lā turru*

[25.] *30 mana erâ x 14 mana annaka u ša ili šuāti*

106. See Borger 1956: 83, *AsBbA* §53 rev. 28: *bīt mumme ašar tedisti ša libbašun ubla* 'the *bīt mummu* (workshop), the place of the renewal for which their (the gods') heart longs'.

107. The more common expression is *ašar* 'where'; cf. Mayer 1976: 178 n. 77; *Racc* p. 54. Perhaps at one time the text read just KI (*ašar*). In line 29 we read *ina* GE_6 KI $GÌR^{II}$ *pár-sat.*

108. See CAD S 150–51 for examples of *sapādu* with *qabû* + *u*ʾ*a*. For a discussion of Akkadian *sapādu*, see Gruber 1980: 449–56.

109. "Work of the/that god" throughout this text refers to the statue or cult image.

[1.] If the work of the god[109] became dilapidated and suffered damage,
[2.] [. . . .] . . . he longs,
[3.] by the command of Shamash, Adad, and Marduk
[4.] [. . . . .] . . . on a favorable day, in the night, when no one has access,
[5.] before [Ea . . . ,] you cover it/him [with . . .];
[6.] you come out and you light a pile of brushwood, (and) make an intercession[110]
[7.] You take away that god from his pedestal and the lamentation priest uncovers his head;
[8.] he beats his breast and utters 'Woe!'
[9.] With a word of lamentation . . . , (and) he takes his hand.
[10.] Until they enter the *bīt mummi* and sit down . . .
[11.] . . . In the courtyard of the *bīt mummi* where that god dwells
[12.] you light a pile of brushwood for Ea and Marduk.
[13.] You offer a sacrifice to Ea and Marduk;
[14.] you sacrifice to that god and make an intercession.
[15.] The king of the land together with his family prostrate themselves on the ground,[111]
[16.] they do not hold back their moanings.
[17.] The city and its people in lamentations in the dust before the temple
[18.] prostrate themselves. The skilled craftsmen[112]
[19.] whose bodies are pure you shall install. Until the work of that god is completed,
[20.] let the lamentation-priest not interrupt the performance of the offerings and intercessions.
[21.] When the (repair) work of that god is completed, on the back of the river
[22.] before Ea, Shamash, and Asalluḫi you shall wash its mouth.
[23.] If the work of that god which has suffered damage
[24.] is not suitable for renewal, he should not be restored![113]
[25.] 30 minas of copper . . . 14 minas of tin and the things which belong to that god[114]

110. See Seux, p. 151 n. 19, p. 165 n. 19.

111. For Akkadian *napalsuḫu*, see Gruber 1980: 470–75.

112. In Esarhaddon's dedication of the Marduk statue (Borger 1956: 83, *AsBbA* §53 29), he uses *ummânī lē'ūti mudê pirišti* 'skilled artisans who know the secrets'.

113. For this idiom, see AHw 1334b. It is probably equivalent to Sumerian *ki-bê mu-na-gi*$_4$ 'he restored to its place'.

114. See *GAG* §137e and Codex Hammurabi VI 61.

[26.] *kī zikir šumīšu tuballalma qīšta tanaddiššu*
[27.] *ina kitî ebbi tarakkas*
[28.] *itti šipir ili šuāti ša niqitta iršû taṣammidma*
[29.] *ina mūši kīma šēpu parsat ana maḫar Ea tašapparšu*

[30.] *lā mūdû lā immar ikkib Enza Maḫza Kizaza*

[31.] *ina pān igāri šidda tašaddad burû tanaddi*
[32.] *ina muḫḫi burê 9 libnāti tanaddi*
[33.] *ina muḫḫi libnāti kalîšina andulla tanaddi*

[34.] *[b]urû tanaddi* □ □ □ □ □ □ □ □ □
[35.] *[o]* ⌜*9*⌝ *libnāti*
[36.] . . . *[o o]* □ *9 paṭirī tarakkas*
[37.] *tanaddi paṭirī* ○ ○ ○ ○ ○ ○ ○ ○ ○
[38.] *ša Nergal*
[39.] *ina muḫḫi paṭirī kalîšunu mutqê tarakkas*
[40.] *miris dišpi ḫimēti tanaddi laḫanna ina muḫḫi tukân ina mê?* [. . .]

[41.] *siḫḫara ša silti ina qaqqari tašakk*⌜*an*⌝
[42.] *libitta* □ *ša Bēlit-ilī tanaddi*
[43.] *ina muḫḫi libitti ša Bēlit-ilī sirqa isarraq*
[44.] *šizba karāna tanaqqi riksu* *iānu*

---

115. Ebeling 1931: 111 note a: "Der Name des Gottes hat einen Zahlenwert." This suggests that the numerical equivalence of the god's name determines the proportions; however, the proportions have already been listed. A *zikir šumišu* can also be a type of offering. This passage is cited in AHw 1525a but without explanation. See also Kraus 1971: 97–112.

116. We do not know exactly what is happening here. Undoubtedly ḪI.ḪI is the logogram for *balālu* 'to mix/alloy'. Mixing copper and tin, of course, is understandable; however, these proportions are unusual; furthermore, it appears that 'the things that belong to the god' (*ša ili šuāti*) are also being intermixed. What exactly does this mean? *Balālu* does not mean simply 'loosely combined', i.e., 'assembled', but 'thoroughly intermixed'. Furthermore, what exactly does *kī zikir šūmišu* mean?

117. We are uncertain exactly what is being bound up in the clean linen cloth; *rakāsu* does not have a direct object. We suggest that it refers to the offering described above.

118. See Thureau-Dangin 1921: 49. The curtain was a device for marking off sacred space (Caplice 1967: 30–31): "the function of the *šiddu* (curtain) was, as it were, to assure the privacy of the divine repast." Similarly, curtains are used in the South Indian ritual for the cult statue, as we see in Waghorne's chapter in this volume.

[26.] according to his name[115] mix together[116] and give him the offering.
[27.] In a cloth of clean linen you shall bind (these things);[117]
[28.] you shall tie (them) together with the work of that god who has suffered damage; and
[29.] on a night when nobody walks before Ea you shall send him.

[30.] The uninitiate must now see (this); it is an abomination against Anu, Enlil, and Ea.

[31.] Before the wall you hang a curtain;[118] you lay down a reed-mat;
[32.] On the reed-mat you lay 9 bricks;
[33.] Over all of the bricks set up a canopy.

[34.] You lay down a reed-mat. □ □ □ □ □ □ □ □ □
[35.] Nine bricks;
[36.] . . . [o o] □ you build up 9 *paṭiru*-altars;
[37.] you lay down *paṭiru*-altars ○ ○ ○ ○ ○ ○ ○ ○ ○
[38.] of Nergal
[39.] On top of all the *paṭiru*-altars you arrange sweet cakes.
[40.] A confection of honey and ghee you lay out; a bottle you set on top; with water? . . .
[41.] A bowl of meal[119] you set on the ground.
[42.] You lay down the brick of Bēlet-ilī[120]
[43.] On the brick of Bēlet-ilī you scatter[121] a scatter-offering (of grain);
[44.] milk (and) wine you libate, the offering set-up is absent[122]

---

119. CAD S 267a does not identify *siltu* but merely calls it "a food used as offering."

120. Bēlet-ilī is the birth goddess (= Dingir-maḫ). "The 'brick' is the brick structure on which a woman lay for her labour" (Lambert 1969: 153). Around her stand the craftsmen, who are now reduced to mere midwives. Thus the renewal of the "work of the god" is understood as a "birthing process," as we shall discuss below (see p. 116).

121. The text reads 'he' scatters: *i-sar-raq*. However, Ebeling is undoubtedly correct (1931: 112) "*i*(!) (falsch für *ta*)-*sar-raq*." The prior plene writing that would indicate the second person is found in line 29. However, sudden switches between second and third person are common in rituals.

122. Ebeling, CAD (I/J 323a), and von Soden (AHw 411b) all take *iânu* with *babu* 'no door'; however, apart from difficulties in understanding why the author would diagram the absence of a door, it is more important to note that *iânu* is not really placed near the diagram inscribed with *babu*. It probably is to be placed in conjunction with the previous *riksu* on the same line. In fact, in most of the examples of *iânu* in the CAD, it negates the preceding noun.

[45.] x x P P P P P P P P P P [P]

[46.] [*ina kut*]*al šiddi 11 nignaqqê tašakkan* — *bâbu*

[47.] — *bîtu*

[48.] *ina tarbaṣi*

[49.] *girakka*

[50.] *tanaddi*

[51.] *igāru šiddu bîtu* [o o]

[52.] *paṭīra ina pān Nergal*

[53.] *tarakkas*

[54.] [*im*]*mera*

[55.] [*tanaqqi*]

Reverse

[1′.] *ina bīt Mu*[*mmi* . . . . . .]

[2′.] . . . . . x [. . . . . .]

[3′.] *10 libnāti a*[*na* . . . . . .]

[4′.] *Apsû* . . . [. . . . . .]

[5′.] AN . . . *tum* [x x] . . . [. . . . . .]

[6′.] x-x-*bu-ma 10 pa*[*ṭirē*] *ina* ⸢*pānīšunu*⸣ [. . . . .]

[7′.] [123]*ina muḫḫi mutqê tarakk*[*as*] *miris dišpi ḫimēti* ⸢*tašakkan*⸣

[8′.] *laḫan*? *šikari ina mu*[*ḫḫi tašak*]*kan u siḫharāte*

[9′.] *ša silti ina q*[*aqqa*]*ri ina pānīšunu tašakkan*

[10′.] *libitta ša Bēlit-ilī* [*ina q*]*aqqari tanaddi ina muḫḫi libitti*

[11′.] *sirqa tasarr*[*aq*] [*siz*]*ba* ⸢*karāna ina maḫar*⸣ *libitti tanaqqi*

[12′.] *ina kutal šiddi* [*11*? *nig*]*nakkē burāši tasarraq*

[13′.] *šizba rēštâ ša ina muḫḫi* [. . . . .] ⸢*tanaqqi*⸣ *ina kutal nignak*[*kē*]

---

123. Ebeling (1931, TuL 27) numbers this as the first line; therefore our numbers are 6 higher than Ebeling's.

124. Sumerian TÙR has been read as *tarbaṣu*, which can mean 'animal stall' or a 'courtyard'. However, this term may reinforce the "birthing" aspect of our ritual. TÙR probably referred originally to the birthing hut in the cattlepen. Sumerian ŠAG$_4$-TÙR (= Akkadian *šassuru*) 'birth-house of the insides' means womb. This term evokes the goddess Nin-tùr, who is equivalent to Bēlit-ilī (CT

[45.]
[46.] Behind the curtain set up 11 censers — gate

[47.] temple
[48.] in the court[124]
[49.] a brazier
[50.] you set up.

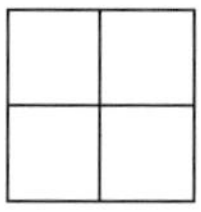

[51.] wall curtain temple

[52.] An offering-table before Nergal
[53.] you set up;
[54.] a sheep
[55.] [you sacrifice].

Reverse

[1′.] in the *bīt Mummi*. . . . .
[2′.]
[3′.] 10 bricks for [. . . . .]
[4′.] Abzu [. . . . . .]
[5′.]
[6′.] [. . .] and 10 *paṭiru*-altars before them [. . .]
[7′.] on top you arrange breads; you place a confection of honey and butter.
[8′.] The bottle of beer you place on top and vessels
[9′.] of meal you place on the ground before them.
[10′.] You lay down on the ground the brick of Bēlit-ilī;[125] on the brick
[11′.] you strew aromatics, before the brick you libate milk (and) wine.

[12′.] Behind the curtain you cense 11 censers of juniper.
[13′.] Best milk[126] which is on [. . . .] you libate; behind the censers

24:12, 15) who is the 'divine midwife' mentioned below in line 10′. See the discussion of TÙR by Jacobsen (1976: 107).

125. See note 120, above.

126. The signs are broken, but [G]A SAG seems more probable than KAŠ SAG. Although the more common expression is indeed KAŠ SAG, GA *reš-tu-u* is attested (Lambert, *Iraq* 27: 11).

[14′.] *7 šiddē tašaddad ina p*[*ān*] *bābi ša dulbāni ištēn šidda tašadda*[*d*]

[15′.] *10 šiddē ša* x *ina pān* ⌜*bābi*⌝ *ša tarbaṣi ṣubāta sāma tašaddad*
[16′.] *ina tarbaṣi girakka ana Nergal tanaddi*
[17′.] *ina* [x x] *girakki paṭīra tarakka*[*s*]
[18′.] . . . . . *girakki tuḫattap miḫḫa tanaqq*[*i*]
[19′.] [. . . . .] *maḫrê u*? *immerē ina pān ilāni tašakkan* ŠÚ [x]
[20′.] [. . . . .] *karāna* GAB *išatti* [*i*]*škun*? *sil*[*ti*]
[21′.] [. . . . .] ⌜KI?⌝ *ina ūmi* ⌜*arkê*⌝ ŠU.BI.AŠ.[ÀM]

[22′.] *išten šidda* ⌜*ša*?⌝ *ina pūt igāri šaddu tašakkan*

127									

[23′.] *išten šiddu ša ina muḫḫi libitti nadû* [o o]
[24′.] *paṭīra tarakkas miḫḫa tanaqqi*

[25′.] *3 šiddū ša ina bīti šaddū ša tabar*[*ri*]

[26′.] *libittu* *2 šiddū*
[27′.] *ša ina muḫḫi bābi*
[28′.] *libittu ša sirqu ina muḫḫi issarraqu*
[29′.] DIŠ *Narudi Bēlit-ilī*
[30′.] *Uraš Ninurta Zababa*
[31′.] *Nabû Nergal Madānu u Pabilsag*
[32′.] *annutu ilāni ša šiddi*

[33′.] [*g*]*irakku ša muḫḫuru ina muḫḫi undaḫḫaru*
[34′.] [*m*]*iḫḫu ša* 〈*ina*〉 *muḫḫuri innaqqû pāni Anšar tukân Nergal*

[35′.] *Anšar Kišar An-gal Enmešarra Apsû tamtim Uttu Ningirsu*
[36′.] *Lugaldukuga Dumuzi u Allatum*

127. Text D has *ḫe-pî* 'missing' here at the beginning of the drawing.

128. Or "birthing area" (see note on line 48 above).

129. This was a cultic act characterized by the "slaughtering of an animal (probably by a special technique)": CAD Ḫ 149a; CAD Ḫ 207b; CAD M/2 50a reads here GI.DU$_8$ *tukân miḫḫa ta*[*naqqi*].

[14′.] you stretch out 7 curtains; before the gate of the passageway you stretch out one curtain.

[15′.] 10 curtains . . . ; before the gate of the courtyard[128] you hang a red cloth;

[16′.] in the courtyard you set up a brazier to Nergal.

[17′.] in [. . .] brazier you set up a *paṭiru*-altar.

[18′.] . . . . . brazier you perform the *ḫitpu*-sacrifice,[129] you libate *miḫḫu*-beer;

[19′.] you arrange first [. . .] and sheep before the gods . . .

[20′.] [. . . . .] wine . . . he drinks(?), he placed(?); meal

[21′.] [. . . . .] . . . on the next day DITTO

[22′.] One curtain, which is stretched on the front side of the wall, you place

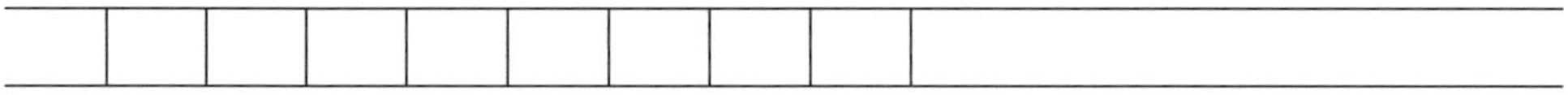

[23′.] One curtain which lies on the brick [. . .]

[24′.] You set up the *paṭiru*-altar; you libate *miḫḫu*-beer.

[25′.] 3 curtains which hang in the temple which are of red wool

---

[26′.] brick 2 curtains

[27′.] which are on the gate[130]

[28′.] The brick on which the scatter offering was scattered

[29′.] Narudi,[131] Bēlit-ilī,

[30′.] Urash, Ninurta, Zababa,

[31′.] Nabû, Nergal, Mandanu and Pabilsag,

[32′.] these are the gods of the curtains.

[33′.] The brazier on which the offering is offered,

[34′.] *miḫḫu*-beer, which is libated on the offering, before Anshar[132] you set up. Nergal,

[35′.] Anshar, Kishar, Anu-rabû, Enmesharra, Apsû of the sea, Uttu, Ningirsu,

[36′.] Lugaldukuga, Dumuzi, and Allatum,

130. Text C is unintelligible: *ina muḫḫi* GUB *šad-du.*

131. For the goddess Narudi, see Tallqvist 1938: 387.

132. For the relationship between Anshar and Ashur see Tadmor and Parpola 1989: 29–30.

[37′.] *annutu ilāni ša ina bīt Mummi libnātīšunu nadâ*

---

mudû mudâ likallim lā mudû lā immar
pirišti ilāni rabûti arna kabta iraššî

én ^{d}utu di-ku$_5$ maḫ en en-en[133] **dingir-re-e-ne-ke$_4$**
kī pî lēʾi Akkade šaṭirma bari
ṭuppi Kiṣir-Nabû mār Šamaš-ibni mašmaššu
mār Nabû-bessun mašmaš bīt Aššur
ḫanṭiš nasḫa

Summary

The creation of the god was a supreme act of synergy between the heavens and the earth (STT 200.11: *ina šamê ibbanu ina erṣeti ibbanu*), for the statue has been produced by earthly and godly artisans: [*ṣa*]*lam* [*bun*]*nanê*[134] *ša ilī u amēli* (STT 200.19). However, the theologically diminished role of the earthly craftsmen is best clarified in the "Mouth Washing" ritual itself and in its incantations. The statue had to be enlivened by the special ceremony called KA.LUḪ.Ù.DA/*mīs pî*, equivalent to Greek *hidrusis* or Roman *dedicatio*.[135] Without this ritual, the statue was only a dead product of human artisans: "This statue cannot smell incense, drink water, or eat food without the Opening of the Mouth!"[136]—a phrase reminiscent of Psalm 135 and Jeremiah 10:5.

Ritual attempts to disassociate the cult image from human artisans are very developed in both the Babylonian and the Nineveh ritual tablets of *mīs pî*. There the artisans have their hands "cut off" with a wooden tamarisk sword while swearing that they did not make the image but that their respective craft deities had. The tools are wrapped in the body of a sacrificed sheep and thrown into the river to denote a return to Nudimmud (Ea), the craft god. In STT 200 (an incantation from tablet 3 of the series) we have the artisans' oath disavowing making the god. All of this is absent from

133. For the epithet, see Tallqvist 1938: 42.

134. Although *bunnanû* usually means 'appearance' or 'Gestalt', here it seems to mean 'product' (from *banû* 'to build'). The Sumerian níg.dím.dim.ma can mean 'product' (see CAD N/2 212). 'Shape' would not really make sense here. See IV R 25 iii 21, "Creation of the gods, work of humans."

135. For references to a rite for dedication of a cult image in Greece and Rome, see Bevan 1940: 31–35.

136. STT 200:43 [*ṣa*$^!$-*lam*$^!$] *an-nu-u ina la pi-it pi-i qut-ri-in-na ul iṣ-ṣi-in a-ka-la ul ik-kal me-e ul i-šat* (see PBS 12/1 No. 6 1–2, duplicating STT 200:43).

[37′.] these are the gods whose bricks were laid in the *bīt mummi.*

Let the initiate show the initiate. The uninitiate must not see (it)!
Mystery of the great gods. He commits a grave offense.

Incantation: "Shamash exalted judge, lord of the divine lords."
Written and collated according to the Akkadian text of a writing-board.
Tablet of Kiṣir-Nabû the son of Shamash-ibni the *mašmaššu*-priest,
the son of Nabû-bessun the *mašmaššu*-priest of the Ashur temple.
Quickly excerpted.

TuL 27, probably because here a statue is restored, not made; consequently, less work by craftsmen is involved; in fact if the "work of the god" cannot be restored, no such attempt should be made (lines 23–24).

Despite the work of human artisans on the cult image, it remains the "work of the god." The gods control and determine: (1) choice of the workers involved, (2) the place, (3) the time, and (4) the "birth" of the god.

Choice of the Artisans

The artisans who worked on the statue had to be carefully chosen. The *ummāni mudûti* should be installed (TuL 27, lines 18–19) and fulfill ritual purity. We know from the Esarhaddon inscriptions that the *mārê ummāni mudê šipri* had to be designated by the great gods themselves; and so Esarhaddon in Borger 1956: 83, *AsBbA* §53, 22–25, arranged diviners in groups: "to determine the experts who should do the work and their initiation . . . they ordered me to enter the *bīt mummi* in Ashur . . . they indicated to me the names of the artisans (fit) for completing the work."

Place of "Rebirth"

The work on the image was done in the temple *bīt mummi* (TuL 27, lines 10, 1′, 37′), also called in *BBR* 31 i line 23 *ašar ilu innepšu* (DÙ-*u*), which is probably the equivalent of Esarhaddon's 'where the gods are created' (*ašar nabnīt ilī innepšuma*) (*AsBbA* §53, p. 88 line 13). As we mentioned concerning line 48 of TuL 27, some of this ritual from Ashur seems to have taken place in an area denoted by the Sumerogram TÙR, which can denote the birthing hut.

Time of "Rebirth"

The sacral menology governed the making of the cult image and apparently its refurbishing. The work was done *ina ūmi magri* ('on a favorable day'), which recalls the beginnings of both the Nineveh and Babylonian versions of the ritual tablet of *mīs pî* and also Esarhaddon's rededication of the Babylonian images: "in a favorable month, on a propitious day."[137] The time would be determined both by calendar and by divination (see Labat 1965: 91 #31).

The Birth of the God: The Ultimate šipir ilī

In Mesopotamian ritual, the cult image was ultimately not a product of human craft (*pace* Deutero-Isaiah) but was born of the gods.[138] Although more elaborately effected in the normal *mīs pî* rituals, in TuL 27 this is suggested by the role of the birth goddess Bēlet-ilī and her brick (lines 42–43, 10′). "The 'brick' is the brick structure on which a woman lay for her labour" (Lambert 1969: 153). Elsewhere she is called ᵈTIBIRA.DINGIR.RE.NE.KA 'Copper-caster of the gods' (Jacobsen 1976: 107 n. 135).[139] Around her stand the craftsmen, who are now reduced to being mere midwives. The three troughs of blood mentioned in the Ninevite Ritual Tablet (line 116) may allude to birth blood. Thus the renewal of the "work of the god" is understood as a "birthing process." When Esarhaddon refers to the refurbishing of Bel, Beltiyya, Belet-Babili, Ea, and Madanu, he says that they were 'ceremoniously born' (*ke-niš im-ma-al-du-ma*).[140]

The use of forms of (*w*)*alādu* for the making of cult statues has occasioned disagreement between R. Borger and B. Landsberger on the precise connotation of (*w*)*alādu*. Borger (1956: 83 n. 35) argues that this verb can simply mean 'to make, to craft' as well as 'to give birth'. Therefore he translates it 'geboren', always using quotation marks. On the other hand, Landsberger (1965: 24–25 n. 38) objects to this "rational" approach; the context supports the more mythical understanding 'were born': "In our late passages it is always a case of the mythological sphere and is to be separated completely from cases involving the verb *epēšu*/*šūpušu* ('to make/have made'). . . . Basically we have here the concept of an organic generation and growth, not of creation through magic of the word (as in Enuma Elish IV 26)."[141] (For Borger's rebuttal, see Borger 1972: 36.) The context seems to support Landsberger's argument. This becomes especially clear when we study the *mīs pî* ritual—particularly in the Babylonian rite BM 45749. In line 23 the *egubbû*-basin is placed 'on the brick stand of Dingirmaḫ' (*libitti ša Dingirmaḫ*). This cult action recalls a similar passage in Atraḫasis where Mami (or Bēlit-kala-ilī) creates mankind on a "brick structure . . . on which

137. *ina arḫi šalmi ūmi emê*, Borger 1956: 83, *AsBbA* §53 27.

138. J. Waghorne, in her essay in this volume, sees a similar theologoumenon in the dedication rituals for the divine image in contemporary south India.

139. For literature on this goddess, see Biggs 1967: 45ff.; Krecher 1966: 199ff.

140. *AsBbA* §53 line 35.

141. Translation by M. Dick.

women performed their labour" (Lambert 1969: 61–62, 153). From this *mīs pî* rite, Ebeling (1931: 111) concludes that "the new god becomes by this process the child of the Mother Goddesses." Therefore the concept of "birth," of a real theogony, is quite strong in the enlivening of Mesopotamian images.

Although Sumerian texts frequently use the Sumerogram TU(D) 'to give birth' in reference to statues (Spycket 1968: 37), this evidence is somewhat more controversial because some scholars would prefer to read the same sign as KU_4 (KUR_9) 'to bring in'; thus the word could refer to the introduction of the statue into the shrine. However, the earliest use of the Sumerogram (Ur III) clearly decides the matter in favor of TU(D) 'to give birth,' because at the time of this earliest attestation, Sumerian differentiated the signs TU(D) and KU_4. An inscription on Statue A of Gudea (ca. 2200 B.C.E.) clearly differentiates these two verbs:

2:6 kur-ma$_2$-gan^{ki}-ta
3:1 ^{na4}esi im-ta-e$_{11}$
3:2 alan-na-ni-šè
3:3 mu-tu
. . .
4:4 é-a mu-na-ni-ku$_4$

From the land of Magan he (Gudea) imported *esi*-stone and (from it) gave birth to his statue . . . he brought it for him (the God) into the temple.[142]

Furthermore, such incantations as lines 3 and 42 of the Babylonian ritual 'Born in heaven of your own power' (**an-na ní-bi-ta tu-ud-da-a**) make it clear that TU(D) 'to be born' is intended.[143] As a late witness to this theologoumenon, Minucius Felix (Octavius xxii:5), a Latin author who wrote in the late second or early third century of the Common Era, refers to a statue as *nascitur* ('being born'):

Nisi forte nondum deus saxum est vel lignum vel argentum. Quando igitur hic nascitur? Ecce funditur, fabricatur, sculpitur: nondum deus est; ecce plumbatur, construitur, erigitur: nec adhuc deus est; ecce ornatur, consecratur, oratur: tunc postremo deus est, cum homo illum voluit et dedicavit.

Say you the stone, or wood, or silver is not yet a god? When then does he come to the birth? See him cast, molded, sculptured—not yet is he a god; see him soldered, assembled, and set up—still not a god; see him bedizened, consecrated, worshiped; hey, presto! he is a god—by a man's will and the act of dedication.

---

142. In some inscriptions, the phrase *mu-na-ni-ku*$_4$ is given in another version as *mu-na-ni-*DU; DU here means 'to install'. See Steible 1991: 4–5. See also Urningirsu II, lines 2: 1–7, for a similar contrast.

143. Winter (1992: 21) has called attention to the fact that the Sumerian verb DÍM 'to craft' is used of cult paraphernalia, stelae, etc., but TU(D) 'to give birth' is used of "making" statues. This distinction, however, cannot be insisted upon too rigorously, because many of the *mīs pî* incantations do in fact refer to the cult statue as DÍM 'crafted': Nineveh Ritual Tablet, line 160 (= *STT* 200:1, Sumerian version) én u$_4$ dingir dím-ma 'Incantation: "day on which the god was crafted".'

Bibliography

Barrelet, M.-Th.

1968 *Figurines et reliefs en terre cuite de la Mésopotamie antique.* Paris.

Bauer, T.

1933 *Das Inschriftenwerk Assurbanipals.* Leipzig.

Bevan, Edwyn

1940 *Holy Images: An Inquiry into Idolatry and Image-Worship in Ancient Paganism and in Christianity.* London: George Allen.

Biggs, R.

1967 *Šà.zi.ga: Ancient Mesopotamian Potency Incantations.* Texts from Cuneiform Sources 2. Locust Valley, N.Y.: J. J. Augustin.

Blackman, Aylward M

1924 "The Rite of Opening of the Mouth in Ancient Egypt and Babylonia." *Journal of Egyptian Archaeology* 10: 47–59.

Boden, Peg

1993 "The *mīs pî*: A Ritual of Transition." Paper read at the Annual Meeting of the American Oriental Society at Chapel Hill, North Carolina.

Borger, R.

1956 *Die Inschriften Asarhaddons, Königs von Assyrien.* AfO Beiheft 9. Graz.

1957–58 "Die Inschriften Asarhaddons (AfO Beiheft 9), Nachtrage und Verbesserungen." *AfO* 18: 113–18.

1967 *Handbuch der Keilschriftliteratur,* Vol. 1. Berlin.

1972 Review of *Brief des Bischofs von Esagila an König Asarhaddon,* by B. Landsberger. *BiOr* 29: 33–37.

Bottéro, J.

1949 "Les inventaires de Qatna," *RA* 43: 1–40, 137–215.

Brinkman, J.

1968 *A Political History of Post-Kassite Babylonia, 1158–722 B.C.* AnOr 43. Rome.

Burrows, E.

1932 "Problems of the Abzu." *Or* N.S. 1: 231–56.

Cagni, L.

1969 *L'epopea di Erra.* Studi Semitici 34. Roma.

1977 *The Poem of Erra.* SANE 1/3. Malibu: Undena.

Caplice, R.

1967 "Namburbi Texts in the British Museum II." *Or* 36: 1–38.

1971 "Namburbi Texts in the British Museum V." *Or* 40: 133–83.

Cassin, E.

1968 *La spendeur divine: Introduction à l'étude de la mentalité mésopotamienne.* Paris.

Civil, M.

1967 "Remarks on 'Sumerian and Bilingual Texts'." *JNES* 26: 200–211.

Curtis, Edward M.

1990 "Images in Mesopotamia and the Bible: A Comparative Study." Pp. 36–56 in William Hallo, Bruce Jones, and Gerald Mattingly (ed.), *Scripture in Context III: The Bible in the Light of Cuneiform Literature.* Ancient Near Eastern Texts and Studies, vol. 8. Lewistown, N.Y.: Edwin Mellen.

Dietrich, M.
1967–68 "Neue Quellen zur Geschichte Babyloniens (I-II)." *WdO* 4: 61–103, 183–251.

van Dijk, J. J.
1980 *Texte aus dem Rēš-Heiligtum in Uruk-Warka.* Baghdader Mitteilungen, Beiheft 2. Berlin.

Ebeling, Erich
1931 *Tod und Leben nach den Vorstellungen der Babylonier.* Berlin and Lepizig.
1937 "Kritische Beiträge zu neueren assyriologischen Veröffentlichungen." *MAOG* 10/2.

Ellis, R. S.
1968 *Foundation Deposits in Ancient Mesopotamia.* YNER 2. New Haven.

Falkenstein, A.
1931 *Die Haupttypen der sumerischen Beschwörung literarisch untersucht.* Leipzig.

Frankfort, H.
1936 *Progress of the Work of the Oriental Institute in Iraq, 1934/35.* Oriental Institute Communications 20. Chicago.

Gelb, I.
1949 "The Date of the Cruciform Monument of Maništušu." *JNES* 8: 346–48.

George, A. R.
1993 *House Most High: The Temples of Ancient Mesopotamia.* Mesopotamian Civilizations 5. Winona Lake, Ind.: Eisenbrauns.

Gruber, Mayer I.
1980 *Aspects of Nonverbal Communication in the Ancient Near East.* Studia Pohl 12. Rome: Biblical Institute Press.

Gurney, O. R.
1952 "The Sultantepe Tablets: A Preliminary Note." *AnSt* 2: 25–35.

Hallo, W. W.
1970 "The Cultic Setting of Sumerian Poetry." Pp. 116–34 in A. Finet (ed.), *Actes de la XVIIe Rencontre Assyriologique Internationale.* CRRAI 17. Ham-sur-Heure, Belgium: Comité belge de recherches en Mésopotamie.
1983 "Cult Statue and Divine Image: A Preliminary Study." Pp. 1–18 in William Hallo, James Moyer, and Leo Purdue (eds.), *Scripture in Context II: More Essays on the Comparative Method.* Winona Lake, Ind.: Eisenbrauns.

Heidel, A.
1948 "The Meaning of *Mummu* in Akkadian Literature." *JNES* 7: 98–105.

Hooke, S. H.
1953 *Babylonian and Assyrian Religion.* London.

Hunger, H.
1968 *Babylonische und assyrische Kolophone.* AOAT 2. Kevelaer and Neukirchen-Vluyn.

Jacobsen, Thorkild
1976 *The Treasures of Darkness: A History of Mesopotamian Religion.* New Haven: Yale University Press.
1987 "The Graven Image." Pp. 15–32 in P. D. Miller, Jr. et al. (eds.), *Ancient Israelite Religion: Essays in Honor of Frank Moore Cross.* Philadelphia: Fortress.

King, L. W.
1912 *Babylonian Boundary Stones.* London.

Kraus, F. R.
1971 "Akkadische Wörter und Ausdrücke, VI–VIII." *RA* 65: 97–112.
Krecher, J.
1966 *Sumerische Kultlyrik.* Wiesbaden: Harrassowitz.
Labat, René.
1965 *Un calendrier babylonien des travaux, des signes et des mois.* BÉHÉ 231. Paris.
1970 *Les religions du proche-orient asiatique.* Paris.
Laessøe, J.
1956 "A Prayer to Ea, Šamaš, and Marduk, from Hama." *Iraq* 18: 60–67.
Lambert, W. G.
1957–58 Review of F. Gössmann, *Das Era Epos. AfO* 18: 395–401.
1959–60 "Two Notes on Šurpu." *AfO* 19: 122.
Lambert, W. G. and A. R. Millard
1969 *Atra-ḫasīs: The Babylonian Story of the Flood.* London: Oxford University Press.
Landsberger, B
1928–29 "Das 'Gute Wort'." *MAOG* 4: 294–321.
1954 "Assyrische Königsliste und 'Dunkles Zeitalter'." *JCS* 8: 31–45, 47–73, 106–33.
1955 "Remarks on the Archive of the Soldier Ubarum." *JCS* 9: 121–31.
1965 *Brief des Bischofs von Esagila an König Asarhaddon.* MKNAW Nieuwe Reeks 28/VI. Amsterdam.
Lloyd, Seton, and Nuri Gökçe
1953 "Sultantepe." *AnSt* 3: 27–51.
Luckenbill, D. D.
1907–8 "The Temples of Babylonia and Assyria." *AJSL* 24: 291ff.
1924 *The Annals of Sennacherib.* OIP 2. Chicago: University of Chicago Press.
Mayer, W. R.
1976 *Untersuchungen zur Formensprache der babylonischen "Gebetsbeschwörungen."* Studia Pohl: Series Maior 5. Rome: Biblical Institute Press.
1978 "Seleukidische Rituale aus Warka mit Emesal-Gebeten." *Or* 47: 431–58.
Meier, Gerhard
1937–39 "Die Ritualtafel der Serie 'Mundwaschung'." *AfO* 12: 40–45.
Michalowski, Piotr
1989 *The Lamentation over the Destruction of Sumer and Ur.* Mesopotamian Civilizations 1. Winona Lake, Ind.: Eisenbrauns.
Miller, Patrick D., Jr., and J. J. M. Roberts
1977 *The Hand of the Lord.* Baltimore: Johns Hopkins University Press.
Moran, W.
1959 "A New Fragment of DIN.TIR.KI = Bābilu and Enūma Eliš VI 61–66." Pp. 257–65 in *Studia Biblica et Orientalia III: Oriens Antiquus.* AnBib 12. Rome: Biblical Institute Press
Moren, Sally M
1980 {In Notes Brèves} *RA* 74: 190–91.
Mullo Weir, C. J.
1958 "The Prayer Cycle in the Assyrian Ritual *bīt rimki,* Tablet IV." *AfO* 18: 371–72.

Parpola, S.
1970 *Letters from Assyrian Scholars to the Kings Esarhaddon and Assurbanipal,* Part I: Texts. AOAT 5/1. Kevelaer and Neukirchen-Vluyn.
1983 "The Assyrian Library Records." *JNES* 42: 1–29.
Porter, Barbara Nevling
1987 *Symbols of Power: Figurative Aspects of Esarhaddon's Babylonian Policy (681–669 B.C.).* Ph.D. Dissertation, University of Pennsylvania.
Rashid, S. A.
1967 "Zur Sonnentafel von Sippar." *BJVF* 7: 297–309.
Sjöberg, Å.
1969 *The Collection of the Sumerian Temple Hymns.* Texts from Cuneiform Sources 3. Locust Valley, N.Y.: Augustin.
Smith, Sidney
1925 "The Babylonian Ritual for the Consecration and Induction of a Divine Statue." *Journal of the Royal Asiatic Society*: 37–60.
Spycket, A.
1968 *Les statues de culte dans les textes Mésopotamiens des origines à la 1re dynastie de Babylon.* Cahiers de la Revue Biblique 9. Paris: J. Gabalda.
Steible, Horst
1991 *Die Neusumerischen Bau- und Weihinschriften,* Teil 2. Stuttgart: Franz Steiner.
Steinkeller, P.
1984 "Studies in Third Millennium Paleography, 2: Signs Šen and Alal: Addendum." *Oriens Antiquus* 23: 39–41.
Streck, M.
1916 *Assurbanipal und die letzen assyrischen Könige.* VAB 7. Leipzig.
Tadmor, Hayim, Benno Landsberger, and Simo Parpola
1989 "The Sin of Sargon and Sennacherib's Last Will." *State Archives of Assyria Bulletin* 3: 3–51.
Tallqvist, K. L.
1938 *Akkadische Götterepitheta.* StOr 7. Helsinki.
Thomsen, Marie-Louise
1984 *The Sumerian Language: An Introduction to its History and Grammatical Structure.* Mesopotamia 10. Copenhagen: Akademisk.
Thureau-Dangin, F.
1921 *Rituels accadiens.* Paris: Leroux.
Weidner, E.
1959–60 "Die älteren Kassiten-Könige." *AfO* 19: 138.
Winter, Irene J.
1992 "'Idols of the King': Royal Images as Recipients of Ritual Action in Ancient Mesopotamia." *Journal of Ritual Studies* 6: 13–42.
Zimmern, Heinrich
1896–1901 *Beiträge zur Kenntnis der babylonische Religion I–II,* pp. 138–45; pls. 46–48, nos. 31–39. Assyriologische Bibliothek 12. Leipzig.
1906 "Das vermutliche babylonische Vorbild des Pehtā und Mambūhā der Mandäer." Pp. 959ff. in vol. 2, *Orientalische Studien Theoldor Nöldeke . . . gewidmet.* Giessen.

The Theology of Cult Statues in Ancient Egypt

DAVID LORTON

Introduction

Whatever the precise intent of the biblical prohibitions and polemics against idols, that is, cult statues,[1] they stem from scruples that were not shared by ancient Israel's Egyptian neighbors. Theirs was a pantheistic and polytheistic faith whose religious imagination played itself out not so much in myths as in a seemingly endless combination and recombination of deities, and of their epithets and iconographic traits, intended to express and further humanity's imperfect understanding of the *mysterium tremendum et fascinans* of the divine.[2] Indeed, so open was the conceptual structure of

1. See "Prophetic Parodies of Making the Cult Image," by M. B. Dick (in this volume).

2. On the paucity of myths in Egypt, see Frankfort 1961: 126–27; and for a review of the problem of myths and their origin in Egypt, see Assmann 1977. But myths might have been transmitted orally, and it now seems that many passing allusions in preserved texts, especially funerary and magical texts, refer to myths otherwise lost to us; see the reconstruction of such a myth by D. Meeks and C. Favard-Meeks (1996: 24–25).

When one considers that the *high* religion of Egypt was not a personal but rather a communal—and perhaps better put, a state—religion (see Assmann 1984: 15–16), it seems inappropriate to apply to it Martin Buber's intensely personal concept of "I and Thou," as is done in Frankfort et al. 1949: 12–14. Rudolph Otto's concept of the numinous as something mysterious that causes both "shuddering" and "fascination" (*mysterium tremendum et fascinans*) seems much better suited to both the personal and the communal experience of the "otherness" of the divine in ancient Egypt. The fascination with and the desire to understand superhuman powers seem to have led to the theological manifestations alluded to: they

> become much more comprehensible, if one considers them as an attempt to transfer entire conceptual complexes of the concept of the divine, developed in one cultic sphere, into another, in order thereby to broaden and deepen the definition of the nature of the divine in the latter cultic sphere. Moreover, it is not so much a matter of heightening the power of the god in question, as of heightening and deepening the understanding of him by the faithful who are devoted to his cult. . . . The motive . . . is always the desire for a progressive perception of the divine. (Spiegel 1973: 1)

On the way that Egyptian religious thinking centered on concrete verbal and visual images that could be combined, recombined, and elaborated on, see especially Rundle Clark 1959 and Tobin 1988.

their religion that, in the New Kingdom (ca. 1575–1087 B.C.E.), when there was a considerable influx of people from western Asia, Syro-Palestinian deities could easily be incorporated into the Egyptian religious system (see Stadelmann 1967).[3] And of course, the state religion of ancient Egypt centered around a care for the deities manifest in their cult statues, residing in shrines in the temples throughout the land.

From the New Kingdom on, in addition to their local significance, the temples of Egypt also functioned as state cults, endowed by the king with lands and cult paraphernalia, including statues, and their priests serving as royal appointees. The situation in earlier periods is not entirely clear from the records that have survived for us, but it is just possible that royal favor of cults was at first sporadic, with local cults attaining the status of state cults on an incremental basis over time (see Goedicke 1979; Kemp 1989: 65). On the Palermo Stone, the remains of an ancient document recording annals of the first five dynasties, there are occasional mentions of the making of a statue of a god or goddess, and once of a king, among the principal events of a year (see Redford 1986: 87–89); the very sporadic nature of these notations suggests that such royal favors did not occur often and tends to support the thesis just mentioned.

These entries on the Palermo Stone consist only of the word "fashioning," followed by the name of the deity or king; only in the single instance of a royal statue is the material specified as copper. From the Middle Kingdom on, private and royal inscriptions occasionally mention the fashioning of statues and other objects for the cults (for a collection of such text passages, see Helck 1980: cols. 859–60). These references do not give us all the details we might like, but at least they sometimes report the materials of which cult statues were made. A single example can suffice here as typical, a passage from a text of Iykhernofret, an official of king Sesostris III (ca. 1878–1843 B.C.E.) of Dynasty XII (ca. 1991–1786 B.C.E.).[4] Iykhernofret reports on what he did in the city of Abydos at the behest of his sovereign:

3. Egypt's polytheism could easily absorb deities from outside, and a forerunner of the New Kingdom phenomenon just mentioned is to be found in the identification of Baal with the Egyptian god Seth at Avaris, home of the Canaanite settlers who were the forerunners of the Hyksos (see Bietak 1979: 255). However, religious thought—like Egyptian thought in general—was so Egyptocentric that the ancients found only limited possibilities for viewing their divine concepts as valid beyond their own borders. The sun is an obvious universal, and their sun-god (as Re, Amun-Re, or *aton* 'the Disk') was viewed in the New Kingdom as the patron of empire in Syria–Palestine and benefactor of the inhabitants there; see, e.g., the oft-translated hymn to the "Aton" (Wilson 1955a: 369–71), a text that itself bears remarkable resemblances to Psalm 104. Hathor, whose name "Realm of Horus" refers to the world of nature, could be viewed as patroness of places where the Egyptian king had special economic interests: Yam (a source of African luxury products, such as ebony and ivory), in the Old Kingdom (ca. 2700–2160 B.C.E.; see Kemp 1983: 129–30); Byblos (where she was identified with the local goddess Baalat as early as the Old Kingdom); the copper-mining area of Sinai (beginning with the Middle Kingdom, ca. 1991–1683 B.C.E.); and in the New Kingdom, Punt (evidently in Somaliland, a source of incense and other valuable products). On the conceptual basis of Hathor's extraterritorial role, see Goedicke 1969–70: 15.

4. Egyptian history up to the Ptolemaic period is divided into 30 (or 31) dynasties, which in turn are grouped into periods (e.g., the "Old Kingdom"). In this study, dates of kings, dynasties, and periods are derived from the king list in Gardiner 1966: 429–53.

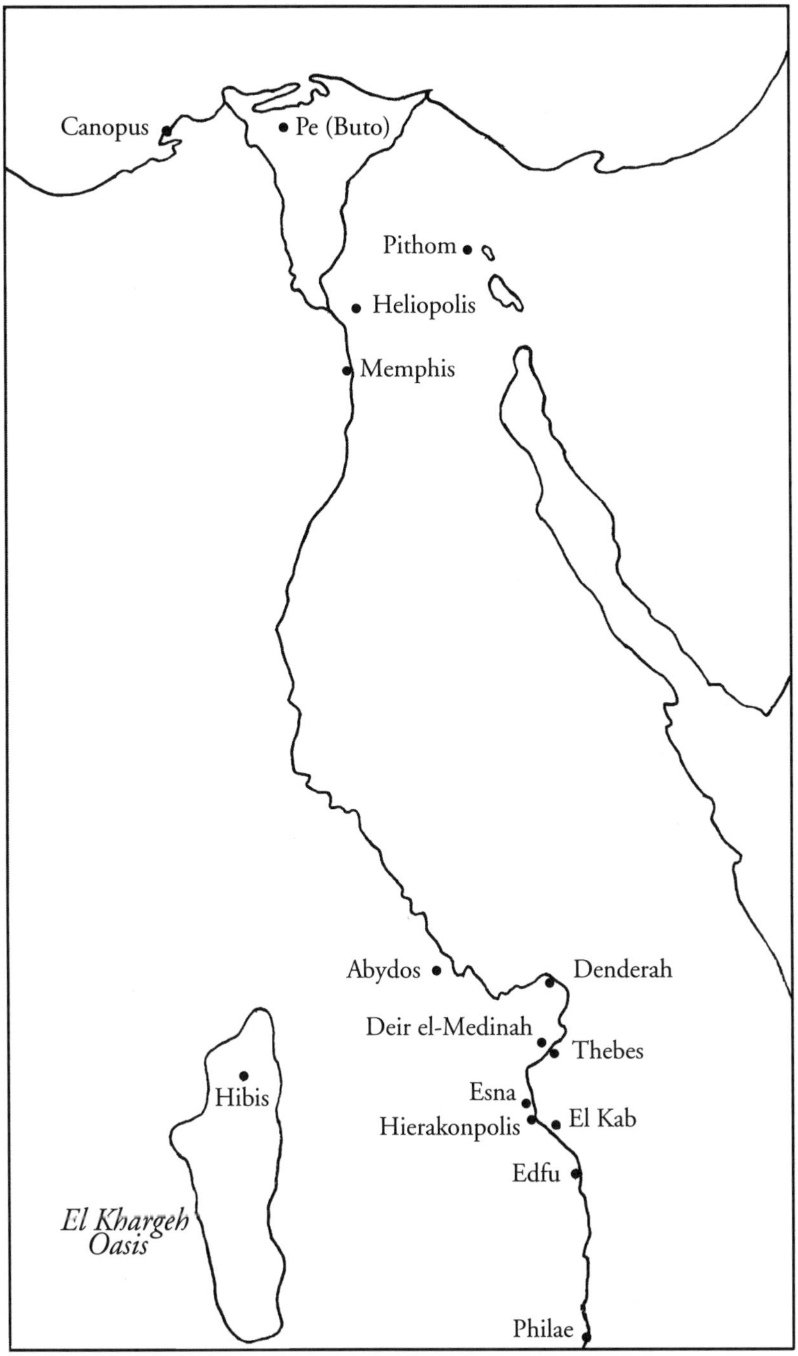

[Figure 1] MAP OF EGYPT, with sites mentioned in this chapter.

> I acted as "loving son" for Osiris Foremost-of-theWesterners and accomplished [. . .] forever and ever and made for him a shrine of "lifting up of the beauty" of Foremost-of-the-Westerners of gold, silver, lapis-lazuli, [cop]per(?), and *sesenedjem*-wood, while the "gods" (i.e., their statutes) were fashioned and their shrines made anew, and set [the professional priests ⟨?⟩] and the lay priests of the temple to their duties, they being caused to know the practice of the daily ritual and seasonal festivals. I directed the work on the *neshmet*-boat. I fashioned (its) cabin. I adorned the breast of the Lord of Abydos (i.e., Osiris) with lapis-lazuli, along with turquoise, electrum, and all kinds of precious minerals that are adornments of the limbs of a god, and provided the god with his regalia in my office of master of the service of the stolist.[5]

It is possible that the earliest cult images were carved from hard stone (see fig. 2). Throughout Egyptian history, some images in the temples—though not necessarily the principal ones—were made of wood covered with a thin sheet of metal. Early examples, preserved because they were buried for some reason in antiquity at the temple of Hierakonpolis, are the copper sheathings of the statues of two Old Kingdom monarchs and, from the same period, a copper falcon's head that, to judge from the nail holes around the base of the neck, was probably attached to a wooden statue (for good photographs, see Aldred 1965: 120–21, figs. 120 and 122). But the passage just cited confirms that, at least as early as the Middle Kingdom, cult statues were made of metal and often embellished with semiprecious stones.

The very fact that the vast majority of cult statues were made of metal, and particularly of precious metals, has worked against their preservation, for they would have been prime targets for melting and reuse. They would certainly have disappeared from the temples as these were closed down in the early centuries of the Christian era (the latest was the temple of Isis at Philae in 535 C.E., under Justinian), but there was an earlier plundering of temples, at some point during the Persian occupations of Egypt (525–404 and 343–332 B.C.E.). After the death of Alexander the Great, the early Ptolemies warred with the rival Seleucid dynasty of Mesopotamia over control of Syria–Palestine, and their records show that they sought the favor of the Egyptian priesthoods by recovering statues that they encountered on their campaigns:

> Having returned the statues of the gods that were found in Asia, together with all kinds of cult equipment and sacred writings of the temples of Upper and Lower Egypt, it was to their proper places that he restored them. (*Satrap Stela of Ptolemy I*)

5. For the passage, with translation and commentary, see Schäfer 1904: 15–20. For an English translation, see Lichtheim 1973: 124. Several idioms and other details require some explanation. "Loving son" indicates Iykhernofret's role in providing for the cult at Abydos; the expression has cultic significance and it will figure in the Opening of the Mouth ritual discussed below. Foremost-of-the-Westerners was the original divine patron of the cemetery of Abydos. This role was eventually assumed by Osiris, and his name became merely an epithet of the latter deity (see Spiegel 1973: 7–37). The identity of the kind of wood called *sesenedjem* seems presently unknown. "Lifting up the beauty" is an idiom for the formal appearance of a cult statue. *Neshmet* is the name of a boat of Osiris that figured in the annual celebration of the "mysteries" of that god at Abydos. A "stolist" was a priest concerned with the clothing and adornment of the cult statue.

[Figure 2] FALCON (presumably the god Horus) of black and white granite flecked with pink; late prehistoric or Dynasty I. Height approximately 6 1/4″; length approximately 9 1/4″. The Brooklyn Museum, L65.2. Guennol Collection, loaned by Mr. and Mrs. Alastair Bradley Martin. For another stone statue of approximately the same date, now in Berlin, see Eaton-Krauss 1980: 20–21.

Having gone off to the province of Asia and reached Palestine, he found numerous "gods" (i.e., their statues) of Egypt there. He returned them to Egypt: they came with the King of Upper and Lower Egypt, Lord [of the Two Lands], Ptolemy, to Hamath, and his majesty dispatched them to Egypt. . . . They (the priests) hastened to come to the place where his majesty was, in the presence of these "gods." After they found that divine image of the Western Harpoon district, and after they spent ten days with his majesty there, the "gods" of Egypt returned to Egypt; and the "gods" of Pithom-Tjeku came to rest there, for it is their eternal home. (*Pithom Stela of Ptolemy II; because the stela was set up in Pithom, the text somewhat awkwardly stresses the city itself and the Western Harpoon district in which it was located.*)

The divine images that the doomed ones of Persia had removed from Egypt, his majesty having set out for the lands of Asia, he rescued them. It was to Egypt that he returned them and to their proper places in the temples, from which they had previously been removed, that he restored them. (*Canopus Decree of Ptolemy III*)

He took every care for the divine images which had been taken out of Egypt to the province of Syria and the province of Phoenicia in the time when the Medes devastated the temples of Egypt. He commanded that they be searched for carefully. Those which were found, apart from those which his father had returned to Egypt, he had them returned to Egypt, while he celebrated a festival and offered sacrifices in their honor, and he had them brought to the temples from which they had previously been taken. (*Trilingual decree in honor of Ptolemy IV*)[6]

There were statues of stone in the Egyptian temples, in addition to cult statues of metal, and it is possible that not all those found were cult statues. But it was the latter that were more portable and more valuable and thus the more likely objects of plunder.

We do not, however, know the fate of cult statues during an earlier period, when the northern part of Egypt was under the domination of foreigners, Canaanites whose rulers bore the title "Hyksos" (ca. 1683–1575 B.C.E.). These people evidently plundered Egyptian tombs and palaces (see Bietak 1979: 242–44), and perhaps temples as well. But we have no evidence for cult statues among the artifacts that left Egypt during their rule,[7] and unlike the Ptolemies, the early kings of Dynasty XVIII, the first of whom expelled the last of the Hyksos dynasts from Egypt, do not boast in their inscriptions of retrieving such objects.

Stone *naoi* (shrines) still surviving in Egyptian temples tend to be no more than 19″ to 23″ in height (see Wildung 1982: 342). Within the stone naos there would have been a portable wooden naos with a two-leaved door. In the reduced height of the wooden naos stood the cult statue itself, with a headdress, though the headdress could have been a separate piece that was attached to or merely set on the statue; the headdress might not have survived with the statue itself. It can be inferred from this that, minus its headdress, a cult statue would have been at most only a foot or so in height if it was anthropomorphic. Theriomorphic (animal-shaped) cult statues would thus probably have been about a foot in length. Remarkably, to date no one has searched through the published and unpublished materials in museum collections to bring together those pieces that, because of their size and the materials of which they are made, stand a good chance of being surviving examples of cult statues. Despite what was said above about circumstances that would have worked against the preservation of these statues, some likely examples do in fact exist. A small number of these are illustrated here (figs. 2–5).

While the objects themselves are of considerable interest, the focus of attention here is the question posed by the biblical polemics against cult statues: if the Israelite prophets claimed that they were nothing but inert material, how is it that other peoples, such as the Egyptians, believed that these statues contained living essence of the deity represented and thus were fit objects of worship? The answer lies in what surviving texts have to say about the matter; as it happens, the earliest date to the New Kingdom, though the beliefs they express, and even their precise contents, could be older. The texts to be

6. For the passages cited and the historical events to which they refer, see Lorton 1971. The Ptolemies continued to build temples to the Egyptian gods and were portrayed on the temple walls in the same manner as their pharaonic predecessors, practices later followed by the Roman emperors as well. Their policy toward the Egyptian priesthood was one of cultivating their favor while controlling their wealth (see Bell 1954: 52–54; Chauveau 1997: 63–65, 140–41, 151–52).

7. Earlier treatments give the impression that objects manufactured in Egypt during the Middle Kingdom and found by excavators in Syria–Palestine are evidence of the trade patterns of that time. Closer study of find contexts has revealed that many, if not most, of these artifacts left Egypt just afterward, during the Hyksos period; see Weinstein 1975.

[Figure 3] CROCODILE (presumably the god Sobek) cast in bronze, with details embellished with inlaid electrum (a natural alloy of gold and silver); Middle Kingdom. Length approximately 8 5/8″. Staatliche Sammlung Ägyptischer Kunst, Munich.

[Figure 4] AMUN CAST IN BRONZE; Dynasty XXII (ca. 945–730 B.C.E.). Height 7 1/8″; the two plumes of the god's headdress are now missing. The god's left hand holds the hieroglyph for 'life', the right hand a scimitar.

[Figure 5] FALCON (presumably the god Horus) cast in silver and electrum; Dynasty XXVII (525–404 B.C.E.). Height approximately 10 9/16″. Staatliche Sammlung Ägyptischer Kunst, Munich.

investigated are both ritual and descriptive: the Daily Cult ritual used in tending the cult statue and the divine essence in it, the Opening of the Mouth ritual that enlivened the statue after its manufacture, and a selection of texts expressing Egyptian beliefs about the relationship between deities and their statues.

Before we proceed, some remarks of a prefatory nature are in order. Notwithstanding the importance of the question addressed here, it has remained uninvestigated, except for very brief treatments by Žabkar (1968: 39–41), Morenz (1973: 151–52), and Assmann (1984: 50–58). It would have been ideal if it had been possible to present here, for readers with comparativist interests, a summary of Egyptian thought based on an existing body of scholarly writing on the topic. Since this is not possible, it has been necessary to prepare a fresh treatment, one that does not pretend to be exhaustive but that will be reasonably representative of Egyptian belief. Additionally, since this is a new topic of investigation, it is necessarily addressed to two audiences with differing needs. Since many points require technical justification for Egyptologists, this has been supplied, though an attempt has been made to keep such material to a minimum. Because technical terms of Egyptology inevitably come into play, and because Egyptian texts translate awkwardly into modern languages and contain allusions to various concepts requiring explanation, an attempt has been made to supply definitions, background information, and explanatory materials for non-Egyptologists.

Ritual Texts

It should not surprise us to learn that a temple, as a focus of respect born of piety and an institution that represented stability and continuity, could play various roles in the life of its town or city. For instance, there is evidence, from the Old Kingdom through the Ptolemaic period, that legal proceedings could take place in temple gateways (see Sauneron 1954 and 1960: 101–2; Van den Boorn 1985: 7–8). In the Old Kingdom, individuals made arrangements with groups of private mortuary priests to conduct their mortuary cult in perpetuity after their death, and some of the written contracts drawn up for this purpose have survived (see Goedicke 1970). Some kind of political and economic collapse that we do not fully understand brought an end to the Old Kingdom and with it a discontinuation of many of these mortuary cults, as indicated in a literary text that reports that "their [i.e., the dead's] offering-stones are desolate" (Lichtheim 1973: 165). The threat that this posed to one's hope for an eternal afterlife found more than one response. Some, for instance, came to hope that a mere recitation of an offering formula by a passerby would somehow be as effective as a real offering for the tomb owner (see Bonnet 1952: 553). Evidently as a means of bypassing physical prerequisites for an afterlife, the First Intermediate Period (the period between the Old and Middle Kingdoms) saw the emergence of the concept of a Judgment of the Dead by which the afterlife could be secured by divine approval of one's conduct during life (see Wilson 1951: 118–19); however, the tradition of physical preparations—mummification, tomb, ritual burial, and mortuary offerings—was too ingrained to be displaced. But it is interesting to note that after the blows to the security of mortuary offerings in both the First and the Second Intermediate Periods, the New Kingdom saw mortuary offerings finally entrusted to the priesthoods of the local temples (see Helck 1975: 254; Allam 1981: 192–93).[8]

But first and foremost, a temple was the abode of a deity or a group of associated deities where they, in the form of their cult statues, were served endlessly—one might almost want to say, relentlessly—by the rituals of the cult. Our own interests, which are influenced by the religious sensibilities of western culture, understandably lead to a fascination with texts that speak to such issues as creation or cosmology or lay down rules for correct or moral conduct. Unfortunately, though, this can lead us to underestimate the central importance of the temple cult in Egypt (and in other ancient civilizations as well), which operated according to the principle of reciprocity, or *do ut des*: just as the resources of the community—and ultimately the nation of Egypt—were put to the service of the god, so the god in return would "protect Egypt" (an important instance of this very phrase occurs in a passage from a text of Tutankhamun that will be discussed below, p. 167 n. 66; see Bonnet 1952: 405–6 and Morenz 1973: 96–97. As we shall see, ritual texts deal with the issue of the living essence in the cult statue.

The Daily Cult Ritual

We have extensive information about the daily cult ritual only starting with the New Kingdom, when select scenes begin to be represented on temple walls[9] and sometimes elsewhere, such as on an obelisk, along with the words that accompany the cult acts, often in abbreviated form. We are fortunate to have the entire ritual of Amun-Re well preserved on Papyrus Berlin 3055, dated to Dynasty XXII (ca. 945–730 B.C.E.).[10]

8. In much the same vein, though thinking more of the Late Period than of the New Kingdom, when they are first attested, Lloyd (1982: 167) states that statues pf deceased persons "were set up in temples and combined the functions of traditional funerary stelae and *ex voto* stelae and statues, their location within the temple illustrating the increasing tendency to regard the gods as a surer guarantee of *post mortem* felicity than the provisions of the traditional mortuary cult." See also Simpson 1982.

9. This statement could be deceptive. Old and Middle Kingdom temples were eventually dismantled and their blocks incorporated within later structures. What might have been represented on the walls of such "lost" structures is therefore presently unknown.

10. On the date, see Möller 1936: 7. An early treatment of the text is von Lemm 1882, but the only full translation and commentary of the text is by Moret (1902). Outdated in some respects and holding up remarkably well in others, it will serve as the focus of the present discussion. For a German translation of the ritual, see Roeder 1960.

A number of scenes from the ritual were depicted on the walls of the cult chapels in the temple of Osiris built by Seti I (ca. 1309–1291 B.C.E.) at Abydos. Unfortunately, in dealing with scenes depicting sequences of events on temple walls, it is not always clear with which wall one should begin or whether one should read the registers (rows of scenes) from the top down or the bottom up. Further, since the titles and contents of the utterances accompanying the scenes of the ritual at Abydos

(A more fragmentary version of the ritual for Amun's consort Mut, of about the same date, has also been preserved on papyrus.) Thanks to the papyrus, we can confirm that each small act was conceived of as a separate stage with a name of its own ("lighting the fire," "taking the censer," "placing the vase on the censer," and so on) and that each was accompanied by a recitation (in Egyptological parlance, an "utterance") that, as will be discussed below, constituted a part of the theological explanation of the ritual's effectiveness and purpose.

From a review of the preserved evidence, it is clear that, with relatively small variations from temple to temple in cult act or accompanying utterance, this was material that was shared by the temples of the land (see Sørensen 1982: 51). Moreover—and this might seem surprising to the non-specialist—Moret (1902: 219–21 et passim) argued that it was in fact the funerary ritual that was adopted by the temples, on the grounds that the cult statue's experience was that of the "Osirian deceased"[11] in needing to be brought to life and maintained by the cult offerings.

This view, however, is questionable. For all Moret's frequent mention of the idea of the cult statue sharing the fate of the "Osirian deceased," the papyrus record of the ritual of Amun-Re does not contain a single explicit reference to Osiris! In the identifications that are set forth in the text by way of "mythic precedents," Amun-Re is in fact identified with Horus, a deity who was considered to be the son of Osiris.[12] Additionally, it is clear

do not always agree with those of the later Amun ritual that is the basis of the discussion here, the latter cannot serve as an unequivocal guide to the order of the scenes at Abydos. Because of these difficulties, several studies have been devoted to the problem of the order of those scenes (see Altenmüller 1969, with reference to the earlier literature).

The scenes at Abydos and their accompanying uttrances are presumably only a selection from the entire ritual and, as just noted, there are some discrepancies in the texts of the two versions. Notwithstanding their many parallels, the versions seem to represent independent traditions of the ritual (ibid., 17), so that even if agreement could be reached regarding the order of scenes at Abydos, this earlier material could not be used to modify or correct the contents of the papyrus containing the Amun ritual.

These points have been made to stress that it would be wrong to conclude, as has one scholar, from any evident differences in the traditions of the ritual at Abydos and Thebes that the contents of the Amun ritual were prepared by a scribe "utterly ignorant or heedless of their purport" (Blackman 1918–19: 27). The papyrus contains the fullest version of the ritual preserved to us, and if we wish to learn what the ancient Egyptians believed about the divine essence in cult statues, we would do best to accord at least a provisional trust to the scribe who recorded this evidence. What is at issue here are the ideas underlying the ritual. If it turns out (as it will) that there is a meaningful development of thought in the text (this contra Sørensen 1982: 59), then our trust in its scribe will have been well placed.

11. Moret is referring to the god Osiris, who was murdered by his brother Seth, brought back to life by his sister Isis, and was ultimately regarded as the prototype of every deceased person, as well as lord of the netherworld where the deceased resided. Writing more recently, Assmann (1984: 61–62) has echoed Moret's views, describing the mortuary cult as the "preparatory school of theology."

12. In the temple of Seti I at Abydos, the representations of the cult of Amun-Re do indeed contain references to Osiris by way of mythic precedent (see thus Moret 1902: 231, 241). However, the god of Abydos was Osiris, and Amun-Re and other deities were worshiped only secondarily there in Seti's temple. These references are thus conditioned by the place in which they occur and do not support Moret's proposition.

from the text itself that there is almost nothing in it that is an obvious borrowing from strictly funerary material. The only real exception is a little material about potential disarticulation of the body; but even this could have a thematic justification, as opposed to being a mindless borrowing of inappropriate material, as will be noted.

Further, we first meet the funerary material in the Pyramid Texts, which were inscribed on the internal walls of a pyramid for the first time at the end of Dynasty V (ca. 2340 B.C.E.), while, as noted above, attestations of the daily cult ritual do not begin until the New Kingdom. While one cannot tell whether these circumstances affected Moret's thinking, it should be clear that one cannot conclude from what amounts to the accidents of preservation of evidence that the development of the royal funerary ritual in fact preceded or thus influenced what happened in the temples—and a *post hoc propter hoc* explanation would in any case be fallacious.

These considerations cannot help but lead to a conclusion that Moret's position is, to say the least, insufficiently nuanced. The real obstacle to understanding is of course our lack of evidence. In the funerary realm, the textual material and the concepts behind it were fixed in virtually their final form by the time we encounter them in the Pyramid Texts, but we are faced with a stony silence from the roughly 700 preceding years of Egypt's history.

Once Egypt was a political unity, how much interchange of ideas about the cult began to be shared among the temples? And what influence did ideas in the realm of the temples have on the funerary realm, or vice versa? Or, did ideas pass between the two realms in both directions? With the raising of such possibilities, it is clear that much could have happened, and that developments might have been slow and complex; but for lack of evidence, these questions must remain unanswered. A solution to the problem can indeed be offered, but it must be one that does not preclude any of the possibilities.

It seems to me that the reason beliefs and practices could be shared was that the problem was shared. In the funerary realm, there was an inert corpse that had to be reanimated by the living self of the deceased so that it could be maintained by the funerary cult. In the realm of the temples, a material object—the cult statue—had to be animated by some part of the living essence of the deity so that it, too, could be maintained by the temple cult. The same problem, that of an inert material substrate that had to be enlivened and then tended with ritual and offerings, received the same solution.

* * * * *

The basic idea behind the daily cult ritual is so simple that it stands every good chance of being the original and "primitive" one: just like any master of a household being tended to by a servant, the god, in the form of his statue, was awakened, washed, fed, dressed, and anointed (wealthy Egyptians, even males, employed unguents and makeup).

But there is an obvious difference between a statue manufactured of natural materials by human hands and a breathing human who is merely unconscious.[13] How could

13. For the funerary realm, the situation inevitably seems more familiar to us, for our culture also allows for the metaphor of death as sleep. But in fact, an inert corpse far more resembles a statue than a breathing, sleeping human.

some part of the divine essence[14] be brought into, or already be in, the statue to be thus awakened?[15] Key statements in the utterances that accompany the ritual acts supply the theological response to the question.

The concept of "theology"—the formulation or systematization of knowledge and belief about the divine—as it applies to ancient Egypt requires comment here. Immersed in our own culture, we are inclined to think of theology as the application of the rigorous logic of the philosophy of Plato and Aristotle to the revealed religion of the holy scriptures. For the Egyptians, thinking about the divine took other forms.

I noted above (p. 123) that syncretisms (identifications of deities with one another) enhanced and enriched thought about the divine for the Egyptians. Aspects of the language also served this purpose. One of these was the wide range of meanings possessed by certain words or roots,[16] all of which would have been present simultaneously for an ancient Egyptian, while we can only indicate the most pertinent meaning or shade of meaning when translating into a modern language. To give one example, the root *ba*, whose basic meaning is evidently 'manifest power', in various contexts would have to be translated as 'power' or 'manifestation'—thus, the 'power' of the god that is 'manifest' in the statue makes the cult image a 'manifestation' of the deity. Additionally, deceased humans were thought to have a 'power' that could leave the body and return to it, which has led some scholars to translate the term *ba* in this sense somewhat misleadingly as 'soul' (see Žabkar 1968: 162).

The other aspect of the language that was turned to this purpose was punning. Far from being a source of humor, as for us, on the principle of the identity of word and thing, puns also served as a source of enrichment of concepts in Egyptian religious thinking.[17] It may be a mistake to think that the words involved in puns were truly

14. One has to make this specific formulation, for it is clear that the statue was not entirely identified with the god; considering only the example of the sun-god, it should be obvious that the essence of the deity was first and foremost in the sun itself, while only part of it could be in his cult statue. Additionally, many deities had cults, and thus cult statues, in more than one of the various temples in the land, and obviously each statue could only have in it a part of the essence of the god.

15. One cannot tell from the words of the ritual itself whether the awakening of the statue entailed bringing the essence into the statue afresh every morning or whether it was in the statue permanently, needing only to be awakened. Texts of the Greco-Roman period inform us that there was both a permanent essence in the statue that slept at night, as well as a daily regeneration of that essence by means of the sunlight (see below, p. 196–97).

16. In Egyptian and the Semitic family of languages to which it is related, a "root" is a basic unit of meaning from which others can be derived. A root can also yield different parts of speech, for example, "to deliver" (a verb) and "delivery" (a noun, though in Egyptian it might really be a participle, "that which is delivered"). Vowels change in these languages in ways that they do not in Indo-European languages, so that we consider a root to be the consonants only.

For the most part, we do not know the vowels of the ancient Egyptian words. Egyptian words discussed in this chapter are written with vowels according to a common scheme that allows them to be pronounced out loud, but these are not to be taken as the actual vowels of the ancient words.

17. See Morenz 1973: 9–10 and Gugliemi 1986. For an interesting discussion of the psychology of the identity of word and thing, which might be a human universal, see Piaget 1951.

"homophones," that is, words that sounded the same or nearly the same. Behind the seeming complexities of the Egyptian writing system is an alphabetic system that represented only the consonants, and we do not know how similar the words may have sounded when pronounced aloud with vowels before, after, and between the consonants. (By way of illustration, consider the similar—and dissimilar—words that can be formed in English using the consonantal sequence *b-r-d.*) But we can say with certainty that the written language employed homo*graphs* for the purpose of punning.

Another feature that characterizes Egyptian religious texts is the citation of "mythic precedent" (see Sørensen 1982: 52 et passim; and the important study of Assmann 1977). This is not at all to say that a text like the daily cult ritual is following along, step by step, the events of a myth conceived of as a story with a beginning, a middle, and an end. Quite the contrary, without any evident rhyme or reason, cult acts or their intended effects refer to various events that once occurred in the divine realm by way of precedent. It has even been suggested, with considerable plausibility, that such mythic precedents were secondarily invented in the context of the cult to explain the effectiveness of the ritual acts (see Otto 1958).

Syncretisms, mythic precedents, wide semantic ranges of roots, and punning—these are a far cry from what we are accustomed to thinking of as theology. But they do not seem so alien if we recall that the monotheistic traditions of Judaism, Christianity, and Islam have within them traditions of spirituality and mysticism that provide emotionally satisfying alternatives to the more cerebral and syllogistically logical theological approach. At the same time, though we are contrasting the allusional and associative qualities of Egyptian theology to the linear form of thinking about the divine with which we are more familiar,[18] it should not be concluded that Egyptian thinking is simply irrational or illogical. When we are able to penetrate beneath the surface, we most certainly find a rational motive for what we encounter. To give an example, as noted above, Amun-Re is identified by way of mythic precedent in our ritual with Horus—but so is the officiant! This would seem contradictory or paradoxical, if we did not note that a recurrent theme of the ritual is that of reciprocity: as mediated through the cult and its offerings (and for these the officiant is responsible), humankind sustains the deity so that the deity will sustain humankind. Cast into the terms of mythic precedent, Horus sustains Horus, so that Horus will sustain Horus. The problem of Egyptian theology has also been taken up by Assmann (1984: 21–23), who calls the western tradition an "explicit" theology and the Egyptian tradition an "implicit" theology.

18. The tension between the two modes of thought was expressed by the author of a Hermetic treatise in the early Christian era, who cautioned against translating from Egyptian into Greek. This corresponds nicely to a statement by the ancient writer Iamblichus that the tracts containing Hermetic doctrine (this was a mode of thought that competed with apostolic Christianity, the old paganism, and other doctrines) contained Egyptian ideas rendered into the technical terms of Greek philosophy (Iversen 1984: 50, 26). On the associational quality of Egyptian religious thinking, see also Hornung 1992: 14.

It should be clear from the preceding discussion that the text considered here weaves a rich tapestry of words that can only be understood by comprehending how the words, and the statements they form, signify. In short, we are dealing with literature, and recognition of this aspect of the ritual puts us in a position to see how the ideas in it are expressed and developed.

In the treatment that follows, comment will focus on the themes that bear directly on the central problem addressed by this volume.

* * * * *

The papyrus begins with the title of the text: "Beginning of the document consisting of the utterances of the divine ritual that is performed for the temple of Amun-Re, king of the gods, during the course of every day by the great priest (lit., 'pure one') who is in his day." The phrase "in his day" seems to imply that at least certain of the temple priests took turns serving as officiant for a day.

After the priest is ritually purified with water—a ritual that precedes the contents of this document—a fresh fire is lit to drive off the enemies of Amun-Re (that is, the hostile powers of darkness), and on a more practical level, to enable the priest to see in the innermost, darkest part of the temple. The priest takes a censer for burning incense and places the incense bowl on it. He then burns pellets of incense, invoking deities who protect the East, the region of the rising sun. Approaching the naos (called *bu djeser*, 'the sacred place'), he invokes the "souls of Heliopolis," the city that was the prime center of the sun cult, and calls upon all the gods of the land (interestingly, neither Amun-Re nor any other deity is mentioned by name) to awaken.

* * * * *

At this point, the naos is touched by the officiant: he breaks the cord and the clay seal that bind the door bolt, and he removes the "finger," that is, the bolt that holds the double door of the naos shut. The utterance that accompanies this last action is rich in allusions, some of them achieved through puns:

> The finger of Seth is drawn as the eye of Horus, so that it (i.e., the Eye) might be sweet; the finger of Seth is loosened (*sefekh*) as the Eye of Horus, so that it might be sweet. The animal-skin around the god having fallen away (*sefekh*), oh Amun-Re, Lord of the thrones of the Two Lands, take to yourself your two feathers and your White Crown: the right Eye of Horus on the right and the left Eye of Horus on the left. Your beauty is yours, oh Amun-Re, Lord of the Thrones of the Two Lands! You who are naked, clothe yourself! You who should be wrapped, wrap yourself! Now, I am a priest: it is the king who sent me to behold the god.

The "Eye of Horus" is alluded to frequently in these utterances, and its referents are on both the practical and mythic plane. Most practically, the word for 'eye' (*iret*) is a pun on words derived from the verb *iri* 'to make/do' that mean 'something that is made' and 'deed': that is, it refers to any offering or ritual act (see Altenmüller 1971: 148, 151; Anthes 1969: 52–53; Goedicke 1969–70: 23). With the phrase "Eye/deed of Horus," we advance toward the mythic plane: the mythic image of the god Horus acting on behalf of his deceased father Osiris was ultimately applied to the king burying his deceased predecessor (presumably his father, though there were numerous instances of succession by a younger brother when there was evidently no surviving heir, as well as of illegitimate succession); to the conduct of both the royal and private mortuary cults; to the concept of the king as ritualist (because first and foremost, the divine quality received by the king upon his coronation was "Horus-ness"[19]); and, as here, to any priestly ritualist (as stated explicitly—"I am Horus"—in the earlier utterance spoken at the approach to the shrine).

The statement "the finger of Seth is drawn as the Eye of Horus" (and that which follows it) contains both pun and mythic allusion. As translated above, it refers to the removal of the doorbolt as a cultic act ("deed of Horus"). But the preposition rendered 'as' has more than one meaning, and one can also translate the sentence as 'the finger of Seth is removed *from* the Eye of Horus'. With this, we arrive at an allusion to the mythic concept of the conflict of Horus and Seth, which is even older than that of Horus and Osiris (Griffiths 1960: 12–22), in the course of which Seth removes the eye (or eyes) of Horus. Thus, the removal of Seth's finger, which is the prelude to the restoration of Horus' sight, is equated with the cultic act of removing the doorbolt, which in its turn is the prelude to opening the doors of the shrine so that the god can look out from it. Obviously, this means that Horus can serve as mythic prototype not only for the officiant, but also for the god! And this has already been made explicit in the text, in the utterance that accompanies the breaking of the cord, in which the priest says to Amun-Re, "It is to you that I have come and brought the Eye of Horus: your Eye is yours, oh Horus!"

There is a special name for the restored Eye (or Eyes) of Horus, the *udjat*-eye(s), which derives from a root that means 'to be whole, healthy'. While the text for the most part employs the basic word *iret* 'eye', there can be no doubt that we are intended to catch the mythic allusion to the *udjat*-eye, for the root has already appeared twice. The two *udjat*-eyes were mentioned in the utterance invoking the deities of the East, and in the utterance of approaching the naos, the priest said, in invoking the "souls of Heliopolis," "May you be healthy (*udja*) as I am healthy, and vice versa! May your vital essence(s)[20] be healthy, for my vital essence is healthy at the head of (i.e., representing) the vital essences of all the living!"

And there is yet another allusion through punning possibly at work at this critical moment of the ritual, an association between *iret* 'eye' and the noun *iru* 'that which acts', which can be used to indicate the active aspect of the visible manifestation (here, the cult image) of the deity (Piankoff 1964 :19).

19. See Lorton 1979: 461. As ministrant to Osiris, the god Horus was Harendotes 'Horus-Who-Cares-for-His-Father'. In the Ramesside Period, this epithet was frequently applied to the king as patron of any cult (Grimal 1986: 70).

20. The Egyptian word for 'vital essence' or 'life force' is *ka.*

The verb *sefekh* 'to loosen', used in slightly different senses, unites the priest's statements about the cultic act that he is performing and the anticipatory references to the clothing of the god that will follow. The animal-skin is mentioned otherwise—though sparingly—in funerary and temple contexts, as noted by Moret (1902: 45–47), who points out that it seems to have been obtained through the ritual slaughter of an animal associated on the mythic level with Seth. The way that the double occurrence of *sefekh* in this text refers both to the finger of Seth and to the skin supports his suggestion. However, Moret does not catch the significance in context of the skin's falling away, banal, in a sense, though it is. In funerary contexts, the mention of the animal-skin is probably a recollection of the wrapping of the corpse in a skin in many late prehistoric burials (Kees 1956: 15). If it were not for a textual mention such as this, we would be in no position to assert that cult statues were covered by anything during the night. But there is some likelihood that by the New Kingdom, the covering was regularly linen: the statuettes in shrines found in the tomb of Tutankhamun were each enveloped in a piece of linen. The operative image drawn from daily life, whether we are to take it as that of a "nightshirt" or even simply a bedsheet, is that of something that is shed upon awakening, leaving the sleeper (here, the cult statue) naked and ready to be dressed for the day.

The references to the two plumes and White Crown might have an Osirian connotation, for the *Atef* crown of Osiris was a double-plumed White Crown, while Amun's crown had the two plumes[21] but not the latter feature. However, one cannot simply relate this stage in the ritual of Amun-Re to Osirian funerary concepts, as does Moret (1902: 47), for the allusions are richer. First, the two plumes are not simply Osirian but also symbolize the two Eyes of Horus that are mentioned in the following sentence, as can be easily shown by textual parallels (so Moret 1902: 47, with n. 3), so that the reference is also Horian and alludes to the concepts of activity (*iri*) and health (*udja*) already discussed. Further, the specific mention of the "White Crown" might have nothing to do with the Atef crown, because it presumably also refers to the Eye of Horus, which could be called a "white eye" in the Pyramid Texts of the Old Kingdom (see Griffiths 1960: 4). Furthermore, it surely refers also to the concept of light, for the root for 'white' (*hedj*) also yields the meaning 'light', and one of the terms for 'dawn'—the time of day when this ritual takes place—is *sehedj ta* 'to make light the earth'.

Given the emphasis on the notion of "eye," it should be borne in mind that when the priest says "it is the king who sent me to behold the god," it is with his own eyes that he will see, and that when he opens the doors of the naos a few moments hence, the god will see him as well.[22]

21. Horus could also be crowned with two plumes. It should be noted that in the "utterance of approaching the sacred place," the priest declares, "I am Horus, . . . with the two high plumes. . . ."

22. We must note that this statement also established a clear differentiation between the person of the king and the person of the priest, quite the contrary to Moret's assertion that the two personae are fused as a "king-priest." The statement should rather be taken as a reference to royal nomination or confirmation of accession to high-ranking priestly offices (Sauneron 1960: 45–47). It is interesting to see how the text alternates freely between the mythic level ("I am Horus") and the practical ("it is the king who sent me"). When the officiant later says, "Pharaoh comes before you," in a hymn, he is clearly substituting for the king as the ideal ritualist, but no identity is asserted: he does not say, "I am Pharaoh."

In all this, there lies the conceptual basis for this stage of the daily activation of the divinity in the statue, and it is, underneath the evident complexity, quite simple: the ability of the statue to act (*iri*) is a response to the cultic act—the deed/Eye (*iret*) of Horus—performed by the officiant. The text expresses this reciprocity clearly, as already noted, even to the point of identifying both parties as Horus. The central concept, of course, is really that of awakening at dawn. But in the case of the cult image, this awakening can only occur in response to the performance of the cult.[23] Light is also a precondition of sight, and the Eye (or two Eyes) also stands for the sun (see, e.g., the texts cited by Moret 1902: 50 n. 2).[24]

* * * * *

The ritual continues with the "opening (i.e., revelation) of the face," that is, the opening of the double door of the shrine and, conceived of as a separate stage, "seeing the god." The utterance that accompanies the former begins by elaborating the image of light that began when the fire was lit and remained implicit in the references to the Eye of Horus and the White Crown and now is made explicit at the break of dawn: "The double door of heaven is opened, the double door of earth is unclosed. 'Greetings to Geb (the earth-god),' so say the gods firm on their seats. The double door of heaven is opened, and the Ennead (*pesdjet*) shines (*pesedj*)." The opening of the double door of the shrine here symbolizes, and on the mythic plane even equals, the opening of the cosmic "double door," that is, the point at the horizon where heaven and earth meet and through which the sun emerges at dawn. The gods who greet Geb are the Ennead themselves, and the statement that they are "firm on their seats" expresses the continued order of creation after the dangers of the night.[25]

The mention of the Ennead (a Greek word meaning 'group of nine') evokes multiple allusions.[26] It is a concept developed in Heliopolis, the main cult center of Re, consisting of nine deities who represent both the stages of creation and the created cosmos

23. Moret's idea (1902: 31–35) that the Eye of Horus is identical to the soul of the god and is offered to the god is only a hypothesis, and it fails to take into account the textual complexities just described.

24. Secondarily, the left Eye can also be the moon, and inconsistencies in the textual references have led to problems in modern scholarly interpretation; for a summary, see Griffiths 1960: 124–27.

25. Other religious texts inform us of the dangers (embodied in the god Apophis) that threaten to prevent the sun from rising in the morning (see Hornung 1982: 158–59). Sørenson (1982: 53–55) stresses the liminal aspect of this segment of the ritual; that is, he sees in it a point in time that is extraordinary, one in which either harm or good can come to the god. He has some support in this from the utterance accompanying the breaking of the seal, when the priest declares, "I do not come to drive the god from his seat! It is to place the god on his seat that I have come!" Sørenson fails, however, to see that the liminality suggested by these words is less likely to project forward through this part of the ritual than it is to refer back to that point in time, during the night, when the sun-god (here, Amun-Re as solar creator-god) had to ward off the attack of Apophis that would have prevented the sunrise. The words of the priest thus seem intended to assure the god that the human realm is ready to receive and support him. For the rest, far from indicating the presence of considerable danger, the utterances of the ritual seem to exude a quiet confidence in its success.

26. This discussion of the Ennead and Re is substantially based on Goedicke 1975a: 207–9.

itself. Its name in Egyptian, *pesdjet*, is derived from the number nine (*pesedj*), which as three × three, or the plural of plurality, expresses the totality of creation.[27] Finally, through a pun, it evokes the concept of "shining" that was all-important to the Egyptians: the created cosmos was a world of light, while darkness (even that of night, though this was safeguarded by the light of the moon and the stars) was the absence of light, and even the "total darkness" of the primeval state of chaos out of which the cosmos was formed and into which it could revert if its order (*maat*) was not maintained through the communal effort of the cult and the personal effort of right action in one's life (on light and darkness, see Morenz 1973: 176 and Hornung 1956: 29–30; on *maat*, see Wilson 1951: 48, 119–23).

Shining light is therefore both the divine source and the nourishing essence of creation, and its principal manifestation—and thus the most potent manifestation of divine power itself—is of course the sun. The sun-god Re was not a member of the Ennead but was secondarily connected with it and considered to be its manifestation. It needs to be noted that our ritual is that of Amun-Re, a syncretistic combination of the Theban god Amun and Re, with a resulting identity here between the divinity of the rising sun and the divinity awakening in the cult statue. The utterance continues, "Amun-Re, Lord of the Thrones of the Two Lands (i.e., both the statue and the sun) is high upon his great seat, and the great Ennead (i.e., both the totality of deities and the shining light of creation) are high upon their seat."

* * * * *

Acts of obeisance to the god follow, wherein the officiant assures Amun-Re that he has not come to do harm. In one of these, he mentions offerings, employing the word *maat*, from a root meaning 'to deliver', quite possibly punning on the concept of *maat* just discussed. He also says, "I bring you your heart in your body, set in its place, as Isis brought the heart of her son Horus to him, set in its place, and vice-versa, and as Thoth brought the heart of Nesret to her. . . ." With this, a new theme is added to that of awakening to light, for to the Egyptians the heart was the seat of emotions and thought, that is, self-consciousness (see Traunecker 1992: 40).

Two hymns follow, evoking the Egyptian custom of praying to the rising sun; in one of them, the cult statue is explicitly called "image (*tut*) of Amun."

There follows an anointing of the statue with perfumed honey and a censing with incense. In the utterance accompanying the former, the purpose of the perfume is said to be "it binds for him (i.e., Amun) his bones, it joins for him his limbs." Texts related to the funerary ritual make it clear that disarticulation of the deceased's body was a major concern (for an interesting discussion, with crosscultural comparisons, see Hermann 1956). Because the attempt to avoid this possibility in the case of the cult statue (now being revivified after its nightly slumber) cannot be taken literally as in the case of a corpse, this wording is indeed a likely borrowing from the rites of the funeral. But the

27. Secondarily, the name could be applied to the "totality" of deities worshiped in any cult center, regardless of their actual number.

concern for the material (in the most literal sense of the word) well-being of the statue is real. Additionally, while these words cannot apply literally to cult images cast from metal, we must recollect that there were images made of wood; and it should be noted that it is also possible that in earlier times, cult statues might well have been made of wood or of wood covered with a sheet of hammered metal. The nature of the wood available to Egyptian craftsmen was such that wooden statues—and other objects as well—were made of any number of pieces carefully fitted together so as to give the impression of being formed from a single piece of wood. From these considerations, it is easy to think that this wording was borrowed from the funerary realm because it was, in its own way, appropriate to the issue of the physical preservation of a wooden statue.

To this point, then, we have seen the following: the awakening to light and arousal of the self-consciousness of the divine essence and the assurance of the physical integrity of its material receptacle.

There follows an "entering" of the "house" and the "shrine" (evidently the naos and the double-doored shrine within it) for the purpose of embracing the statue; because these are too small for a real entering, we must conclude that the officiant is simply inserting his outstretched arms. The utterances at this point make it clear that the "embrace" is really the placement of a headdress adorned with a uraeus (a cobra) on the head of the statue. The uraeus is identified with the Eye, once again as a pun on the notion of cultic act, but there is also a mythic allusion to the Eye as the effective force (by the pun *iret* 'eye' = *iret* 'that which acts') of the sun. The uraeus is also identified with *maat* (on this identification, see also Rundle Clark 1959: 242), evoking again the notion of reciprocity: the cultic act is man's *maat* toward the god as "right action," while the god's effective activity (*iret*) will also be *maat*. Reciprocity is evoked in another way in these utterances. The officiant refers to himself as a *ba* and as the goddess Sekhmet, punning on the notions of *ba* and *sekhem* that are introduced at this point.

There is here a fourth main stage in the quickening of the divine essence within the statue. To the awakening to light, self-consciousness, and the integrity of the physical body there is now added the capacity to act. This completes the quickening, and in the process, the divine essence is finally identified: "oh living *ba* who smites his enemies, your *ba* is with you and your *sekhem* is at your side." The terms *ba* and *sekhem* do not have any appropriate single translation equivalents in English. It seems best to take *ba* here as 'manifestation' and *sekhem* as 'power', though the root *ba* also has the connotation of 'power' (on the term, see p. 134 above). But even with this limited understanding, it can be seen why these words entailing the notion of "power" are introduced precisely at the point when the god's capacity to act (*iret*) is confirmed.

There is clearly something special about the 'embrace' (*sekhen*) that culminates the quickening process (the gesture also occurs in the funerary literature; see Moret 1902: 86–89; Englund 1978: 158). On the level of the operative image of everyday life, it is clearly a sign of affection in the morning after awakening. But what is its religious significance in the cult? Given the fact that the officiant identifies himself as a *ba* at the point when he intends to embrace the statue, it is certainly possible that we have here an allusion to or ritual enactment of the divine *ba*'s embrace of his cult statue, which we find mentioned in texts of the Ptolemaic period, as discussed below (pp. 196–97).[28]

* * * * *

At this point, the officiant closes the doors of the shrine, turns away, and then returns and opens the doors once again. Here, there is much repetition in the cultic acts and the words of the utterances that accompany them. Moret (1902: 102) supposes that this duplication stems from the dual nature of Egypt itself in ancient thought: this portion of the ritual is performed once for Upper Egypt (the Nile valley) and once for Lower Egypt (the delta), while Blackman (1918–19: 42–43, 46) has argued that these were merely alternate versions of this portion of the ritual and that both versions were never performed together. Either view could be correct, but we should note that there is also some progression in the activity. Offerings, alluded to only in passing in the last utterance accompanying the preceding portion of the ritual, are stressed in the very first utterance of this second opening of the doors: perhaps we are to see in the second opening of the shrine a reflection of everyday human life in which the now-awakened master of the house leaves his bedroom to take breakfast in another room.

Ba and *sekhem*, also introduced at the end of the preceding part of the ritual, are mentioned again at the very beginning of this part, which can be taken as further evidence against Blackman's point of view because of the obvious implication of consecutiveness: "Your manifestation (*ba*) is powerful (*sekhem*) in Southern Heliopolis, awe of you having taken the south, and your name is sacred,[29] the north being in fear of you." Upper and Lower Egypt might be included in these references, but the use of the more generic terms "south" and "north" implies foreign regions as well. In the period before that from which this papyrus stems, Egypt had empire in both Nubia to the south and Syria–Palestine to the north, and the chief god of the Egyptian state and its empire was the syncretistic deity Amun-Re, whose cult ritual is preserved here: Amun, the god of Thebes, home city of the kings of Dynasty XVIII (ca. 1575–1308 B.C.E.) and sacred to the monarchs of the succeeding dynasties, combined with Re, the god of the sun that can be seen the world over. That foreign lands are to be understood here is confirmed a few sentences later: "Your power (*bau*) overthrows the lands, and your fame (*hemhemet*) is throughout every country." The word *bau*, itself derived from the root *ba*, can have the connotation 'fame, reputation', so that it is aptly used in parallelism with *hemhemet*. But it also means 'power', and it is the god's power, manifest in the king and his army, that "overthrew" lands and created empire.

28. Once again, we must note the unsuitability of Moret's idea, presented in his account of the ritual up to this point, that the officiant is presenting the god with the eye of Horus and in so doing presenting him with his soul. What is really important to the workings of the text are the rich allusions at the center of which stand the word for "Eye." Further, the god's "soul" is scarcely the officiant's to give! The divine essence is the god's alone, and the purpose of the cult is to serve it.

29. As is frequently the case, there is no single term in English that can convey all the senses of the word. Powers that are "sacred" are also potentially threatening if not appeased, and the root *djeser*, here rendered 'sacred', also has connotations of aggressive behavior (Hodges 1985).

In what follows—further prostrations of the officiant, burning of incense, and hymns to the god—it is clear that food is being burned and that the god was thought to consume its aroma, mixed with that of the incense (see Moret 1902: 119–20).

It is at this stage that the concept of *ka* 'vital essence' or 'life force', before mentioned only in passing, is now stressed. After statements concerning the gods when they see Amun-Re as the sun in the sky, the officiant states: "Maat mounts you as your effectiveness (*akh*, here also with the meaning 'light'; that is, she actualizes the effective power of the sunlight), she places her arms around you, so that your *ka* will exist through her, your daughter having formed you and you having formed her, you having come into existence with the *ka*s of all the gods, you having protected them, you having made them, oh image (*tut*) who makes their *ka*s. . . ." Once again, mere translation cannot capture the multiple allusions in these apparently simple statements. *Maat*, referred to here as a goddess, is to be associated with the offerings (*maat*) but also, as before, with the plumes of the god's crown. When she is said to place her arms around the god, the image is a very specific one in Egyptian thought: the outstretched and embracing arms are in fact the distinctive hieroglyph for the word *ka*. Further, the reference to Amun-Re's *ka* is written unambiguously as his vital force, but the plural form *ka*s (*kau*) is written in such a way as to make an allusion to a word *kau* 'food' (see Moret 1902: 128 n. 1). The passage thus equates the plumes of the god's crown and the light they represent as the Eyes of Horus with the offerings that sustain and in some sense constitute the life force of the god. It also again implies the issue of reciprocity: just as the god sustains his creation, his creation—as mediated by the cult—sustains him.

The term 'image' (*tut*) in the passage is also played upon further: ". . . oh image (*tut*) and *ka* of all the gods, image of Amun, image of Atum, image of Kheperi, image of the lord of the entire land (i.e., the king), image of the lord of appearances, the King of Upper and Lower Egypt, image of him who fashioned the gods, who fashioned humankind, and who fashioned every living thing. . . ." The cult statue ("image of Amun") is here placed in a mediating role, expressed metaphorically as the image of gods associated with creation (Atum is the creator-god of the Ennead) and the sun (here called Kheperi), because the sun is the visible manifestation of the divine creative power and the image of the divine qualities that are in the king in his own role as mediator between the human and divine realms.

Finally, there are also references to the concept of opening the mouth. "You open your mouth that you might speak with it, and you establish heaven with your arms. . . "; ". . . to whom those in the netherworld pay homage, Re above the living (written clearly as indicating humankind), goodly opener of the mouth for those in heaven, and goodly guide for those in the netherworld. . . ." In the cultic context, one cannot help but think that the god is expected to open his mouth to consume the offerings. But the utterances of the officiant, perphaps on the principle of reciprocity, mythologize the act by referring it to speech, both as an act of creation and as a means of sustaining creation.

This portion of the ritual, though it formally duplicates the preceding portion, adds an important new concept: the divine essence that is in the statue is the vital force (*ka*) of the god, and it is to be sustained through the cult offerings (*kau*).

The portion concludes with a presentation of a figurine of the goddess Maat to Amun-Re; the lengthy utterance that accompanies this act draws together the themes that have been introduced to this point (for discussion, see Gugliemi 1980). A censing is then done that is intended to make the preceding offerings valid for the images of the other deities in the temple: "all the great Ennead who are in the following of Amun in his temple."

* * * * *

We need not linger over the remaining stages of the ritual, for the concepts that most concern us have already been dealt with. After purifications with water and incense, colored cloths that stand for items of clothing are presented to the god, followed by unguents and the like used for bodily and facial adornment. Not surprisingly, most of the objects are identified with the Eye of Horus. There are a number of correspondences between these presentations and those made in the Opening of the Mouth ritual (see Moret 1902: 196; Otto 1960: 2.37–44, 112–22). One of the utterances, which accompanies the presentation of an unknown substance called *semien*,[30] opens with the words "*Semien, semien*: open your mouth, that you may taste its taste. . . ."

The papyrus ends with the replacement of the statue into the naos and final purifications (Blackman [1918–19:27, 47] has argued that these belong at the beginning of the ritual and were written down at this point on the papyrus by error), including a repetition of the material concerning *semien* just mentioned. The very last utterance, unfortunately a little broken by lacunae, seems to imply that offerings were left behind. Though the text does not mention it, it is clear from the fact that the shrine had to be unsealed at the beginning of the ritual that it was now resealed (see Moret 1902: 212). Also not in the text, but attested elsewhere (on temple walls: see Nelson 1949; and in the Opening of the Mouth ritual: see Otto 1960: 2.157), is the ceremony of "Removing the Footprint," wherein the officiant left the sanctuary walking backward, sweeping away the traces of his footprints as he went.[31]

Though the words are rich, there was a stark simplicity in the ritual itself, performed by a sole officiant confronting the statue of the deity. Though couched in purple prose, the account by Sauneron (1960: 78–83) of how the entire temple might have shared in the ritual carried out in the holy of holies is quite plausible.

What were essentially simpler versions of the morning ritual were conducted at midday and evening (Sauneron 1960: 88–89).[32] There, over the service entrance lead-

30. Erman and Grapow (1971: 3.453) do not seem right in taking the word as it occurs here as some sort of exclamation. This seems clear from the wording ("taste its taste") that follows; and it is further established that *semien* is a substance by the fact that it is identified with "the spittle of Horus and Seth" in the Opening of the Mouth ritual (see Otto 1960: 2.44).

31. Altenmüller (1971) has suggested that this is a reinterpretation of a ceremony of "Bringing Holy Water," with the problem of the meaning of its title being one of homophones.

32. For more detailed information from the Greco-Roman period temple at Edfu, see Alliot 1949: 107–32.

ing from a side corridor to the first of two rooms in front of the holy of holies, is carved a text that states: "Its double door opens on the hall of offerings in order to worship Re three times each day. Duty-priests who perform their rituals within it enter it three times each day" (Alliot 1949: 102).[33]

Religious Festivals

On festival occasions[34]—preserved temple calendars tell us that by the late New Kingdom, there could be as many as ten religious holidays in a month!—the cult statue left the temple and was carried about in a procession. At least beginning with the New Kingdom, some deities were not only hidden from view in their naoi, but the naos was within the cabin of a portable model boat. These boats were of varying sizes and could be so large as to require thirty bearers.[35] Again beginning with the New Kingdom, we have evidence that individuals could take advantage of these "public appearances" of the

33. The word translated 'duty-priests' seems, in this period, to indicate a relatively low rank in the clergy (Gauthier 1931: 10–11), and they are known from earlier periods as lay-priests. Because of the fact that they entered the pronaos (vestibule) by a side door, it is likely that their function was to bring in the objects that the officiant would employ in the cult ritual.

34. Where not otherwise noted, the information in this discussion is derived from Sauneron 1960: 90–96.

35. While the invisibility of the deity within the cabin of a portable boat was the general rule, it was not universal. Sometimes at least the shrines were visible within baldachins (light-weight frames with holes on the sides for the insertion of carrying-poles). The "Gurob Shrine Papyrus," evidently of New Kingdom date, shows front and side views of a temple shrine suspended by short ropes, both top and bottom, within a baldachin; the drawings are made with accurate proportions on a ruled grid, presumably for the use of the carpenter who was to build the object. The front and side panels of the naos are clearly indicated as being only half the height of the naos, and in the most recent discussion of the papyrus, Smith and Stewart (1984: 57–58 with n. 14) conclude, somewhat reluctantly, that at least the front of the naos might have been left exposed. While one might choose to think that both sides and front (and back, if need be) were protected with curtains or even that the baldachin was curtained, there is really nothing to necessitate such a conclusion. As shown by the examples regarding the god Min, we know for a fact that not all cult statues were entirely hidden from view in public processions, and this creates every good possibility that the Gurob shrine was intended to leave its occupant half visible to the public. As in so many problem areas, the evidence is too scanty to allow firm conclusions. But I am inclined to think that we are dealing with practices that varied from temple to temple and/or, as again suggested by the examples of Min, from deity to deity. Statues of forms of the god Min, whether Min himself (at Abydos) or the syncretistic Amun-Min-Kamutef (at Thebes), were carried in full view of those who beheld the procession (see "Abydos" 1988: 10; L. D. Bell 1986: 30). We even know of a case where a cult statue—again of Min—came to be transported in a chariot (see Sauneron 1960: 73). Though they were presumably not cult statues from temples, there is evidence that statues of deities, conveyed in chariots of their own, accompanied the king when he led his army into foreign lands (see Schulman 1986b: 47–48). In another attested instance of the practice of taking along divine protection, a man named Wenamun (ca. 1090 B.C.E.), who voyaged abroad with an official commission to obtain wood for a new boat for the god Amun, was accompanied by a statuette of "Amun-of-the-Road" (see Lichtheim 1976: 225, 230 n. 8; Goedicke [1975b: 49] connects his possession of the statuette with the fact that his mission was specifically on behalf of Amun himself.)

cult statues to solicit oracular responses from them. There is even a unique instance, from the middle of Dynasty XVIII, in which a man claims that the statue of Amun-Re cured him of blindness during such a procession (Posener 1975: 202–5).

Though the occasions that entailed such public processions could be frequent, some of them were especially important events that occurred only once a year. One of these, "The Beautiful Feast of the Valley" at Thebes, is well known from its depiction on the third pylon (monumental gateway) of the temple of Karnak; the fascinating history of this depiction, which was mutilated by the "heretic" king Akhenaten and restored by his successors, has been discussed at length by Murnane (1979). Another such important occasion (whose depiction had a nearly identical history), when the cult statue of Amun at Karnak visited the temple of Luxor, was the Festival of Opet (for a discussion of the festival and an illustration of its depiction, see Murnane 1986; Johnson 1986). There were other such visits from temple to temple, perhaps the best known being the festival of the "happy reunion," when Hathor of Denderah sailed to Edfu to visit the god Horus (Sauneron 1960: 102–3). Also, at Edfu and Denderah in the Greco-Roman period, there was a New Year's ceremony in which the cult statues were taken to the roofs of the temples, where they experienced what the ancient Egyptians called a "union with the sun disk" (texts alluding to this ritual are discussed below, pp. 189–94). The walls surrounding the roofs prevented the populace from observing the rite; but interestingly enough, at Esna in the same period, this ceremony was carried out before the entrance to the temple, where it could be seen by all (see Badawy 1975: 7).

We might easily surmise that the removal of the cult statue from its abode in the holy of holies of a temple and its transport elsewhere were the occasion of special ritual attention, even though the texts of these rituals have not survived. As it happens, what would otherwise be a reasonable guess is confirmed by a text that lists the contents of the library of the temple of Edfu. There, in addition to the "book for the conduct of the cult," which was presumably Edfu's version of the daily cult ritual, we find listed "all ritual relating to the exodus of the god from his temple on feast days" (see Sauneron 1960: 138). Another reasonable guess, namely that these festival occasions needed considerable organizing efforts on the part of both the temple and the civil administrations, is confirmed by a statement in the inscription on a statue of a vizier of the Late Period (ca. 945–343 B.C.E.), who informs us of his many duties, including the fact that he was "one who gave instructions for the temples in the conducting of the month-festivals and the festivals of the fifteenth day of the month" (de Meulenaere 1982: 139).

An overwhelming proportion of our evidence for ancient Egyptian life and thought consists of the monumental record of tombs and temples; relatively little has survived of the texts that were written on papyrus. Among the records written on papyrus on an ongoing basis were the annals and daybooks of the royal administration. One of the few documents we have that preserves, or is derived from, these records is Papyrus Boulaq 18, a fragment of the records of a royal residence of Dynasty XIII (ca. 1785–1678 B.C.E.), possibly belonging to King Sobekhotep III. Among its entries, we find two that take note of a royal banquet that was held on the occasion of a festival of the god Montju (Redford 1986: 108–9; Gardiner 1966: 152–53). This accidentally-preserved evidence is precious, for it tells us that religious festivals could serve as the occasion for social events at the royal level. We might well imagine that dinner parties were given in private households as well, and we are fortunate to have evidence of an instance of this practice in a text from Deir el-Medina.[36]

Since we have just been concerned at some length with the daily cult ritual, we may close by noting that, on these special days, the ritual was expanded by the insertion of additional presentations to the deity. When we find depictions of scenes from the ritual in temples, some of these extra presentations are included (see Moret 1902: 3–4; and for a detailed discussion based on the Greco-Roman period temple of Edfu, see Alliot 1949: 133–79).

The Opening of the Mouth Ritual

By an interesting coincidence, Egypt, like Mesopotamia, had a ritual performed on newly-fashioned statues called the "Opening of the Mouth" (and sometimes, in extended form, "Opening of the Mouth and the Eyes").[37] The full title of the Egyptian ritual is, "Performing the Opening of the Mouth in the workshop for the statue (*tut*) of N" (see Otto 1960: 2.34).[38] The text of the ritual has been published and studied by

36. In a paper on the economic/social significance of gift-giving in ancient Egypt that should be of interest to comparative anthropologists, Janssen (1982) has discussed several texts from Deir el-Medina (a village in the Theban cemetery area that was the home of the workmen of the royal tombs and their families) that record gifts given on special occasions, including the contributions of dinner guests to private feasts. In some instances, the occasions in question are not noted (at least, not in the portion of the text preserved), but in three cases they are. One is in connection with a wedding, and another is on the occasion of the birth of a child (the text assures us that "hard drinking" took place!). The third instance, which is the one of interest to us here, specifies the festival of the deified king Amenophis I, who was the patron god of the village.

37. In a paper that is in many ways interesting, though dated, Blackman (1924) suggested with at least a degree of optimism that the Mesopotamians borrowed the ritual from Egypt (see esp. p. 59). But there are clear problems of fixing the time of such a borrowing and of fixing the circumstances as well, given the distance between the two areas of civilization. The similar comparative approach taken by Baly (1930: 183) is open to much the same objections. In both cultures, there was clearly a perceived need to transform the object ritually into something that was not "just" an inert piece of natural material fashioned by human hands. Going hand in glove with this consideration is another, based on a natural image from everyday life, that the ability of the quickened effigy to serve as a focal point for the consumption of offerings is predicated upon its ability to open its mouth. (The added concept in New Kingdom Egypt of opening the eyes should be connected with the image of awakening that we have met with in the daily cult ritual. In the Old Kingdom, while the focus of the ritual was on the mouth, as shown by its title even in that period, there is clear evidence that it was thought to involve the endowment of faculties in a more general sense: as pointed out by Mercer [1952: 36–37], the Pyramid Texts mention the opening of the nose and ears as well as of the mouth and eyes.) But the identical titles and similarities between the rituals to which Blackman has drawn attention are best viewed as coincidental: as will become clear in the discussion below, there are actually profound differences in the concepts that underlie the two rituals.

38. *N* stands for the "name" of the individual for whose statue the ritual is performed, written out in full in each of the preserved versions.

Budge (1909) and more recently by Otto (1960); a translation with some helpful commentary has been supplied by Goyon (1972).

We do not have pictorial representations of the ritual prior to the New Kingdom, and the examples extant are all from the funerary realm, facts that raise serious problems concerning its origins. But the central concept that gave rise to the ritual is quite old: the phrase *Opening of the Mouth*, with no special explanation, first occurs in the tomb of Metjen, an important official early in Dynasty IV (ca. 2600 B.C.E.) (see Goyon 1972: 6), while in the realm of the temples, clearly referring to a statue, the words "Fashioning and Opening of the Mouth in the workshop" have survived on a fragment from the sun temple built by Nyuserre of Dynasty V (ca. 2400 B.C.E.) (see Helck 1977: pl. III, line 5). In addition to statues, the ritual was performed on mummies, anthropoid sarcophagi, ushabtis, and heart scarabs,[39] while there is evidence that in the land of the living, it could also be performed on a figurine fashioned for magical purposes (see Blackman 1924: 53, 57; Otto 1960: 2.26–27). From the New Kingdom, there is also evidence for the performance of the ritual on the figurehead on the prow of the boat of Amun (see Goyon 1972: 90 n. 1).

Like the daily cult ritual, the Opening of the Mouth was conceived of by the Egyptians as comprised of a large number of separate stages and, depending on the amount of available wall space, a larger or smaller number of these could be represented; the words of the ritual could also be written on the deceased's coffin or on a roll of papyrus. Because of the practice of representing the ritual with visual material on tomb walls, we refer to these stages as "scenes." Stated as briefly as possible, the course of the ritual is as follows. After purifications and the awakening and dressing of the *sem*-priest, the artisans are brought before the statue. The next significant stages comprise a change of garb by the *sem*-priest followed by the presentation to the statue of the foreleg and heart of a slaughtered bull. Then follows the touching of the mouth with various implements that

39. Ushabtis were small figurines of the deceased that were placed in the tomb; it was thought that if the deceased were called upon to do manual labor in the afterlife, the figurines would somehow come to life and perform the required tasks (see Schlögl 1986). Heart scarabs, inscribed with a plea that the heart (that is, the conscience) of the deceased not betray him at the Judgment of the Dead, were typically placed on or in the chest of the mummy or formed part of a pectoral attached to a necklace worn by the mummy (see Feucht 1977).

Artistic representations show the ritual being performed on bandaged mummies. Examination of human remains has turned up evidence that could indicate the performance of the ritual on mummified corpses prior to wrapping (Pahl 1986).

There has been a debate as to whether the ritual is better understood in the funerary realm, as intended to benefit the deceased (so Bjerke 1965: esp. pp. 214–15) or whether it is better taken as directed toward the objects (statue, mummy, sarcophagus) on which it is performed (so Finnestad 1978: esp. pp. 131–34). The debate has in part to do with the interpretation of specific pieces of evidence that are not of concern to the present discussion; here, it is pertinent to note that in principle, both scholars are correct. The ritual is performed on inanimate objects, as Finnestad rightly stresses, and our concern will be how the ritual was thought to quicken them. But Bjerke is also right, for if there were no entity (i.e., deceased person or deity) beyond the objects, standing to benefit from the performance of the ritual on the objects, the ritual itself would have no *raison d'être*.

were evidently artisans' tools, as well as with the little finger of the *sem*-priest. One of these, the touching of the mouth with an adze called *netjerty*, was evidently of such importance that the entire ritual could be called to mind by the representation of this scene alone (see Otto 1960: 2.83).[40] This might have less to do with the importance of the object itself as an artisan's implement than with its name, which is formed from the root *netjer* 'god': to show it touched to the statue's mouth symbolizes the purpose of the entire ritual, which was to make the statue a fit object for the cult.[41] During the course of these scenes, the "loving son" (that is, the deceased's son who was entrusted with the duties of arranging his funeral and assuring the continuance of his mortuary cult) is introduced into the workshop. A few scenes later, the "loving son" leaves and some of the earlier scenes are repeated. The scenes that follow mostly comprise material that is shared with the daily cult ritual, including nearly identical utterances accompanying the ritual acts: the clothing of the statue with various cloths, anointing it, providing it with scepters, fumigations, and the presentation of an elaborate offering. The ritual removal of footprints then occurs, and finally, the statue is removed from the workshop and installed in its shrine. Unlike the corresponding ritual in Mesopotamia, there was nothing elaborate about this journey: the elaborate ritual was confined to the workshop. The primary celebrants of the ritual were a *sem*-priest (we do not know what the title means) and the *chery-hebet* or 'ritualist', whose title literally means 'the one who holds the ritual (i.e., the papyrus on which the words of the ritual are written)'.

Quite in contrast to the utterances of the daily cult ritual, those of most of the Opening of the Mouth ritual are brief and rather cryptic, a situation that is not helped by a fair amount of textual variation and corruption in the preserved examples. Nevertheless, it will prove possible to analyze the ritual and determine how it was intended to quicken the statue for its function as recipient of cult offerings—and this rather more from the utterances than from the visual evidence of the representations. First, however, we should consider questions of the origin and applications of the ritual.

As noted, the attestations of the ritual are all from funerary contexts. This raises the question of whether it, or something quite like it, might have been performed on cult statues as well: the question is of importance, because the justification for including any discussion of the ritual in the present context hinges on its answer. There is hard evidence, plus considerations of some weight, that combine to yield an affirmative reply:

1. As already mentioned, the phrase *fashioning and opening of the mouth* occurs on a fragment of inscription found in the sun temple of Nyuserre. Although there

40. While Otto's observation is valid for representations on tomb walls and Book of the Dead papyri, it is not true for stelae. A corpus of twenty-eight New Kingdom stelae with representations of the Opening of the Mouth ritual has been collected and studied by Schulman (1984), who has noted (pp. 173–75) that they show a wide range of scenes from the ritual and sometimes a conflation of two or more scenes in a single depiction.

41. Just like the deities of the Egyptian pantheon, the ritually-buried deceased who was the object of a mortuary cult and its offerings was called a *netjer*. On *netjer* as that which has been divine since creation, as well as that which is made divine through ritual, see Meeks 1988.

is unforunately no explanatory detail, the occurrence is important, because it indicates that a ceremony by this name was performed on temple statues at this time and that it was perceived as distinct from, and occurred after, the physical manufacture (the "fashioning") of the statues.

2. In the discussion of the daily cult ritual above, a number of instances were noted where the god was enjoined to open his mouth. Moret (1902: 204) suggested that these had the force of the Opening of the Mouth ritual,[42] a characterization that seems doubtful. In my view, these statements reveal that to the Egyptians, the ability of the deity (as present in the cult statue) to consume the offering presupposes the deity's/statue's ability to "open the mouth." Given this point, it is difficult not to think that a ritual intended to effect this purpose was performed on temple statues, just as it was on statues intended for the funerary realm.
3. In a similar vein, I stressed in the discussion of the daily cult ritual that certain concepts were shared by the temple and funerary realms, because they supplied a shared solution to what was perceived by the ancients as a shared problem. The problem of quickening inert matter to be served by a cult after undergoing a technical process—whether a treated corpse (a mummy) or a statue, and in the latter case whether for a funerary cult or a temple cult—was a shared problem that was likely to have had a shared solution.
4. There are a few instances in New Kingdom temples where mention of "opening of the mouth" is connected, in text and/or representation, with offerings or purifications; one of these entails touching the mouth with the *netjerty* implement. There are a few similar occurrences in the Greco-Roman period temples at Edfu and Denderah, one of which also involves the *netjerty* adze, while another mentions that the activity was performed "according to the prescriptions of the workshop." These references have been collected by Otto (1960: 2.31–32; cf. also p. 4 n. 1) who, because they are without explanatory detail, prefers to stress their ambiguity. Are these in some way based on the injunctions to open the mouth that we have encountered in the daily cult ritual, perhaps even to the point of including in certain temples the scene of the *netjerty* implement from the Opening of the Mouth ritual itself, or do they serve to confirm that the ritual was performed on the cult statues prior to their installation in the temple? When the alternatives for explanation are formulated thus, the ambiguity claimed by Otto diminishes considerably: these occurrences confirm what was noted regarding the injunctions in the daily cult ritual—namely that they

42. More specifically, Moret is referring to a single instance in which one of the utterances for presenting *semien* is made to stand for the Opening of the Mouth ritual, where we might rather have expected the touching of the mouth with the *netjerty* implement. In my opinion, Moret has overinterpreted here: this odd occurrence would better be taken simply as a confirmation of the close connection between the *opening of the mouth* concept and the offering cult. Otto's discussion (1960: 2.6–7) recognizes the connection, but only in the funerary realm.

presuppose the ability of the manufactured object to open its mouth, an ability that surely did not arise on its own, but rather had to be effected by ritual—and this in turn implies that the Opening of the Mouth ritual was not confined to the funerary realm. We may also note that the dedicatory ceremonies of the Ptolemaic temple at Edfu included an Opening of the Mouth ceremony that was in some way considered valid for the building as a whole (see Otto 1960: 2.32). This application of the ritual (perhaps directed to the carvings on the walls) seems to be a very late development, but the very existence of the application confirms the sense of appropriateness of the ritual to the temple realm implied by the earlier examples just mentioned.

Otto begins his evaluation of the ritual with an admission that his original hope of reconstructing an original ritual from what has been preserved proved impossible (Otto 1960: 2.ix), but his discussion remains historically oriented. He suggests that the ritual as we have it has its origin in the funerary realm in the fashioning of royal statues (2.15–16). If I understand Otto correctly, he is thinking of statues fashioned for the *sed*-festival, a sort of royal "jubilee" that entailed aspects of ritual renewal (2.3). Otto views the ritual that is preserved as having been created at the beginning of the New Kingdom out of elements that could theoretically have been taken from several sources: a statue ritual, an offering ritual, the ritual for embalming bodies, the temple ritual, a slaughtering ritual, and the funerary ritual (1960: 2.2).[43] His reason for concluding that the ritual in its final form is of New Kingdom origin is, by his admission, the argument from silence (1960: 2.10). Finally, he sees the ritual as we have it as an eclectic compilation derived from a number of sources that, even though it was never fully edited into a harmonious whole (thus the repeated scenes), nevertheless was structured in a way that was meaningful.

The evident complications in Otto's interpretation of the sources for parts of the ritual stem from his methodological determination to work out a complex history for the various parts of the ritual entailing sources in various realms in which the concept of *opening the mouth* was involved, rather than envisioning the possibility that a single ritual was applied across the board. It is not Otto's position that there was no ritual opening of the mouth performed outside the funerary realm but rather that more than one ritual with this name existed, differing to some greater or lesser extent from what has been preserved regarding tomb statues. But it must be noted that in the Opening of the Mouth ritual, just as in the daily cult ritual, there is virtually nothing whose origin necessarily lies specifically in the funerary realm: the concerns addressed by the ritual would have been equally applicable to all of the objects upon which we know that an opening of the mouth ritual was performed. This being the case, and taking into consideration the points detailed above, the easier conclusion might be that there was a

43. But cf. also pp. 15–16, where Otto views the personnel of the ritual to be an argument against its originating in the funerary realm, though on p. 22 he notes that at least some of the implements that appear in the ritual could point to the embalming ritual.

single Opening of the Mouth ritual and that, if differences existed at all in the various realms of its application (statues for temples, objects in the funerary realm, magical figurines and the like), the differences would have been marginal, in wording and perhaps in specific personnel. With this in mind, we can address Otto's points as outlined in the previous paragraph. Except for the last point, it would be helpful to address them in reverse order.

Absence of evidence is not necessarily evidence of absence, which always means that the argument from silence is potentially a misleading argument. We can only note that there seems to have been no interest in representing the ritual in tomb contexts prior to the New Kingdom and that we are in no position to posit the point in time when the ritual achieved the form in which we finally meet it. At best, we can note that there is some reason to think that some form of an opening of the mouth began in the realm of the temples and passed quite early into the funerary realm (Otto 1960: 2.1, citing an earlier study by Gardiner; we can also note, with Baly (1930: 178–79), that the artisans' scenes can only have originated in regard to statues, whether temple or funerary, and not with mummies). Otto's discussion of the ritual prior to the New Kingdom, however illuminating in some respects, leads, as we have seen, to no satisfactory conclusion: relatively little can be gleaned from references to the opening of the mouth in earlier funerary texts, that is, materials that relate first and foremost to the funeral ceremonies and the mortuary cult that they in some sense inaugurate,[44] particularly in regard to the form and content of the ritual itself.

By the same token, Otto's suggestion that what he terms the "statue ritual" might have originated with royal statues could also easily be a blind alley. The earliest attestation of fashioning and opening of the mouth in the royal context of the *sed*-festival (see Otto 1960: 2.3) is from the reign of Pepi II of Dynasty VI (see Sethe 1933: 114), which is later than the attestation in the sun temple of Nyuserre. Further, Otto's argument regarding the personnel of the ritual is an uncertain one, for he himself (1960: 2.1) acknowledges that the personnel could have differed according to the type of statue on which the ritual was performed. As in the case of the daily cult ritual, the search for origins is frustrated by the silence or relative silence of sources prior to the New Kingdom. And, as in the former case, it is therefore better to set aside the question of origins as unproductive, noting only that a shared problem—in this case, the quickening of the statue so that it could open the mouth—led to a shared solution in more than one realm. The more productive approach to these rituals is to consider their salient features, trying to find some movement of thought through the ritual and to determine how the elements function within the overall structure, or *Gestalt*.

44. From the New Kingdom, we have evidence that the Opening of the Mouth ritual was performed in the tomb on the occasion of the funeral (Otto 1960: 2.27), though for all we know, this could have been in a highly abbreviated form intended to recall its effectiveness (see also the observations by Schulman [1984:177] in this regard)—and it is certainly possible that it was this performance, whether in full or abbreviated form, that led to its representation in tombs. A New Kingdom text composed for the dedication of a statue in a temple makes no mention of the ritual, which leaves it uncertain whether or not this was done in the temples as well (see Otto 1960: 2.30).

Turning to the last of Otto's observations cited above,we find one part of the ritual that clearly represents a secondary development, namely, the material shared with the daily cult ritual, complete with its lengthy utterances that differ markedly from the short utterances that otherwise characterize the ritual. At this point in the ritual, with the statue quickened so that it can receive the cult offerings, it is provided with its first instance of cult attention, even prior to its being carried to its ultimate place of cult function. It is impossible to judge whether this is entirely a fresh intrusion or whether it replaces an earlier and simpler sequence, with shorter utterances; but in either case, the material essentially doubles what we shall see is the function of the second presentation of the foreleg and heart. This helps us to see that the material involving the placement of the statue in its ultimate cult place is simply the necessary complement to the essential ritual that has occurred in the workshop, while the earliest scenes of the ritual can be viewed as preparatory. The real essence of the ritual, then, lies in four major parts, which will be the focus of our discussion: the artisans' scenes; the *sem*-priest's change of garb and the first presentation of the foreleg and heart; the scenes of touching the mouth; and the second presentation of the foreleg and heart (for a similar identification of the core of the ritual, see Goyon 1972: 103).

A further observation can be offered here. While the latter part of the Opening of the Mouth ritual as we have it and the latter portion of the daily cult ritual constitute a significant amount of shared material, the earlier portions of the two rituals contain very little that is shared, whether ritual acts or specific words. This is significant, because the earlier portion of the daily cult ritual is concerned with the concept of wakening and comprises an elaborate theological explanation of what the awakening of the divine essence in the statue entails, while such concepts—and indeed, the very word "to awake"—are entirely absent from the earlier part of the Opening of the Mouth ritual. Even as a secondary development, the latter ritual conceivably could have included the concept of a *first awakening*, just as it came to entail a first dressing, anointing, and feeding—but in point of fact it did not. It would be impossible to say why this is so, but the point itself can be noted: the distinctively different content of the respective rituals make it clear that, to the ancient Egyptians, the purpose of the Opening of the Mouth ritual was not identical, or even analogous, to that of the daily cult ritual.

* * * * *

In the case of statues, the Opening of the Mouth ritual was performed in the workshop upon completion of the manufacture, as already noted. Because of the close connection between the manufacture and the ritual, it is not surprising that artisans are present in early scenes that follow closely upon the initial purifications that, it seems, serve to establish the sacral nature of the space (here, the usually profane space of the workshop) and time of the ritual.[45] In considering the utterances that accompany these

45. A scene that precedes those of the artisans is entitled by Otto (1960: 2.15) in his commentary, "animation (German *Beseelung*, more literally 'endowing with a soul') of the statue." Otto's title is entirely idiosyncratic, for there is nothing in the representation or the words spoken to suggest that

scenes, it should be noted for the non-specialist reader that here, as throughout the discussion, technical difficulties in the textual material will be glossed over to the extent that they do not affect the overall analysis. In the first of these scenes, the *sem*-priest says, "'Branded' for me is my father, made for me is my father, made perfect (the verb *setut* can also be understood as a pun on *tut* 'statue', thus 'made as a statue'; on these associated meanings, see Fischer 1963: 27–28) for me is my father!—(But) who has made him perfect for me?"[46]

In the following scene, the questioning continues: "Who might approach my father? Who has smitten my father? Who has seized his head? Who has smitten my father?" (Certain versions give the last not as a question but rather as a response: "Behold, the smiter of your father!")

In the next scene, the *sem*-priest touches the mouth of the statue with the little finger of his right hand, saying, "I have come to meet you—I am Horus! I press for you your mouth—I am your loving son!" One could view the presence of this scene as problematic. The touching of the mouth with the little finger will be repeated later, and the introduction of the (presumably) real "loving son" (here played as a role by the *sem*-priest and identified with Horus by way of mythological precedent) will also occur later.[47] Thus, the scene could be taken as an "accidental" doubling caused by the accretional process that Otto has seen as informing the ritual as we have it. But it could equally be viewed as intentional, introducing here a motif that will in fact be repeated in each of the following main stages of the ritual. The practical purpose of applying the

the statue is quickened at this point. Scarcely more plausible is Goyon's (1972: 115) suggestion that the intent of the scene is to capture the soul so that it can be given to the statue: there is nothing to confirm this intent. The actual meaning of this scene must remain obscure.

46. One technical point will be addressed here for the reader who can consult the Egyptian text. Otto (1960: 2.61 n. 2) takes the verb 'to brand' in the highly metaphorical sense 'to take possession of'. Since it occurs in parallelism with the verbs "to make" and "to make perfect," I think it is more logical to take it as referring to the endowment of the statue with its necessary characteristics. In the funerary realm, this could refer to facial (and sometimes bodily) features, but especially to the inscribing of the name of the deceased on the statue. In the case of cult statues, it could refer to the appropriate iconographic attributes of the deity.

47. Goyon (1972: 96–97) has argued that the assumption of the role of "loving son" was a secondary development in the history of the *sem*-priest, based on the fact that at Memphis in early times, there was a *sem*-priest in charge of dressing the statue of Ptah and also a *sem*-priest in the clergy of the local funerary deity Sokar. On the other hand, Schmitz (1984) has argued that *sem* was a function of the "loving son" that secondarily developed into a priestly office. Yet another explanation has been offered by Griffiths (1982: 234): "'The son whom he loves' [an alternative translation of the expression here rendered "loving son"] is normally the son of the deceased, patterned on the *pietas* of Horus towards Osiris; if a son was not available, an Osirian priest would act instead of him, and such a priest bore the title of *sꜣ-mr.f* [i.e., "loving son]" (here, Griffiths cites Goyon 1972: 98—evidently a typographical error for p. 97—but the interpretation is not Goyon's, as we have just seen). It should be clear that these interpretations cannot all be correct. The "melding" (if that is the right term for it) of the functions of the "loving son" and of the role/functions of the *sem*-priest seems to be one of those problems of historical origin in Egyptian religion that, for lack of surviving evidence, cannot be addressed except by means of speculation.

finger to the mouth of the statue would have been to wipe away the last traces of manufacture from the mouth (depending on the material of the statue, bits or slivers of metal or wood, or stone powder), as recognized by Otto (1960: 2.95).

In the following scene, the *sem*-priest says, "Lo, my father has been smitten!" (or, perhaps, "Who has smitten my father?").[48] The artisans reply, "Lo, may those who might smite your father be exempt!" The verb rendered "exempt," which has a basic meaning "to protect," is well attested in legal contexts with the meaning "exemption" from taxes or obligations to perform duties (i.e., labor on state-sponsored projects) that assume the character of taxes. In the present context, this nuance is clearly applied to the possibility of prosecution or punishment of those who would do harm to the statue.[49]

What lies behind this little drama is clear enough from the implications of the verbs in the first two scenes and the final statement of the artisans. In the first scene, the verbs all have a positive connotation: "to 'brand'" (in the sense of endowing the statue with the characteristics that make it an appropriate image), "to make" (a very basic word, to be sure, but incontestably positive in the context of making a statue), and "to make perfect." By contrast, the verbs of the following scene assume a sinister character: "has smitten my father" and "has seized his head." The initial question, "who might approach my father?" suggests the possibility of still more negative activity.[50] The key to understanding the abrupt change from positive to negative connotation is supplied by Otto's insight (1960: 2.65) that the activities of the manufacturing process—depending on the material of the statue, smelting, sawing, chiseling, polishing, and the like—are all actions that would represent deadly attacks if directed against a living human body. (This point has been recognized by Munro [1984: 920–21], though he offers a different interpretation of the scene.) The *sem*-priest, who is here playing the role of one beholding the statue for the first time, clearly undergoes a change of reaction: from appreciation of the result of the artisans' handiwork, he turns to a realization that the latter was accomplished by what amounts to a violent and life-threatening assault upon the "body" and a fear that further hostile action might occur.

48. The fact that such different translations are possible is a clear indication of the technical difficulties of the text that have been alluded to. In the present instance, the interrogative pronoun "who?" and the exclamatory particle "behold!" have nearly identical spellings, and the confusion results from the inconsistent spellings in the preserved versions. Otto (1960: 2.66) renders this sentence 'Come, smite my father!' I would reject this interpretation: while "come!" is indeed yet a third word with nearly identical spelling, none of the preserved versions has the specific spelling that would justify it; see Otto 1960: 1.34.

49. Whether or not the verb was ever applied in legal contexts other than those involving taxation is an open question: such a usage does not appear in the documentation that has survived. The specialist reader will note that the verb form here is adapted from formulations of casuistic law: "As for anyone who might do such-and-such. . . ," with the remainder of the statement specifying the punishment (see Lorton 1977a: 53–54).

50. The pejorative, hostile connotation of the expression rendered here 'to approach' is well attested (see Erman and Grapow 1971: 3.336–37). Goyon (1972: 117–19) sees elements in these scenes as implying the final modeling of the statue's face. This suggestion is in a sense a variant of a suggestion made by Helck, on the basis of puns within the text, that will be discussed below.

That the following scene is more likely to be intentional than an accidental doubling now becomes clearer. When the *sem*-priest identifies himself with Horus (on the level of mythological precedent, as son and avenger of the murdered god Osiris) and otherwise as the "loving son" (in the human realm, the son who arranges his father's funeral; one can imagine that this identification was not included in the ritual when it was performed on cult statues[51]), an explanation for his prior references to the statue as "my father" is provided that in and of itself suggests that the scene always belonged here. The statement "I have come to meet you" in some of the preserved versions of the scene is important in context: what has been rendered "to meet" literally means "in the embrace of," with the embrace having a positive and protective connotation. Other versions of the scene have a different wording that confirms this interpretation: "I have come to you that I might embrace you" (employing an entirely different word for "embrace"). In short, in this dramatic episode, the ritual persona's reaction to his first sight of the statue changes from one of pleasure to horror at the thought of the violent implications of the manufacturing process and fear of further violence, and he rushes to the statue, crying out—translating literally at this point, though the result is not idiomatic English—"I have come in protective embrace of you!" Then, when he touches the mouth of the statue with his little finger, the gesture agrees thematically with the context in several ways. First, it is an affectionate gesture that accords with the protective intent of his approaching the statue. Second, the gesture is directed toward the mouth, which is in keeping with both the overall intent of the Opening of the Mouth ritual and with the specific question "who has seized his head?" of the previous scene. And finally, in wiping away the remaining extraneous bits left behind by the manufacturing process, he is also wiping away the last traces of the "violence."

When the artisans exclaim, "Lo, may those who might smite your father be exempt," two things can be observed. The first is that the verb form, whose nuance is as clear in the Egyptian as in the English translation, sets the perceived violent assault into the hypothetical future: with an element of psychological deflection supplied by the specific choice of the verb form, the artisans implicitly deny that they have participated in any "assault." The second is that any putative violence that might yet occur (there will in fact be none, since their role is finished) is declared to be something that, given the fact that it is necessary to create the statue, ought to be forgiven and not prosecuted.

In a highly technical discussion that cannot easily be summarized here, Helck (1967: 33–36) has shown that the utterances of these scenes also contain an elaborate series of puns on words for materials involved in the manufacturing process and for artisans. While Helck is undoubtedly correct overall in the puns he has identified, I am reluctant to follow him in thinking that we have here a clue to historical origins, specif-

51. Even though all preserved versions of the ritual are in funerary contexts, there is precious little that could be viewed as strictly funerary and in no way appropriate to a cult statue. Perhaps the most strikingly funerary statements occur when the mouth of the statue is touched with the *wer-hekau* implement, and the accompanying utterance states that the purpose of the act is to prevent death (see the discussion below).

ically, that the ritual was originally derived from the manufacture of statues made of ivory: his historical hypothesis depends ultimately on a single pun on words for "panther" and "ivory" that, while conceivably correct, is one of the less certain among the puns that he proposes. I would therefore prefer to apply Helck's valuable insights instead to an attempt to understand the *structure* of the ritual, which is the purpose of the present essay, and to view the puns as entailing a *transvaluation* of the manufacturing process, through the ritual, to a new and higher purpose, namely the quickening of the statue. The issue of transvaluation will concern us again later. This point can be taken on its own but, in view of the preceding discussion, we are led to propose that the latent element represented by the puns is also linked to the more overt theme of violence and provides a means of transvaluing the potentially violent aspect of the manufacturing process into something that is life-giving. The transvaluation and subsuming of violence to ordered human purposes will occur again in the next section of the ritual, in a very different context.

This brings us to the point where we can begin to compare the Egyptian Opening of the Mouth ritual with the ritual attested from Mesopotamia. Both could be said to share a negative evaluation of the manufacturing process, but this point of comparison is tricky: in the Egyptian ritual, the negative evaluation is treated as only potential, something that could be effectively denied in ritual context, and we shall see in the next paragraph that the manufacturing process itself was in fact valued positively. More significant is the contrast between the two rituals in this regard. In the Mesopotamian ritual, the artisan's hand is symbolically severed and he is made to declare that he had no role in making the statue, events that transpire in the context of a ritual enacted outside the workshop that was intended to symbolize a birthing process occurring in the divine realm. In the Egyptian ritual, which transpires within the place of manufacture, the negative evaluation characterized as violence is presented as only potential and is effectively dealt with by denial and transvaluation.

If one looks outside the ritual itself, there is abundant evidence that the Egyptians acknowledged—indeed, even celebrated—the physical aspect of statues as well as the manufacturing process. It is well known that in two-dimensional art (paintings and relief), the Egyptians preferred to show the human figure in an unnatural way, with the lower part of the body in profile and the shoulders full-front. But as early as the Old Kingdom, Egyptian artists tended to represent statues naturalistically in full profile, without the cliché of shoulder frontality (see, e.g., Junker 1951: 402; on the representation of statues and their manufacture in the Old Kingdom, see Eaton-Krauss 1984), thus stressing the difference between a statue as an object that has been manufactured—notwithstanding the fact that it was intended to be the receptacle of living essence—and a real human being. They were also not averse to depicting the manufacturing process itself, and the reader can conveniently be referred in this connection to the study of Eaton-Krauss (1984) for the Old Kingdom. In the realm of texts, we have noted that kings and officials proudly recorded their role in the manufacture of cult statues, sometimes including the materials of which they are made.

The point is made with special emphasis by a representation that has survived from a New Kingdom tomb (see Otto 1960: vol. 2, fig. 13). To the left, artisans apply the finishing touches to two anthropoid sarcophagi (one of these will contain the body of the deceased and nestle inside the other). At the lower right, a man holds an open papyrus on which the words "performing the Opening of the Mouth" are written, while at the upper right, a man with an axe is felling a tree. The representation should not be taken as contradicting the point that the ritual was performed after the manufacture of the object. Rather, using limited available wall space, the artist has encapsulated three separate stages, as proved by the fact that the felling of a tree is shown. And, by taking the unusual step of depicting the last-mentioned element, he has demonstrated what we have otherwise noted from diverse sources: to the Egyptians, the raw materials and the process of manufacture were at least as important as the ritual that ultimately endowed the object with life and effectiveness. The significance of this fact will emerge more clearly when we consider the scenes in which implements are touched to the statue's mouth.

A final scene involving the artisans (or, at least, one of them) follows, and its precise meaning is unclear. At best, we can note that the *sem*-priest forbids some form of harm that might come to the head of his "father" (i.e., the statue), and that in this scene, as in yet another unclear one that follows, Horus, Seth, and Isis are invoked by way of mythological precedent. Finally, there is a scene in which the ritualist says to the *sem*-priest, "Run, that you may see your father!"

* * * * *

At this point, the *sem*-priest changes his garb, donning a panther skin, a clear sign that an important transition point has been reached. The accompanying utterances, however, are difficult. The *sem*-priest states, "I snatch his Eye (some versions have "Eye of Horus") from his mouth! I tear off his foreleg!" The ritualist declares, "I 'brand' for you your Eye, that you may be *ba* by means of it!" Some versions of the latter statement have "Oh, N.! 'Branded' for you is your Eye (variants, "this Eye," "his Eye"), that you may be *ba* by means of it!" Otto (1960: 2.72) is surely correct in thinking that these words accompanying the *sem*-priest's change of clothing are most properly taken as addressed to him, so that we must conclude that there is a secondary reinterpretation of the ritualist's speech in the versions that take it as addressed to the statue. We must agree with Otto in thinking that the utterance accompanies the act being performed at this point in the ritual, and it must be inferred from this that the ritualist's speech is directed to the *sem*-priest. This can only mean that the "Eye" refers in both utterances to the object of the ritual action, that is to say, the panther skin. The snatching of the "Eye" from the very mouth of the voracious beast of prey is a dramatic image, but in context it entails an incongruity that neither Otto nor I can explain. The reference to the mouth will, however, have its echo in a reference to the lips and mouth of the slaughtered bull, so that however mysterious it must remain for us in its literal sense (the visual material of the representations at this point also offers no help in this regard), a clear thematic linkage is introduced here between the material regarding the panther skin and the material regarding the slaughtered bull.[52] Much the same is true of the *sem*-priest's second statement, "I have ripped off his foreleg," because in point of fact the panther skin as worn in Egyptian ritual contexts (abundant references are cited by Otto [1960: 2.72–73]) was not missing any of its legs; but at the same time, a linkage is provided with the material to follow, where the foreleg will also be stressed. However impenetrable these statements of the *sem*-priest might be on the literal level, it is actually on the metaphorical level—that is to say in this case, the use of puns—that their intent becomes clear. The pun on the word for 'eye' (*iret*) and the verb 'to do, to act' (*iri*, with its infinitive *iret*) was discussed above. I should add here that *khepesh*, the word for 'foreleg', forms a pun on (or is derived from the same root as) the word *khepesh* 'physical strength'.[53] It can thus be postulated that the *sem*-priest dons the panther skin at this point so that the actions he is about to perform will be ritually effective. When this motive is taken into account, the wording of the text suggests that this effectiveness, or ability to perform (*iret*) the ritual act, is derived from the physical power (*khepesh*) of the panther as the priest dons its skin. In the statement "I snatch this Eye from his mouth," the word *iret* might thus contain a double allusion, to both the panther skin itself as the object that is being ritually handled (*iret*) and the ability to act with ritual effectiveness that the skin confers on the priest.

When the ritualist states to the *sem*-priest, "I 'brand' for you your Eye, that you may be *ba* by means of it," the literal meaning of the utterance is again unclear; the most we can say at this level is that because "this (i.e., the panther's) Eye" has now become "your (i.e., the *sem*-priest's) Eye," it is clear that the utterances reflect a *process* of empowering the *sem*-priest that is occurring. But once again, on the metaphorical level, there is meaning to be found. The application of the concept *ba* 'manifest power' to the *sem*-priest must again refer to his ability to act with ritual effectiveness. However, we must also note that there is a word (perhaps from the same root) *ba* that means 'panther'.[54] Thus, when the ritualist says that the *sem*-priest will be "manifestly powerful" or will "manifest power," the statement (through the punning meaning "that you may be a panther") implies that he will specifically manifest the power of the animal whose skin he is wearing.[55]

52. At this point, it would be useful to note that in much Egyptian textual material, particularly religious material, the concepts that underlie what appears or the motives for mentioning something remain unstated. This is probably because they needed no explicit mention or explanation for the ancients themselves. However, the inevitable result of this phenomenon for the modern investigator is all too often perplexity and frustration.

53. On this figurative interpretation, see Munro 1984: 924, though with a different interpretation of the significance.

54. See Erman and Grapow 1971: 1.415. Though it is listed there as first being attested in the Middle Kingdom, there is no certainty that it is not older. The Egyptian language, in any event, had no other word for the animal (see Erman and Grapow 1971: 6.116).

55. While the specific connotation of the verb *ab* 'to brand' is uncertain in the present context, it can be noted that, on one level, it might be functioning as a secondary pun on *ba*. Through a metathesis of radicals, the word *ba* 'panther' takes the form *aby* beginning in Dynasty XVIII (see Erman

Otto (1960: 2.75) interprets the material involving the slaughtered bull that is to follow as reflecting an old hunting ritual, while in an earlier study to which he refers (1950: 169), he thinks that the animal entailed was domesticated by preagricultural pastoralists. It is certainly possible to address the question of historical origins, and it is tempting to see in the donning of the panther skin a reflection of the hunting and gathering stage of Egypt's prehistory, with the slaughter of the wild and dangerous beast and the ritual donning of its skin representing an attempt to absorb and thereby control the untamed forces of nature, and to see in the slaughter of the bull a later, similarly-intended ritual from the agricultural phase of prehistory (the Neolithic) whose central importance replaced that of the earlier ritual without entirely displacing it. But I would prefer to refrain from such an approach to these materials: when all is said and done, there is no reason why ritual material that "seems" old could not have been developed, perhaps with a deliberately archaic flavor, at a later time than we might think, and it is thus dangerous to read a diachronic (historical) dimension into material that we encounter and need to account for synchronically. This is not to deny that these materials seem quite old indeed and might even be so. Rather, the point to be emphasized is that even if we could fix the point in time of the origin of the panther-skin and slaughtered bull materials, it would not necessarily lead to a productive understanding of how and why they are functioning together at this point in the ritual.[56]

Erman and Grapow 1971: 1.7). The puns here have already been noted by Goyon (1972: 120 n. 4); on the skin conferring the power of the panther on the *sem*-priest, see Helck 1987: 51.

56. It might be recalled that, early in the daily cult ritual, there was a reference to a skin in which the cult statue was draped. In a lengthy discussion of the reference, Moret (1902: 43–47) drew together a number of references to animal skins in religious contexts—including the material just discussed here—and suggested that they all derive from an early ritual in which a "Typhonian" animal (one representing wild or chaotic powers) was sacrificed and its skin donned for the purpose of investing the human sacrificer with the powers of the animal. Additionally, Moret (pp. 74–76 and 222–25) argued that a primitive dismemberment of the body of the deceased preceded the concerns about preserving the body intact that underlay the mummification process, and—since it was his opinion that the divine cult was nothing more than the mortuary cult applied to deities—he proposed that "The tradition of dismemberment seems to correspond to this concept, common to many religions, that makes the god the very victim of the sacrifice that is offered to the divinity. The *sacrifice* of the god constitutes the cult" (p. 222; italics Moret's). That is to say, it was his belief that dismemberment of the deceased and sacrifice and dismemberment of the deity historically preceded the tradition of sacrificing an animal to the deceased or the deity.

It has already been argued that we are best off regarding material shared by the funerary and temple realms as shared solutions to shared problems, rather than positing explanations of historical development generally, or more specifically the explanation that the material passed wholesale from one realm into another, for which there is no solid evidence. Additionally, it is clear from a reading of Moret's treatment of religious contexts mentioning an animal skin that while the skin is an element that they all have in common, there is nothing so homogeneous about these contexts as to commend Moret's proposal of a single primitive sacrificial ritual that underlies all of it. In fact, Moret's explanation seems forced and unsatisfying, as can be adequately illustrated by the two ritual contexts treated in this chapter, wherein the following observations can be made: (1) the daily cult ritual does not identify

If we eschew, then, the quest for origins and focus our attention on what can be observed intratextually, some resolution of what is problematic in this material may be at hand. Beyond the pun on *ba* in the text, there is nothing extratextual that can help us understand why the *sem*-priest dons the panther skin at this point. But within the *Gestalt* of the ritual, there is a single explanation that presents itself. Clothed in the panther skin, the *sem*-priest himself is, as it were, the wild beast of prey who stalked, killed, and tore apart his victim. To be sure, we know from the textual material (see Otto 1960: 2.74) that he did not personally perform the slaughter, while visual material (cf. Otto 1960: fig. 1) equally confirms that it was not he who removed the foreleg and heart from the bull. And while we might hypothesize that he did perform these functions at some earlier point in time, in doing so we again place ourselves in the speculative area of origins, which does not really help us understand what is happening here. Rather, the points to be stressed are the following: first, through the pun on *ba* 'panther' and *ba* 'manifest power', the *sem*-priest dons the skin so that the actions he is about to perform will be ritually effective (his effectiveness is also alluded to by the verb *khepesh*); and second, when the *sem*-priest, clad in the panther skin, will present the foreleg and heart of the slaughtered bull to the statue, it will be as though the beast were carrying pieces of the prey that has been torn apart.

The ensuing material begins with the bull—evidently already slaughtered[57]—on the scene. The ritualist says, "*sem*-priest, extend (your) arm towards the male Upper Egyptian[58] *nega* (a kind of cattle with long spreading horns; see Montet 1954: 47–54)! Slaughterer, cut off his foreleg (*khepesh*), cut out his heart!" At this point, a female who

the statue's leather garment as coming from a *ritually sacrificed* animal; and (2) the panther skin in the Opening of the Mouth ritual is donned by an *officiant* of the ritual and not by the statue that is the beneficiary of the ritual. Thus, the only quality that the two have in common is the putatively coincidental one that they both entail the hide of some animal or other (in the former case, we are not even sure what animal).

Finally, we should note that while the sacrifice of a deity may well be a part of the overall human religious experience that has been noted in some cultures by ethnographers, there is nothing to support Moret's outdated, evolutionary approach that would see this phenomenon as a human universal that once existed in Egypt as well, and thus as a precursor of historically attested religious practices. Egypt's prototypical murdered deity, Osiris, was murdered by another deity, his brother Seth; he is never presented as the sacrificial victim of humankind. The one deity who is sacrificed by man—or at least by individuals who act ritually on behalf of mankind—is in fact Seth himself: in the form of a hippopotamus, for instance, he can be harpooned by the king (see Altenmüller 1967: 20–24). But in the case of Seth, the slaughtered deity is one who is negatively valued as the embodiment of death and the wild forces in nature, not a positively valued deity.

57. Given the value of a bull, we might wonder whether one was freshly slaughtered for every ritual in the funerary realm, and we might prefer to think that a single sacrificial bull was put to the service of all rituals in a given locale on any single day. But these are only speculations, and they do not speak to the intent of the ritual text.

58. On the basis of extratextual material, Otto (1960: 2.74) notes that "Upper Egyptian" is likely to be a reinterpretation of an original "royal." This is not by way of a pun, but because of very similar signs employed in the writings of the two words.

is present and who is identified as "the great (female) falcon,"[59] is said to "speak (presumably, whisper) into his (i.e., the bull's) ear" the statement, "It is your lips that did it to you," followed by the sarcastic question, "Is your mouth open (now)?" No explanation is given for the woman's speech, so that it seems quite mysterious. Is she accusing the bull of having said something "evil" so as to justify his death? In this connection, we may note that it is easy to draw a connection between the slaughtered bull and the machinations of the evil Seth, slayer of his brother Osiris (so Otto 1960: 2.76, on the basis of extratextual material), but nothing here specifically authorizes making the connection. Or, are we to understand a more basic, natural image—that by uttering some sound, the bull made his location known to the ravenous beast of prey and is thus responsible, however inadvertently, for his own death (so Otto 1950: 170)? In either case, we can see that the woman's speech is intended to explain, or perhaps better put, to justify, the death of the bull: in short, the victim is blamed for being the victim. The next words are evidently spoken by the ritualist: "Bring the goat, cut off its head! Bring the goose, cut off its head!" Then, the ritualist says—evidently to the statue, though the instructions specify that he is facing the *sem*-priest at this point—"I grasp them for you! I bring you your enemies! It (evidently either the goat or the goose) is delivered, at your disposal, its limbs upon it!"[60] He then says, "It is entirely slaughtered for you," and his final words could be directed to the sacrificed animals considered as "enemies" or to any potential enemy: "Do not approach that god (i.e., the statue)!"

At this juncture, we can note two points. The first is of comparative interest. In a study of sacrificial cult in Mesopotamia, Hallo (1987: 3–5) has noted ethnographic evidence suggesting that cult sacrifice can be accompanied psychologically by guilt and terror at taking a life, concern lest taking the life of the animal touch off a cycle of revenge, and/or an intent to defuse the violent aspect of the human psyche. It should be of interest to anthropologists and students of comparative religion to note that the words of the female "great falcon" justifying the slaughter of the bull clearly fit into this wider pattern of ambivalent attitudes to the act of sacrifice. But from the purely intratextual point of view, we should also note that when the woman focuses attention on the "lips" and "mouth" of the bull, there is a clear thematic allusion to the central intent of the Open-

59. Outside this ritual, the goddesses Isis and Nephthys are known as "the greater kite" and "the lesser kite" (Egyptologists prefer to use this nearly obsolete term for the bird) in their role of mourners of their deceased brother Osiris. Interestingly, though, only one female falcon is present here, and no mythological allusion to the Osirian cycle is made, as has been noted by Otto (1950: 166). Within the context of the ritual, we can note that the falcon, like the panther, is a beast of prey; and although falcons can be tamed for hunting purposes, one has rather the impression (see Otto 1950: 170) that it is a wild falcon that is envisioned in the present context and that deadly forces of nature are being arrayed against the bull.

60. The phrase rendered "at your disposal" is otherwise attested as indicating subjection; see Lorton 1974: 124–25. "Its limbs (literally, "arms")" likely refers to a way in which the arms of a captive were tied together above his head: (see Otto 1960: 2.75) and, by extension, to the bound limbs of the sacrificial animal.

ing of the Mouth ritual,[61] and further, that in justifying the slaughter of a bull, she effects a degree of denial of violence that echoes, in its own way, the content of the artisans' scenes. Returning to the comparative aspect, it is perhaps this vantage point that can help explain what otherwise seems to me to be problematic in this material. That the creation and maintenance of order out of chaos was a basic concept of Egyptian religion scarcely needs documentation here. Yet, in this material, individuals impersonate animals (panther, falcon) that represent ferocious elements in nature when harm is done to the bull, which one cannot avoid recognizing as a domestic animal that falls within the ambiance of civilization and order. Any attempt to resolve this evident contradiction necessarily entails a speculative element, and to be sure, we can plausibly surmise that these wild forces are brought into the realm of civilization and order by the mechanism of ritual personification; but this would not explain why they are directed against the bull. Without denying the explanation just proferred, for it is not an either–or issue, we can offer the equally plausible hypothesis that, just as the "great falcon's" words provide an excuse for taking the bull's life, so the assuming of wild personae shifts the burden of guilt for this phase of the ritual, with its aspect of violence, away from civilized man.[62]

We cannot fail to note here that the major portions of the ritual to this point—the artisans' scenes and the scenes involving the slaughtered bull—are conceptually linked by the theme of violence. In the earlier material, it is denied that the forceful techniques that are necessary to form the statue are to be viewed as a violent assault on the "body." In the present material, the slaughter of the bull is denied to be an act of unjustified violence, while we may otherwise view the material as ritually bringing the violent forces of nature into the service of the statue and/or view it as ritually deflecting the burden of guilt for what is done to the bull onto these violent forces.

61. To be sure, this material occurs elsewhere in cult context (see Otto 1960: 2.75–76). However, it should be noted that the focus of the cult was on the consumption of offerings, for which the ability to open the mouth was essential; we have seen this point emphasized in the words of the daily cult ritual. In the woman's speech, there are also special puns on *septy* 'lips' and *setep* 'to cut off (the foreleg)', and on *sesh* 'open' and *sheser*, a word for the bull that appears in some versions (see Otto 1950: 168).

62. We should not fail to note the ambivalence inherent even in the domestic bull, which can and does exhibit savage behavior (perhaps it was the need to lasso an unwilling bull, an act that is well-attested in ancient Egyptian representations, that has given Otto and others a potentially mistaken impression that there was some kind of prehistoric "ritual hunting" of bulls), thus making it a fit object for sacrifice that could, in a cult context, conceptually entail the maintenance of order. It seems to me that what underlies both ambivalences—the subsuming of wild forces into the ritual and the possibility of viewing the bull as both a domestic animal and an avatar of savage power—is a deeper ambivalence involving force as a necessary means of maintaining order versus the savagery of sheer violence. We see this clearly in the epithet "victorious bull," referring to military force, that appears frequently in the royal titulary in the New Kingdom and later (specifically, in the Horus name; see Von Beckerath 1984: 154–55). But the image of the bull's incarnating force directed against those outside society or the state can be traced much farther back, to late prehistory in the powerful visual images produced on the "bull palette" and one of the representations on the Narmer palette, conveniently represented together by Emery (1963: pl. 3).

The second point to be noted is that the introduction of the goat and the goose is perhaps secondary or, at the very least, of secondary importance (see Otto 1950: 165). As noted by Otto, the word for goat employed by the text (*ar*) forms a pun on the verb "to approach" in the injunction "do not approach that god." There is no intratextual justification, whether by pun or otherwise, for the inclusion of the goose here, but the word for it (*semen*) puns easily on a common word meaning "to cause to endure," an association that would make sense in context. Additionally, the head of course entails the mouth, and a concern with both (note the question "who has seized his head?" in the artisans' scenes) is otherwise present in the ritual. We can also note in this connection the concern that the head remain joined to the skeleton in the daily cult ritual: it is possible to hypothesize that the severing of these heads is intended ritually to prevent the statue's head from suffering the same fate. Alternatively, we can note that with the sacrifice of a bull (large cattle), a goat (small cattle), and a goose (bird), the three main categories of sacrificial animals are included. But in the last analysis, it is clear from both the visual material and the words that accompany the ritual acts that the presentation of the foreleg and heart of the bull are the real focus of this portion of the ritual.

In the next scene—the utterances will not concern us here—the butcher gives the foreleg of the bull to the ritualist and its heart to another individual present called the "companion," and these in turn present them to the statue. With the latter act, the foreleg is dubbed the "Eye of Horus," with an obvious double pun on the ritual "deed" or "object handled" and the ability to "act" in the sense of the quickening of the statue so that it can open its mouth, the mention of Horus potentially implying at the same time both the beneficiary of the ritual act and the one who executes it, as we have seen in the daily cult ritual. With rather less ado in the words of the ritual, the goat and the bird are then presented.

The ensuing "scene" appears to be in reality a longer utterance (formulated in the first-person singular, though it may have been spoken by both the ritualist and the *sem*-priest, in turn or in unison) that continues the content of what has preceded. However, only the foreleg is mentioned, which shows that it was considered to be even more important than the heart. The goat and the goose are not mentioned at all. In this utterance, it is made clear that the presentation of the foreleg is intended to "open the mouth" (and the eyes) of the statue. The speaker identifies himself with Horus and the "loving son" and speaks of "embracing" the statue and "pressing" its mouth, all of which we have met with in the previous portion of the ritual and which clearly serve as intentional linkages between the two portions: the protective attitude of the speaker in the earlier portion, when he considered the possibility of violence committed against the statue, can thus also be viewed as implying a promise of action on behalf of the statue that is carried out in the present portion.[63] The pressing of the mouth also serves as a linkage with the portion of the ritual that will follow, as do two statements on which

63. This speech also contains a reference to the "mother" of the individual represented by the statue. This feature will be commented on below (see n. 65 below).

comment will be reserved for the moment: "How *heneg* is your mouth! I 'weigh' for you your mouth over against your bones!"

What, then, is the point of the presentation of the foreleg and the heart of the slaughtered bull, which the words of the last utterance identify as the effective moment when the opening of the statue's mouth, and thus its quickening, is effected? From observations already made, the reader is likely already to have inferred the answer. With the presentation of the foreleg and the heart,[64] the statue is endowed with physical strength (*khepesh*) and consciousness, the essential attributes of individual life.

But the full significance of this presentation goes beyond the force of language alone, however much language might be thought to accomplish in the charged atmosphere of ritual. It has been shown by laboratory experiment that the freshly severed foreleg of a bull, at a temperature just above seventy degrees fahrenheit, will exhibit spontaneous muscle contractions and tremors for up to twenty minutes and that these could continue to be induced artificially for up to two hours after the slaughter of the bull by such means as percussion with an instrument or even stimulation with a finger (see Schwabe 1986: 150 and Schwabe et al. 1989: 9–11). The scientific reason for this is that muscle enzymes continue to produce adenosine triphosphate (ATP) for some time after the limb is excised (see Schwabe et al. 1989: 12–13), but to an ancient Egyptian, who of course would not have known this, the phenomenon would have seemed like "magic." Now, the representations of the presentation, as is typical of Egyptian art, are quite antiseptic: a man is shown calmly extending a neat foreleg—in fact, an outsized *khepesh*-hieroglyph—to the statue. But when we consider the reality—a twitching, writhing mass of "live flesh," blood streaming from its severed end (and it is this end that is pressed to the mouth of the statue!)—a new dimension is added to our appreciation of the ritual's preoccupation with the theme of violence.

It was noted above that the Opening of the Mouth ritual did not serve as a "first awakening" of the statue that would be continued by the daily awakening to the cult attention it was intended to enjoy. Considering metaphors that might easily be derived from human existence, one could wonder whether it was a birthing ritual, like the one attested from Mesopotamia. But now that we have seen the statue quickened by endowing it with physical strength and consciousness derived from a slaughtered bull, we can see that it is not. The fact that the verb *mesi* that is used for the crafting of a statue can also mean 'to give birth' or sometimes even refers to male engendering (see Erman and Grapow 1971: 2.137–38) probably has no special weight here. At best, we can note that since the result of the fashioning of a statue was something that resembled a living creature, the technical processes that resulted in the finished object were thought somehow to be analogous to the process of procreation. However, if we were to go so far as to

64. The word *ib* is used for 'heart' in the daily cult ritual, while the Opening of the Mouth ritual employs *haty*. Both terms can be used for the heart as the seat of thought and emotions, while of the two, it is *haty* that tends to be employed to express the specific connotation of the heart as a physical organ, which is especially appropriate to the sacrificial context here. On the nuances of meaning of the words for 'heart', see Piankoff 1930: 10–13 and Long 1986: 484–85.

wonder whether the use of the verb *mesi* might imply that the manufacturing process was once completed by a birthing ritual that was later replaced by the present ritual, we would be in a hopelessly speculative area.[65] What needs to be stressed is that the essential processes by which cult statues were thought to be quickened in the Egyptian and Mesopotamian rituals, as the extant texts stand, were profoundly different.

* * * * *

The ensuing section of the ritual is concerned primarily with the touching of the mouth of the statue with various objects. The first is the *netjerty*, called by other names as well in the preserved versions (there is no certainty whether this variance is deliberate or a matter of scribal confusion; see Otto 1960: 2.80), and the accompanying utterance contains the statement that the mouth of the individual (as represented by the statue) is opened "that he may go and speak personally (literally, 'bodily', quite in keeping with the idea of the statue as physical object) to the Great Ennead in the House of the Prince, which is in Heliopolis." This is material that is strictly appropriate only to the funerary realm and would presumably have been absent from the ritual when performed on cult statues or replaced by a statement about creative utterance such as we have seen in the daily cult ritual. The material is also quite old and can be traced back to the specifically royal funerary ritual of the Pyramid Texts, where it refers to the need of Horus to plead his case for legitimate award of the kingship to him rather than to his brother, the evil Seth. This material is pre-Osirian (see Griffiths 1960: 67–68), and it has been demonstrated that its inclusion in the royal burial ritual, which includes the recrowning of the king at the inauguration of his afterlife, recalls a procedure in real life in which the legiti-

65. A reference to a mother in this part of the text was alluded to above. Between the statement "I am your loving son! I open for you your mouth!" and the cryptic statement with which the section concludes is inserted "who unites him with his mother who weeps for him, who unites him with the one who unites (herself) with him." The grammar is quite awkward because of the shift to the third person ("him" instead of "you"), and this as well as the reference to weeping suggests that the statement is a secondary insertion, intended to make the passage more appropriate to the context of a funerary statue; in this connection it should be remembered that all our preserved versions of the ritual are concerned with statues intended for the funerary realm. (Goyon 1972: 123 n. 4 has also noted that this material seems to be a secondary insertion, though he takes it as a "gloss.") While the mention of a mother can be taken to imply a birth, this is no way makes the ritual a birthing ritual. Additionally, there are difficulties in identifying the mother. A reference to a mother is not always appropriate in the temple realm. While some deities were assigned mothers (such as those of the Ennead, which was structured into generations; or Horus, son of Isis; or the child deities of triads), this was not universally the case. Moreover, since most persons do not predecease their parents, a reference to a natural mother is also not appropriate to the funerary realm, unless—as is not impossible in this highly unclear context—the reference is to the individual joining his already deceased mother in the afterlife. However, we might also consider the possibility that the reference is to a female divinity—perhaps to the "great female falcon" present at this stage in the ritual and here considered a mourner, a role we have noted that she can play, or perhaps to a goddess who will receive the deceased in a nurturing and thus motherly way, such as the Beautiful West, who personifies the cemetery, or Nut, who will receive the deceased for a celestial afterlife in the company of the sun-god Re during the daytime or the stars at night.

macy of the individual about to be crowned was affirmed, if need be, against the rival claims of a pretender (see Anthes 1954; Lorton 1979: 462). After the Old Kingdom, when the royal burial ritual passed into the private sphere, there also arose a concept of a Judgment of the Dead, both royal and private, by moral standards, as a prerequisite for the afterlife, and it was possible to attach this new concept to the older textual material (see Griffiths 1980: 3): in short, the allusion is to the Judgment of the Dead. However, it needs to be noted that this ritual, like the daily cult ritual, culminates in an offering, so that allusions to the ability to speak are understandable but secondary. The primary purpose of opening the mouth in these rituals is to consume food in the form of offerings, which was the prime requisite for continuing life for gods and deceased persons, just as it was for living persons.[66]

In the next scene, the mouth is touched with an implement called "great-of-magic" (evidently a staff of some sort, rather than an artisan's implement; see Otto 1960: 2.19–20), after which there follow scenes of obscure intent involving a "noble" (mention of "his mother who mourns him" occurs again at this point), actors called "he who is in the front" and "he who is in the following of Horus," and artisans once again. In the first scene, the "great-of-magic" instrument calls to mind a royal crown called "great-of-magic," as a result of which material that was originally royal occurs at this point. There also occur here two statements mentioning death that could only be appropriate to funerary rather than temple statues: "beware lest he die" (the addressee is uncertain; the goddess Nut, here assimilated to the "great-of-magic" crown, has been alluded to in this utterance, but there follow statements in the second-person masculine singular), and "May you exercise your protection of life for N., your protection being behind him for

66. The dependence of a local god upon the "largesse" of the community of worshipers in his village is an indubitably primitive concept that entails an inherent inconsistency with more sophisticated concepts of the relationship between an actual deity and some part of his divine essence that resides and is manifest in a statue of him in one or more locales; Jacobsen's (1987: 17–18) remarks concerning Mesopotamian deities in this regard are equally true for Egypt. But it was easy for the tradition of a primitive offering cult to be continued on the principle of inherent religious conservatism, and because it is hardly plausible that the minds of intelligent people were not inquiring, we can easily suppose that cult offerings came to be regarded as symbolic of a positive intent toward deities who did not literally need them to survive and even that the gods required such service from humankind as a prerequisite for their own reciprocal beneficence toward man. The latter valuation of the cult as something not needed but required is clearly attested in Mesopotamia; see thus a statement in a text translated by Speiser (1955: 68). There is also an Egyptian text that has to be understood as implying this valuation. In the Amarna Period, King Akhenaten concentrated his attention on the worship of the sun-disk and withdrew royal patronage from the traditional cults; according to the Restoration Stela of Tutankhamun, which commemorates the return to traditional beliefs and cult patronage after Akhenaten's death, the temples and their cults were abandoned. The Egyptians, however, did not believe that their deities had died of starvation in the meanwhile: rather, the text states that Egypt was sick at home and her foreign ventures unsuccessful, because the gods "turned their backs" on the land. Tutankhamun restored the temples, furnishing them with new cult statues and reestablishing the daily offering cult, so that the gods would, in the words of the stela, "protect Egypt." For a translation of the text of the Restoration Stela, see Wilson 1955b.

the sake of life, so that he will not die!" (addressed to Shu, god of light and air, who could conceivably be the addressee of the earlier statements as well). Are these purely insertions intended for the funerary realm, or could the mentions of death be rewordings of statements stressing life that occurred in the ritual as it was applied to cult statues? It has gone unnoticed by previous commentators that this group of scenes has a rough parallel in the Pyramid Texts (utterances 642–50, Sethe 1910: 443–49). Without offering a full translation here, I raise the following salient points:

1. In the Pyramid Texts material, Shu is asked to protect the beneficiary of the ritual, as here, while mention is also made of Nut as the sky who "bears him alive every day like Re" (it was noted above that the "mother" who appears at this point in our text may be Nut);
2. the assumption of the "great-of-magic" crown is stressed, as here;
3. references are made to the *ka* in both texts: in the Pyramid Texts we find "may your *ka* stand among [the gods] . . . a *ka* is raised up behind you (or: "in your following") and "[Oh Osiris] N., you are the *ka* of all the gods. Horus having protected you, you have become [his *ka*]," while in the Opening of the Mouth ritual we have "you have become the *ka*s of all the gods, may you appear as King of Upper and Lower Egypt, assuming power over the gods, lord of their *ka*s." Note also in the Pyramid Texts, "Oh Osiris, N., Geb having given you [all the gods of Upper and Lower Egypt, may they raise] you up, may you be powerful through [them]" (on the restoration, which is based on a version discovered after Sethe's edition was published, see Faulkner 1969: 1.267–68); and
4. the Pyramid Texts at this point make, not negative references to death, but positive references to life: "Oh that Osiris N. [. . .] that he may live," "His mother the sky bears him alive every day like Re," and "His son provides this N. with life." Additionally, these utterances of the Pyramid Texts make references to the carrying and lifting of the deceased king into the sacred *henu*-boat of the god Sokar by Horus and the divine figures called the "children" or "sons" of Horus and to the protection of the deceased king by the gods Geb and Horus.

These respective ritual materials give every appearance of being related, even though we are not able to trace the history of the textual transmission. In the Opening of the Mouth ritual, the celestial role of Nut is deemphasized in favor of her identification with the crown, and she is otherwise demythologized as the "mother." This point leads to the suggestion that otherwise obscure scenes in the Opening of the Mouth ritual, involving actors bearing nonmythical designations, are a demythologized version of the Pyramid Texts' reference to the help afforded the deceased by the various divine figures or at the very least of material derived from or bearing a close conceptual relationship to material that we have found in utterances 642–50 of the Pyramid Texts. There is yet a further connection to be made between the material from the Pyramid Texts and the Opening of the Mouth ritual that will be noted below. What is important for our purposes here is that we have found conceptually related material containing affirmations of life without references to death (and in a funerary context!), from which we can conclude with some degree of probability that the references to death at this point in our preserved versions of the Opening of the Mouth ritual constitute a special wording that was occasioned by their application to funerary statues. After yet another obscure scene, the "loving son" is brought into the workshop, in the words of text, "to see the 'god' " (in the funerary context, the "god" is the statue of the deceased father), and the statue is addressed with the words, "Oh, N., I bring you your loving son, that he may open your mouth!" It seems that it is only at this point in the ritual that the surviving son who is responsible for executing the funeral arrangements had the opportunity to see the statue for the first time and, concomitantly, assumed a role in the ritual.[67]

The "loving son," according to the visual material, now wears the panther skin; as noted above (p. 154 n. 47), scholars have offered differing interpretations of the relationship between the functions of the *sem*-priest and the role of the "loving son." The son touches the mouth of the statue with two implements in quick succession, a chisel called *medjedfet* made of iron[68] and a representation of a finger made of electrum.[69] Although the term *medjedfet* is likely to be based on a root *djedef* (see Otto 1960: 2.20), the accompanying utterance evidently makes a pun on it and the verb *medjed* 'to press' in the statements "Oh, N.! I press for you your mouth" and "N., Horus presses for you your mouth!" The utterance also includes "How *heneg* is your mouth! I weigh for you your mouth over against your bones!"

In the following scene, the *sem*-priest touches the statue's mouth with his own little finger, an act he performed earlier in the artisans' scenes. It may not be too fanciful to suppose that the finger implement of the preceding scene is a "double" of his human

67. An impression might arise here that the person whose statue is the object of the ritual is deceased and that his son, naturally enough, is now coming for the statue. This cannot be correct, however, for it is commonly understood that whenever possible, individuals secured their tombs and tomb furnishing, including statues, during their lifetimes. Bolshakov (1991) has pointed out instances where it is clear that a person's mortuary cult began during his lifetime, which he states (p. 217) to have been possible upon completion of the decoration of the tomb walls. The latter point does not take into consideration the undecorated tombs that have survived, and it should be clear enough that in tombs, just as in temples, it was the statue (or more strictly speaking, the life force in the statue) that was the beneficiary of the cult offerings. Thus, neither when the son designated to oversee the funeral and the mortuary cult appears at this point in the ritual, nor when the statue is carried to the tomb at the end of the ritual, are we necessarily to infer that the individual is deceased. Anticipating the discussion below (p. 181 n. 75), I would conclude from all this that just as the presence of some part of the life force of a deity in a cult statue in a temple did not, for the Egyptians, contradict the living reality of the god or goddess, the same was true of humans.

68. There continues to be confusion in scholarship about the words *bia* and *hemty*, now taken by most to be 'iron' and 'copper', respectively: thus, Otto (1960: 2.20 and 91) renders the term *bia* in our text as 'copper', while Goyon (1972: 130) takes it as 'iron'. It is possible that both terms originally referred to copper, with *bia* being used exclusively for 'iron' only in the New Kingdom. This evident change in usage might seem surprising, but it seems that *bia* originally referred not to copper exclusively but rather to the overall results of the copper-refining process, which yields both copper and droplets of iron when the ore contains hematite (see Nibbi 1977: esp. 60).

69. Electrum is a naturally occurring alloy of gold and silver (for a discussion, see Gale and Stos-Gale 1981).

finger, at least in terms of its ritual function, though in fact the implement represents both the index and middle fingers (see Goyon 1972: 100). The accompanying utterance features the exclamations noted before. Here, however, the verbal material juxtaposes the word *heneg* with a sort of label *hemag*, written with a scale as its determinative, while the word 'weigh' (*mekha*) is accompanied by a label *mekha* 'scale'.

In the three scenes that follow, the *sem*-priest employs an object called *nemes*, the 'companion' employs an object called *abet*, and the "loving son" employs four *abets*. The objects themselves are obscure: the *nemes* could be a cloth and the *abet* an implement for polishing (see Otto 1960: 2.20–21). The utterances that accompany the first and third of these scenes specify that the mouth and eyes of the statue are being cleaned at this point, an act that seems to recapitulate the end of the manufacturing process. This inference is supported by the fact that there are no further repetitions of the exclamations "How *heneg* . . . ," and so forth, in the new (as opposed to the repeated) scenes that follow.

In the next scene, the *sem*-priest touches the mouth of the statue with an implement called *pesesh-kef*, a sharp instrument whose end is shaped like the tail of a fish.[70] The accompanying utterance is "I make firm (*semen*) for you your jaws (*arty*), they being split (*pesesh*)." As just noted, the imitation of the manufacturing process seems to be complete, and the present ritual gesture and its utterance give every impression of having a confirming function, assuring that the mouth will be able to function by the opening and closing (the "splitting") of the jaws. It was noted earlier that the introduction of a sacrificial goat (*ar*) is connected in its more immediate context with a pun on the word *ar* 'approach'; at this juncture, we are obliged to recognize that the goose (*semen*), which also appears there, and the goat clearly prefigure, through puns, the wording of this scene. The juxtaposition of the goose and the goat in a clearly secondary connection to the slaughtered bull, while the punning roots *semen* and *arty* in the present scene are another clear indication of the intentionality and artifice behind the tapestry of the ritual. It only needs to be added that the verb *semen*, rendered here simply as 'to make firm', has its own wide range of meanings. It can mean 'to make lasting, enduring', which is appropriate to the function of a statue that is to enjoy the benefit of a cult in perpetuity, but it also has a nuance 'to confirm' (for convenience, see Faulkner 1962: 228)[71] that is appropriate to the interpretation of the scene offered here: with the ritual

70. On the implement, see Otto 1960: 2.16–17; Graefe 1971; the discussions cited by Schulman 1984: 174 n. 53; and Roth 1992. The last-mentioned study takes the appearance of the *pesesh-kef* in a ritual to imply the concept of birthing, while my analysis here takes an essentially opposite tack. It should be borne in mind that although this knife or knife-like implement could have been used to cut an umbilical cord, as Roth argues, this need not have been its only use, either in daily life or in rituals.

71. As should be evident from context, a nuance of immobility that unfortunately attaches to the English "make firm" is not present in the Egyptian word. The nuances 'to make lasting' and 'to confirm (the validity of something)' are simultaneously present in the word *semen* when it is used in the sense 'to enforce' laws (on this usage, see Lorton 1986: 54–55).

"resumé" of the manufacturing process completed, the present scene "confirms" the ability of the statue (or more specifically, its mouth) to perform its intended function.

In the next scene, the *sem*-priest presents a container of grapes to the statue, and the accompanying utterance refers to the presentation as the "Eye of Horus." The word for grapes, *iarut,* is written in such a way that it is clearly intended to pun on *iret* 'Eye' and *iri* 'to make, do'. Since the function of the statue's mouth is to consume cult offerings, the presentation of the grapes can be seen as encapsulating two main purposes of the ritual: it endows the statue with its ability to perform (*iri*) this function, while the grapes prefigure the offerings (*iret,* ritual 'act' as we have seen it in the daily cult ritual, also mythologized as *iret* 'Eye' of Horus) that are to be made later.

In the ensuing scene, the *sem*-priest presents an ostrich feather (*shu*) to the statue. The accompanying utterance states, "Take to yourself the Eye of Horus! Your face will not be empty/deprived (*shu*) because of it!" The pun is obvious, and the mention of the statue's "face" is consonant with the focus of the ritual. We cannot help but note that the presentation of the grapes and the ostrich feather somehow form a pair, but the precise intention behind the juxtaposition of the two does not seem to be recoverable.[72]

The next scene, which occurs in only two of the preserved versions, repeats two earlier elements of the ritual: the donning of the panther skin by the *sem*-priest and the "loving son's" presentation of the four *abet*s. The juxtaposition confirms the already-noted ambiguity in the ritual functions of the *sem*-priest and the "loving son," but its occurrence at this juncture must remain mysterious. We may note, however, that the present group of scenes that begins with the *pesesh-kef* scene seems somehow intended to confirm the ritual validity of the scenes that precede and that it was the scene entailing the four *abet*s (polishing implements?) that was the culmination of the recapitulation of the manufacturing process. It can also be noted that the panther skin was transferred from the *sem*-priest (who is shown no longer wearing it) to the "loving son" just before the latter's scene involving the *medjedfet*-chisel and finger of electrum.

In the following scene, a small bowl of water is presented to the statue by the *sem*-priest. The accompanying utterance does not clarify whether the statue is to drink the water, in which case it could be connected with the presentation of the grapes, or whether the water is to wash the mouth of the statue, in which case the scene could be connected with the culmination of the manufacturing process. There could, of course, be an intentionally ambiguous invocation of both of these possibilities; the insertion of the preceding, repeated scene in two of the versions suggests that at least some of the ancients preferred the latter of the two alternative interpretations.

Finally, in the scene that follows, the "loving son" is escorted out of the workshop; in the ensuing portion of the ritual, it is again the *sem*-priest who is wearing the panther skin.

72. Otto (1960: 2.21) notes that the feather may imply a fan, and this in turn could entail the idea of the statue's being able to breathe. Unfortunately, the inference is not confirmed by anything in the verbal or visual material of the ritual.

This section of the ritual has presented its fair share of obscure and puzzling features, some of which could be addressed at some length and some of which were best passed over quickly. The task that remains is to transcend the particulars and the obscurities and to render some account of the ultimate significance of this sequence of scenes. Comment on why they appear at just this point in the overall ritual is best reserved for the end of the discussion. What concerns us here is their more immediate contextual meaning.

It should be clear enough to the reader that what this portion of the ritual was intended to accomplish is somehow expressed by the oft-repeated "How *heneg* is your mouth! I 'weigh' your mouth over against your bones!" Unfortunately, however, the meaning of these exclamations is quite obscure. The word *heneg* is not otherwise attested in Egyptian texts, so that its meaning is unknown. Intratextually, we have noted that a nearly equally obscure word *hemag*, evidently meaning 'scale', is once connected with *heneg*. Otto (1960: 2.94) has cautioned that this ancient "gloss" could well involve a secondary interpretation, but we in fact cannot discount the possibility that the meaning of *heneg* is conceptually connected with that of *mekha* 'weigh' in the accompanying exclamation. Referring to the same scene that includes these labels but taking quite a different tack and relying on extratextual evidence, Helck (1967: 34–35) has suggested that the words entail puns on red-colored materials used in the manufacturing process: *heneg*/*hemag* can pun on *hemaget* 'carnelian', while *mekha*/*mekhat* (the latter "label" written in some versions as *kha* or as *khem*) could pun on *mekhenet* 'jasper'. While an interpretation along the lines of "how red are your lips" is quite tempting in context, there are obstacles to its acceptance. First, it is based on "labels" that might themselves be secondary, as Otto warns, and second, the latter of the proposed puns is clearly somewhat far-fetched. We would thus best content ourselves with the observation of Goyon (1972: 123 n. 5) that *heneg*, whatever its precise meaning, represents a positively-valued condition or function of the mouth that results from the ritual acts performed on it.

While the second exclamation is more amenable to translation than the first, its actual meaning is equally unclear. Attempts to assign *mekha* 'to weigh' the metaphorical meaning 'to join' (so Otto) or 'to readjust' (so Goyon) are ad hoc and unsatisfactory. "I join/readjust your mouth to your bones" might recall the concern we have encountered in the daily cult ritual that the head be connected to the "bones," that is, the skeleton. But while the concept makes sense when the entire head is entailed, what sense is there in thinking of the mouth alone as joined to the bones? An object can be "weighed" for the purpose of assigning it "value," and the exclamation might thus be taken as meaning "I weigh/give weight/value your mouth over against your bones (i.e., the rest of the body)," though with no certainty as to whether the preposition rendered neutrally here as "over against" is to be taken as implying "more than" (a frequently attested meaning) or as implying only equal weight. However, this explanation is also ad hoc and speculative. The most we can say with certainty about the two exclamations is that they both serve to privilege the mouth, which is consistent with the purpose of the ritual.

If we must remain frustrated in our attempt to understand these statements, then we must turn to what is implicit in this portion of the ritual to account for its function.

It has already been noted that the employment of artisans' tools in these scenes, as well as the wiping of the mouth with the finger, serve to recall or recapitulate the actual manufacturing process. It was mentioned above that not every pun proposed by Helck in his provocative study of these scenes is equally plausible, but most of them are likely to be correct, and I see the significance of Helck's observations as a confirmation of this recollection of the statue's manufacture, in this instance by *encoding* it into the text through puns. Finally, Otto (1960: 2.22) has noted that while artisans' tools are employed in these scenes, the names that they are given are mostly not attested outside the text of this ritual. He concludes from this that these are not the names of the implements as tools of everyday use but rather special names that were applied to the tools for purposes of the ritual or very old names that had long since been replaced by others. The symbolic touching of the statue's mouth with artisans' tools that recall the making of the statue, the "encoding" of references to the physical materials of the manufacturing process into the text through puns, and the endowing of implements with alternative names are all clues pointing to the same conclusion. The handiwork of the artisans had produced an inert object that could serve as a representation or likeness of the individual for whom it was made. The basic thrust of this portion of the ritual, then, is to *transvalue* the manufacturing process into something of ritual effectiveness in quickening the statue by endowing it with it faculties, especially the ability to open its mouth. Since this transvaluation of the manufacturing process serves to privilege it, we again see a deep contrast with the Mesopotamian ritual, wherein the physical process of manufacture is ritually denied and a birthing process introduced to quicken the statue.

We have seen that at the end of the preceding portion of the ritual, the presentation of the foreleg and heart of the slaughtered bull is accompanied by the cryptic exclamations that typify—or at least seem more properly at home in—the portion of the ritual under consideration here. Whether based on this repeated verbal material or on more general thematic considerations (unfortunately, he is not explicit on this matter), Goyon (1972: 103) has noted that a connection can be made between these portions of the ritual, though he accords primacy to "the heart and the leg of the sacrificed animal, for which all the consecrated objects that are subsequently used to touch the openings of the head are merely substitutes." I would accord considerable importance to the connection that Goyon has established, while disagreeing strongly with his evaluation of its significance. The present portion of the ritual, with its transvaluation of the manufacturing process into a quickening process, is a solution to the problem of quickening inert matter that could theoretically stand on its own—there is nothing in the ritual itself to suggest that this material has a "secondary" or "substitute" status. By the same token, the presentation of the foreleg and heart of the sacrificed bull, endowing the statue symbolically with strength and consciousness, is an equally valid, though quite different, solution to the problem of quickening that can also hypothetically stand on its own. But while these solutions to the problem are hypothetically separable, they are in fact both present in the ritual, and more specifically, they are immediately juxtaposed to one another, a fact that demands that we view them as intentionally complementary solutions to the problem. The inclusion of the exclamations "How *heneg* is your mouth!

I 'weigh' your mouth over against your bones!" at the end of the preceding portion of the ritual thus serves not only as a clear textual linkage between the two portions but also as a clear indication that we are intended to understand them as a unity comprised of two elements of equal weight that embody complementary approaches to the central purpose of the ritual.

* * * * *

In the ensuing portion of the ritual, the *sem*-priest is once again clad in the panther skin, and we have essentially a repetition of the earlier material concerning the slaughtered bull, along with the goat and the goose. The only significant differences between the two portions of the ritual are first, that in the earlier version the bull is called an "Upper Egyptian male *nega*," while in the present portion he is called an "Upper Egyptian male *sheser*" in some preserved versions, while other versions change the specification to "Lower Egyptian"; and second, that the "great female falcon" of the earlier portion is here called the "lesser female falcon." If we were to follow Otto in viewing the ritual as an eclectic combination of elements from various sources that could and did result in repetitions of material in an almost accidental manner, we might view the differences just cited as secondary attempts to justify the repetition. We must, however, consider the alternative possibility that whatever the history of the ritual might have been, and regardless of whether or not the repetition of this material was original or secondary, what we meet with synchronically is informed by intentionality (what we have seen to this point certainly justifies taking this tack), and its compiler(s) intended it to be meaningful in the form that they imparted to it. In exploring this possbility, we must look at the differences just noted and then turn to the deeper significance they might be signaling.

The "great" and "lesser" female falcons are a scarcely veiled, demythologized reference to Isis and Nephthys, the sisters of Osiris (and of his murderer, Seth) who mourned their slain brother in this particular falcon form. But the references are indeed demythologized, and they are scarcely mourners here—this is not strictly funerary material. What is striking, of course, is that a complementary pair is involved, which invites us to consider the two appearances of the slaughtered bull material as expressing a deeper complementarity. The same is true of the "Upper Egyptian" and "Lower Egyptian" designations of the bull, though the variations in the textual evidence for the second occurrence render it unclear whether this added distinction is a secondary one, or whether there is simply some scribal confusion entailed. Perhaps the more significant distinction is the introduction of the term *sheser* to designate the bull in the second occurrence of the material. We have noted that there are puns in the material relating to the slaughtered bull, and that the word *sesh* 'to open' in the "falcon's" question "Is your mouth open now?" puns on the term *sesher* that we encounter here. But the fact that the punning cycle in this material cannot be completed until we encounter the word *sesher* at just this point is the clearest possible indication that the repetition is informed by intentionality and that the double occurrence of the material in some way indicates both a unity (as implied by the overall repetition) and a complementarity. But, turning now to the deeper level, how exactly are we to understand all this?

We must note here two juxtapositions within the overall ritual. One is the juxtaposition of the presentation of the foreleg and heart of the slaughtered bull with the material involving the touching of the mouth with various implements as complementary means of quickening the statue. The second is the juxtaposition of the second presentation of the foreleg and heart with the material shared with the daily cult ritual (adornment of the statue and, especially, offerings) that comprises most of the latter portion of the Opening of the Mouth ritual. These juxtapositions help us to understand an error on Otto's part, which, when recognized as such, facilitates an understanding of the repetition of the scenes involving the presentation of the foreleg and heart.

The repetition of the material is indeed a doubling, and Otto (1960: 2.103) is right in sensing that the ritual does not involve two slaughtered bulls but rather a double presentation stemming from a single slaughter, and, as noted above, the surface complementarities expressed in the text suggest a deeper complementary motive behind the doubling. Otto's mistake is in viewing the first occurrence of the presentation as a "first meal" for the statue (1960: 2.75), a mistake that was perhaps easy to make, given that he did not recognize the symbolic value of the foreleg and the heart. Taking the symbolic value into account, it is certainly true that the presentation could have had both meanings, the endowment of the statue with physical strength and consciousness and with it the ability to consume offerings and, at the same time, an actual or symbolic first meal. But the doubling of presentation suggests, in a very natural way, that these respective meanings are distributed between the two presentations in a complementary manner, an interpretation that is supported by the juxtapositions noted in the preceding paragraph. The fact that the quickening effect of the presentation of the foreleg and heart has its own complement in the quickening of the statue by touching its mouth with various implements (or, to put it another way, the insertion of the latter material between the two presentations) has the effect of delaying the second meaning of the presentation until its second occurrence. This interpretation is confirmed by the elaborate offering material shared with the daily cult ritual that occupies so many of the later scenes of the ritual. One could also approach the issue of the "first offering" by noting thematic linkages. The first real intimation of a food offering occurs after the quickening by means of artisans' implements, with the presentation of grapes; and by means of a pun that was noted, it is this presentation that first embodies the double sense of quickening effect and first offering. This simple presentation has further, progressively resounding, echoes in the second presentation of the foreleg and heart and in the subsequent, more elaborate offering.

* * * * *

In the preceding discussion, we have focused on the deeper meaning of each of the four main components of what is taken here to be the core of the Opening of the Mouth ritual, concentrating primarily on the intratextual evidence by way of a direct response to its content. Various linkages among the sections, which point to a larger *Gestalt*, have also been noted; for the most part, these need not be repeated here. What remains is to articulate the ways in which the four main portions of the ritual combine to comprise a comprehensible whole, informed by an overall intentionality.

The first and second portions of the ritual share the theme of violence. In the first, the idea of the manufacturing process as a violent physical assault is denied, while in the second, untamed natural violence is brought into the service of order. The second and third sections serve as complementary quickening processes. In the second, the foreleg and the heart endow the beneficiary of the ritual with physical strength and consciousness, while in the third, the manufacturing process is transvalued into one that is life-giving. A doubling, in which the implements of the third part in some sense substitute for the foreleg of the second part, has been noted as a conceptual means of establishing this complementarity. The third (with the presentation of grapes) and the fourth parts share the theme of "first offering" that finds its fullest expression in the more elaborate offering that occurs later in the ritual. Perhaps more significant is their shared function as respective complements to the first and second parts. This complementarity is especially clear in the repetition of the sacrificial materials of the second and fourth parts, where their separation by the third part enforces a separation of the two implicit functions of the sacrificial material, that is, as a quickening ritual and as a first meal. By the same token, the first part, which is concerned with the denial of a violent or negative aspect of the manufacturing process, finds its complement in the third part, which privileges the process by transvaluing it into a quickening ritual.

The observations made in the preceding paragraph imply a *Gestalt* whose articulation can be viewed in more than one way. For convenience, we shall label the four sections thus: (A) manufacturing process (denial of violence); (B) sacrificial material (subsuming of violence to the ordered purposes of humankind; quickening effect); (C) manufacturing process (quickening effect; first meal); and (D) sacrificial material (first meal). The progressive thematic linkages that we have noted allow us to express the relationships between the successive sections as

$$A \rightarrow B \rightarrow C \rightarrow D$$

At the same time, the thematic alternation between manufacturing process and sacrificial material, when considered as complementary approaches to the same problem, allow us to express the relationships as

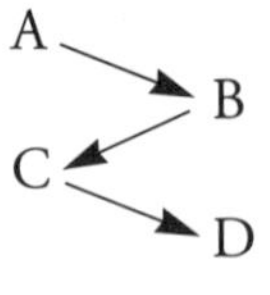

or as

$$\begin{cases} A \\ B \end{cases}$$
$$\begin{cases} C \\ D \end{cases}$$

But when the complementary aspects are viewed from another angle, the respective relationships between A and C, on the one hand, and B and D, on the other, can be expressed as A : C :: B : D or

that is, a chiastic relationship.

We can see, then, that the core of the ritual is indeed a *Gestalt* whose sections relate to one another by means of a richly elaborate set of associations. I stated at the outset of this discussion that literary analysis could serve to elucidate the ritual, but it would be anachronistic to view the ritual as simply a piece of literature wanting an explication of its subtext. The ritual is not really a literary text, of course, and we must recognize that it expresses beliefs that were sincerely held by the ancients. What we can experience as the intellectual satisfaction of a literary analysis surely resounded for them on the emotional level. This ritual, like the daily cult ritual, begins with purifications that established the sacred character of its space and time, creating a sort of "dream time" (to borrow an expression from the beliefs of Australian aborigines) transcending the realm of mundane concerns, in which the ritual acts and words could have their creative effect of bringing wishes or intentions to fulfillment. We should also bear in mind that there were probably many small ritual gestures required, as well as special intonation or cantillation of the words, to enhance the psychological experience of the participants. Thus, the act of intellection, which grasps how the ritual signifies, would have had for them the psychological and emotional effect of confirming the ritual's effectiveness: a material object (mummy, statue, etc.) exists, and in sacred space and time, it is quickened and transformed into the receptacle of a living essence.

* * * * *

The remainder of the ritual does not need very detailed comment here. The very next scene is a repetition of the scene in which the *netjerty*-adze was touched to the mouth of the statue. Otto (1960: 2.108) has noted that the repetition seems secondary, while serving to stress the completion of the opening of the mouth itself. In view of the preceding analysis, we must recognize that this additional element implies yet another structure in the ritual, insofar as its major portions deal either with the manufacturing process (artisans, implements) or the slaughtered bull:

manufacture → slaughter → manufacture → slaughter → manufacture

But a single scene ought not to have the same status as a portion of the ritual made up of several scenes, and this observation confirms the idea that the inclusion of this repeated scene is in some sense secondary. Our concentration on the *Gestalt* of the ritual indicates, however, an intention behind the insertion that goes beyond, though it does not contradict, Otto's suggested motive of finality: in returning to the theme of manufacture, the scene can be viewed as creating a structure in which the latter now frames, and in so doing, outweighs that of the slaughtered bull. The emphasis that is thus created is especially interesting for purposes of comparing the Egyptian ritual to the ritual attested from Mesopotamia where, as we have seen, the physical manufacture of the statue is ritually denied.

It is at this point that the concerns of the ritual turn to the adornment of the statue and elaborate offerings. Overall, this is material that is shared with—and one might easily suspect, borrowed from—the daily cult ritual. As already noted, a theme of "first offering," which began with the offering of grapes and continued with the second presentation of the foreleg and heart of the slaughtered bull, is here expanded into the first occasion of what is to become ongoing cult attention.

While the transport of the statue from the workshop to the shrine where it was to reside could easily have been a festive occasion, it is only nominally a part of the ritual itself. The process—or perhaps just its very beginning, still in the workshop—is represented by a single scene that begins with extremely brief utterances. The ritualist says to nine "companions," "Carry him on your arms!" The next statement is quite cryptic, and there is considerable variation in the preserved versions. The simplest version states, as translated by Otto (1960: 2.165), "The god comes! Beware, oh earth!" Goyon (1972: 178) does not translate the second exclamation but takes it to be a reference by title to a hymn that would have been recited at this point. Otto's translation makes no real sense, and we cannot be sure whether Goyon's suggestion is correct; in any event, what follows could not have been the hymn in question. It is a short address to the "children" or "sons of Horus," who are to carry their father (in the present context, the statue) so that he can take his place in the sacred *henu*-boat of the god Sokar. This utterance is interesting for several reasons.

First, its inclusion in this scene provides us with an illuminating juxtaposition of an unmythologized (carrying by the nine "companions") and a mythologized (carrying by the "sons of Horus") version of a ritual act. Second, we may note that not only the words of the utterance, which have some parallels in the Pyramid Texts (see Otto 1960: 2.166), but also the basic concepts they articulated, are quite old. After the Old Kingdom, the "sons of Horus" were regarded as patron gods of the canopic jars that contained the internal organs of the deceased, and they were thus brought into close connection with Osiris as prototype of the mummified deceased. The secondary nature of the latter connection is shown by their very name, which reveals an original connection with Horus (see Lorton 1985: 120), and in the Pyramid Texts of the Old Kingdom, they perform more generally helpful functions for the deceased (as here), including the performance of the Opening of the Mouth itself (see Mercer 1952: 36). From this we can see the antiquity not only of the material itself but of its association with this ritual. Finally, we also saw the concern with the *henu*-boat in the Pyramid Text materials that were cited above in a discussion of a sequence of scenes in the present ritual, and its occurrence in the mythologized material of the scene discussed here serves to confirm the appropriateness of the connection that was drawn above.

Direct ritual concerns mount again at the completion of the journey, when the statue is placed in its shrine, where, the text affirms, it will "live, prominent among the 'gods' (i.e., in the funerary realm, the other deceased), forever" (see Goyon 1972: 180, whose translation at this point is more accurate than Otto's). And with this, the ceremony is over.

Theology

In discussing the daily cult ritual, we saw that, in addition to *tut* 'statue', the cult statue could be called the *ba* or the *sekhem* of the deity, the first term meaning 'power that is manifest' or 'manifestation' and the second implying the 'empowerment' of the statue by some part of the divine essence that has entered into it. These are eloquent terms indeed, and in a very real sense they answer the question with which we are ultimately concerned here: how it is that the ancient Egyptians thought that their cult statues were something other than useless, inanimate objects. But Egyptian thinking could be complex, and of course there is more.

From time to time in the course of this chapter, we have noted that the animate force in the statue was some part of the divine essence. The essence in question, both of deities and of deceased humans in the case of mortuary statues, was the *ka*. Basically—and perhaps as most primitively—conceived, the *ka* was the 'vital essence' or 'life force' of an individual (see esp. Frankfort 1948: 62–63, 67; according to Schweitzer [1956: 14], this was first proposed by Erman in 1909), both in this life and the next, which was transmitted from generation to generation by the act of procreation: "He is your son, whom your *ka* has begotten for you," says a collection of teachings known as the Maxims of Ptahhotep (see Frankfort 1948: 67, and Schweitzer 33–36, for personal names that express the same idea). It is to the *ka* of the deceased that the food offerings were directed,[73] and though it is sparser, there is evidence from the New Kingdom on that this was true of divine offerings as well.[74] Thus, in a papyrus containing hymns to Amun that probably dates to late in the reign of Ramesses II, we find the statement, "The river flows downstream and the north wind, it travels upstream (the Nile flowed from south to north), making deliveries (i.e., offerings) to your *ka* of everything that exists" (see Gardiner 1905: 16). Again, a papyrus listing the benefactions of Ramesses III to the deities of Egypt contains, inter alia, the following statement addressed to Ptah, god of Memphis: "I appointed archers, bee-keepers, and incense-bearers, and I established steersmen for them to transport them for the collection of their annual imposts for your august treasury, so as to fill the storehouse of your temple with many things and double your offerings, in order to offer to your *ka*" (see the translations of Breasted 1906: 4.167; and Bleiberg 1988: 159). In a similar vein, the caption of an offering scene in the

73. Steindorff (1911: 155) notes that the phrase "for the *ka* of so-and-so" does not appear in the standard mortuary offering formula known as *hotep-di-nesut* until the Middle Kingdom. However, Schweitzer (1956: 82, with n. 12) has shown that the phrase is attested in the formula by the end of the Old Kingdom and that it is well attested outside the formula as well in this period (pp. 81–82).

74. There is also evidence that worship in general was directed to the *ka* of deity; for a convenient collection of some examples, see Lichtheim 1976: 91–109.

Greco-Roman period temple of Horus at Edfu states of the king, "delivering an offering to his august father, feeding his *ka* with millions of things" (see Chassinat 1918: 36, lines 1–2). In the Greco-Roman period temple of Hathor at Denderah, a row of priests is depicted carrying portable shrines containing the statues of deities in connection with the New Year's rite of the Union with the Sun Disk. For variety, the caption accompanying each priest contains a different verb for the act of carrying or lifting and a different expression for the shrine and its contents, as well as a different expression for the purpose of the activity. In one case, the caption has the priest say, "I lift up the shrine containing the divine *ka* of Uniter-of-the-Two-Lands (a form of the god Horus) to be suffused with his rays" (i.e., the rays of the sun-god; see Sauneron 1960: 75). Finally, we must note that the *serdab* (a small enclosed chamber) that contained the statue of the deceased in many Old Kingdom tombs was called the "house of the *ka*," an expression that could also be applied to the entire tomb and which, beginning with the New Kingdom, could refer to temples as well (see Schweitzer 1956: 84–85). The term just rendered "house" actually refers also to the landed estates that produced food to support its inhabitants (see Robichon and Varille 1936: 7–8; Schweitzer 1956: 86; and Goedicke 1970: 15 n. 10, 126, n. 11), which reinforces the connection between nourishment and the *ka*.

At this point, we should not be surprised to learn that there is an Egyptian word *kau* that means 'food'. The connection between the *ka* and food is well established in texts, as already noted (see also Frankfort 1948: 66 and Schweitzer 1956: 50–51), but the fact that our first attestations of the term *kau* do not occur until the Middle Kingdom has raised questions of etymology and origins. Both philological and artistic considerations can help us with the question of etymology. Philologically, the near certainty of an etymological connection between the terms is supported by the existence of other words that are also clearly related to the concepts of "vital essence" and procreation—*ka* 'bull', *kat* 'vagina', and *kat* 'work', the last including not only labor of the usual sort, both conscript labor performed as a kind of tax and craftsmanship but also the deadly 'work' of warfare (on these, which are all written with the hieroglyph for *ka* 'vital essence', see Faulkner 1962: 283). Iconographically, we may note two representations from Dynasty XVIII. In the tomb of Ahmose son of Ebana, which was decorated early in the dynasty, there is a scene in which the hieroglyph for *ka* rests on a standard before the deceased in the place where an offering table would normally appear, while the offerings themselves are depicted just beyond the *ka* (see fig. 6; the caption over Ahmose's outstretched arm reads "reaching for his *ka*"). A later representation pictures the offerings on their table before the deceased in rather the usual manner, but enclosed within the *ka* hieroglyph (see Frankfort 1948: fig. 21).

In the Old Kingdom, an expression for passing from this life was "going to one's *ka*." It is nearly certain that the meaning of the expression was that death caused a temporary separation of the individual and his or her *ka*, the two being reunited after mummification, at the funeral (see Greven 1952: 33 with n. 91). The depictions described above, besides providing a new "wrinkle" on an old idea, serve to reinforce the connection between the *ka* and food. As to which came first, it is a "chicken-and-egg" dilemma

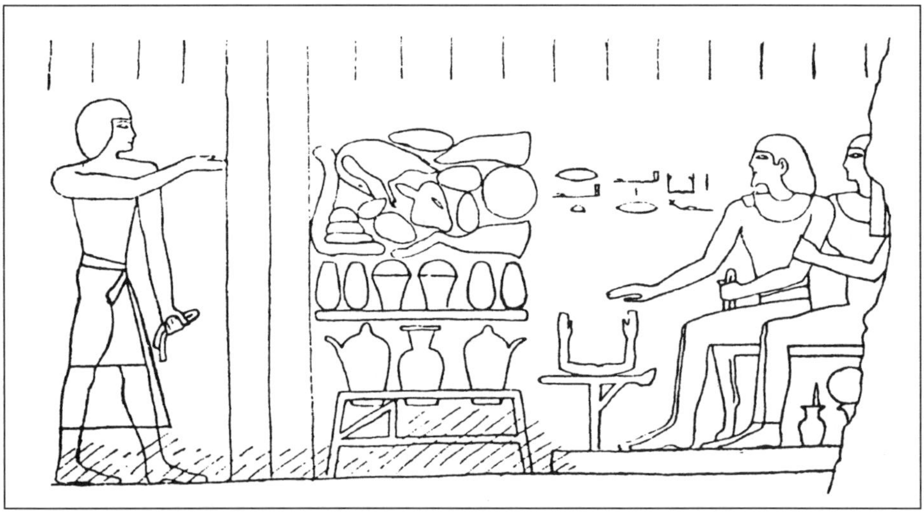

[Figure 6] FROM THE TOMB OF AHMOSE, son of Ebana, at El Kab. From Weigall 1911: 173.

that remains irresolvable, especially because we cannot be sure whether a relatively late date for our first attestation of a term might be just an accident of the preservation of evidence. Thus, we cannot really tell whether *kau* 'food' and the related terms are derived from *ka* 'vital force' or whether the latter is derived from one or another of them. The realm of art, however, comes to our rescue in assuring us that the conceptual connection between nourishment and *ka* was a very early one. An Archaic Period platter for receiving libations is composed of the hieroglyph for *ankh* 'life', embraced in what was to become a standard iconographical gesture of support and protection by the hieroglyph for *ka* (for a photograph, see Aldred 1965: 57: fig. 45). This marvellous piece, in which language literally is art, confirms that, from an early date, it was thought that life was sustained by the *ka*, which in its turn was sustained by nourishment (in this case, drink-offerings). All of this is an area that has not received enough attention in the scholarly literature as it relates to cult statues. But the evidence just cited is sufficient to show that just as in the case of mortuary statues, the *ka* of the deity—or some part of it, because more than one statue of a deity existed simultaneously—could be thought to quicken the cult statue.[75]

75. We have observed above (pp. 132–33) that shared problems found shared solutions in the temple and funerary realms: the similar functions of cult and mortuary statues have been noted by Simpson (1982: 267). Writing on Mesopotamian beliefs, Jacobsen (1987: 17) has offered the useful example of the sun-god Shamash and noted that he was incarnate in cult statues in a number of cities while at the same time visibly manifest in his heavenly body. What was true of Shamash and the rest of the Mesopotamian pantheon applies equally to the gods of Egypt, so that we are constrained to say

We can now proceed to the more abstract, and presumably secondary, thinking about *ka*. According to the Heliopolitan Cosmogony (an account of both the origin and the continuing nature of the world that is attested as early as the Pyramid Texts of the Old Kingdom), a part of the primeval chaos spontaneously emerged as the divine, absolute "being" of our cosmos. This being was a monad, and it differentiated itself, through three stages conceived of as generations of deities, into the cosmos; the group of deities thus created was the Ennead noted above (see the treatment of this idea by Allen 1988: 8–10). Most important for us here is the concept that when the divine absolute, Atum (whose name means 'the All'; see Allen 1988: 9), generated Shu and Tefnut, the first generation, he imparted his *ka*, or 'vital force', to them by embracing them, thus forming a *ka* hieroglyph with his outstretched arms (the Pyramid Text source for this has been much discussed; see esp. Otto 1955 and Allen 1988: 14). With this act, the life force of the absolute being that created, permeates, and is the cosmos became the life force of all that is part of it, all the generations of deities, kings, and ordinary humans.[76]

One might expect it to follow from this that *ka* is an independent, abstract force permeating the cosmos, like *Maat* 'cosmic order',[77] but this was not so. Life force, like being, might ultimately have been a monad, but with the creation of the world in which we live, when the "One" became the "many"—and here we must also bear in mind that this abstract idea was grafted onto a more "naive" concept of an individual's life force (see Schweitzer 1956: 38)—each deity and mortal came into possession of his or her

that it was some part of the divine essence—which could be expressed as *ka*—that was present in a cult statue. Interestingly, though most Egyptians contented themselves with one funerary statue, the same beliefs must have applied when individuals had more than one such statue (on this practice, see Schweitzer 1956: 87–88) and presumably also when, in addition to the statue in the tomb, an ancient Egyptian attempted to render his mortuary offering-cult more secure by dedicating a statue of himself to a temple (on this practice, see Simpson 1982: 267). In the Old and Middle Kingdoms, private individuals could have a *ka*-house in a temple (see Schweitzer 1956: 85). That these memorial chapels contained statues is confirmed by statements in royal decrees of the Old Kingdom and the First Intermediate Period (see Goedicke 1967: 81, 214).

In the funerary realm, there was yet another important concept that involved statues, that of *akh*, which means something like 'effective one'. While a passage in the daily cult ritual credits Amun with providing deities with *akh*, there is no special reason to think that the reference is to the same specific concept that is known from the funerary realm, as opposed to just the more basic sense of 'that which is effective', thus referring to rituals (an attested meaning of the root) and offerings. In fact, the passage occurs in a list in the ritual: "their *ka*(s) (which Moret suggests is a pun on *kau* 'food'), their *akh*(s), their provisions (i.e., offerings), and everything of theirs" (see Moret 1902: 128). In any event, this is not a productive concept in the theology of cult statues; for the funerary realm and its statues, see the studies by Demareae (1983), Friedman (1985), and Schulman (1986).

76. See Greven 1952: 15–19, 25. Some of the passages from the Pyramid Texts that she cites refer to deceased royal predecessors, however, rather than deities (see Redford 1986: 137). I also do not agree with her treatment of divine and royal *ka*s as constituting a conceptual nexus quite different from the one pertaining to the rest of mankind; there are important similarities as well, particularly in the funerary realm.

77. Frankfort (1948: 65–66) suggests that the plural form *kau* could function in this abstract sense.

own *ka*. Indeed, it is interesting to note that the term itself can even take on shades of meaning such as 'will', 'personality', and 'mood' (see Frankfort 1948: 67; Schweitzer 1956: 79–80; and Faulkner 1962: 283), which show how intimately the concept was connected to the individual.

What relationship existed between the concepts of *ba* and *ka*, in both the funerary and the temple realms, is a problem. No satisfactory explanation has yet been offered, and for lack of very early evidence, perhaps ultimately none can be.[78] Nevertheless, a suggestion, albeit a speculative one, will be offered here in the hope that it might lend some clarity to the discussion. Perhaps the two concepts developed in prehistory in different parts of the land, each indicating a kind of ghost-like existence after death or a supernatural being; whether either concept was linked to cult statues by the end of prehistory is unknowable. The forging of a single state in the Nile floodplain was evidently followed by a process of cultural homogenization, including religious belief and practice. Under these conditions, it is easy to suppose that because *ba* and *ka* were different lexical roots and thus entailed concepts that partly overlapped and partly complemented one another, neither prevailed at the expense of the other but, rather, both were maintained in a relationship that was evidently less uncomfortable for the ancients than it is for us.

At this point, let us return to the rituals that were treated above (see the section on Ritual Texts, pp. 130–79). In the daily cult ritual—after the stages of waking to the light of dawn, arousal of self-consciousness, confirmation of physical well-being, and affirmation of power (using the terms *ba* and *sekhem*)—it is at this point that the god's *ka* is first stressed. The aroma of food mixed with that of incense is employed to nourish the *ka*, just before this stress occurs.

The situation is quite different in the Opening of the Mouth ritual. Bearing in mind that our preserved examples all stem from the funerary realm, there are statements here and there in the text in which it is simply taken for granted that the deceased will have a *ka* in the afterlife. These occur both before and after the quickening of the statue, and significantly, there is no statement to the effect that, "*Now* the *ka* is in the statue." Yet the *ka* somehow did enter the statue, which could even happen during the lifetime of the individual (see n. 67 above). It follows from these observations that, for the Egyptians, in some way *ka* was divisible without diminishment. We never find a suggestion in any Egyptian text that a deity or human had any less life force because of what we have been calling "some part" of it was in a cult statue, nor is there any suggestion that the *ka* in a statue was anything less than a whole *ka*. This seems quite abstruse, but the statement quoted above, "he is your son, whom your *ka* has begotten for you," suggests that the notion is derived from practical, everyday observation: just as whole life is passed along from generation to generation, without diminishment of the life force of either the older or the new generation, so life force of an individual (divine or human) can pass into statues.

78. The discussion by Frankfort (1948: 64) suffers, in my view, from its forced attempt to find a contrast between the two concepts by asserting an impersonal nature of the *ka*.

* * * * *

As it happens, there is only scattered textual information about the relationship between deities and their cult statues, apart from the words of the rituals already considered. Without making any claim of being exhaustive, I will cite relevant text passages that are known to me. They will be presented in chronological order, except for the following, which is discussed first because of its special interest.[79]

At the temple of Hibis at el Khargeh oasis, a hymn to Amun-Re carved in the reign of Darius (521–486 B.C.E.) states,

> . . . who made (*iri*) the gods, who built (*qedi*) those who were built, who nursed those who were nursed, Chnum (*Chenem*), who made (*iri*) those who were modeled (*chenem*), wise one excellent of being, intelligent one, lord of those who are, who began all existence . . . who made great his image (*sšm*) to exalt his beauty, who fashioned (*nebi*) his image (*qi*) according to his desire, he having graced it with the grace of his breath, his respect being its respect, awe of him being greater than all the (other gods),[80] he having created (*qema*) himself, he having created (*qema*) his self, having begotten (*setji*) himself as the great image (*tut*). . . ." (Davies et al. 1953: pl. 32, middle register, lines 6–10; for translations, see Assmann 1975: 294–95 and Cruz-Uribe 1988: 126–27).

This passage contains most of what is in the passages to follow, but the material is handled in a particularly artful manner. We can clearly see that Amun-Re is here cast in the

79. In addition to the concepts in the passages to be discussed here, it is possible that textual material in the Greco-Roman period temple at Esna distinguishes between *seshta* 'mystery' in reference to the hidden, celestial form of a deity, and *kheperu* 'form', referring to the deity's perceptible aspect (see Sauneron 1982: 12). It should be noted, however, that Sauneron presents this interpretation as uncertain and that he does not explicitly identify *kheperu* with cult statues, though the latter is an attested usage.

80. For 'his respect being its respect', what seems to be a corrupt passage is taken here as *feqauef em feqauef.* The translation of this and the following 'awe (*shefyt*) of him greater than all the (other) gods' are inevitably inexact. The passage does not describe the here and now, when humankind feels respect for and awe of Amun-Re, but rather the process of creation, when the god establishes himself as the source of these reactions. On this nuance of the term *shefyt*, which in nonreligious contexts can even take on the connotation of a 'legal right' (which must be 'respected') see Lorton 1974: 132–36.

Earlier in the passage, where 'excellent of being (*wen*)' is followed by 'who began all existence (*kheper*)', an important ontological statement is made. The verb *wenen* 'to be' indicates existence "at all," while the verb *kheper* 'to come into being, to become' is used in religious texts to indicate the dynamic mode of being of creation, in which individual beings pass into and out of existence (see Allen 1988: 25). Here, the text alludes to the emergence of the creator-god (originally Atum, here replaced by Amun-Re) from the watery chaos of Nun, when he therefore 'was' (*wen*) and then to the process of self-differentiation (*kheper* 'becoming') by which he made himself into the cosmos (it was noted at the beginning of this chapter that Egyptian religious thought was pantheistic), which began with his creation of the deities Shu and Tefnut, that is, air and moisture, which 'began' *kheper*, that is, the state of dynamic being of the cosmos. This allusion echoes a much earlier statement in a text of the Middle Kingdom, where Atum is said to create Shu and Tefnut 'when he was (*wen*) one, when he became (*kheper*) as three' (that is, by turning himself into two further deities without losing his own identity, the one god became three; see de Buck 1938: 39).

role of ultimate source of creation and being, that is, the role of Atum that was discussed above. Here, however, in the first part of the passage, an important word for this creative act (*qema*) is preceded by the basic word for 'to make, do' (*iri*) and two verbs (*qedi, chenem*) that normally describe the work of artisans. And, when the verb *qema* is finally introduced, combined with a sexual metaphor (there is nothing unusual in this, in Egyptian thought), the result, remarkably enough, is the god as 'Great Image' (*tut*), a common word for cult statues that we have seen in the rituals. But the "image" is not presented as the result of a drawn-out manufacturing process nor is it really an "image" in the sense of "representation" that our word implies, as much as a "model." What is described is the instant of self-creation (commonly called "the first moment" in religious texts) in which the divine Absolute appeared and began to "unfold" itself as the cosmos that we perceive with our senses (for an Egyptian text that concentrates on this moment, see Lorton 1977b), while the creator is called an "image" in the reverse sense that what he creates is an image of him. Thus, in the daily cult ritual, Amun is called "*tut* who made their (i.e., the gods') *ka*s" (see Moret 1902: 126; see also pp. 128, 130), "divine *tut* who came into being in the first moment, when no god existed and no name of anything was known" (see p. 129), and "*tut* of the *ka*s of all the gods" (see p. 130; on *tut* 'image' with the meaning 'model, example', see Kaplony 1966). The temple of Hibis is unique, in that it was somehow intended to be a temple of all of the gods of Egypt, considered as aspects of Amun-Re, with approximately 650 deities represented there (see Cruz-Uribe 1989: 50–52), and the artfulness of the scribe is well suited to the context of the temple: by his choice of words, we are led to understand this earlier part of the passage on two levels as referring both to creation itself and to the cult statues of the temple. The phrase 'to exalt his beauty' not only calls to mind the idea of a divine epiphany in the temple in the form of the god's presence in the statue but is, more specifically, the technical expression for a deity's public appearance in a festival procession (see Erman and Grapow 1971: 1.383).

We had noted earlier in this chapter that the Egyptians placed great emphasis in their texts on the physical manufacture of their cult statues. This text shares with those to follow the characteristic of ignoring the human manufacture of these statues, attributing their creation instead to a deity. But what is unique to this text is its explicit crediting of the presence of deities on earth, in the person of their cult statues, to divine will and divine grace.

A papyrus from the reign of Ramesses II contains the earliest passages in the group considered here. In one, Amun is described as "fashioning (*hem*) himself, none knowing his shape (*qi*), goodly nature who came into being as the sacred, secret image (*bes*)[81] who built (*qed*) his images (*seshemu*), who himself created (*qema*) himself, goodly power

81. The term *bes* is attested in reference to the form of the Absolute in the "first moment" of his self-creation, which is unknowable to humankind (see Faulkner 1962: 34). The root also has connotations of 'entering' and 'revealing' (see p. 34), which suggests that like *tut* above, it has a double meaning, indicating that the creator-god is the model of his own creation, referred to here as "his images"; this idea is quite explicit in a text of Ptolemy XII cited below.

(*sekhem*) who made good his desire (*ib*),[82] who joined his seed with his body to bring his 'egg' into being within his secret self, being (*kheper*) who came into being (*kheper*), image (or 'model', *tut*) of what is fashioned (*mesut*)" (compare the translation of Allen 1988: 49). Here, seven centuries before the text just considered, we see its concepts and some of its vocabulary already in place: Amun's creation is described in terms that also apply to the cult statues in which the deities he created are manifest in the human realm. It is also interesting to see creation attributed to an act of volition (*ib*), though this concept is not explicitly related to cult statues, as in the text from the Hibis temple.

A second passage from this papyrus also addresses these issues: "He is the All-lord, the beginning of what exists. What is above is his *ba*, it is said. He is the one who is in the netherworld, (just) before the east, his *ba* in heaven, his body in the west, and his image (*khenty*) in Southern Heliopolis, bearing his appearances" (compare the translations of Wilson 1955c and Assmann 1975: 318). This passage seems odd at first glance, because it alludes to concepts that it does not explicitly state. The most important is the amalgamation of Re and Osiris in the New Kingdom that made these two gods into aspects of one another, Re being the daytime sun and lord of this world and Osiris the nighttime sun and lord of the netherworld (see, e.g., Hornung 1999: passim). This concept could be attached to Amun in his own syncretistic form of Amun-Re. Additionally, the "netherworld" is referred to in a manner that stresses that part of it which adjoined the eastern horizon where the sun rose, thus recalling an old concept that was especially important in the Pyramid Texts of the Old Kingdom (see Mercer 1952: 33–34). Finally, we must note that the "west," the area both of the sunset and where cemeteries were typically located, and the "netherworld" both refer to the realm of the dead. We can thus see that the passage, with an internal consistency of its own, refers to the Re aspect of the amalgamated deity as his *ba*, the source of his manifest power, to his Osirian aspect as his body, which is appropriate to the realm of the dead, and to his cult statue in Southern Heliopolis as his earthly epiphany.[83] Secondarily, *utjes khau* 'bearing his appearances' could also serve here as a variant of *utjes neferu* in reference to the public processions of the god in religion festivals, as above. The references to Amun's *ba* in heaven do not contradict what has already been said about the cult statue as *ba*. This word has a wide semantic range and, similarly to *tut* as discussed above, can refer both to the heavenly source of the god's power and to the cult statue as an earthly locus where his power is made manifest.[84] The reference to Amun's *ba* also serves as a precedent for

82. While the meaning 'to gladden the heart' has been ascribed to the expression *senefer ib*, it certainly makes no sense in this context. *Senefer* can also mean 'to carry out (business)' (see Faulkner 1962: 232), a meaning that is much more appropriate here.

83. There could be a reference here to the king as well, who is often called the image of a god, as in the royal name Tutankhamun, 'Living Image of Amun'. Bonnet (1952: 293) has noted that before he took the name Akhenaten, Amenophis IV included this very phrase as an epithet in his titulary. He translates 'who has assumed the crowns in Hermonthis', and primarily on the strength of this evidence, he has suggested that an Upper Egyptian coronation ceremony occurred in this city. Southern Heliopolis, however, could easily be Thebes (see Kees 1949: 432–36).

84. The way in which these senses of the word can be played on becomes clearer if we take into account a reference to Amun as "that *ba* who is in Thebes" (see Lichtheim 1980: 26).

a central concept of a group of texts from the temples of Edfu and Denderah that will be discussed below.

A text known as "The Memphite Theology," once thought to be quite ancient, is now understood to be a relatively late composition that could have been written at any time from the reign of Ramesses II to that of Shabaka (ca. 716–695 B.C.E.) of Dynasty XXV, with a later date in this time range being the more likely.[85] A main concern of the text is to equate Atum and his creation with the god Ptah, thus making the chief god of Memphis the creator-god and guarantor of the institution of kingship. A detailed description of these matters concludes with a summary that also relates Ptah's creation to the realm of human affairs:

> Ptah rested, after he made everything and every divine word, having fashioned (*mesi*) the gods, having made the cities, having founded the nomes (i.e., administrative districts), having placed the gods in their shrines, and having made perfect[86] their bodies for the satisfaction of their desires.[87] The gods entered into their bodies, (which were made) of every kind of wood, every kind of stone, and every kind of clay, and everything that grows all over him (i.e., Ptah), as that which they had become,[88] he having united the gods (i.e., their statues) and their *ka*s and they being satisfied and associated with the Lord of the Two Lands"[89] (compare especially the translation of Allen 1988: 44).

This passage is particularly interesting for its clear insistence on the divine origin of cult statues: not only are statues said to be the work of the creator-god, but the gods are said to "become" their statues by entering them (or, to be more precise, by their *ka*s entering them), quite in contrast to the mundane reality of the quickening of the statues through ritual. The phrase "everything that grows all over him" derives from a conception of Ptah as an earth-god, notwithstanding its evident incongruity in the present context: perhaps we are to understand the image as referring to veins of ore, because a mention of metal statues is otherwise lacking. The word "shrines" could conceivably mean house shrines as well as those in temples, thus accounting for the relatively humble materials wood and clay.

A hymn to Isis in the temple of Philae, carved under Ptolemy II, states, "You are the mother of Horus, the mighty bull, who established the temples of the Ennead (i.e., of all the gods) and made (*iri*) every cult statue (*nen*)" (see Žabkar 1988: 19, fig. 2). This is the only text in the group to use *nen*, a term first attested in the Greco-Roman period that Erman and Grapow (1971: 2.274) suggest is derived from an older term *senen* 'image, statue'. An alternative suggestion can be offered that "who made *nen*" is a deliberate archaism, harking back to the well-attested Old Kingdom expression *iri nu* (an older form of *nen*) 'to make this', in which 'this' refers to the tomb and its furnishings, a phrase that was also used in the New Kingdom in reference to the building and

85. On the problem of dating this text, see Junge 1973; Goedicke 1977; and Allen 1988: 43.

86. *Setut* (see pp. 153–54 above).

87. This is a clear reference to the gods' statues and their offering cults.

88. *Kheper*; though the phrase is more awkward in translation than in the Egyptian original, it clearly means that, when the gods entered their statues, they in some sense "became" their statues.

89. A title of the king, here given to Ptah.

dedication of temples and obelisks (see Erman and Grapow 1971: 2.216). The divine concept Horus-mighty-bull also harks back to an earlier usage: "bull" and "mighty bull" were an element in the Horus name of nearly every king of Dynasties XVIII to XX, whose monuments would have been, if anything, even more ubiquitous in Ptolemy II's time than they are to this very day.[90] The ascription of cult statues to a deity other than a creator-god is another unique feature within this group. Since "Horus-mighty-bull" is a clear allusion to Horus as prototype of the human institution of kingship, this otherwise unpretentious passage assumes an important mediating function between the parallel "realities"[91] in Egyptian thinking about cult statues: their origin in the divine realm and their origin in royal patronage of the temples.

At the temple of Edfu, a text dating to Ptolemy IV echoes, in part, "The Memphite Theology":

> King of Upper and Lower Egypt, who made (*iri*) the earth and fashioned (*mesi*) the Ennead, father of the fathers of all the gods, who began what was begun, who formed forms (*sekheper kheperu*), who made (*iri*) what is, who created (*tema* for *qema*) what exists, who cast (*nebi*) what is cast, who built (*qedi*) what is built, *Ta-Tjenen* (a name of Ptah), fashioner (*mesi*) of the gods (see Chassinat 1918: 37, lines 9–10).

This passage plays on the same themes as the others, adding the word *nebi* 'to cast', which refers to the activities of the goldsmith (see Faulkner 1962: 129). Because of its immediate proximity to *qedi*, we might question whether we are to take the latter in its more general sense 'to build', which can imply architectural activity, or in its more specific sense that refers to the work of a potter (on the latter, see Faulkner 1962: 281–82). Though nether *seshem* nor *tut* occurs to provide an explicit reference to cult statues, a comparison with other passages in this group as well as consideration of the vocabulary derived from human crafts (including *mesi*, which in addition to its general meaning is a term for fashioning statues) clearly suggest that these cosmological statements also serve implicitly as an etiological references to statues.[92]

The last text in this group is from the temple of Mut (Amun's consort) at Karnak and was carved under Ptolemy XII. The passage says of Amun-Re, "[. . . heaven] for his *ka*, earth for his image (*seshem*), the Two Lands bearing his images (*sekhemu*) and breath in everything, nothing lacking [. . . he is with]in everything—but if not, if departed,

90. Alexander the Great's younger brother and successor, Philip Arrhidaeus, had the Horus name "Mighty Bull," which was otherwise only used later in the Lagide dynasty, by Ptolemy I and Ptolemy XV, while Horus-mighty-bull appears in the Horus name of Ptolemy XII as a divine concept. Ptolemy II's own Horus name "valiant (or 'mighty') youth" alludes to the same militaristic ideal, though with quite different words. On all this, see von Beckerath 1984: 224–52; 285–95.

91. On expressions of the "parallel" worlds of human and divine realities, see Bryan 1989: cols. 581–82.

92. This implication of the passage has been recognized by Žabkar (1988: 24). I do not concur, however, with his rendering 'fashioner of fashioners, builder of builders', in which the 'fashioners' and 'builders' appear as strangely anonymous creators. From the overall tenor of the passage, which deals with 'flowing' of the creator-god into his creation, we do better to take these as passive, not active, participles. For similar pleonastic constructions, see van den Boorn 1988: 42–43.

they die" (see Goyon et al. 1983: 54). With a remarkable sparseness and beauty of language that can only be approximated in translation, this passage incorporates the ideas that we have seen again and again: not just the god's statue (*seshem*) but all of creation is an image (expressed in the plural, *sekhemu*) of the creator. This text is unique in the group, however, in its emphasis on creation's dependence on the creator for its continued existence. The restoration of "heaven" in the lacuna at the beginning of the passage is demanded both by context and by many parallel references in Egyptian texts to heaven and earth. But once again, the phraseology does not contradict what has been said above: the idea expressed is that the *ka* of the god is an entity above and beyond the part of it that resides in any single cult statue and that the "vital essence" or "life force" of the creator is more basic than its manifestations in the realm of human perceptions.

Considered as a group, these texts reflect a common feature in Egyptian religious literature: they express precise concepts, though expressing them in varied ways, playing freely with terminology and the semantic ranges of the terms they use.

* * * * *

We had occasion above (see p. 146) to note the ritual of "Uniting with the Sun Disk" at New Year's attested in temples of the Greco-Roman period. In the temple of Horus at Edfu, where the ritual was celebrated on the roof, there are small windows for light and ventilation in the area of the staircase used by the procession of priests who carried the temple's divine statues to their "union" with the rays of the sun. An inscription under one of these windows records a hymn describing the rising of the sun, and it provides a good beginning for the next group of texts we shall consider here—indeed, would it be too romantic a notion to think that the recitation of this hymn when the light of dawn appeared through the window was the signal for the procession to begin?

> The Sun Disk shining on the eastern side,
> Earth's Consort[93] clear of clouds,
> Horus-of-the-East[94] glows,
> shining in the sky,
> having entered the window of the Great Place (i.e., the temple)!
>
> * * *
>
> The Eastern *Ba* (i.e., the rising sun), as he races (up) to heaven
> his beams make light in the window!
> As Horus-of-Horuses goes out,
> having distanced himself to the sky,
> may his rays unite with (his) august "body"![95]

---

93. That is, the sky. The alliteration in the translation reflects an alliteration in the text itself: *Gebet gati em igep*.

94. That is, the sun, here stressed as a form of Horus, which is only natural in a temple of Horus. The allusion is to the divine form Re-Harakhty, 'Re (the sun-god)-Horus of the horizon'.

95. The word for 'body' is *sah*, a term well attested in reference to a mummy (see Erman and Grapow 1971: 4.51–52). As we have already noted, mummies, like statues, were subject to the Opening of the Mouth ritual, and we see here an explicit recognition of the similar status of the two, as inert

* * *

He of the dawn, He-who-comes-into-being-in-the-Netherworld[96] at daybreak, his brilliance in [his] house!—
Re presents himself in the eastern highlands,
having flown to the sky,
his sunlight ⟨upon⟩ the Place-of-the-two-deities.[97]

* * *

Divider-of-sides, having divided the skies,[98]
his brightness illuminates the House of Horus (i.e., the temple)!
As He-who-is-in-the-sky shines on the arms of the Two Sisters,[99]
may his "birthing"[100] mingle (*sensen*) with his image (*sekhem*)!

* * *

Re-the-Great shines in the East,
having cast (his) light on his Seat (i.e., the temple)!
He goes out from Nun,[101]
having left Punt (a land to the southeast of Egypt), having lit up [the temple(?)]
[. . . As he rises] in the eastern highlands, and as he sets in the western highlands (i.e., during the entire course of the day),
his care is upon his Great Place!

---

matter needing to be quickened. Another text passage from Edfu makes an interesting connection between *sah* and the concepts that were discussed above, stating that the king has come to the god "to 'lift things' (i.e., to make offerings) in the presence of his 'body' (*sah*), to fill his house, to endow his temple, to deliver offerings to his *ka*, to adore his *ba*, to glorify his image (*sekhem*), to satisfy his 'majesty' (*hem*, another word whose real meaning is 'body', as noted above) with prayer" (for the text, with translation, see Alliot 1949: 54).

96. The phrase alludes to a belief that the dead lived in an netherworld beneath ours and that during the night, the sun shone upon them. The next phrase evidently contains another allusion to the sunlight entering the window.

97. In this name of Edfu and its temple, the identity of the "two deities" is uncertain. Horus and Hathor, whose statues lead the procession (see below) are likely possibilities; Alliot (1949: 322), however, sees "the two deities" as two aspects of Horus represented by the "Dappled-of-plumage" and "Falcon-of-gold" statues kept in the Mesnet chapel of the temple.

98. "Divider-of-sides" might refer to the sun-god as a judge, a function that is occasionally attested (see Bonnet 1952: 628). In any event, the text makes a pun here on *rit* 'side' and *rit* 'skies, heaven'.

99. The allusion is to the pylon (monumental gateway) of the temple, envisioned as the sister goddesses Isis and Nephthys (see Bonnet 1952: 520). The pylon at the eastern end (i.e., the entrance) of the temple, with its two towers and lintel over the doorway, is here imaged as the two goddesses with their arms outstretched; for someone within the temple looking toward the entrance, this would have been symbolic of the eastern horizon.

100. The word 'birthing' (but compare the variant wording at Denderah discussed in n. 102), referring to the sunrise as the daily (re)birth of Re, is also likely to be an allusion to "Birth-of-Re," a name of New Year's day and of the New Year's festival.

101. Unlike the earlier image of the Netherworld, out of which the sun rises every day, there is here an allusion to sunrise as a reenactment of the "first moment" when the creator-god—here referred to as the sun—emerged from primeval chaos (Nun).

* * *

May he alight (*khen*) upon his statue (*bes*) [. . .] his "majesty" (*hem*)!
The god, his heart rejoices in goodness,
lasting forever,
shining above,
his statues glowing in Pe![102]

Unfortunately, the flow of thought in the last stanza is interrupted by a worn spot. But it is clear that in the first five stanzas, time and again and with ever-different imagery, reference is made to the rising sun and its appearance at Edfu. When the sun is referred to as the "Eastern *Ba*," that is, the 'manifest power' that arises on the eastern horizon, we see a reference to the concept expressed in the passages that follow.

A passage carved on the wall at the bottom of the staircase also alludes to the "Union" on the rooftop terrace. It is a label to a depiction of the procession:

> Arrival of ⟨his⟩ "majesty" (*hem*, i.e., the statue of the god Horus) at the Place-of-the-first-occasion,[103] so that his *ba* might unite (*sema*) with his image (*sekhem*).[104]

Another text, carved on one of the two doorways leading out from the corridor linking the various chapels of the temple and opening on the area in front of the holy of holies, which is adjacent to the area of the staircase, also describes the festival:

> The doorway of going . . . to bring in procession the great god, lord of Edfu, He-of-Edfu, the great god, lord of heaven, to elevate the lord of Mesnet,[105] dappled-of-plumage, and Hathor, mistress of Denderah, in order to go out as their statues (*bes*) to the Seat of the First Festival,[106] which is upon the terrace of the [staircase], and to see

102. Pe, a city of religious importance in the Delta, is here identified with Edfu. The statues "glow" because of the sunlight that shines on them during the ritual. For the text, with a translation, see Alliot 1949: 413–14. A close copy of the hymn also appears in connection with two staircase windows in the Roman period mammisi ("birth-house") at the temple of Hathor at Denderah (see Daumas 1951: 397–98). Unfortunately, the end of the text is entirely destroyed and thus affords no help in filling in the lacunas at the end of the Edfu version. The Denderah copy has numerous small variations in writings, as well as two features worth noting here. Where we rendered "his brilliance in [his] house," the Denderah version has "his brilliance in the house of 'appearance.'" The word "appearance" could also have been in the now-worn spot in the Edfu version; the reference would have been to the appearance of the statue when the door of the shrine is opened at daybreak, which cultically replicates the sunrise (the word used is in fact the most commonly-attested one for the "appearance" of the sun at dawn). Second, where the Edfu version has *mesu* 'birthing', the Denderah copy has *meskhau* 'brilliance, splendor'.

103. Carved at the bottom of the staircase, the text anticipates the arrival of the procession at its top. The "first occasion" or "first moment" is the creation of the universe, which is symbolically repeated every day at sunrise and also at New Year's (see Morenz 1973: 166–68; Frankfort 1948: 150).

104. For the text and a translation, see Alliot 1949: 306.

105. At Edfu, the statue of Horus in the holy of holies was not the statue that headed the procession on the New Year's festival. Rather, it was one of the two statues of the god located in the Mesnet chapel just behind the holy of holies, as well as a statue of Hathor of Denderah that was also in the Mesnet chapel (see Alliot 1949: 327).

106. The "First Festival" of the year is, of course, the New Year's festival. For "Seat of the First Festival" as one of the designations of the rooftop terrace, see Alliot 1949: 417. Here, the text alludes to "Seeing the Sun Disk," another name of the ritual, for which see Finnestad 1985: 102–3.

> the sun-disk in the eastern horizon,[107] so that his (i.e., the sun-god's) rays might pass over their [im]ages (*sekhem*), so that their "flesh" (i.e., the statues) might be rejuvenated, so that their statues (*seshem*) might be renewed, and so that they might live by seeing his rays. . . .[108]

A second passage on the doorway states that the purpose of the ritual is

> so that their images (*sekhem*; the reference is to Horus, Hathor, and the other deities whose statues are in the temple) might unite (*chenem*) with their *ba*s in the horizon[109] so that the *ba* of Re might be established upon their images (*tit*), so that the deities[110] might depart with them (i.e., with their *bas*). . . .[111]

A passage on the other doorway leading into the area adds further information:

> bringing in procession He-of-Edfu, in his august shrine, as his statue (*bes*), to the Seat of the First Festival, She-of-Denderah with him, his (*sic*) Ennead of his "majesty" (i.e., the other cult statues of the temple) [behind him] and the sacred emblems preceding him, in order to unite with the sun-disk[112] on the New Year's day, and on other festival days as well. . . .[113]

Yet another text passage, carved on a nearby wall, describes the purpose of the stairway:

> The Eastern *Ba* goes out by means of it to the "horizon" in his great mysterious form of He-of-Edfu; his "majesty" causes his image (*sekhem*) to go in procession to the "sky" to see his *ba* in the "heavens."[114]

Despite the brevity of the passage, its wording is important. The "Eastern *ba*," which we saw as a description of the sun in the hymn cited above, is here equated with the statue of Horus that led the procession to the rooftop, thus stressing the identity of the god

107. The mention of the horizon calls to mind a passage in a New Kingdom text, the Wisdom of Ani, which describes the god as "the sun on the horizon, while his images (*tut*) are on earth" (see Erman 1966: 239; in the generally better translation by Lichtheim [1976: 141], the word for 'horizon' is erroneously rendered 'sky'). Since the word for 'sun' in this passage from Ani has the basic meaning 'sunlight', we have here a likely allusion to the underlying concept of the ritual, namely that sunlight is the means by which divine essence enters the cult statue. Unfortunately, this falls short of a confirmation that the ritual itself was already celebrated during the New Kingdom.

108. For the text and a translation, see Alliot 1949: 333–34.

109. In context here, "horizon" refers to the rooftop terrace.

110. The word *semen* 'to establish' has, in legal texts, the nuance 'to confirm', as to confirm something as true or to confirm someone in possession of something, e.g., an inheritance (see Morschauser 1988a: 100; Gilula 1977: 39, with 40 n. 21; note also the usage of the word discussed in n. 71 above). Here, the *ba* of Re will ritually take possession of the cult images. This is not, of course, a legal "possession"; as the text makes clear, when the *ba* of Re shines upon each statue, the statue receives from it its own rejuvenated *ba*.

111. For the text and a translation, see Alliot 1949: 332–33.

112. The text here alludes to the other, more usual, name of the ritual.

113. For the text and a translation, see Alliot 1949: 331–32.

114. "Horizon," "sky," and "heavens" all refer to the roof of the temple in this passage. For the text and a translation, see Alliot 1949: 385.

and the statue. The phrase "to see his *ba*," however, emphasizes that there is divine *ba* above and beyond the statue, some of which is to enter the statue in the course of the ritual. Alliot (1949: 433 n. 2) is therefore far too simplistic when he interprets the sunlight itself as the *ba* of the god in his discussion of the New Year's ritual. The sun-god himself, a power within him, power flowing from him through the medium of the sunlight, as well as the cult statue, are *all* implicated in the notion of *ba*, even though no single text passage mentions all of them.

The staircase used by the procession to the rooftop was in the southeast corner of the inner part of the temple, that is, the corner oriented toward the rising sun. Thus, Horus's ascent within the microcosm of the temple[115] mirrored the rising of the sun in the world outside. Not surprisingly, then, at the end of the ritual, the procession descended into the temple by another staircase, whose rooftop opening was at the northwest corner. Two texts describing this staircase contain passages reflecting the ritual that has occurred and anticipating the statues' return to their shrines. The first states that the staircase has been built for the "dappled-of-plumage,"

> for hurrying to his Great Place after the "revelation of the face"[116] atop his temple, together with the Ennead that is in his following, so as to come (back) satisfied to his august house on his beautiful festival of New Year's, as well as calendrical festivals, when his "majesty" goes out to see the sun-disk and to join (*sema*) ⟨his⟩ statue (*senen*) with his *ba* in the horizon, his rays in sight of his nome. . . .[117]

The second text adds further information about the expected result of the ritual:

> The god (i.e., the statue) rests in his august shrine afer ⟨his⟩ *ba* has united (*sema*) with the image (*sekhem*) of his *ka* and his (i.e., the sun-god's) rays have united (*abekh*) with his "flesh." The Ennead, secret of forms and whose beauty is hidden, the great "powers" (*sekhem*, a reference to the statues as well as the divine essences in them, which are "secret" and "hidden" because they are not seen by profane eyes) of the Great Place, they come along their way to rest in their shrines, for the rays of the sun-disk have united (*ab*) upon them. . . .[118]

115. The notion of sacred spaces, especially temples, as embodying the site of creation and microcosm of creation, is widespread in human religious experience; see the brief account by Eliade (1963: 367–87). On the symbolism of the temple of Edfu, which falls into this pattern, see Finnestad 1985: 8–16, 42–68.

116. "Revelation-of-the-face" is the name of the ritual act of opening the shrine, when the officiating priest(s) can see the face of the cult statue. The expression also occurs in the daily cult ritual (see above, p. 139).

117. The "nomes" were the districts into which Egypt was divided for administrative purposes. Presumably, the people of the district gathered in crowds around the temple on special festivals. In the temple of Denderah (the same might be true of Edfu, though the texts do not confirm it), we know that the procession from the rooftop proceeded to the inner part of the temple by way of one of the outer rooms, where at least the more privileged persons of the district were gathered to see it (see Fairman 1954: 187–88). For the text and translation, see Alliot 1949: 423–24.

118. For the text and transliteration, see Alliot 1949: 422–23.

This passage is particularly important because of its mention of the concept of *ka* in connection with that of *ba*. It was noted above that *ba* and *ka* were concepts that partly overlapped and partly complemented one another; one might even wonder, though there is no way to prove it, whether the Egyptians thought of them as two aspects of the same animating force. In any event, the theology expressed in the text passages just cited makes it clear that it was the *ba* of the sun-god that was thought to 'empower' ('power' is a meaning of the root *ba*) and rejuvenate the cult statues as focal points for human service of the divine through the medium of the cult. We have already noted evidence, from the Old Kingdom through the Greco-Roman period, that points consistently to a belief that it was the animate force in the form of *ka* that was resident in a statue and enjoyed the benefits of the cult (whether the funerary or the temple cult). This, then, is the meaning of the statement "*ba* has united with the image of his *ka*": when the god's *ba* has suffused the statue, the *ka*-life of the statue, that is, its ability to enjoy cult attention, is made possible.[119]

119. Addressing this problem (though not the same group of texts), Finnestad (1985: 134–37) has described the god as *ba* as "a dynamic being in the act of manifesting himself," which she contrasts with *ka*, defined as "the life-quality as such. . . . As long as god lives he is, or has, his *ka*." However, we noted above a passage from the Pyramid Texts that described Atum's imparting of his own essence to Shu and Tefnut through the medium of the *ka*, and with this, it has to be conceded that the thinkers responsible for these texts could have referred to the *ka* alone to express the process effected by the New Year's ritual. Evidently, however, they had something specific in mind, that induced them to employ both of the concepts for a "life force" or "power" that animates otherwise inert material; this problem will be addressed below. In similar texts from Denderah, the *ba* is typically represented as a human-headed bird, making it possible to envision the relationship between the deity and the image it inhabits and animates as effected by the *ba* as a bird that flies down from the sky and alights upon the statue. The verb "to alight" is common in the Denderah texts; various verbs meaning "to join" and "to mingle" are more common at Edfu, but "to alight" also occurs there; see the text cited on p. 197 below. This simple, natural image, as well as the sense of "manifestation" inherent in the root *ba*, is a sufficient basis for explaining the concepts as we find them in the theologies of Edfu and Denderah. The difference of opinion expressed here might seem minor. However, there underlies it a fundamental difference in methodological assumptions. Finnestad's approach to the problem has, in my opinion, two basic weaknesses. First, in the group of texts quoted earlier (pp. 184–190), we saw the basic concepts combined and recombined, no two formulations quite alike. Finnestad ignores this phenomenon and, considering only one combination of concepts, accords it the status of a theological absolute. Second, Finnestad attempts to articulate this absolute in philosophical terms that in this context are anachronistic and potentially misleading, as when she states, "*ba* thus implies ontological transition . . ." (p. 135). Elsewhere (p. 83), Finnestad cites a text passage at Edfu that states, "the *ka* arrived as the flying *ba*." In this passage, *ka* and *ba* are clearly treated as two aspects of the same thing, as becomes even clearer if we render the statement "the life force arrived as a flying manifestation of power." With this understanding, one can wonder whether Finnestad's concept of "ontological transition" is even applicable. But if one wishes to see the crystallization of the "manifestation of power" into a "life force" that will be served in the temple by cult offerings as some sort of "transition," it should be clear that such "transition" as is implied here is expressed neither by *ba* nor by *ka* but by the acts of "flying" and "arriving"; that is to say, the transition is not expressed as ontological but rather as spatial, from heaven to earth. The spatial nature of this transition has been noted by Assmann (1984: 50–58), who refers to it by the Latin term *descensio* 'descent'.

There is a very real connection to be drawn between the ideas here and the progression of thought in the daily cult ritual. In the latter, after the awakening to light at dawn and the assurance of consciousness and physical soundness, the cult statue is addressed as a "living *ba*," that is, as a living manifestation of the god. But it is only after offerings are presented to the statue that reference is made to the *ka*.

On the facade of Edfu's holy of holies, the focal point of the daily cult ritual in the temple, there are several texts referring to the daily waking of the god and its cosmic significance. One short text contains statements of special relevance for the problems at issue here:

> (Just as) the sky exists far off bearing Re, while Mesnet (a chapel just behind the holy of holies and also a reference to the temple itself) is holy bearing his image (*sekhem*), (so also) there exists the "secret horizon" in it (i.e., in the temple), the Great Place (here, the name of the holy of holies) hidden in Edfu. When the winged sun-disk has come from the netherworld sky every day to see his statue (*bes*) in his Great Place, he descends upon his image (*sekhem*) with his images (*achem*), and his heart is satisfied in his shrine.[120]

Short though it is, this text is hypercharged with symbolic references. We had noted that it was one of the cult statues of Horus in the Mesnet chapel behind the holy of holies (specifically, the dappled-of-plumage mentioned in two of the texts just cited) that led the New Year's procession to the temple roof and thus was the primary beneficiary of the ritual of Uniting with the Sun-Disk. It was another statue of the god, in the holy of holies itself, that was the focus of the daily cult ritual. This elaboration of chapels and statues of course served to enhance the aura of divine mystery, though the historical origin of this elaboration, as well as its special theological justification or explanation, unfortunately eludes us. But it is clear that there had to have been a reciprocal relationship between the statues: in the respective rituals, what primarily benefited one of them was of cultic relevance to the other. The text alludes to this relationship when it employs the term Mesnet, referring in context to the Mesnet chapel itself but also serving as a designation of the entire temple.[121] The "secret horizon" is specified as the holy of holies, "secret" because it is well hidden from profane eyes, deep within the darkness of the temple.[122] The designation is a direct allusion to the point in the daily

120. For the text and a translation, see Blackman and Fairman 1941: 398–99. Their translation differs somewhat from the one offered here mainly because of different interpretations of the nuances of verbal constructions. This leads, however, to only one principal divergence in interpretation: they take the "horizon" to be the horizon of heaven itself, while here, the "secret horizon" is taken as a reference to the holy of holies. Both translations agree, however, in seeing the text as asserting a relationship between heaven and the temple.

121. Blackman and Fairman (1941: 422 n. 2) note the wider reference of Mesnet but do not recognize its simultaneous, more specific reference.

122. The forecourt and outer halls of the temple, to which at least some members of the public evidently had access, were well lit by the light of day. However, except for small windows in the area of the stairway leading to the roof, the inner portion of the temple was windowless and could only be lit in three ways: first, by the daylight that penetrated through the central axis of the temple when all

cult ritual when the doors of the statue's shrine are opened and the officiant states, "The double door of heaven is opened, the double door of earth is unclosed" (see p. 139 above): the appearance of the sun above the horizon and the appearance of the cult statue when the shrine is opened are, on the symbolic level, identical. As Finnestad has pointed out, the "netherworld sky" refers both to the real heaven below the horizon and to the farthest interior of the temple, while the "winged sun-disk" is both the sun itself and the many images of the winged sun-disk carved along the main axis of the temple, both on the ceiling and above each doorway; in her words,

> with the effect that the Winged Disk seems literally to fly out from the underworld when the ingoing rays of the sun are reflected by the reliefs. They seem to be emerging from the dark interior. In this way the ingoing cosmic theophany of the sun-god is made to coincide with the outgoing cultic epiphany; by this ingenious decorative feature the notion is conveyed of the Winged Disk coming out of the underworld united with his image (1985: 111–12).

Thus, the specific wording of our text, which is reinforced by the iconography of the temple axis, makes an explicit connection between heaven and the Mesnet chapel, where there resided the ultimate (literally, because the chapel is at the very rear of the temple), most potent cult image of Horus at Edfu, and between heaven and the holy of holies where the daily cult ritual was performed, as well as an implicit connection between the Mesnet chapel and the holy of holies, establishing an interrelationship between the two chapels and the cult images in them.[123]

From all this, one might have the impression that divine essence was absent from the cult statue during the night and returned to it in the morning by means of the sunlight. However, this is not so. Several other texts on the facade of the holy of holies—incorporating the portion of Edfu's daily cult ritual wherein the god in the shrine is called upon to awaken—identify him with the sun-god, who is turn is referred to as "he who comes to life in the eastern mountains and goes down in the western mountains and sleeps in Edfu, daily" (see Blackman and Fairman 1941: 400–410). A text passage from an interior wall of the holy of holies conveys much the same information: "The

the doors were opened (see Finnestad 1985: 111); second, by means of a system of holes in the roof, which allowed light to filter into the chapels on either side of the holy of holies and play upon the reliefs on their walls (Finnestad 1985: 95); and third, by means of the smokeless light of lamps burning pure oil.

123. There is a companion text to the one that we have been considering that deals only with heaven above and the Mesnet chapel (see Blackman and Fairman 1941: 398–99). This text reads, "(Just as) the horizon exists in heaven, bearing Him-of-the-horizon (i.e., the sun), (so) there is another one on earth bearing his image, the western horizon in the sky bearing Re and Mesnet on earth bearing He-of-Edfu. The double doors of Mesnet are opened, and the sun-disk shines, like Re shining in the horizon." When the two texts are taken together, they clearly allude to the "mystery"—which is not explained—of the relationship between the cult statue in the holy of holies that receives the attention of the daily cult ritual, as well as the daylight that passes along the central axis of the temple, and the statue in the Mesnet chapel that was the center of attention in the ritual of Uniting with the Disk on the roof of the temple.

august winged sun-disk, he goes down in the night, and he, Re, takes possession of the nome (i.e., the district of Edfu), his delight: it is his Great Place upon earth, and he sleeps in it until dawn" (de Rochemonteix and Chassinat 1897: 35). From these statements, it is absolutely clear that the cult statue, once it was quickened by the Opening of the Mouth ritual, was thought permanently to contain some part of the living essence of the god, which (like any human) slept at night and woke at dawn. The texts we have been considering show that this simple concept was elaborated in the temple theology: with each new dawn, divine essence further permeated the cult statue through the medium of the daylight, while at New Year's (and on certain other festivals, unfortunately unspecified at Edfu), a special rejuvenation by sunlight occurred.

From this evidence it would seem that once quickened by divine essence, a cult statue enjoyed a life that consisted of two "parallel" existences.[124] In one existence, the *ka* of the deity slept and woke and was sustained by its human worshipers through the offerings of the daily cult. In its parallel existence, the statue maintained an ongoing relationship with the creator-god (manifested in the sun), periodically rejuvenated and daily regenerated by the creator's *ba* through the medium of the sunlight. From this point of view, the group of texts cited at the beginning of this section (pp. 184–188), which treat cult statues as special instances of the divine creation of the world and discount their human manufacture, take on a new dimension of significance. But we must note that these parallel existences were simultaneous and in some way interrelated, as typified by the following statements at Edfu:

> The people worship your *ka*, (while) your *ba* in heaven joins (*chenem*) your image (*sekhem*), as the one mingles (*sensen*) with the other.[125]

> (The king has come) to "lift things" (i.e., make offerings) in the presence of his (i.e., the god's) "body" (*sah*), to fill his house and to endow his temple, to deliver offerings to his *ka*, to adore his *ba*, to glorify his image (*sekhem*), and to satisfy his "majesty" (*hem*) with prayer.[126]

Both *ka* and *ba* are thus objects of worship, while the statement "the *ka* arrived as the flying *ba*" cited in n. 119 above makes it clear that both had a celestial origin. Nevertheless, the parallels means of sustaining the existence of the deity in the statue are made abundantly clear in the texts: it is the *ka* that receives the offerings of the cult (on this point, see also the discussion by Finnestad 1985: 136–37), while the heavenly regeneration of the divine essence in the statue is effected by the *ba*.

Another short text passage from the interior of the holy of holies is notable for the richness of the vocabulary with which it expresses the union of god and statue:

> He alights (*khen*) upon his statue (*bes*), he mingles with (*sensen*) his idol (*achem*), he embraces (*sekhen*) his image (*sekhem*).[127]

---

124. Again, on the concept of parallel realities, see Bryan 1989.
125. For the text and a translation, see Alliot 1954: 553–54.
126. For the text and a translation, see Alliot 1949: 54–55.
127. For the text, see de Rochemonteix and Chassinat 1897: 22.

Thus far, we have considered only texts from Edfu, the Greco-Roman period temple that, as it happens, has received the most scholarly study (for some further relevant passages expressing much the same thoughts, see de Wit 1961a; 1961b; Gutbub 1986). However, there are texts from the nearly contemporary temple at Denderah expressing the same theological concepts, though with an additional complication. Two passages can suffice as illustrative. These are from the "building texts," which were carved in the various rooms of the temple. They give the name of the king and, playing on the rich vocabulary of terms for building, chapels, images, and the like, they state that he has built the room for certain purposes. The "building texts" usually consist of a single sentence, but with the insertion of numerous subordinate clauses, the sentence becomes long and complex. These texts are from two of the subsidiary chapels located to the east of the holy of holies.

> (the king), he has built the House-of-Uniter-of-the-Two-Lands for He-who-shines-as-gold, the Serpent in the House-of-the-Serpent,[128] to guard the image (*semen*) of his body (*djet*) in his sanctuary and to protect his "majesty" (*hem*) in his [shri]ne, the images (*seshem*) of his [mysteriousness][129] carved (*sepecher*) in his chapel as beautiful expressions of Isden (i.e., Thoth, the god of writing), (so that) when he has seen his court (i.e., the chapel) and embraced his images (*sekhem*), he might alight (*khen*) upon his statue (*bes*) in his chapel and praise Re for his city in sweetness of heart, his body enveloped in joy,[130] and give great kingship to the king.[131] before the *ka*s of the living, forever.[132]

> (The king), he has constructed Uhemkheperchat,[133] built as an excellent work of eternity, great divine images (*sekhem*) incised (*kheti*) within it as effective works of Perception (i.e., Thoth), decorated with two-thirds gold and shining like sunlight more gleaming to the sight than heaven, (so that) when the *ba* of He-who-shines-as-gold has seen them, he might alight (*khen*) upon them in joy, and (so that) when he has embraced (*sekhen*) his images (*sekhem*) incised (*kheti*) upon the wall, he might make excellent the kingship of the king before the *ka*s of the living, forever.[134]

---

128. Chapels can have more than one name. This one, whose principal cult image was a serpent arising from a lotus, was called both House-of-Uniter-of-the-Two-Lands and House-of-the-Serpent. Uniter-of-the-Two-Lands and He-who-shines-as-gold were both names of the serpent.

129. The word is now lost, but Chassinat saw a trace that seemed to confirm the reading in an earlier copy of the text by Mariette.

130. This clause, in which the hieroglyph of a lotus is employed in the writing of the word for 'joy', puns verbally on the cult image of the serpent emerging from the lotus and makes a connection between the god's actions on behalf of Denderah and the king and his divine essence's permeation of the statue.

131. Chassinat's publication adds the word "Re" after "king"; this makes no sense in context, and the word does not appear in Mariette's copy.

132. For the text, see Chassinat 1934: 172.

133. This reading of the name of the chapel is given by Daumas (1969: 51). He is unable, however, to translate it.

134. For the text, see Chassinat 1934: 73. A group of passages principally from Denderah, expressing these concepts, is cited by Morenz (1973: 151–52) and Assmann (1984: 50–58). In a text frequently copied in the later periods of Egyptian history, the *ba* of the deceased is also said to 'embrace' (*sekhem*) his body and heart (see Goyon 1974: 123).

In the first of these passages, the *ba* does not happen to be mentioned explicitly. That the *ba* is to be understood, however, is clear from comparison with all the other texts we have considered, and it is confirmed by two other "building texts" in the same room: "(so that) when his *ba* has come from the sky to the House-of-the-Serpent, his/its heart might mingle with his statue" (Chassinat 1934: 174) and "(so that) when his *ba* has come from above and he/it has embraced his image on the wall" (Chassinat 1934: 174–75; the first of these adds the interesting information that the *ba* has something to do with the "heart/consciousness" of the statue). In any event, the passage states that the god (understanding that his *ba* is meant here) enters the images (in the plural) carved on the wall and—evidently, from the fact that the word is singular—the cult statue itself. In the second passage, the allusion is only to the images on the wall. The "complication," then, is the difficulty we sometimes have, in reading the building texts from Denderah, in judging whether a passage is referring to cult statues or to the carvings on the wall (the fluidity of the reference has already been noted by Morenz 1973: 151–52). But the complication can only be frustrating in the context of our focus on the cult statues themselves: it is clear enough that the scribes who composed the Denderah texts meant to convey the information that the divine *ba*s entered both the statues and the images on the walls. This in turn is interesting because, while there is no reference at Denderah, as there is at Edfu, to an Opening of the Mouth ceremony performed on the images on the walls, the content of these texts implies that such a ceremony was performed.

* * * * *

With this, we have reached the end of our quest for information on how the ancient Egyptians believed that their cult statues were alive with divine essence. We can close with two passages that interestingly echo the prophetic polemics against idols.

The first is from a story fictitiously set in the reign of Ramesses II (ca. 1290–1224 B.C.E.). The copy we have is from the Ptolemaic period, but the story could have been written as early as the period of the first Persian occupation of Egypt (525–404 B.C.E.), and it seems to reflect Egyptian concerns about the removal of cult statues from Egypt, perhaps at that time (see Morschauser 1988b: 216–23; texts recording the return of at least some of these statues to Egypt by the early Ptolemies were quoted above, pp. 126–27). In the tale, a cult statue of the god Khonsu of Thebes is sent to the far-off land of Bakhtan, where it cures a princess of an illness caused by an evil spirit that has possessed her. Once expelled, the evil spirit says to Khonsu, "Welcome in peace, great god who expels disease demons! Bakhtan is your home, its people are your servants. . . ." These seemingly welcome words are a ruse. The statue should have been returned to Egypt once its mission had been fulfilled, but it is the troublemaking spirit who evidently puts it in the mind of the Prince of Bakhtan to make Khonsu a god of his own land, as the spirit's own words already implied. The text goes on to say of the prince of Bakhtan:

> Then he schemed with his heart, saying: "I will make the god stay here in Bakhtan. I will not let him go to Egypt." So the god spent three years and nine months in Bakhtan.

> Then, as the prince of Bakhtan slept on his bed, he saw the god come out of his shrine as a falcon of gold and fly up toward Egypt. He awoke in terror and said to the priest of Khons-the-Provider-in-Thebes: "The god is still here with us! He shall go to Thebes! His chariot shall go to Egypt!" Then the prince of Bakhtan let the god proceed to Egypt, having given him many gifts of every good thing and very many horses and soldiers (the translations are from Lichtheim 1980: 92–93).

We have just been considering texts that describe how the divine *ba*, sometimes imaged as a bird, comes down from the sky and "alights" on the cult statue and "embraces" or "mingles with" it. Khonsu's dream threat to the prince is precisely this process, but in reverse: if the prince insists on keeping the statue in Bakhtan, the god's divine presence will depart from the statue and return to Egypt, leaving the prince with no god at all but only an inert material object. The prince then realizes the futility of his scheme, and he returns the statue to Egypt.

The second passage is:

> [. . . the wri]tings (or "drawings") of the manual of their primeval bodies [. . .] they have ceased, one after the other, (whether) of precious stones, gol[d . . .] (Redford 1981: 89, 102).

Carved on a block found reused in the Tenth Pylon of the temple at Karnak, the text preserves fragments of a speech of Akhenaten (ca. 1367–1350 B.C.E.). It is unfortunate that we do not have the entire inscription, because it was evidently a proclamation of essential elements of his "heretic" religious doctrine. In any event, the statement with which we are concerned clearly deals with cult statues, whose iconographic features, as we know from other surviving sources, were recorded in the form of drawings in manuals (Redford 1981: 93–94). For Redford, who published the text, this passage refers to "the evanescence of all other gods who, while perhaps once existing, have now 'ceased,' in contrast to the eternal, matchless sun. To me, at least, this text militates strongly in favour of the view that Akhenaten's beliefs approached the status of monotheism, rather than merely a pale, henotheistic tendency" (Redford 1981: 98; see also Redford 1984: 172). But a monotheistic statement would deny the existence of other gods, which this statement does not explicitly do. Coming as it does between reference to manuals containing drawings and a reference to precious stones and gold, the "they" of "they have ceased" cannot be deities per se but rather cult statues (see already Murnane 1995: 31). Akhenaten's form of worship was focused directly on the sun in the sky (the Aton, or 'sun-disk'); even the temples of Aton were open-air for this purpose, and no cult statues were used (see Redford 1984: 235).[135] Even if an explicitly monotheistic statement appeared in a now-lost portion of this inscription, the most obvious and direct reference

135. An evident attempt at a theological justification for this practice can be found in a statement from another text of Akhenaten, which calls the Aton "the one who built himself by himself, with his (own) hands—no craftsman knows him" (for the translation, see Redford 1981: 95). This formulation should be compared with the group of texts discussed at the outset of this section (pp. 184–88), which treat cult statues themselves as divine creations.

of the statement in question is to the king's decision not to employ cult statues in his own religious practice. Understood thus, this derision of cult statues as made of precious, but perishable, materials is a remarkable presaging of the polemics of the Hebrew prophets.

Bibliography

Abydos

1988 "Abydos." In *Report for the Year 1987/88*, pp. 9–10. London: The Egypt Exploration Society.

Aldred, C.

1965 *Egypt to the End of the Old Kingdom.* New York: McGraw-Hill.

Allam, S.

1981 Review of W. Helck, *Wirtschaftsgeschichte des Alten Agypten im 3. and 2. Jahrtausend vor Chr. The Journal of Egyptian Archaeology* 67: 192–94.

Allen, J. P.

1988 *Genesis in Egypt: The Philosophy of Ancient Egyptian Creation Accounts.* Yale Egyptological Studies 2. New Haven: Yale Egyptological Seminar.

Alliot, M.

1949 *Le Culte d'Horus à Edfou au temps des Ptolémées*, vol. 1. Bibliothèque d'Étude 20/1. Cairo: Institut Français d'Archéologie Orientale.

1954 *Le Culte d'Horus à Edfou au temps des Ptolémées*, vol. 2. Bibliothèque d'Étude 20/2. Cairo: Institut Français d'Archéologie Orientale.

Altenmüller, H.

1967 *Darstellungen der Jagd im Alten Ägypten.* Hamburg and Berlin: Paul Parey.

1969 "Die abydenische Version des Kultbildrituals." *Mitteilungen des Deutschen Archäologischen Instituts Abteilung Kairo* 24: 16–25.

1971 "Eine neue Deutung der Zeremonie des *Init Rd*." *The Journal of Egyptian Archaeology* 57: 146–53.

Anthes, R.

1954 "Note concerning the Great Corporation of Heliopolis." *Journal of Near Eastern Studies* 13: 191–92.

1969 "Das objektlose *Iri n* 'Handeln für' in den Pyramidentexten." *The Journal of Egyptian Archaeology* 55: 41–54.

Assmann, J.

1975 *Ägyptische Hymnen und Gebete.* Zurich and Munich: Artemis.

1977 "Die Verborgenheit des Mythos in Ägypten." *Göttinger Miszellen* 25:7–43.

1984 *Ägypten—Theologie und Frömmigkeit einer frühen Hochkultur.* Stuttgart: W. Kohlhammer.

Badawy, A. M.

1975 "L'Accès au temple égyptien de Basse Époque et d'époque gréco-romaine." Pp. 5–8 in vol. 1 of *Actes du XXIXe Congrès International des Orientalistes: Égyptologie.* Paris: L'Asiathèque.

Baly, T. J. C.

1930 "Notes on the Ritual of Opening the Mouth." *The Journal of Egyptian Archaeology* 16: 173–86.

Beckerath, J. von
1984 *Handbuch der ägyptischen Königsnamen.* Münchner Ägyptologische Studien 20. Munich: Deutscher Kunstverlag.
Bell, H. I.
1954 *Cults and Creeds in Graeco-Roman Egypt.* Liverpool: Liverpool University Press.
Bell, L. D.
1986 "Les Parcours Processionnels." *Dossiers Histoire et Archéologie* 101: 29–30.
Bietak, M.
1979 "Avaris and Piramesse: Archaeological Exploration in the Eastern Nile Delta." *Proceedings of the British Academy* 65: 225–90.
Bjerke, S.
1965 "Remarks on the Egyptian Ritual of 'Opening the Mouth' and Its Interpretation." *Numen: International Review for the History of Religions* 12: 201–16.
Blackman, A. M.
1918–19 "The Sequence of the Episodes in the Egyptian Daily Temple Liturgy." *Journal of the Manchester Egyptian and Oriential Society* 8: 27–53.
1924 "The Rite of Opening the Mouth in Ancient Egypt and Babylonia." *The Journal of Egyptian Archaeology* 10: 47–59.
Blackman, A. M., and Fairman, H. W.
1941 "A Group of Texts Inscribed on the Facade of the Sanctuary in the Temple of Horus at Edfu." Pp. 397–428 in *Miscellanea Gregoriana: Raccolta di scritti pubblicati nel centenario dalla fondazione del Pont. Museo Egizio.* Rome: Poliglotta Vaticana.
Bleiberg, E.
1988 "The Redistributive Economy in New Kingdom Egypt: An Examination of *B3kw(t)*." *Journal of the American Research Center in Egypt* 25: 157–68.
Bolshakov, A. O.
1991 "The Moment of the Establishment of the Tomb-Cult in Ancient Egypt." *Altorientalische Forschungen* 18: 204–18.
Bonnet, H.
1952 *Reallexikon der ägyptischen Religionsgeschichte.* Berlin: de Gruyter.
Boorn, G. P. F. van den
1985 "*Wḏꜥ-ryt* and Justice at the Gate." *Journal of Near Eastern Studies.* 44: 1–25.
1988 *The Duties of the Vizier: Civil Administration in the Early New Kingdom.* London: Kegan Paul International.
Breasted, J. H.
1906 *Ancient Records of Egypt: Historical Documents from the Earliest Times to the Persian Conquest, Collected, Edited, and Translated with Commentary.* 5 vols. New York: Russell & Russell.
Bryan, B. M.
1989 Review of K. Myśaliwiec, *Eighteenth Dynasty before the Amarna Period. Bibliotheca Orientalis* 46: 579–82.
Buck, A. de
1938 *The Egyptian Coffin Texts,* Vol. 2: *Texts of Spells 76–163.* Oriental Institute Publications 49. Chicago: University of Chicago Press.
Budge, E. A. W.
1909 *The Book of Opening the Mouth: The Egyptian Texts with English Translations.* Books on Egypt and Chaldaea 26–27. London: Kegan Paul, Trench, Trübner.
Chassinat, E.
1918 *Le Temple d'Edfou,* Vol. 2. Mémoires publiés par les membres de la Mission Archéologique Française au Caire 11. Cairo: Institut Français d'Archéologie Orientale.

1934 *Le Temple de Dendara,* Vol. 2. Cairo: Institut Français d'Archéologie Orientale.

Chauveau, M.
1997 *L'Égypte au temps de Cléopâtre: 180–30 av. J.-C.* Paris: Hachette.

Cruz-Uribe, E.
1988 *Hibis Temple Project,* Vol. 1: *Translations, Commentary, Discussions, and Sign List.* San Antonio: Van Siclen.
1989 "Oasis of the Spirit." *Archaeology* 42/5: 48–53.

Daumas, F.
1951 "Sur trois representations de Nout à Dendara." *Annales du Service des Antiquités de l'Égypte* 51: 373–400.
1969 *Dendara et le temple d'Hathor: Notice sommaire.* Recherches d'Archéologie, de Philologie et d'Histoire 29. Cairo: Institut Français d'Archéologie Orientale.

Davies, N. de G. et al.
1953 *The Temple of Hibis in el Khargeh Oasis,* Vol. 3: *The Decoration.* Publications of The Metropolitan Museum of Art 17. New York: The Metropolitan Museum of Art.

Demarée, R. J.
1983 *The ꜣḫ iḳr n Rꜥ-Stelae: On Ancestor Worship in Ancient Egypt.* Egyptologische Uitgaven 3. Leiden: Nederlands Instituut voor het Nabije Oosten.

Eaton-Krauss, M.
1980 "Kultbild eines Falken." Pp. 20–21 in *Ägyptisches Museum: Staatliche Museen, Preussischer Kulturbesitz.* Stuttgart / Zurich: Belser.
1984 *The Representations of Statuary in Private Tombs of the Old Kingdom.* Ägyptologische Abhandlungen 39. Wiesbaden: Harrassowitz.

Eliade, M.
1963 *Patterns in Comparative Religion.* Trans. Rosemary Sheed. Cleveland / New York: World.

Emery, W. B.
1963 *Archaic Egypt.* Baltimore: Penguin.

Englund, G.
1978 *Akh—une notion religieuse dans l'Égypte pharaonique.* Boreas: Uppsala Studies in Ancient Mediterranean and Near Eastern Civilizations 11. Stockholm: Almqvist & Wiksell.

Erman, A.
1966 *The Ancient Egyptians: A Sourcebook of Their Writings.* Trans. A. M. Blackman. New York: Harper.

Erman, A., and Grapow, H., eds.
1971 *Wörterbuch der ägyptische Sprache im Auftrage der deutschen Akademien.* 7 vols. Berlin: Akademie.

Fairman, H. W.
1954 "Worship and Festivals in an Egyptian Temple." *Bulletin of the John Rylands Library Manchester* 37: 165–203.

Faulkner, R. O.
1962 *A Concise Dictionary of Middle Egyptian.* Oxford: Oxford University.
1969 *The Ancient Egyptian Pyramid Texts.* 2 vols. Oxford: Clarendon.

Feucht, E.
1977 "Herzskarabaüs." Cols. 1168–70 in vol. 2 of *Lexikon der Ägyptologie,* ed. W. Helck and W. Westendorf. Wiesbaden: Harrassowitz.

Finnestad, R. B.
1978 "The Meaning and Purpose of *Opening the Mouth* in Mortuary Contexts." *Numen: International Review for the History of Religions* 25: 118–34.

1985 *Image of the World and Symbol of the Creator: On the Cosmological and Iconological Values of the Temple of Edfu.* Studies in Oriental Religions 10. Wiesbaden: Harrassowitz.

Fischer, H. G.

1963 "Varia Aegyptiaca." *Journal of the American Research Center in Egypt* 2: 17–51.

Frankfort, H.

1948 *Kingship and the Gods: A Study of Ancient Near Eastern Religion as the Integration of Society and Nature.* Chicago: University of Chicago Press.

1961 *Ancient Egyptian Religion: An Interpretation.* New York: Harper and Row.

Frankfort, H. et al.

1949 *Before Philosophy: The Intellectual Adventure of Ancient Man.* Baltimore: Penguin.

Friedman, F.

1985 "On the Meaning of Some Anthropoid Busts from Deir el-Medina." *The Journal of Egyptian Archaeology* 71: 82– 97.

Gale, N. H., and Stos-Gale, Z. A.

1981 "Ancient Egyptian Silver." *The Journal of Egyptian Archaeology* 67: 103–15.

Gardiner, A. H.

1905 "Hymns to Amon from a Leiden Papyrus." *Zeitschrift für ägyptische Sprache und Altertumskunde* 42: 12–42.

1966 *Egypt of the Pharaohs.* New York: Oxford University Press.

Gauthier, H.

1928 *Dictionnaire des noms géographiques contenus dans les textes hiéroglyphiques*, vol. 5. Cairo: Société Royale de Géographie d'Égypte.

1931 *Le Personnel du dieu Min.* Recherches d'archéologie, de philologie et d'histoire 3. Cairo: Institut Français d'Archéologie Orientale.

Gilula, M.

1977 "The Stative Form of the Verb *sḏm* 'To Hear'." *Journal of the American Research Center in Egypt* 14: 37–40.

Goedicke, H.

1967 Königliche Dokumente aus dem Alten Reich. Ägyptologische Abhandlungen 14. Wiesbaden: Harrassowitz.

1969–70 "An Egyptian Claim to Asia." *Journal of the American Research Center in Egypt* 8: 11–27.

1970 *Die privaten Rechtsinschriften aus dem Alten Reich.* Beihefte zur Wiener Zeitschrift für die Kunde des Morgenlandes 5. Vienna: Notring.

1975a "Unity and Diversity in the Oldest Religion of Ancient Egypt." Pp. 201–17 in *Unity and Diversity: Essays in the History, Literature, and Religion of the Ancient Near East*, ed. H. Goedicke and J. J. M. Roberts. Baltimore: Johns Hopkins University Press.

1975b *The Report of Wenamun.* Baltimore: Johns Hopkins University Press.

1977 "727 vor Christus." *Wiener Zeitschrift für die Kunde des Morgenlandes* 69: 1–19.

1979 "Cult-Temple and 'State' during the Old Kingdom in Egypt." Pp. 113–31 in vol. 1 of *State and Temple Economy in the Ancient Near East*, ed. E. Lipiński. Orientalia Lovaniensa Analecta 5. Leuven: Leuven University.

Goyon, J.-C.

1972 *Rituels funéraires de l'ancienne Égypte: Le Rituel de l'ouverture de la bouche, les Livres des respirations.* Paris: du Cerf.

1974 "La véritable attribution des soi-disant chapitres 191 et 192 du Livre des Morts." *Studia Aegyptiaca* 1:117–27.

Goyon, J.-C. et al.
1983 "Inscriptions tardives du temple de Mout à Karnak." *Journal of the American Research Center in Egypt* 20: 47–63.

Graefe, E.
1971 "Das sog. Mundöffnungsgerät '*psš-kf*'." *The Journal of Egyptian Archaeology* 57: 203.

Greven, L.
1952 *Der Ka in Theologie und Königskult der Ägypter des Alten Reiches.* Ägyptologische Forschungen 17. Glückstadt / Hamburg / New York: J. J. Augustin.

Griffiths, J. G.
1960 *The Conflict of Horus and Seth from Egyptian and Classical Sources: A Study in ancient Mythology.* Liverpool: Liverpool University Press.
1980 *The Origins of Osiris and His Cult.* Studies in the History of Religions (Supplement to *Numen*) 40. Leiden: Brill.
1982 "Eight Funerary Paintings with Judgement Scenes in the Swansea Wellcome Museum." *The Journal of Egyptian Archaeology* 68: 228–52.

Gugliemi, W.
1980 "Bemerkungen zum Maatopfer im Amunsritual." *Göttinger Miszellen* 40:23–28.
1986 "Wortspiel." Cols. 1287–91 in vol. 6 of *Lexikon der Ägyptologie,* ed. W. Helck and E. Otto. Wiesbaden: Harrassowitz.

Gutbub, A.
1986 "À propos de quelques textes dogmatiques concernant la dédicace du temple et sa prise de possession par la divinité à Edfou." Pp. 389–407 in vol. 2 of *Hommages à François Daumas.* Montpellier: Université de Montpellier.

Hallo, W. W.
1987 "The Origins of the Sacrificial Cult: New Evidence from Mesopotamia and Israel." Pp. 3–13 in *Ancient Israelite Religion: Essays in Honor of Frank Moore Cross,* ed. P. D. Miller Jr., et al. Philadelphia: Fortress.

Helck, W.
1967 "Einige Bemerkungen zum Mundöffnungsritual." *Mitteilungen des Deutschen Archäologischen Instituts Abteilung Kairo* 22: 27–41.
1975 *Wirtschaftsgeschichte des Alten Ägypten im 3. und 2. Jahrtausend vor Chr.* Handbuch der Orientalistik, Erste Abteilung: Der Nahe und der Mittlere Osten, Erster Band, Fünfter Abschnitt. Leiden: Brill.
1977 "Die 'Weihinschriften' aus dem Taltempel des Sonnenheiligtums des Königs Neuserre bei Abu Gurob." *Studien zur altägyptischen Kultur* 5: 47–77.
1980 "Kultstatue." Cols. 859–63 in vol. 3 of *Lexikon der Ägyptologie,* ed. W. Helck and W. Westendorf. Wiesbaden: Harrassowitz.
1987 *Untersuchungen zur Thinitenzeit.* Ägyptologische Abhandlungen 45. Wiesbaden: Harrassowitz.

Hermann, A.
1956 "Zergliedern und Zusammenfügen: Religionsgeschichtliches zur Mumifizierung." *Numen: International Review for the History of Religions* 3: 81–96.

Hodge, C. T.
1985 Review of J. K. Hoffmeier, *Sacred in the Vocabulary of Ancient Egypt. Anthropological Linguistics* 27: 327–31.

Hornung, E.
1956 "Chaotische Bereiche in der geordneten Welt." *Zeitschrift für agyptische Sprache und Altertumskunde* 81: 28–32.

1982 *Conceptions of God in Ancient Egypt: The One and the Many.* Trans. J. Baines. Ithaca: Cornell University Press.

1992 *Idea into Image: Essays on Ancient Egyptian Thought.* Trans. Elizabeth Bredeck. New York: Timken.

1999 *The Ancient Egyptian Books of the Afterlife.* Trans. D. Lorton. Ithaca: Cornell University Press.

Iversen, E.

1984 *Egyptian and Hermetic Doctrine.* Opuscula Graecolatina (Supplementa Musei Tusculani) 27. Copenhagen: Museum Tusculanum Press.

Jacobsen, T.

1987 "The Graven Image." Pp. 15–32 in *Ancient Israelite Religion: Essays in Honor of Frank Moore Cross,* ed. P. D. Miller Jr. et al. Philadelphia: Fortress.

Janssen, J. J.

1982 "Gift-Giving in Ancient Egypt as an Economic Feature." *The Journal of Egyptian Archaeology* 68: 253–58.

Johnson, W. R.

1986 "À la recherche des décors perdus." *Dossiers Histoire et Archéologie* 101: 50–52.

Junge, F.

1973 "Zur Fehldatierung des sog. Denkmals memphitischer Theologie oder der Beitrag der ägyptische Theologie zur Geistesgeschichte der Spätzeit." *Mitteilungen des Deutschen Archäologischen Instituts Abteilung Kairo* 29: 195–204.

Junker, H.

1951 *Das lebenswahre Bildnis in der Rundplastik des Alten Reiches.* Anzeiger der phil.-hist. Klasse der Österreichischen Akademie der Wissenschaften, Jahrgang 1950, Nr. 19. Vienna: Hölder-Pichler-Tempsky.

Kaplony, P.

1966 "Das Vorbild des Königs unter Sesostris III." *Orientalia* n.s. 35: 403–12.

Kees, H.

1949 "Ein Sonnengeiligtum im Amonstempel von Karnak." *Orientalia* n.s. 18: 427–42.

1956 *Totenglauben und Jenseitsvorstellung der alten Ägypter: Grundlagen und Entwicklung bis zum Ende des Mittleren Reiches.* 2d ed. Berlin: Akademie.

Kemp, B. J.

1983 "Old Kingdom, Middle Kingdom and Second Intermediate Period c. 2686–1552 B.C." Pp. 71–182 in *Ancient Egypt: A Social History,* ed. B. J. Trigger. Cambridge: Cambridge University Press.

1989 *Ancient Egypt: Anatomy of a Civilization.* London / New York: Routledge.

Lemm, O. von

1882 *Das Ritualbuch des Ammondienstes.* Leipzig: Hinrichs.

Lichtheim, M.

1973 *Ancient Egyptian Literature: A Book of Readings,* vol. 1: *The Old and Middle Kingdoms.* Berkeley / Los Angeles / London: University of California Press.

1976 *Ancient Egyptian Literature: A Book of Readings,* vol. 2: *The New Kingdom.* Berkeley / Los Angeles / London: University of California Press.

1980 *Ancient Egyptian Literature: A Book of Readings,* vol. 3: *The Late Period.* Berkeley / Los Angeles / London: University of California Press.

Lloyd, A. B.

1982 "The Inscription of Udjahorresnet: A Collaborator's Testament." *The Journal of Egyptian Archaeology* 68: 166–80.

Long, B.

1986 "Le *ib* et le *ḥ3ty* dans les textes médicaux de l'Égypte ancienne." Pp. 483–94 in vol. 2 of *Hommages à Francois Daumas.* Montpellier: Université de Montpellier.

Lorton, D.
1971 "The Supposed Expedition of Ptolemy II to Persia." *The Journal of Egyptian Archaeology* 57: 160–64.
1974 *The Juridical Terminology of International Relations in Egyptian Texts through Dyn. XVIII.* Baltimore: Johns Hopkins University Press.
1977a "The Treatment of Criminals in Ancient Egypt through the New Kingdom." *Journal of the Social and Economic History of the Orient* 20: 2–64.
1977b "The 'Triumphal Poem' of the Creator in Papyrus Bremner-Rhind." *The Newsletter of The Society for the Study of Egyptian Antiquities* 7/4: 17–23.
1979 "Towards a Constitutional Approach to Ancient Egyptian Kingship." *Journal of the American Oriential Society* 99: 460–65.
1985 "Considerations on the Origin and Name of Osiris." *Varia Aegyptiaca* 1: 113–26.
1986 "The King and the Law." *Varia Aegyptiaca* 2: 53–62.

Meeks, D.
1988 "Notion de 'dieu' et structure du panthéon dans l'Égypte ancienne." *Revue de l'Histoire des Religions* 204: 425–46.

Meeks, D., and Favard-Meeks, C.
1996 *Daily Life of the Egyptian Gods.* Trans. G. M. Goshgarian. Ithaca: Cornell University Press.

Mercer, S. A. B.
1952 *The Pyramid Texts in Translation and Commentary*, vol. 4. New York / London / Toronto: Longmans, Green.

Meulenaere, H. de
1982 "La Statue d'un vizier thébain." *The Journal of Egyptian Archaeology* 68: 139–44.

Möller, G.
1936 *Hieratische Paläographie: Die aegyptische Buchschrift in ihrer Entwicklung von der Fünften Dynastie bis zur römischen Kaiserzeit*, Vol. 3. 2d ed. Osnabrück: Otto Zeller (reprinted, 1965).

Montet, P.
1954 "Les Boeufs égyptiens." *Kêmi* 13: 43–58.

Morenz, S.
1973 *Egyptian Religion.* Trans. A. E. Keep. Ithaca: Cornell University Press.

Moret, A.
1902 *Le Rituel du culte divin journalier en Égypte d'après les papyrus de Berlin et les textes du temple de Séti Ier à Abydos.* Geneva: Slatkine (reprinted, 1988).

Morschauser, S. N.
1988a "The End of the *Sdf(3)-Tr(yt)* 'Oath'." *Journal of the American Research Center in Egypt* 25: 93–103.
1988b "Using History: Reflections on the Bentresh Stela." *Studien zur altägyptischen Kultur* 15: 203–23.

Munro, P.
1984 "Die Nacht vor der Thronbesteigung—zum ältesten Teil des Mundöffnungsrituals." Pp. 907–28 in vol. 2 of *Studien zu Sprache und Religion Ägyptens zu Ehren von Wolfhart Westendorf.* Göttingen: Hubert.

Murnane, W. J.
1979 "The Bark of Amun on the Third Pylon at Karnak." *Journal of the American Research Center in Egypt* 16: 11– 27.
1986 "La Grande Fête d'Opet." *Dossiers Histoire et Archéologie* 101: 22–25.
1995 *Texts from the Amarna Period in Egypt.* Writings from the Ancient World 5. Atlanta: Scholars Press.

Nelson, H. R.
1949 "The Rite of 'Bringing the Foot' as Portrayed in Temple Reliefs." *The Journal of Egyptian Archaeology* 35: 82– 86.
Nibbi, A.
1977 "Some Remarks on Copper." *Journal of the American Research Center in Egypt* 14: 59–66.
Otto, E.
1950 "An Ancient Egyptian Hunting Ritual." *Journal of Near Eastern Studies* 9: 164–77.
1955 "Zur überlieferung eines Pyramidenspruches." Pp. 223–37 in vol. 2 of *Studi in memoria di Ippolito Rosellini nel primo centenario della morte (4 giugno 1843–4 giugno 1943).* Pisa: V. Lischi & Figli.
1958 *Das Verhältnis von Rite und Mythus im Ägyptischen.* Sitzungsberichte der Heidelberger Akademie der Wissenschaften, Philologisch-historische Klasse, Jahrgang 1958, 1. Abhandlung. Heidelberg: Carl Winter.
1960 *Das Ägyptische Mundöffnungsritual.* 2 vols. Ägyptologische Abhandlungen 3. Wiesbaden: Harrassowitz.
Pahl, W. M.
1986 "The Ritual of the Opening of the Mouth: Arguments for an Actual-Body-Ritual from the Viewpoint of Mummy Research." Pp. 212–17 in *Science in Egyptology*, ed. A. R. David. Manchester: Manchester University Press.
Piaget, J.
1951 *The Child's Conception of the World.* Trans. J. and A. Tomblinson. New York: Humanities.
Piankoff, A.
1930 *Le "Coeur" dans les textes égyptiens depuis l'Ancien jusqu'à la fin du Nouvel Empire.* Paris: Geuthner.
1964 *The Litany of Re: Texts Translated with Commentary.* Bollingen Series 40/4. New York: Pantheon.
Posener, G.
1975 "La Piété personelle avant l'âge amarnien." *Revue d'Égyptologie* 27: 195–210.
Redford, D. B.
1981 "A Royal Speech from the Blocks of the 10th Pylon." *Bulletin of the Egyptological Seminar* 3: 87–102.
1984 *Akhenaten: The Heretic Pharaoh.* Princeton: Princeton University Press.
1986 *Pharaonic King-Lists, Annals and Daybooks: A Contribution to the Egyptian Sense of History.* SSEA Publication 4. Mississauga: Benben.
Robichon, C., and Varille, A.
1936 *Le Temple du scribe royal Amenhotep fils de Hapou.* Fouilles de l'Institut Français d'Archéologie Orientale au Caire 11. Cairo: Institut Français d'Archéologie Orientale.
Rochemonteix, M. de, and Chassinat, E.
1897 *Le Temple d'Edfou*, vol. I. Paris: Librairie de la Société Asiatique, de l'École du Louvre, etc.
Roeder, G.
1960 *Kulte, Orakel und Naturverehrung im alten Ägypten.* Zurich / Stuttgart: Artemis.
Roth, A. M.
1992 "The *Psš-kf* and the 'Opening of the Mouth' Ceremony: A Ritual of Birth and Rebirth." *The Journal of Egyptian Archaeology* 78:113–47.
Rundle Clark, R. T.
1959 *Myth and Symbol in Ancient Egypt.* London: Thames and Hudson.

Sauneron, S.
1954 "La Justice à la porte des temples (à propos du nom égyptien des propylées)." *Bulletin de l'Institut Français d'Archéologie Orientale au Caire* 54: 117–27.
1960 *The Priests of Ancient Egypt.* Trans. Ann Morrissett. New York: Grove.
1982 *Esna,* vol. 8: *L'Écriture figurative dans les textes d'Esna.* Cairo: Institut Français d'Archéologie Orientale.
Schäfer, H.
1904 *Die Mysterien des Osiris in Abydos unter König Sesostris III nach dem Denkstein des Oberschatzmeisters I-cher-nofret im Berliner Museum.* Untersuchungen zur Geschichte und Altertumskunde Ägyptens 4/2. Leipzig: Hinrichs.
Schlögl, H.
1986 "Uschebti." Cols. 896–99 in vol. 6 of *Lexikon der Ägyptologie,* ed. W. Helck and W. Westendorf. Wiesbaden: Harrassowitz.
Schmitz, B.
1984 "Sem (priester)." Cols. 833–36 in vol. 5 of *Lexikon der Ägyptologie,* ed. W. Helck and W. Westendorf. Wiesbaden: Harrassowitz.
Schulman, A. R.
1984 "The Iconographic Theme: 'Opening of the Mouth' on Stelae." *Journal of the American Research Center in Egypt* 21: 169–96.
1986 "Some Observations on the *3ḫ iḳr n Rʿ*-Stelae." *Bibliotheca Orientalis* 43: 302–48.
Schwabe, C. W.
1986 "Bull Semen and Muscle ATP: Some Evidence of the Dawn of Medical Science in Ancient Egypt." *Canadian Journal of Veterinary Research* 50: 145–53.
Schwabe, C. W. et al.
1989 *"Live Flesh": Rudiments of Muscle Physiology in Ancient Egypt.* Working Paper Series No. 54. Davis: Agricultural History Center, University of California.
Schweitzer, U.
1956 *Das Wesen des Ka im Diesseits und Jenseits der alten Ägypter.* Ägyptologische Forschungen 19. Glückstadt / Hamburg / New York: J.J. Augustin.
Sethe, K.
1910 *Die altägyptische Pyramidentexte nach den Papierabdrücken und Photographien des Berliner Museums.* Leipzig: Hinrichs.
1933 *Urkunden des Alten Reichs.* Leipzig: Hinrichs.
Simpson, W. K.
1982 "Egyptian Sculpture and Two-Dimensional Representation as Propaganda." *The Journal of Egyptian Archaeology* 68: 266–71.
Smith, H. S., and Stewart, H. M.
1984 "The Gurob Shrine Papyrus." *The Journal of Egyptian Archaeology* 70: 54–64.
Sørensen, J. P.
1982 "Redundans og abstraktion i det aegyptiske daglige tempelritual." *Chaos* 1:49–60.
Speiser, E. A.
1955 "The Creation Epic." Pp. 60–72 in *Ancient Near Eastern Texts Relating to the Old Testament,* ed. J. B. Pritchard. 2d ed. Princeton: Princeton University Press.
Spiegel, J.
1939 "Die Grundbedeutung des Stammes *ḥm*." *Zeitschrift für ägyptische Sprache und Altertumskunde* 75: 112–21.
1973 *Die Götter von Abydos: Studien zum ägyptischen Synkretismus.* Göttinger Orientforschungen, 4. Reihe, Band 1. Wiesbaden: Harrassowitz.
Stadelmann, R.
1967 *Syrische-palästinensche Gottheiten in Ägypten.* Probleme der Ägyptologie 5. Leiden: Brill.

Steindorff, G.
1911 "Der Ka und die Grabstatuen." *Zeitschrift für ägyptische Sprache und Altertumskunde* 48: 152–59.
Tobin, V. A.
1988 "Mytho-Theology in Ancient Egypt." *Journal of the American Research Center in Egypt* 25: 169–83.
Traunecker, C.
1992 *Les Dieux de l'Égypte.* Paris: Presses Universitaires de France.
Weigall, A. E. P.
1911 "Miscellaneous Notes." *Annales du Service des Antiquités de l'Égypte* 11: 170–76.
Weinstein, J. M.
1975 "Egyptian Relations with Palestine in the Middle Kingdom." *Bulletin of the American Schools of Oriential Research* 217: 1–16.
Wildung, D.
1982 "Naos." Cols. 341–42 in vol. 4 of *Lexikon der Ägyptologie*, ed. W. Helck and E. Otto. Wiesbaden: Harrassowitz.
Wilson, J. A.
1951 *The Culture of Ancient Egypt.* Chicago: University of Chicago Press.
1955a "The Hymn to the Aton." Pp. 369–71 in *Ancient Near Eastern Texts Relating to the Old Testament*, ed. J. B. Pritchard. 2d ed. Princeton: Princeton University Press.
1955b "Tut-ankh-Amon's Restoration after the Amarna Revolution." Pp. 251–52 in *Ancient Near Eastern Texts Relating to the Old Testament*, ed. J. B. Pritchard. 2d ed. Princeton: Princeton University Press.
1955c "Amon as the Sole God." Pp. 368–69 in *Ancient Near Eastern Texts Relating to the Old Testament*, ed. J. B. Pritchard. 2d ed. Princeton: Princeton University Press.
Wit, C. de
1961a "Inscriptions dédicatoires du temple d'Edfou." *Chronique d'Égypte* 36: 56–97.
1961b "Inscriptions dédicatoires du temple d'Edfou." *Chronique d'Égypte* 36: 277–320.
Žabkar, L. V.
1968 *A Study of the Ba Concept in Ancient Egyptian Texts.* Studies in Ancient Oriential Civilization 34. Chicago: University of Chicago Press.
1988 *Hymns to Isis in Her Temple at Philae.* Hanover / London: University Press of New England.

The Divine Image in Contemporary South India: The Renaissance of a Once Maligned Tradition

Joanne Punzo Waghorne

No Hindoo who has received an English education ever remains sincerely attached to his religion. . . . It is my firm belief that if our plans of education are followed up there will be not a single idolater among the respectable classes in Bengal thirty years hence.

—Lord Macauley, 1831[1]

It may seen incredible to you that educated men should stand up today and defend idolatry. Has India learned nothing? . . . India is a land of contradictions. The most metaphysical of races is still the most polytheistic and the most idolatrous.

—John Henry Barrows, 1896[2]

Author's note: The title of this paper is adapted from Partha Mitter's fine history of the Western reaction to Indian images of gods, *Much Maligned Monsters* (1977).

1. Quoted from a letter by Macaulay to his father in 1835 (Smith 1879: 193). Lord Macaulay wrote a famous Minute (the British bureaucratic term for a memorandum) that outlined the new British policy to support higher education on the model of English universities and in the English language. Prior to this, the East India Company had support schools for Sanskrit and the Indian vernacular languages.

2. Barrows was the president of the now famous World Parliament of Religions held in conjunction with the Columbia Exhibition in Chicago in 1893. Inspired by the Parliament, Mrs. Caroline Haskell founded a lectureship on comparative religion at the University of Chicago that continues today and also established another lectureship to be delivered in India. Barrows was chosen to go to India in 1896 and arrived just after the triumphant return of Swami Vivekananda, whose impassioned defense of Hinduism at the World's Parliament made him a celebrity among educated Hindus in India and among the advocates for the new comparative study of religion in America. Barrows in his lectures, quickly published as *Christianity, the World Religion,* tried (unsuccessfully) to silence Vivekanda's thunder (1897: 73).

In the opening days of the nineteenth century, the British East India Company consolidated a new empire in India. No longer primarily traders or merchants, as they had been for nearly a hundred years, these new foreign masters of India began to structure their rule and to justify their new power to a sometimes suspicious British public and an often hostile Parliament at home. At the same time, a new evangelical movement was sweeping England and spilling over into the discussion of a righteous rule of India, as the fervor to save souls at home became a passion to convert the world. And, significantly, during this period of the consolidation of an Eastern empire in an age-old land, Britons had their first glimpse of the recently garnered artifacts of the ancient Mediterranean world. Gods from the ruins of Egypt were for the first time displayed in the new British Museum in 1802 (James 1981: 4–6).[3] For many educated Europeans, these ancient sculptures exemplified great wonders of human ingenuity, as did the newly discovered religious texts and temples of India. But for others, India, with its temples still thriving and alive with ritual activity, became a manifestation of an idolatry as pervasive as any in the ancient world. The missionaries and many British civil servants, under the influence of the new evangelical ethos, closed their eyes to the India in front of them and heard instead the sharp voices of the prophets and the cutting wit of the Hellenistic rationalists against the foolish idolater. For nearly a century, India provided a theater in which Victorian gentlemen could play the new prophet or the enlightened Greek rationalist or both, as they strode into this land of living idolatry to denounce its ignorance and announce their own formulas for its salvation.

This new crusade against idolatry adopted, as we will see, much of the "logic" of the last stages of the prophetic parodies against idolatry and merged this with the Hellenistic rationalism that had found new life in the eighteenth-century Enlightenment. The major charge against Indian idolatry focused on the deluded mind of the idolater, who was drained of all moral fiber, enslaved to custom, and bankrupted by crafty priests who filled their bloated bellies by maintaining these delusions. Thus the cries against idolatry were immediately linked with crusades for education in India and the founding of new universities and colleges on the "enlightened" model of British education. British education, with the English language as the medium of instruction, was introduced into India in 1835.

A century and a half later, the drama of the crusade against "idolatry" played itself out with superb irony. Young Indians took to British sciences, social sciences and phi-

3. The core of what was to become the Egyptian collection of the British Museum began with a small collection donated by members of "the Egyptian Society" of London. Napoleon, however, inadvertently did far more for the collection. His military expedition to Egypt to secure domination of the new Eastern trade routes to India was joined by French scholars who began a serious collection of ancient objects. These were confiscated by the victorious British army and sent back to England as trophies of war. This collection, along with the finds of Giovanni Belazoni's early archaeological expeditions to Egypt, were finally installed in the new Egyptian sculpture gallery in 1835 (James 1981: 12–18). Thus, ironically, the defeat of Napoleon's own ambitions toward India led to establishment of museums in Britain that displayed ancient images during the same years that the British rediscovered "idolatry" in India.

losophy with gusto. They took the English language, mastered it, and made it their own. India has produced major literary figures, scientists, philosophers, and a large middle-class of journalists, scientists, engineers, administrators, and businessmen. But in India, especially in South India, "idolatry" has also persisted. Here living iconic traditions continued through unbroken lineages of sculptors (S/*śilpin*),[4] temple architects (S/*sthapati*), and learned priests (T/*ācāriyaṉ*). In modern urban India, Hindu scholars (S/*paṇḍita*, 'pandit') continue to teach the complex ritual texts in Sanskrit, the *āgamas*,[5] which like the Mesopotamian and Egyptian sources focus on worship in the temple and combine how-to instructions with theological reflections (Davis 1991: 9–14; Bhatt 1984: 10–18, 1988: 24–45; Brunner-Lachaux 1963: i–xlvii).

The environs of Madras city in South India is an especially vital area for modern Hinduism. New schools and universities continue to be built, industry expands, and technology advances, as computer companies begin to rise around this city like their counterparts in the Silicon Valley in San Jose or on Route 128 in Boston. At the same time, the industrial middle-class actively supports building new temples as never before, sometimes on the same grounds as the English medium school or the modern new industry. As Philip Ashby pointed out fifteen years ago, Western and Indian intellectuals who "de-emphasize the roles of the intimate family social group and the cult in daily religious life . . . are not aware of or they ignore reports like that of an Indian political scientist in 1961 who said that more Hindu temples has been built in the preceding ten years than in the previous two generations" (Ashby 1974: 131). All such construction and the rituals that accompany the proper consecration of these temples are expensive, but committees of lay devotees seem to have no trouble raising funds from individuals,

4. Transliterating liturgical and technical terms for temple rituals used in modern Madras is a nightmare. Many of the publication of temples are in English. Although the priests most often use Sanskrit terms, they write them in Tamil script and thoroughly Tamilize their form, following the common practice for the last several centuries. The English publications in India usually do not italicize technical terms but capitalize them. In the context of this volume, I will use the proper Sanskrit or Tamil form of the word of the most commonly used term in each case. In some cases, the term that is most used is Tamil but with part of its form borrowed from Sanskrit. I will indicate the formation of such terms. When each term is first used, I will give its language of origin as S/ = Sanskrit or T/ = Tamil, followed by the transliteration of the original term. Following the practice in anthropological descriptions, I will not continue to use diacritics and italic on frequently used terms.

5. These scriptures date from the 10th century to the 12th century C.E. Madras city and the broad surrounding area is a center for the study of these ritual texts. Temples such as the Kapaleeswara Temple in Mylapore have traditional schools (S/*bhaṭṭaṣāla*; T/*paṭṭasālai*) attached to the temple grounds to train young priests. Traditional pandits and university-trained scholars work together to edit, translate, and publish texts in such institutions as the Kuppuswami Sastri Research Institute in Madras, the Institut Français d'Indologie in Pondichéry, the Sarasvati Mahal Library in Tanjore, and the Government School in Mahabalipuram. The Anathacharya Indological Research Institute in Bombay, directed by K. K. A. Venkatachari has sponsored several important conferences on the *agamas*, temples, and temple rituals. A new institute in Mahabalipuram, a center for traditional sculpture and architecture, has been founded by V. Ganapati Stapathi, a celebrated contemporary temple architect who has designed several Hindu temples in the United States.

small businesses, and larger corporations in the area. Today there is a renewal of temple culture in progress, a renaissance that embraces modernity and expresses it in the very cultic forms supposed to be so antithetical to it.

The worship of the divine image in South India, then, is vital for the contemporary context that it adds to this volume's study of the making of the cult image. But, even a survey of the making of cult images in modern India and the rituals that consecrate these images would be a book-length project. For this chapter, I will present the position of the modern iconoclasts, the "educated" British and Americans who argued for over a century against this "heinous practice" in the context of my observation[6] in Madras of the "All India Sai Samaj Mangalabhishekam for Shri Sai Baba Murthi," as it was announced in the newpapers, held on March 22, 1987. This was the 48th day and final ceremony for the installation of a life-size marble image of a modern saint, Sai Baba of Shirdi (1835–1917), who was considered an embodiment of the supreme Godhead by devotees.

The devotees of Sai Baba of Shirdi are found all over India and are distinctive in many respects but also typical of many modern religious movements there that have included the installation and the worship of an image-body (S/*mūrti*) of their founder-teacher as the "Gurudev" (S/*gurudēva*, 'teacher-God'). The members of the Sai Samaj, the congregation of devotees located in the Mylapore neighborhood of Madras, tend to be well-educated professionals from many caste and community backgrounds who share in the common fellowship that the now-living presence of Sai Baba in the image-body, the *mūrti*, is said to foster. The Sai Baba community, again like many modern religious movements, emphasizes social service as an important part of their mission in Madras. These image-worshippers hardly fit the picture of members of the incredulous masses or of socially insensitive hoodwinkers that filled the pages of the nineteenth-century polemics against idolatry. The members of Sai Samaj in Madras are articulate members of the modern world. Their rationality and their theology, nonetheless, allows for the expectation that their own actions in ritual will bring the living presence of divinity into a marble image formed by human hands. In the gulf between the modern iconoclasm

6. In addition to this consecration ritual, I witnessed several more such rituals installing the divine images in new temples in Madras in 1986–87. My husband Dick Waghorne and I observed and he photographed the *mahakumpabhiṣēka* (consecration ritual) of the (1) Sri Tyagaraja Sami Temple in Tirupati, April 15–19; (2) Sri Ayyappan Temple, Madipakkam, May 29, 1987; (3) Sri Kalyana Kandaswamy Temple Madipakkam, Madras, June 1, 1987; (4) Tyagaraja Ashraman, Tiruvaiyaru, June, 9, 10, 11. When we returned to the United States, we began to document the same installation rituals for the Sri Siva-Vishnu Temple in Lanham, Maryland, just outside of Washington, D.C. The divine images in this grand new temple have been installed over a period of four years, with major rituals happening in the summers of 1990, 1991, 1992, and 1993. The temple, along with many others in major metropolitan cities and even smaller towns across the United States, have been built by the new Indian communities here. Thus, the temple-building boom witnessed in Madras in 1987 has extended to the United States as part of the Hindu diaspora of the last twenty years. We returned to India in 1994–95 to continue this study at new temples.

and this living practice of iconolatry in modern India lies the potential to understand how concretized religion, materialized divinity, functions and thrives in the new urban cosmos of modern times as it once did in the urban centers of the ancient world.

The Modern Iconoclasts

> *This ignorance could not annihilate the principle of religion in the spirit of man, but in removing the awful repression of the idea of one exclusive sovereign Divinity, it left that spirit to form its religion in its own manner . . . depraved and insane invention took this direction with ardour . . . the promiscuous numberless crowd of almost all shapes of fancy and of matter, became . . . mounted into gods. They were alternately the toys and the tyrants of their miserable creators.*
>
> —John Foster, 1821

India, although the jewel of the Empire, became the most glaring illustration of the nineteenth-century's definition of "idolatry." The word "idolatry" came to function in Britain and in America as an amorphous term to be readily applied to any form of religion, at home or abroad, that did not properly acknowledge the biblical word of revelation and did not conform to an enshrined standard of rationality. The term implied a set of interconnected assumptions that came to seem so right and so reasonable that it passed into the twentieth century sometimes even in the guises of social-science theory and development studies. The process of the modernization of the old prophetic polemic began, ironically, with the rise of classical humanism.

The age of revolutions in Europe and America, from 1750 through the 1820s, produced a wave of humanism in the Western world that coincided with the early period of British expansion in India. For a brief time, the desire to know and understand overpowered the need to judge and distance this foreign culture. Journals of travels in India kept by early officials of the East India Trading Company were often notably free from the language of judgment. A British officer traveling in the employ of an Indian prince in 1773 describes a Christian missionary as "haranguing" the priests in the great temple of Srirangam and creating such a disturbance that his own tour was disrupted.[7] That this same missionary would become a heroic figure for later generations of British highlights the nature of the change in attitudes that occurred in the next fifty years. With the rise of the evangelical movement in Britain in the 1820s, a new modern style of the polemic against idolatry took form. The campaign for education and social justice

7. This appears in the Diary of George Patterson, 1772–73, a manuscript in the India Office Library (European Manuscripts E379/vol. 9:224). Patterson was referring to Christian Frederick Swartz, whose early work in South India was used to spur the later rise of missionary evangelicalism in Britain.

borrowed from the earlier period of humanism was recast in biblical language and turned into a new crusade against "idolatry."

The early polemic against idolatry quoted above was initially directed against the ancient pagans, but as the author put it, it is "applicable to modern heathens" (Foster 1821: 39). Published in 1821, John Foster's *Essay on the Evils of Popular Ignorance* is a superb example of the new critique of "idolatry" that would fall most heavily on India as the British began to consolidate their empire. Although the book never mentions India, it was misclassified in the card catalogs of the nineteenth century under "missions-India," betraying its probable use, and was only recently recataloged in the library in which I found it. The work, a plea for educating the "lower orders" in Britain, nonetheless assumes a connection between the ignorance of the uneducated in Britain and the profound ignorance of all deluded souls who are without the holy word of the One God. The essay begins with a quotation from Hosea, "My people are destroyed for lack of knowledge." In his preface to the American edition, John Foster explains that this quotation remained the "motto" for his essay, which was originally given as a series of lectures for the Bristol Auxiliary British and Foreign School Society, a missionary group. He confesses the essay to be "but as an echo, of that sentence of sacred language" (vi).

Foster's essay encapsulated the nineteenth-century notions about idolatry that became as congealed as the millennia-old concoction of Greek satires with the prophets' polemics outlined earlier in this volume by Michael Dick. This latter-day meeting of Greek with Hebrew, however, occurred in individuals whose classic education in school and university bridged to a later period of evangelical piety. Their own meeting of Greek and Hebrew filtered through Reformation Protestant theology produced a Christianity of the Book and of books. Such was John Foster's essay in which he defined the human mind as "the supremely valuable thing in man" (p. 274) and yet with certainty equated all intellectual development with knowledge of the revealed word of God. Thus *ignorance = spiritual depravity,* while *education = rationality = knowledge of the Bible.* His essay is a "history" of such ignorance in which he asks his readers to

> behold the different spectacle of numerous national tribes, or any small selection of persons, on whose *minds* are displayed the full effects of knowledge denied; who are under the process of whatever destruction it is, that spirits can suffer from want of the vital aliment to the intellectual nature, especially from 'famine of the words of the Lord' (p. 67).

In Foster's history, all people once knew the one true God but some fell away because of their vanity and lust for power. Once deprived of divine Truth, humans were now ruled by their own passions and not by God's reason. They created their gods in their own image out of the material which their own senses and fantasy could provide. The clever among them saw the untruth in these gods but also saw the opportunity to play on the ignorance of the masses and learned to exploit popular faith in these gods to gain power. Thus, tyranny was born. Idolatry remained rampant among the masses, who were assumed to be especially lustful and unreasonable. The elite should have known better but enjoyed the power that their control over these puppet gods provided. Idolatry was thus connected to:

1. the ignorance of the masses,
2. the duplicity of the elite,
3. the general rule of the sense over reason,
4. the rise of social injustice and
5. the degeneration of the entire human race from God's pure creation.[8]

Foster said nothing of India and only a little of modern pagan religion but saved his venom for his arch idolaters—the Catholic Church.[9] By the mid-nineteenth century, however, the "popish" priests lost their first place among tyrant-idolaters to the Hindu priests and the Hindu pandits.

The voices of the prophets continues to echo throughout the nineteenth century, as missionary activity increased when the British Parliament renewed the East India Company's charter in 1813, granting them power to rule India but adding a pro-missionary clause after a rancorous debate. The clause in the new charter was not an open endorsement of missionary activities but was couched in terms of advocating support for those who brought "useful knowledge and moral improvement" to the "the native inhabitants of British dominions in India" (Richter 1908: 150–51). In the 1820s, a coterie of British civil servants had made Foster's same connections between rationality, education, and civilization in a neo-prophetic formula that lumped ritual, cult, priestcraft, ignorance, injustice, vanity into one "heinous" evil—idolatry.[10] That education would "naturally" predispose the Indian mind to rationality and thereby lay the very groundwork for the destruction of idolatry and the acceptance of a book-based Christianity. Other civil servants, however, stood fast to an Enlightenment relativism about truth and falsehood in religion and maintained an adventurous spirit that continued a give-and-take relationship with Indian culture. These were the "Orientalists," a long line of British bureaucrat-scholars who continued to defend Indian culture and religion throughout the nineteenth century. A letter of 1831 from Henry Young well illustrates how this young pro-missionary civil officer portrays the distinctions between education of Indians in the famous "Hindoo College" championed by H. H. Wilson, the leader of the

8. It is not hard to see how a holistic reading of Hosea could well be used as a motto for such an equation. Foster makes no careful distinctions, as does Michael Dick, between Hosea's concern for the erection of pillars or offerings under trees, or sacrifices on hills within the Israelite cult and the prophets' discussion against Mesopotamian "idolatry." Foster's essay predates modern biblical criticism and did not anticipate the effect that humanistic scholarship on the Bible itself would have on his natural equation of intellectual achievement with knowledge of *the* Book.

9. For example, Foster describes a scene in the Catholic church: ". . . with the darkness of the shadow of death in their souls, they prostrated themselves to their saints or to their 'queen of heaven,' nay to painted images and toys of wood or wax, to some ounce or two of bread and wine, to fragments of old bones, and rags of clothing" (p. 62).

10. In this period, from 1793–1833, a growing number of missionaries not only fought Hindu society with its idolatry from the outside but began to try to "reform" the overly Hindu habits of their own converts. Within Indian Christian communities, the hold-out from Hinduism was not idolatry per se but the continuance of caste practices among the converts. Here also many missionaries held that "education" of the community would naturally lead to the end of these practices (Ingram 1956: 20ff.).

Orientalists, and new Christian school founded by the Reverend Doctor Alexander Duff:

> The Hindoo College is a fine quadrangular building, the inner area being very small, so as to give the house the shape of a native building; I do not say appearance for it is built after a regular Grecian order, and, like most houses in Calcutta, is very handsome and elegant. The ground-floor students are exclusively engaged in the study of Sanscrit [Sanskrit] which occupies them seven or eight years, and one can not help grieving at the sad and cruel waste of precious time and talent at this unprofitable study. English has been introduced recently, that is to say, since the last two or three years; and I observed one class going over a proposition of Euclid, which they seemed to enter into con amore. The first class had just returned from a lecture on some branch of natural philosophy, and seeing some essays of their composing I asked for one or two, which with some hesitation they granted. . . . The subject was: 'Is Paley's definition of virtue, viz., that it is doing good for mankind for the sake of everlasting happiness, correct?' and the writer contended that after death the soul vanished into thin air, etc. (quoted in George Smith 1879: 169–70).

This was written at the height of the campaign to introduce English as the exclusive medium of instruction, as Duff has already done in his new school. Here the old British civil servants of the East India Company are accused of supporting a school that merely rejoined the Hindu mind to the pagan Greek. Now these neo-pagans dwelt in this Hindu-Greek house, happily spinning fruitless philosophy that denied a knowledge of real virtue to the soul and the spirit, which Young hints could so easily be found by reading a good English Bible. The Reverend Duff, who is credited with providing a model of true education in his own school, already had the prophets on the tip of his pen when he wrote in his journal in 1832, "Here there is little change: much work of preparation silently carried on, little of the practical work of conversion from dumb idols to serve the living God" (Smith 1979: 171). From this point on, the voices of the new prophets would try to silence any rationalism that did not harken to the Word of God.

Once India was opened to missionary activity, the subcontinent was imagined in truly Biblical proportions as a mighty stage for grand expansion of God's Kingdom. As early as 1811, vice-provost of the official government college of Calcutta wrote:

> No Christian nation ever possessed such an extensive field for the propagation of the Christian faith, as that afforded to us by our influence over the hundred million natives of Hindoo-stan. . . . Why should it be though incredible that Providence hath been pleased, in a course of years to subjugate this Eastern Empire to the most civilized nation in the world, for this very purpose? (Buchanan 1811: 41).

And, almost a century later that same untainted sense that the nineteenth century marked a new great extension of biblical times echoed in the lectures of the president of the now famous 1893 World Parliament of Religions:[11]

11. The World's Parliament in many was marked the entrance of America into the world's scholarly community. The centenary of this event has produced new scholarly interest in the Parliament.

> The religion of Christ has in this century of intellectual progress, when superstitions have been dispelled by the light of truth, made more rapid and memorable conquests than any previous periods since the downfall of Roman paganism (Barrows 1897: 23).

The sense was that this was a time when scenes from the prophets and the Gospels made India a living museum of idolatry, Satan's very kingdom.

In the published "memoirs" of missionaries and in the many biographies about them—very popular genres in the nineteenth century—the book-based Christianity came back to life. Here the living presence of an ancient temple-based religion set a stage for the arguments against idolatry that turned learned references to the Bible into vibrant evocations of Biblical times in which the participants in the debate wandered over this vast continent, not simply quoting the prophets, but standing once again in their sandals, seeing themselves like a Second Isaiah pitted against the vast wealth of an undying Babylon. But the much-accepted theory that all humanity had once known God's true word allowed the missionary also to hurl the learned Hindu into the role of Hosea's own Israelites, once God's chosen nation of priests who "rejected knowledge" for the sake of their fat bellies and unquenchable desires. In a journal entry from 1847 later published by his brother, the Reverend Henry Fox describes his debates with a group of learned Brahmins:

> I walked into the village to get into the shade of the houses and went to a street full of Brahmins, where I has been treated somewhat rudely in the morning. In a few minutes I had the whole horde upon me, and there ensued a discussion most utterly profitless, except to myself, to whom it served as a grindstone to sharpen me for further contests. About two o'clock, Brahmins, old and young, with pride and impudence strongly marked in their faces, surrounded me, and sometimes one, but more commonly three or four at once, assailed me with childish and ludicrous questions, many of them of a quite unanswerable character: "Why are some men born rich and others poor?" . . . "Is there any difference between God and your body?" "Who knows the difference between right and wrong?" "Is your God, the God of the whole world or only of your country?" . . . I could only feel at the end, that God had graciously delivered me out of the hand of the enemy, and also I felt sorry at these poor men willingly refusing the light and the treasure. But I rejoiced to find Satan alive to the fact of his kingdom being disturbed; anything is better than the deadness of some places (Fox 1852: 229–30).

In another version of a discussion that he had with a group that came to his tent, Fox writes in 1847:

> Several have harped on the trite topics, that all things are God, and that he is materially the substance of all: others again, that our bodies are created by him, but that he is the soul of all men, that there is but one spirit, ours and his being the same; others that God is the author of sin, "for if He is not," they say "who is?" . . . It is quite remarkable how

To mark the occasion, religious leaders met again in Chicago in August, 1993, for a second parliament. For an introduction and an edited collection of the many speeches given at the 1893 event, see Seager 1993.

> readily they fly off from the subject: pretending to answer some questions I have asked, they will go on with a long rigmarole about what has no more to do with it than the man in the moon[12] (Fox 1853: 227).

Both of these descriptions reveal Fox as the heroic prophet faced with the blind "wise man"—wise in their own conceit. He must stride out "alone in the midst of Satan's kingdom" (p. 224) to debate with these utterly foolish questioners. Here, of course, Fox is not only a modern Hosea but also the prophet Jesus confronting the Pharisees.

Images of the prophets in the den of idolatry crying to save the widow and the orphan from social injustice also linger in the verbal images created in another earlier "memoir" of the missionary John Chamberlain, whose biographer describes his heroic labors in the backcounty of Bengal:

> At the ghaut [ghat], or landing place, are great numbers of persons bathing and performing their morning ceremonies; and among them, a poor woman laid on a low bed, raised only a few inches above the ground, in dying circumstances, left exposed to the blazing sun, totally unheeded by all around her, with a young man, her son, sitting behind her waiting, to appearance destitute of all anxiety, to see her breathe her last. Above, are the ruins of a large idol temple, grown over with weeds and scrubs; not far distant from it, the hut of a Brahmun [Brahmin] filled with images, constant objects of his veneration and confidence; and behind this a bazaar, where numbers of people collect together for purpose of traffick. These and such like scenes meet the eye in every direction while floating on this river, and it was to these haunts of idolatry that our friend penetrated to preach the everlasting gospel (Yates 1831: 139–40).

The memoir of Rev. Fox has a similar scene on the theme of the greedy priest who sits with his idols while the poor are robbed of life and livelihood:

> As we drew near to the river, we passed several small raree shows [portable peep shows] consisting each of a box gaily painted with mythological figures, and opening with folding-doors so as to display inside the tawdry image of either Vishnu or Siva; these were placed in the road by the owner, who stood by begging for money, and reaping a rich harvest from the piety of the people. When I asked some of them why they provided mere toys for worship instead of serving God, they made the common answer of patting their stomachs, to show that it was their livelihood (Fox 1852: 219–20).

The same themes of the crafty priest and the blind pandits persisted to the very end of the century. Describing the holiest city in India in the first Haskell lectures, Dr. Borrows the President of the now famous World Parliament of Religion of 1893, says of the city of Benares:

> In the bewildering scene one becomes confused and asks himself if he is visiting Bedlam. Is this the nineteenth century? Where is our boasted civilization? Are all men maniacs here? Is insanity the natural conditions of some portions of the human race? There is a temple to the goddess of small-pox; here are idols of almost inconceivable

12. The concept that the divine and human body share the same subtle substance is common in Hindu theology. See Narayanan 1985: 54; Davis 1991: 101–4.

> hideousness; there are men carrying a dead body to lay it in the sacred waters before it is burned; here others are pounding the fragments of a human form that has only been partly incinerated; there hundreds of poor wrenches are crowding down toward a noisome well with copper coins in their fingers and wreaths of yellow flowers, eager to dip their hands and feet in its infested depths. . . . One walks through the crowds that press down to the Ganges . . . with the feeling that here priestly tyranny has achieved its most diabolical triumphs; it has enslaved and degraded and almost bestialized a proud and intelligent people (Barrows 1899: 67).[13]

Again we meet the unenlightened educated of this den of idolatry:

> Now I know what excuses are offered for these idolatries. I once spent a whole morning in Madras listening to excuses and palliations. My lectures in that city, following immediately those of the famous apostle of Hinduism, Swami Vivekananda, had aroused a good deal of discussion, and naturally there was an eager desire on the part of the Hindu Pundits and the sharped-tongued Hindu lawyers to get even with the Christian apologist, who was invited to attend a reception given at eight o'clock and to speak on American and the Columbian Fair. . . . Perhaps a hundred and fifty lawyers, well educated and glib-tongued men, were present. They filled the hall, and were evidently expecting no ordinary sport (Barrows 1899: 68).

Thus, for nearly a century the British and later the American missionaries who attacked "idolatry" maintained an interconnected set of assumptions that linked idolatry to unreason, guile, ignorance, social and ultimately economic injustice, and poverty.

In the late nineteenth and early twentieth centuries, a rising new class of university-educated Indian intellectuals, the beneficiaries of those earlier cries for universal education, began in earnest to apologize in the classical sense of the term for Hindu "idolatry." Beginning in the 1870s, there was a gradual revival of the "Orientalists," those British intellectuals and civil servants who discovered and extolled the value of the ancient East. These new Orientalists began to underplay the current state of Hindu religion as being a deviation from a once glorious past. Anxious to make the most of this small offering for a new pride, the Indian intellectuals lost no time in appropriating this academic theory as an intellectual resource for a growing nationalism. Accepted as axiomatic by both Indian and Western theorists was the inferiority of modern image-worship compared to India's ancient philosophical tradition. Theories of the origins of modern idolatry followed the earlier general theory of devolution: India had simply fallen into degeneracy from its once glorious past. The "ignorant masses" were predictably blamed for introducing this practice into India.[14]

As the theory of the evolution of human history reversed the earlier theory of a primal Golden Age gone amuck, image-worship came to be defended by Indian intellectu-

13. My thanks to Jeremy Lehrer, a student-member of our seminar "Visions and Journeys: Orientalism" in the Department of Religious Studies at The University of North Carolina, Chapel, Hill, for this reference.

14. This theory has persisted in India among scholars and is still popular. Examples of recent adherents include J. N. Banerjea (1954: 66–72) and the very respected P. V. Kane (1941: 707–13).

als by arguing in the fashion of the famous Sanskritist F. Max Müller that the practice was a necessary step for those not sufficiently evolved spiritually to deal directly with abstract concepts of God (Müller 1964[1878]: 360–78). Swami Vivekananda, in a fiery speech before the 1893 World Congress of Religions in Chicago, turned the iconoclasms of the missionaries inside-out by arguing that Hindus recognized "idolatry" as a legitimate first step to God, but only as a first step. While Hindus matured beyond the need for all material forms to direct worship, the Christian West could never relinquish its own idolatrous clinging to holy books, churches, or even doctrines:

> Hindus associated the ideas of holiness, purity, truth, omnipresence, and all other ideas with different images and forms. But with this difference: upon certain actions some are drawn their whole lives to their idol of a church and never rise higher, because with them religion means an intellectual assent to certain doctrines and doing good to their fellows, the whole religion of the Hindu is centered in realization. Man is to become Divine, realizing the Divine, and, therefore, idol or temple or church or books, are only the supports, the helps of his spiritual childhood, but on and on he must progress (Seager 1993: 429).

Vivekananda's defense of idolatry satisfied the late nineteenth century's liberal tastes for a seemingly rational explanation of religious phenomenon, but Vivekananda was not telling all to his Chicago audience. Subtly placing the actual practice of image-worship beyond Western view and Western criticism by his powerful intellect and masterful use of the English language, Vivekananda never revealed the extent to which the practice continued for those Hindus he implied were now above it. His great spiritual master, Sri Ramakrishna, had never ceased to worship God in incarnated form. Sri Ramakrishna was a priest whose duty was to serve and care for the holy image in the Kali Temple in Calcutta where he spent most of his life. A modern guide to that famous temple tells the pilgrim that Sri Ramakrishna "experimented on the full spectrum of spiritual life" by study and worship of many deities and many religions, including Islam and Christianity, "which culminated in the worship of the Shodasi in the person of Sri Sarada Devi, his divine consort" (Bodhaswarupananda 1974: 31). Ramakrishna never left the precincts of the temple to carry out his experiments. His birthplace as well as this temple remain a shrine to all of his followers. This same guidebook calls the temple "the Abode par excellence of his spiritual presence" (p. 31) and earlier tells the devotee that at the birthplace of Sri Ramakrishna, in a village in Bengal, a temple has been built to Sri Ramakrishna himself and that the "marble image of Sri Ramakrishna in the temple was installed on May 11, 1951, and since then has been and is worshiped daily" (p. 15). But, Sri Ramakrishna did not have to wait until the twentieth century to receive worship as a divine icon; Vivekananda himself installed his Master's ashes in the headquarters for the new Ramakrishna order of monks and began worship of both the vessel of ashes and a holy portrait of the Master within twelve years of his Master's death (Gambhirananda 1983[1957]: 103–4. The experience of the Ramakrishna Mission, of moving from intellectualism and apology back to the practice of ritual, is repeated, as we will see later, in many other movements in India that began in reaction to the devaluation of Hinduism.

Charges of idolatry for India, however, were not silenced by Vivekananda or the elegant arguments of others like him even in the West. In the early twentieth century a a new critique of Hinduism can be detected in some of the new social scientists who were fearful of the negative effects that such a strata of religion would have on economic development. The charge of "idolatry" per se never entered the new critique nor does the word even pass their pens or lips; but the general wastage of time, money, and energy in the "ritualism" that image-worship in fact enjoins remained a culprit that impedes modern development. A striking example of this continuity occurs in a recent college textbook on world religions. The picture of idolatry-for-profit that the Rev. Fox portrayed in his 1852 memoirs (Fox 1852: 219–20), as he described the portable peep shows of the gods wheeled out on the streets to solicit a few pennies from the deluded poor, reincarnates once again in a photograph that illustrates a section on "Hinduism Today" in *The Religious World: The Communities of Faith* (Converse 1988). The photograph, taken by the author, shows a "Portable Deity" wheeled out into the streets, with a bedraggled man sitting nearby. The caption explains to the student that the offerings made to this image "provide a living for the owner." The text explains that:

> Modern Hindu liberals regard the hundreds of religious holidays (national, religious, personal) as "bad news," for the many millions of hours are lost to production and the tasks of nation building. Similarly, absenteeism for the sake of performing pilgrimages is a drain on manpower, and the news that two and a half million pilgrims attended a holy festival for ten days is bad news for the economy (Converse 1988: 104).

Given the enormous range of modern Hinduism and the constricted space of a textbook entry, the inclusion of such a description becomes an overarching image of the religion in India for yet another generation of educated Britons and Americans.

Nevertheless, the fact remains that India in the twentieth century is now a major manufacturing nation. Economic development has not stood still and neither has temple worhsip with its divine images—an ornamented world of living Gods. As technology and industrialization progress, the rationalizing tendencies of Vivekananda alive in the "modern Hindu liberals" become less important to a younger generation. Things may well have changed rapidly during the last decade, for even the anthropologist Milton Singer in 1972 argued that modernization in Madras city was characterized by "'deritualization,' the decline in ritual observance represented by the abbreviation, consolidation, or omission of many domestic rites" and the rise of devotionalism (Singer 1972: 149). But today the rationalizing process, if it is carried on at all, is carried on in a very Indian manner of using ritual itself to make transitions, to make statements, to reconfigure the society working its way toward technology with surprising speed.

Thus the old thesis against "idolatry" fails to see that ritual itself can communicate, but more than this, that it can transform a society. Ritual can effect transition, and more specifically, the very making of the divine image—the divine body of the God—can bring about the necessary configuration of the world so that a new mode of life-making and life-producing can be absorbed in a former trading and agricultural society. A closer look at the consecration rituals for the marble image of Sai Baba in the Sai Mandira in Madras city can begin to prove this point.

Image-Making and Modernization in Madras

The image-body of Shirdi Sai Baba is not ancillary but primary to devotees and has been so from the beginning of the movement.[15] Unlike India's most famous modern saint, Mahatma Gandhi, Sai Baba was not concerned with ideology but with religious practice. Sai Baba of Shirdi taught in what is now Maharashtra state from 1854 to 1917. He preached the absolute importance of the person of the guru, the spiritual teacher, for the welfare of the devotee (Rigopoulos 1993: 172–77). Sai Baba declared that he had realized God and that his identity was merged with the universal Godhead. As the *Sai Sudhā*, the magazine of the movement explains:

> He emphasized pure love and surrender to the Gurudev —the Almighty—and considered no other sadhana [spiritual practice] as more effective than absolute surrender and service of the Gurudev. One-pointed devotion to the Guru—surrender of mind, thought, and body—at the feet of the Gurudev was all that was required. The guru takes over the entire care of the devotee disciple and the disciple is lifted up stage by stage if necessary until the disciple obtains full grace ([Venkataraman] 1987: 1).

Sai Baba's teachings were later propagated after his death by a former lawyer from Madras who had never met the guru but who wrote the definitive biography of the saint "by means of radiation or unseen influences [which] came to me in flashes to fill up the picture (of Baba) that I was trying to draw" (Saipadananda 1973: 29). Sri Narasimhaswamiji, as he is now called,

> discovered that Sai Baba was really the incarnation of Sri Rama [an incarnation of Vishnu, the preserver of the universe] and Sri Krishna [also an incarnation of Vishnu] and that His power for good was as potent even after his Samadhi [his "death" viewed as only the end of his life in the flesh] as it had been when He was alive and that He was worthy of worship as God Incarnate (Kalidas 1987: 27).

Sri Narasimhaswamiji is always portrayed carrying the picture of Sai Baba, which he worshiped as the embodied guru.

Devotion to Sai Baba, then, is not modeled on an interpersonal relationship with God such as that defined by the nineteenth-century theology of a Foster or a Barrows in which God commands, reasons, and otherwise "talks" to his devotees. Sai Baba stressed what could be called an inter-bodily relationship in which the devotee experiences divinity in the sight, the sound, and the touch of the Master and in acts of service to

15. For a detailed treatment of Sai Baba's life, see Rigopoulos 1992.

Him. Service to such a master in India means physical service—washing the guru's feet, feeding him—while he is alive in the flesh. After death, the embodiment of the guru must continue, for His presence can not be separated from His teaching. This, then, is a system in which learning is assumed to take place as much through bodily action as through that equally mysterious process whereby the Divine Mind meets the human mind. Here the much-maligned notion in the West of "thinking with the heart" is revered as the path to God, not to perdition. When the body—both human and divine—becomes necessary for the realization of God, much of the logic of nineteenth-century Western theo-rationalism—if I may coin the term—falters. Ritual, as recent anthropology has clarified, is not "magic"—a mere mechanistic means to an end and therefore opposed to education. Ritual is itself both effectual and intellectual.[16] Ritual is not a part of the never-never land of vain hopes but rather a very real way to effect change—the personal transformation of the devotee, and the transformation of the community as a new social entity.

But beyond these social and personal aspects, ritual is also the means whereby stone comes alive. For the Sai Samaj, it is this latter theomorphic transformation of matter into God that is central to all else. The final installation rituals of the new marble mūrti of Sai Baba at the Sai Mandira, the temple of Sai Baba, on Sunday, March 22, 1987 was the central transformative ritual. Devotees to the new mūrti of Sai Baba told me emphatically that this new image-body of the guru allowed them to do real service now to His body and thus to Him. And the making of this divine image also allowed for the renewal of a new social body of devotees. The ritual of the "making" of the divine image was all about bodies—human, divine, social, and metasocial. An analysis of the details of ritual actions of that Sunday morning will provide precision to the argument that rituals that make stone into holy flesh do not harden a society but rather create a supple matter in which life can be conceived.

Embodying Sai Baba in Living Stone

The 48th-day final ceremony took place in two adjacent halls, with the two crucial parts of the ritual sometimes going on synchronically. The temple complex that houses the image of Sai Baba is divided into two major rooms joined by a narrow passageway. As the devotee enters the temple complex, the main gate directly faces a large open room with a raised stage that functions as the sanctum on which the marble image of Sai Baba, consecrated that day, now stands. This is the temple (S/*mandira*) proper. In the *mandira*, behind the marble image of Sai Baba stands a silver throne on which rests the painted portrait of this divine teacher, the Gurudev, that for years had been the primary object of devotion for the community (fig. 1; all photographs are by Dick Waghorne).

16. For a cogent account of recent theory in ritual studies as well as an explication of ritual as meaning, see Catherine Bell's *Ritual Theory, Ritual Practice* (1992: 30–54).

[Figure 1] THE AGAMA SASTRIAR, the priest who is expert in the ritual texts for this installation, presents a garland to the painting of Sai Baba, here enthroned on a silver stand with lion guards; the painting had served as the principal image for the community until this day, when the marble image of the Master would supersede it.

To the left of the sanctum-stage is another small room in which a flame continually burns. This flame was kindled from the fire at the temple in Shirdi, Sai Baba's earthly home, which had burned unceasingly since the guru's death. To the right of the *mandira* is a room used for meetings, lectures, or religious discourses. On the final day of the consecration rituals, this room was transformed into "the hall of the sacrifice" (S/*yajaśāla*).

[Figure 2] WOMEN DEVOTEES OF SAI BABA prepare raw fruit in the *yajaśāla* just before the priests begin to chant. The holy pots, the *kumpam*, can be seen in the background, each seated on a bed of grain, covered with a cloth crisscrossed with strings, then topped with a coconut and flowers.

The ritual process moved back and forth during the day between the two major rooms, the *mandira* and the *yajaśāla*. The priests in the *yajaśāla* were all men and the chief actors in the ceremony with the exception of the wife of the lay head of the temple. The ritual harkened back to the ancient Vedic fire sacrifice and in this context functioned as the font of ancientness, of old normative tradition for this modern ritual. The actions in the *mandira*, on the other hand, were dominated by women and by the lay devotees. In architectural appearance and in ritual actions, it evoked invention and modern values. The two parts of the ritual were carefully synthesized in the end, and

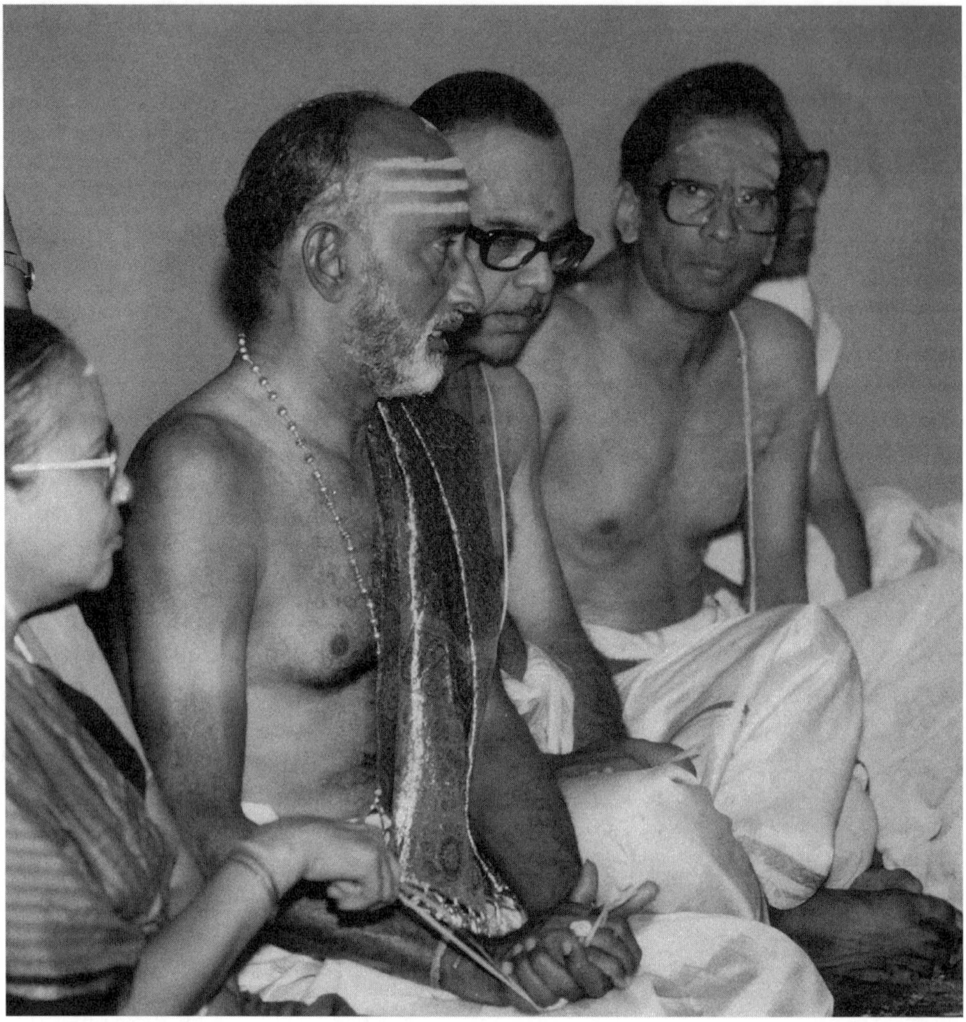

[Figure 3] DR. MUTHU VENKATARAMAN, acting as the *yajamāna*, is supported by his wife, who sits beside him in a gesture reflecting the ancient form of the Vedic sacrifice. Here, representing female power, she transfers her power to her husband and thus to the ritual.

this synthesis is key to understanding the ritual. A careful description of each stage of the observances will reveal the importance of this final synthesis.

The first stage of the ritual began in the mandira where the image-body of Sai Baba now sat "firmly" in the sanctum. The installation ritual (S/*pratiṣṭhā*) performed 48 days before had established the image on its permanent base and "made it firm," as the word in Sanskrit denotes. The sanctum, unlike the small room that holds the deity in a traditional temple, is an otherwise plain stage with a curtain in front that priests could open

[Figure 4] THE PAINTING OF SAI BABA, which at first covered the main *kumpam*, has been set aside so that the ritual can proceed. The juxtaposition of the portrait and the pot began a transmutation of power from the image to pot that the ritual will complete by then transferring the contents of the empowered pot to the new image-body.

to the audience at key points and then close at others. As the ritual began, the curtain was open and Sai Baba's *mūrti* was clothed in a formal white dhoti (a loincloth worn by traditional Hindu men). The temple priests made an offering of burning camphor and incense to the divine image-body, and the curtain closed.

The action now shifted to the *yajaśāla*. At the middle of this rectangular hall stood an altar in three tiers. In front of this altar was a fire pit constructed from bricks covered

[Figure 5] THE CHIEF PRIEST, dressed ornately for the occasion, begins to stoke the sacred fire with ghee.

in stucco. Such fire pits have been used for offering sacrifice in India since the time of the Vedas (1200 B.C.E.). To the left of the pit sat the priests, adorned with gold jewelry and with golden trimmed dhotis and brocade shawls and head turbans. On the right of fire pit sat a large group of women who were preparing food. Bananas and other raw fruits were set on trays. The women sat chopping and arranging while the priests were chanting mantras (S/*mantra*), the holy locutions that acted here much like "incantations" (fig. 2). When the women finished their work, the Secretary of the Sai Samaj and his wife acted as the 'sacrificer' (S/*yajamāna*), the patron of the ritual representing those

[Figure 6] WOMEN DEVOTEES BRING FRUIT from the *yajaśāla* to the *mandira.* Their saris are an important clue to the range of Sai Baba devotees. Two wear traditional Tamil Brahmin saris (right and next to left), one wears a very fashionable modern sari (left), and another a traditional North Indian silk sari with a very modern style bodice.

who had donated the funds for this rite. The patron and his wife pledged to protect and support the ritual. The wife sat next to her husband's right shoulder, holding a long grass (S/*darbha*), pointed toward him as she readily transferred her own power as a woman (S/*śakti*) to the ritual work at hand (fig. 3). In front of this ceremonial area, which was demarcated by decorative paintings on the floor, sat the congregation, who at this point simply watched the ceremonies.

[Figure 7] SAI BABA IS BATHED IN MILK and rose water with great delight by his women devotees.

The central feature of the *yajaśāla* were the fire pit and the brass pots (T/*kumpam*) filled with holy waters. The ritual action in the first portion of the ritual moved from the fire pit to the brass pots. There were 21 pots at each of the cardinal points and 16 surrounding the central tiered altar, 4 on each side. The first tier of the altar held 8, 2 on each side, and thus the sum of pots yielded the important Vedic number 108. The top tier had a golden lion-headed throne with peacocks at each side. On the throne seat was the major *kumpam*, larger than all the others, with a painting of Sai Baba covering it from view (fig. 4). At the top was a royal umbrella. All of the pots were "dressed" alike

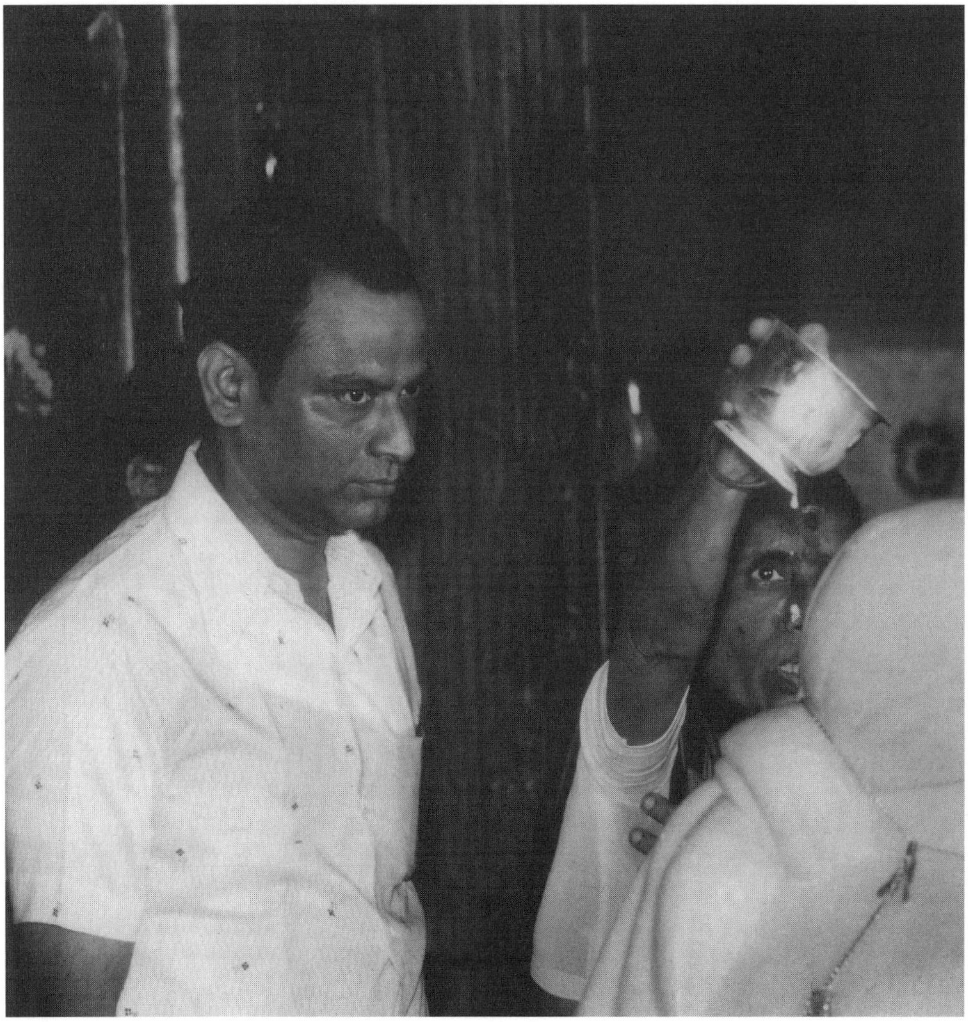

[Figure 8] DEVOTEES OF ALL AGES take the silver cup to bathe their Master.

and differed only in size, with the exception of the major pot, which alone had garlands. Each pot was wrapped in a small dhoti, tied with string, topped with leaves, and capped with a coconut and a few jasmine flowers. Each sat on a bed of rice.

The ceremony proper began at the fire pit. The fire was burning, but at this point only mantras, holy chants, were offered into the fire. After the chanting, the chief priest went to each of the pots on the altar and offered flowers and rang a bell; the assisting priest offered flowers to each of the smaller pots. Darbha grass continued to function as a conduit of power, as the chief priest used small broom-like bundles of this grass to pass offerings between the fire and himself. Sitting in front of the fire pit, he began to pour

[Figure 9] GRADUALLY, LIFE AND POWER are transfused into the image of Sai Baba as the holy waters in each pot are poured over him. A priest collects these waters, which will be sprinkled into the crowd seated below.

ghee, clarified butter, on the fire by first dipping both ends of the grass into the ghee and then an end of the grass in the fire. Then he kept pouring ghee into the fire with a wooden bowl and a wooden spoon (fig. 5). Surrounding the fire pit now were many large containers of cooked food, the kind of delicacies used in South India to satisfy a hungry guest. When the fire blazed, all of the food was slowly offered into the pit.

While all of this occurred in the *yajaśāla*, the women, who had prepared the raw food at the inception of the ritual, brought the food on brass trays in procession from

[Figure 10] DEVOTEES HAVE THEIR FIRST SIGHT of the divine image.

the *yajaśāla* to the sanctum of the *mandira,* singing while they walked (fig. 6). At this point, the curtain was closed, as the women offered the image-body of Sai Baba the fruit and then undressed Him for His ritual bath.

While the offerings of food continued in the *yajaśāla,* the congregation of devotees returned to the *mandira.* The women who had undressed and prepared the image-body now began to mix the ingredients for the milk bath (*pālabhiṣēka,* T/*pal,* 'milk' + S/*abhiṣēka,* 'ritual bath'). To a vat of milk, they added rose water and other spices. Each then dipped a silver cup, normally made of brass as a household bathing vessel, into the vat and carefully poured it over the marble *mūrti.* The milk poured down the body and "pots" that were so prominent in the hall of sacrifice. These *kumpam* are filled with holy water that acts as the medium for life-power that is gradually infused into the pot during the long ritual. These pots echo the Indian conception of impregnation, the male placing the "seed," a tiny embryonic child, into the uterine waters to grow. When the life-giving power gestated in the "water" is poured over the *mūrti*, it too vivifies. The pots, cradled on a lotus leaf strewn with raw rice, conflate two processes of quickening: the pots are like the earth in whose dark soil the seed germinates but they are also like the womb in whose warm waters the embryo grows.

The curious point of ritual is that things are not made naturally as in the Occidental sense of the effortless generation of life by God's will alone. Even the seemingly natural process of cultivating plants and conceiving babies is not understood as a spontaneous, "natural" process in India. All the corresponding processes are a kind of manufacturing, requiring great human effort. This effort is the act of ritual. The notion is hardly new in India, for the Sanskrit word for ritual, *karman*, is also the word for 'work'. Thus, this type of ritual in particular has much to say about the interrelationship of what the Enlightenment West too easily demarcated as the "artificial" versus the "natural." This sense of the sin of "artificial" creation is at the heart of Foster's polemic against idolatry: it obscured God's natural plan for humanity and created a counterfeit. Here, in the Hindu system, the natural things of this world are re-created by human effort, *karman*/ work, into living usable form for the benefit of both the Gods and humankind.

The end product of this ritual is indeed "artificial." The nature of the body which is created is not normal flesh, though its sees and hears, eats and sleeps, as a living entity. It was made, like a human baby, from the synthesis of "work" done by men on the one side and women on the other. However, the materials each donated were seemingly inert matter not the "natural" substances of their own bodies.

What is the "male" work and what is the "female?" In the *yajaśāla*, where the men do their work, the pots are transformed into embryo-like bodies. The pots are the first stage of a process of what could be called a theomorphism—the production of a god-body. Priests assert that the *kumpam* are a basic body with skeleton (the brass pot itself), veins (the wrapped strings), blood and other essential fluids (the yellow and red power), skin (the cloth), head (the coconut) and hair (the leaves). It is a naked, transitional body. The *mahakumpabhiśēka* in the *yajaśāla* effects a transfer of essentially disembodied powers from various sources through the medium of the fire to the pots, which act as a transitional body that is then "poured" into the image-body. The powers originate from the holy words chanted by the priests, that is, by their own controlled breath (S/ *prāna*). Power also comes from the raw food, "natural" substance, offered to the *mūrti* and then returned to the fire. The cooked food and the garments are all human products given to the God and then also added to the fire pit. The very fire itself was an extension of the eternal flame lit by Sai Baba in Shirdi. Thus, like the cycles in nature, the powers of Sai Baba are in a sense concentrated and returned to him again. The mantras were His own names; the food, His own food; and the garments, His also. But human "work" gave the raw product form as cooked food, arranged flowers, and woven cloth. The devotees have taken what was God's and returned it back to Him transformed.

This same process mirrors the Vedic sacrifice, in which human work is the work of "cultivation" and of "manufacturing"—of fabricating what is a given by the Gods into goods for the use of both Gods and men.

The *yajaśāla* itself is both a "natural" and an "artificial" setting for the ritual. In Vedic times, priests did not construct permanent temples to house the Gods but instead built temporary shelters to cover the fire pits, which then were the place for the union of the Gods and humankind. Even today, the base element of the God's body is raw stone, clay, or wood from the "natural" world. Like their Mesopotamian counterparts, such bodies are then carved into recognizable form by the hand of the sculptor but then must undergo a birthing process initally away from the city and temple[17] and close to "nature."

Ironically, in this ritual, the "natural" side of divine life is associated with men, not women. The women's work did not share in the agricultural metaphor so important to the male side. Rather, women worked through direct service to the very body of their divine teacher. Here the milk bath, the *pālabhiṣēka* was more literally a "bath" than an unction. The act of loving service to God is perceived as a productive enterprise modeled after the loving service that women give to their husbands and their children. Such nurturing is considered as essential for life as air, water, or food. Remarking on the reasons for the sanctity of the old sacred portrait of Sai Baba that once stood alone in the sanctum, a contributor to the monthly magazine of the movement reminded the community that "the power that it has gained through the course of time due to the constant prayers and poojas [ritual offerings] performed all through the year have made it a very sacred one punctuated with the power of giving anything that has been asked by His devotees" (Kumara Raj 1987: 18). Hence, while the men made the things needed to birth the image, the women provide the service that also gave it life.

The *mahākumpābhiṣēka,* then, depended as much on the metaphor of cooperative work as it did on the imagery of food, holy water, or holy pots. Or to put it another way, the ritual existed as much as a series of verbs as of nouns. The priests chanted together, joining their breath into one force. They added various ingredients into the fire, much like a group of old cooks pooling their skills to make a master meal. The women, always working as a group, chopped food, mixed the bath water, dressed and undressed their Lord, and bathed his body. The devotees of both sexes and all ages sang, prayed, listened, looked, and gave their own acts of service to the feet of the Master. The "men" and the "women," the "actors" in the ritual and the "audience" who watched and performed at crucial points, were all necessary to do this ritual-discipline (S/*karmayoga*) and to make this ritual work.

---

17. This has been the practice with every consecration ritual I have witnessed. If possible, the *yajaśāla* is constructed outside on the temple grounds or, if there are no grounds, as in the case of the Sai Mandir, a portion of the temple is ritually set aside as a sacrificial ground. Even when the *yajaśāla* remains within the temple, its borders are always clearly marked and access to all but Brahmin priests is usually forbidden.

The ritual, then, not only "made" God, but it also made the social body, the Samaj. The Sai Samaj, the community of devotees, chose to name itself by a term that derives from the Sanskrit word *saṃyāja*, meaning those joining together in a sacrifice. Unlike the perception of the nineteenth-century iconoclasts or of their prophetic progenitors, the consecration ritual did not destroy the social fabric but rather reinforced it—not to enslave the devotee to passions but to bond each to the service of God-incarnate and to each other.

The modernity of this new social body was apparent not only in the innovations in the ritual but also in the general ethos of the social and spatial environment that it created. The esprit of this ceremony was strikingly inclusive and not exclusive. At no point were the doorways guarded nor were there any signs, literal or figurative, that forbade anyone entrance and the right to participate, although I noticed that the street people who are fed regularly as an act of service were not inside the *mandira*. The ceremonies in the *yajaśāla* were modeled after the traditional Vedic rites, but the ancient codes that demanded ritual purity were, within the bounds of a kind of middle-class solidarity, flexibly defined. In order to photograph, my husband had to walk between the sacred fire and the altar and among the many pots. The chief priest was disturbed over the impropriety of this and called my husband over for a talk. It was decided that this photographer was, after all, a functionary of the ritual, and so the priests took him in the back room and tied a special dhoti over his pants. With a broad smile, the Secretary announced to me that they had made my husband a Brahmin and he was now free to roam the sacred precincts! Such was the social environment in this modern temple. This environment sustained the claims of the devotees that they had established a democratic organization within the parameters of their own social world.

Sai Baba had preached the oneness of all religions and all peoples and the spatial context, the architecture, of the Sai Mandira evokes and enforces this sensibility. The "temple" is sometimes called a "mosque" because Sai Samaj had members from many Hindu castes and Muslims as well and Sai Baba himself may have been born a Muslim (Rigopoulos 1993: 1–27). Unlike a mosque, this structure houses an embodied God, but unlike a traditional Hindu temple, the God does not reside in a dark "womb-chamber" (S/*garbhaghṛa*) that is usually reached by long hallways and a series of antechambers. The divine image of Sai Baba sits "on stage," in public view. So public is the sanctum that even a curiosity seeker peeking into the front door of the Sai Mandira would be rewarded with the sight of the divine image. The aspect of the mosque clearly borrowed by the architect of the *mandira* is the area in front of the sanctum that has the openness of a mosque rather than the long, dark, pillared halls with the complex divisions of space that characterize a traditional South Indian temple. This open hall ensures that no members would have greater to access to God through what in Christian churches would be the front row seats or in Hindu temples thoroughfare to the antechamber closest to the deity. Even the sanctum, which like the altars in many Christian churches and in most Hindu temples is usually restricted to the ordained, could be reached by two small staircases on each side, permitting the devotees access during the *pālabhiṣēka.* In this sanctum-stage could stand all those who had acted in the ritual. Thus the only ritual division that can be made is between the "audience" and the "actors." The only social division is the separation of men on one side of this hall and women on the other during rituals. Here the Sai Samaj adheres to social custom practiced in almost all public contexts in Madras. Thus, space confirms what word declared: the Sai Baba movement has attempted, within the bounds of broadly shared social customs in Madras, to create an inclusive modern social body.

The theology, then, of the Sai Baba Samaj is broadly Universalist but not in the Occidental sense of the term. A nineteenth-century British writer like Foster assumed that a God's sovereignty would be compromised by the particularity and the plurality that divine embodiment would imply. That is, once the principle of "one exclusive sovereign Divinity" was lost, then the plurality of man-made visible gods took his place. For Foster, God's very universal power rendered him abstract in all but mind, will, and thought. Devotees of Sai Baba also understood their Gurudev to be the sovereign God—all forms of God. But at the same time they consider Him to be incarnate in the marble image in front of their eyes, which is like the divine image of Sai Baba at Shirdi or even like one which they may have in their own homes. One of the most ardent women devotees told me that she did not need other Gods now, because Sai Baba was all Gods. This did not mean, however, that she or other devotees stopped worshiping at other temples. In India, there are obligations to family Gods as well as to neighborhood deities that can no more be ignored than the obligations to parents or children. But, for the devotees of Sai Baba, he remains their chosen God (*S/ iṣṭadēvata*) and therefore of final sovereignty in their lives. Thus for the devotee, Sai Baba is both the lord of the universe and a very particular personage available "in the flesh" to each of them.

Conclusions

The modern polemic against idolatry so carefully developed by the university-educated Christian apologists of the nineteenth century can, after a hundred and fifty years, be brought to the bench not before Hosea's angry God but before the very academic norms of rationality that these modern iconoclasts claimed as their own. That old assumption that somehow ritual thinking is opposed to rational "scientific" thinking or that ritual hoodwinks the user or that it is incompatible with modern education needs serious reconsideration, if any such theory of the relationship of the theological suppositions of a culture are to be related to its capacity to advance socially, morally, or even economically, as Foster so strongly argued. I believe that it is possible to argue that the theology of ritual embodiment of God is compatible with the logic of modern technology and of modern democracy.

One of the hallmarks of modernity for Foster, and for many others since, had been the theory that a society must learn to separate religion from work in a very important sense. The work of Vedic ritual, the *karmayoga,* just like the ritual work of the Mesopotamian or Egyptian priests, has its own instrumentality. Something does get done. The difficult issue is, what? Stone turns to flesh, God is reborn in the temple, and somehow the world is reformed and remade. "How ridiculous," says the iconoclast; "how important," says the iconolater. What really is at stake in the still raging debate between the iconoclast and the iconolater? Certainly neither the ancient Mesopotamians nor the modern devotees of Sai Baba ever say that they have made God from nothing. They do re-form God from water, earth, stone, and their own thin air, their own life breath. The marble *mūrti* of Sai Baba is the great Master but is not all of Him. Humans have given Him life among their community in their own world. In such iconic cultures, humans retain the right to share in the process of life-making within the realm of their earthly life. In the theological formulation of John Foster, a wise human can communicate with the Great Communicator but humans know not to violate His sole right to make life. The humans have been given the earth to do work but not to do ritual work. The formulas, those words that God spoke to create the world, must remain hidden. But the Hindu priest knows these holy locutions, words that do not merely command but create. The Hindu priests know the mantras, just as the ancient priests knew the spells in the days when the prophets confronted Babylon with God's own holy word. But in iconic cultures humans do not cede to the Gods all of the power of creation. In their time and in their place, priests have ritual as a means of re-making, re-doing, re-creating a body and a home for the Gods when They deign to dwell in the human world.

Ironically, the West had to do many mental gymnastics both to maintain the concept of the all-sovereign God and to come to grips with the stark materialism of science. The theory of evolution, for example, presents the genesis of the human body as a problem in the nature of living matter. Neither God's will nor His thought made man. Material body transformed into another type of body, and so forth. Manufacturing also shares this essential materialism with science. Manufacturing creates the Life of our society in a very artificial way. Humanity makes goods without which many modern people could not survive: cars, refrigerators, stoves, and even frozen food. We depend on nature much the same way that the Sai Baba devotees depended on the natural ingredients—the food, fire, stone, breath—that they used to make a body for their Gurudev. But the making process is not in God's hands; that is human work. It is human work to make daily life possible in industrial societies just as it is human work to make God live in ancient as well as in modern iconic cultures. The arguments against "idolatry" will likely continue in the West. But the evidence remains that at least in modern South India, education, industry, and rationality are living most compatibly with the making and the worship of the divine image.

Bibliography

Ashby, Philip
1974 *Modern Trends in Hinduism.* New York / London: Columbia University Press.

Atmaprana, Pravrajika, ed.
1986 *Sri Ramakrishna's Dakshineswar.* New Delhi: Ramakrishna Sarada Mission.

Banerjea, J. N.
1956 *The Development of Hindu Iconography.* Calcutta: University of Calcutta.

Barrows, John Henry
1897 *Christianity, the World Religion: Lectures Delivered in India.* Madras: Christian Literature Society.
1899 *The Christian Conquest of Asia.* New York: Scribner.

Bell, Catherine
1992 *Ritual Theory / Ritual Practice.* New York: Oxford University Press.

Bhatt, N. R.
1984 "Śaiva Āgmas." Pp. 10–28 in *Agama and Silpa,* ed. K. K. A. Venkatachari. Bombay: Ananthacharya Indological Research Institute.
1988 "Development of Temple Rituals." Pp. 24–45 in *Siva Temple and Temple Rituals,* ed. S. Janaki. Madras: Kuppuswami Sastri Research Institute.

Bodhaswarupananda, Swami
1974 *The Ramakrishna Leelasthans: Pilgrim Centers of Modern India.* Madras: Sri Ramakrishna Math.

Brunner-Lachaux, Hèlène
1963 *Somasambhupaddhati, première partie.* Pondichèry: Institut français d'Indologie.

Buchanan, Claudius
1811 *Memoir of the Expediency of a Ecclesistical Establishment for British India: Both as a Means of Perpetuating the Christian Religion Amoung Our Own Countymen and as a Foundation for the Ultimate Civilization of the Natives.* Cambridge: Hillard and Metcalf.

Campbell, William
1839 *British India and Its Relation to the Decline of Hinduism and the Progress of Christianity.* London: John Snow.

Converse, Hyla S.
1988 "Hinduism." Pp. 61–117 in *The Religious World: Communities of Faith.* 2d ed. London / New York: Macmillan.

Davis, Richard H.
1991 *Ritual in an Oscillating Universe: Worshipping Siva in Medieval India.* Princeton: Princeton University Press.

Foster, John
1821 *An Essay on the Evils of Popular Ignorance.* 2d American ed. New York: William B. Gilley.

Fox, George Townshend
1852 *A Memoir of the Rev. Henry Watson Fox, B.A.* New York: Robert Carter & Brothers.

Gambhirananda, Swami
1983[1957] *History of the Ramakrishna Math and Ramakrishna Mission.* 3d rev. ed. Calcutta: Advaita Ashrama.

Ingram, Kenneth
1956 *Reformers in India, 1793–1833.* Cambridge: Cambridge University Press.

James, T. G. H.
1981 *The British Museum and Ancient Egypt.* London: British Museum Publications.

Kalidas, Vuppuluri
1987 "Sri Narasimhaswamiji, the Apostle of Sai Baba." *Bhavan's Journal* 33: 26–29.

Kane, P. V.
1941 *History of Dharmasastra.* Vol. 2, part 2. Poona: Bhandarkar Oriental Research Institute.

Kumara Raj, T. A.
1987 "The Holy Portrait of Sainath at His Mylapore Mandira." *Sai Sudhā* 47: 3–4.
Max Müller, F.
1964[1878] *Lectures on the Origin and Growth of Religion as Illustrated by the Religions of India.* Reprint. Varanasi: Indological Book House.
Mitter, Partha
1977 *Much Maligned Monsters: History of European Reactions to Indian Art.* Oxford: Clarendon Press.
Narayanan, Vasudha
1985 "Arcavatara: On Earth as He is in Heaven." Pp. 53–66 in *Gods of Flesh / Gods of Stone: The Embodiment of Divinity in India,* ed. Joanne Punzo Waghorne and Norman Cutler. Chambersbrug, Penn.: Anima.
Ramakrishniah, D.
1987 "Ever Protecting Sai Bhagavan." *Sai Sudhā* 47: 5–10.
Richter, Julius
1908 *A History of Missions in India.* London: Oliphant Anderson & Ferrier.
Rigopoulos, Antonio
1992 *The Life and Teachings of Saint Sai Baba of Shirdi.* Albany: State University of New York Press.
Saipadananda, Swami
1973 *Sri Narasimha Swamiji, Apostle of Sri Sai Baba, the Saint of Shirdi.* Madras: All-India Sai Samaj, Mylapore.
Seager, Richard Hughes, ed.
1993 *The Dawn of Religious Pluralism: Voices form the World's Parliament of Religions, 1893.* La Salle, Ill.: Open Court.
Singer, Milton
1972 *When a Great Tradition Modernizes: An Anthropological Approach to Indian Civilization.* Chicago: University of Chicago Press.
Smith, George E.
1879 *The Life of Alexander Duff, D.D., LL.D.* New York: American Tract Society.
Tejasananda, Swami
1983 *Holy Kamapukur.* Calcutta: Advaita Ashrama.
[Venkataraman, Muthu]
1987 "All India Sai Devotees' Convention and Sri Sai Baba's Marble Murthy." *Sai Sudhā* 47: 1–3.
Yates, William
1831 *Memoirs of the Early Life of John Chamberlain, Late Missionary in India.* Boston: James Loring.

spilled over the raised foot of the guru into another vat placed at his feet (fig. 7). After the women finished their bathing of Sai Baba, every member of the congregation, following each other in an orderly line, came up to the sanctum and also took the silver cup and bathed their Master (fig. 8). No one was excluded from the rite. My husband was asked to put down his cameras and come, and we too offered the *abhiṣēka* along with all of the others. Finally, when each devotee had done this service for their Gurudev, the bells rang, calling all devotees back into the *yajaśāla*.

The early offerings of raw food, the garlands and the clothes that the *mūrti* had worn that morning were brought into the *yajaśāla*. With bells clanging and trumpets blowing, the food, garlands, and clothes were added to the conflagration in the fire pit. The chief priest then took the same ghee that had fueled the sacred fire and anointed the major pots on the altar. The officers of the Sai Samaj, including the patron and the chief priest, then anointed each other as they prepared themselves for the crucial ritual work that followed. All of those who were to carry the pots from the *yajaśāla* to the sanctum in the *mandira* tied turbans on their heads in preparation for receiving the pots. A special priest took the major *kumpam* at the top of the altar onto his head. Each of the officers of the Samaj took one of the other pots on the altar. Other devotees in turn took the pots from the floor onto their heads. The chief priest, carrying a tray of fire and followed by the chief patron and the priests carrying the main pots, then led the long procession of 108 singing and chanting devotees. The procession wound its way around the inner parameters of the temple complex and finally entered the main doorway facing the sanctum. With the curtain opened and the rest of the community seated in front of the sanctum-stage, each pot was poured in turn over the head of the marble Gurudev (fig. 9), After the final pot had been poured, the Secretary-patron took the holy water collected from the "bath" and sprinkled it over the crowd, whose eyes were riveted on the image (fig. 10). The curtain closed again. The women devotees then dried and dressed their Master in purple garments and decorated him with garlands. The curtain opened for the first auspicious sight of the deity in full dress. The priest slowly waved a flaming lamp (T/*ārāti*, S/*ārātrika*) in front of the now reembodied Gurudev. The *ārāti* lamp was lit from the flame brought from the fire pit in the *yajaśāla*. The glimmering light from the lamp revealed the face of God to the devotees seated below. The curtain closed. The ritual work had ended.

This complex ritual process ultimately "made" a body for God. Yet the "making" process is difficult to interpret. It is neither a natural process nor is it simply artificial. Certainly the "laws" of nature do not prevail when stone becomes a living thing. It is this sort of "magic" that the modern iconoclasts saw as violating rationality. Yet, the ritual does mirror the natural world, with pots and all of the implied womb imagery, at the same time that it asserts that humankind must work through ritual to make life happen.

Making God from God's Own World

The full 48-day ritual of enlivening the divine *mūrti*, the *mahakumpabhiṣēka* (S/*mahā*, 'great' + T/*kumpam*, 'brass pot' + S/*abhiṣēka*, 'bathing') takes its name from the